Mozume .

D1715044

Edited by

Rachel Spilka

Writing in the Workplace

New
Research
Perspectives

Carbondale and Edwardsville

**Southern
Illinois
University
Press**

Copyright © 1993 by the Board of Trustees,
Southern Illinois University
All rights reserved
Printed in the United States of America
Edited by Julie Riley Bush
Design and production by Natalia Nadraga
96 95 94 93   4 3 2 1

Library of Congress Cataloging-in-Publication Data

Writing in the workplace : new research perspectives / edited by
   Rachel Spilka.
       p.   cm.
    Includes bibliographical references and index.
    1. English language—Rhetoric—Study and teaching. 2. English
language—Technical English—Research. 3. English language—
Business English—Research. 4. English language—Rhetoric—
Research. 5. Technical writing—Research. 6. Business writing—
Research. I. Spilka, Rachel, 1953–   .
    PE1404.W7266   1993
    808'.0666—dc20   92-13211
    ISBN 0-8093-1724-9   CIP

The paper used in this publication meets the minimum requirements
of American National Standard for Information Sciences—Permanence
of Paper for Printed Library Materials, ANSI Z39.48-1984. ∞

Contents

Preface

This anthology is about possibilities. Although some consider the discipline of professional writing to be at its maturity (see, for example, Souther, 1989), this text takes a different stance by assuming that too many questions have yet to be asked, too much research has yet to be conducted, and too much knowledge has yet to be discovered before this discipline can reach its maturity. Instead of attempting to provide answers for the discipline, this collection attempts, instead, to ask helpful questions intended to provide more direction to the discipline and therefore assist in its continuous growth. Therefore, readers will find in this collection a deliberate focus on future possibilities for professional writing research.

Before the discipline can mature further, it needs to determine where it has been and where it needs to go next. It needs to discuss research conducted so far of workplace writing and to identify new research directions that can help the discipline move closer to fulfilling its goals. This type of self-analysis is critically important if the discipline is to advance significantly in strengthening the integrity of its research, which, in turn, seems a prerequisite for strengthening the integrity of its approaches to theory, pedagogy, and practice. This anthology, by evaluating research advances to date and proposing research directions for tomorrow, suggests how future research on workplace writing might be conducted. In fact, every chapter in this volume identifies gaps in or new directions for research, or asks questions aimed at inspiring new empirical directions that can help promote the discipline's continued maturation.

In many respects, this book is a follow-up to the 1985 anthology *Writing in Nonacademic Settings*, edited by Lee Odell and Dixie Goswami. If there were ever a watershed event in the evolution of professional writing research, it was that collection of essays, which inspired a new generation of researchers to conduct studies of workplace writing and which motivated professional writing veterans as well to approach the discipline in new, more expansive ways. In particular, the two articles in that anthology authored by Odell and Faigley, who both called for more research about the "social perspective," provided valuable theoretical focus and guidance that resulted in a new energy and spirit among researchers in the discipline.

During the middle and late 1980s, most researchers of workplace writing, inspired by the Odell and Goswami anthology, chose the social perspective for textual analyses, surveys and interviews, and other types of research. An increasing number of these researchers initiated qualitative studies aimed at exploring the relationship between social contexts and the composing process in workplace settings, and these studies often introduced new approaches to research design, methodology, and analysis. Whereas previous researchers of workplace writing tended to rely heavily on prewriting and postwriting measures (mostly surveys and interviews), these qualitative researchers now relied, as well, on "process measures" designed to trace cognitive and social behavior throughout the writing process (these process measures included observations of informal social interactions and formal meetings, writing and reading protocols, the recording in log books of data about social interactions, discourse-based interviews of drafts, and interviews conducted consistently throughout the evolution of documents). With expanded research designs and methodology, writing researchers were able to discover new and interesting patterns of rhetorical and social behavior. As more qualitative studies of workplace writing were in progress and completed, and as more preliminary and final research findings were reported at conferences and in publications, excitement grew among scholars about what these patterns might mean for advances in the discipline.

The idea for this book emerged from a number of informal discussions among these scholars about the need for the discipline to develop a clearer perspective of what researchers have been discovering since Odell and Faigley's 1985 call for more qualitative research on the social perspective of workplace writing, how these researchers have been designing, conducting, and analyzing their studies, and what these research discoveries and approaches might mean for continued growth of the discipline. Scholars agreed that the time had come for the discipline to collect its thoughts and assess where it has been, where it is now, and where it wants to head next in light of recent research discoveries and innovations. In particular, there is a growing consensus that if the profession intends to take significant strides forward in research, theory, pedagogy, and practice, it needs to gain more certainty about research advances to date. If researchers are unaware of what other researchers have been discovering or of how other researchers have been conducting their studies, they will have difficulty initiating new studies that build on knowledge already gained, and the discipline will have difficulty determining how to strengthen the integrity of its research on workplace writing. This book attempts to be a healthy boost toward realization of all these goals.

In a sense, this volume is a snapshot of the best-quality research, and thinking about research, among professional writing specialists approximately a decade after publication of the first results of initial qualitative studies of composing processes in the workplace. Besides serving as a follow-up to Odell and Goswami's *Writing in Nonacademic Settings*, I envision this anthology fulfilling multiple purposes for the discipline: providing a history of research inspired by that anthology; capturing (and describing) what is, in my opinion, the best-quality research that has emerged in the past decade and the best scholarly thinking on professional writing in the discipline today; and raising questions aimed at inspiring and providing direction for future professional writing research and, subsequently, for future advances in professional writing theory, pedagogy, and practice.

While designing this anthology, I was interested in two types of contributions: reports of quality, completed studies of workplace writing since the mid-1980s, and essays introducing new and important arguments about research to date on workplace writing and future research directions for the discipline. Another aim was to include a variety of contributors and contributions to represent as many different perspectives and viewpoints in the discipline as possible. To solicit high-quality contributions, I sent letters of invitation to two types of professionals: professional writing researchers who had completed (or were close to completing) well-regarded studies on workplace writing, and professional writing scholars who already had made valuable empirical and theoretical contributions to the discipline. From the proposals received, I selected contributions representing a diverse cross section of the discipline's best researchers and thinkers. Among this volume's contributors are both newcomers to writing research and veterans in the field, both professional writing specialists in academia and those in the workplace, both Americans and Canadians. Yet I consider all these contributors similar in being pioneers in the discipline. All of them assume an important role, here, of evaluating how research to date might influence the research of tomorrow. In a sense, this anthology makes all of them collaborators in carving out new directions for the discipline's future empirical and theoretical inquiries.

The ideal audience for this anthology consists of current and future professional writing researchers, as well as all those in the profession who perceive high-quality research as key to the continuing progress and maturity of this discipline. The anthology's structure is designed to accommodate the needs and interests of both types of readers.

Part One is a collection of chapters reporting on specific studies of workplace writing. These chapters represent research since the 1980s of the social perspective of workplace writing and can serve a number of roles. First, each chapter presents a unique perspective on the relationship between social contexts and workplace writing and can inspire new ideas for empirical and theoretical inquiry in their respective areas of inquiry. Part One contributors were encouraged to speculate on how their studies contribute to growth in professional writing theory, practice, and pedagogy, and readers of this anthology are invited to make their own conclusions about these studies' contributions, as well. Second, each Part One chapter describes an approach to writing research that current and future professional writing researchers can analyze, critique, and either emulate or modify as they deem best.

Part Two authors assess the implications of recent professional writing research of the social perspective for professional writing theory, pedagogy and practice, and future research directions. Before composing their first drafts, all Part Two authors had the opportunity to read Part One chapters, so they would have the option of responding in their arguments to those studies along with other studies of workplace writing completed since the mid-1980s. The key role of Part Two chapters is to inspire new ideas, discussions, and debate so the discipline can make significant and responsible strides forward toward strengthening its research programs, thereby strengthening as well its future approaches to professional writing theory, pedagogy, and practice.

Part One and Part Two chapters do not aim to exhaust their respective subject areas; to do so would be impossible in the scope of a single anthology. They do attempt, however, to provide a sense of recent research advances and future research needs at this exciting juncture in the discipline's continued growth. Above all else, this volume exists to invite the discipline to make a more concerted effort to discuss the important issues raised here. The discipline needs to make greater progress toward reaching a consensus perspective as to which research approaches it considers most valuable, and to have the most potential, in strengthening the integrity of its scholarly inquiries. Perhaps this collection of essays will be an important first step toward this type of initiative.

In closing, I wish to thank Barbara Mirel, who assisted me so ably in editing first drafts of the anthology's chapters; her comments were instrumental in sharpening the arguments of those drafts and in helping contributors think through issues more expansively than they might have done otherwise. I also thank the anonymous reviewer chosen by the publisher, whose comments on second drafts led, as well, to significant improvements. All contributors to this collection have my highest admiration and respect for the originality of their thinking and the importance of their insights; I thank them, too, for their patience with revision requests and deadline pressures. Of great assistance in project management, copyediting, and production decisions were Kenney Withers, Curtis Clark, Carol Burns, Julie Bush, and Natalia Nadraga of Southern Illinois University Press; I especially thank Kenney Withers for his wonderful enthusiasm throughout this project. Of great assistance in keeping me strong and healthy during initial phases of manuscript editing were Dr. Jerremy M. Ramp and Dr. Madalyn K. Squires. In addition, my colleagues in the rhetoric and composition program at Purdue have kept me intellectually strong. I am grateful, as well, to Mark, Jane, and Aaron Spilka for their continued love, support, and encouragement of my scholarly efforts.

Finally, I would like to dedicate this anthology in memory of my mother, Ellen Potter Spilka, 1926–1990. As a professional librarian and onetime social worker, a lifelong scholar of social history, and an advocate for mill workers and the poor in New England industrial towns, she believed strongly in the social dimensions and possibilities of this project. She would have enjoyed seeing this book through to its completion and would have appreciated, especially, its potential to inspire the type of intellectual curiosity, debate, creativity, and growth needed to discover ways to use communication altruistically to enrich the social contexts of our worksites, and not just the social fabrics of our own lives.

Part One

Research Studies of Writing in the Workplace

Part One is a collection of chapters reporting on research on workplace writing conducted by the authors in the late 1980s or early 1990s. While most authors report on qualitative studies of composing processes in the workplace, three authors (Couture and Rymer, Mirel) report on surveys they conducted, and one author (Segal) reports on a textual analysis of medical discourse. Yet, all authors use "the social perspective" in their approach to the research of workplace writing.

The first three chapters of Part One present research findings on social perceptions of workplace professionals and strategies of learning about and then analyzing social effects on composing behavior in workplace settings. In the first two chapters, the authors report on surveys they conducted in which they relied on the social perspective both to design survey instruments and to analyze survey data. In a survey of over four hundred professionals in a variety of business and technical occupations, Couture and Rymer found that two writing variables—whether the type of writing task is routine or special, and whether the writer is a professional who writes or a career writer—can shape writers' initial social perceptions and subsequent composing behavior at work. They suggest that such global situational exigencies as a writer's functional relationship to writing and the importance of a writing task can have far greater impact on composing processes than the writer's discipline or occupation, or the genre of a document. Mirel reports on other surveys suggesting that if manual writers hope to develop manuals that meet user needs, they need to understand not just what users need to learn, but also how users learn; they need to consider that users' instructional needs "have a social and organizational base, not just a cognitive one." In particular, Mirel suggests that manual writers need to analyze what workers wish they could do, what strategies they have relied on to do what they want, and what they have been unable to do and why. In the third chapter, MacKinnon reports on a qualitative study describing what workplace professionals might need to learn about social contexts and workplace writing and how they might need to learn it, and then analyzes this learning process in light of social cognition theory. According to MacKinnon, for new employees, writing can serve as a form of apprenticeship that can result in more active participation in a corporate community. From his research, MacKinnon concludes that "context would appear to be a critical element in any speculative model of rhetorical development of on-the-job writing ability."

In the next two chapters, Kleimann and Spilka report on multiple case studies they conducted that help explain the value during the composing process of social interaction between the participants of a rhetorical situation. Kleimann describes how social interaction at a federal agency can open up opportunities for negotiation between writers and multiple reviewers. She argues that a dynamic relationship exists between the organization and the review process. Her findings demonstrate how organizational cultures can affect every aspect of the review process, including the structure of the process and reviewers' decisions and behavior. Whereas Kleimann describes social contexts influencing social interaction in the workplace, Spilka describes social interaction influencing social contexts. Her study of the composing process in state government suggests that in some workplace cultures, oral and written discourse may have an interdependent relationship that encourages and facilitates a back-and-forth movement throughout the composing process between oral and written modes of expression. Her results suggest that this back-and-forth movement can serve rhetorical functions that, in turn, can help fulfill social goals critical to the success of individual projects and contribute, as well, to social acculturation in the long term.

In the remaining chapters of Part One, the authors discuss various aspects of the reciprocal relationship between social contexts and workplace writing. Segal reports on a textual analysis that explores the negotiation between the character of Western medicine and the nature of its professional discourse. With a textual case study, she examines the relationship between the authority of texts and the authority of doctors and the ways in which the conversation of a profession can perpetuate the values of that profession. Her study suggests that the effect of some medical writing is not so much to inform as to affirm what the community already knows. Dautermann then describes a qualitative study in which a group of nurses, while revising policy and procedure manuals, were influenced by social contexts, but also attempted to influence both their own nursing division and the greater hospital community. "Composing together," Dautermann notes, "enabled [the] nurses to mediate their own experience through language, to recognize the discourses of others, and to begin to carve out a place for their own voices in the community." In a case study of writing done by social workers attached to a juvenile court system, Paré describes the tension that can exist "between individual vision and community expectations" during the evolution of workplace documents. He found that these social workers struggled to determine what they could or could not write in their reports and that this struggle was influenced by both official and unofficial discourse community restrictions. According to Paré, because discourse communities act as arbiters of appropriate discourse, both allowing and disallowing certain types of writing, writing in any context can be constrained heavily by socially imposed limitations and restrictions.

The last two chapters explore various roles of genre in workplace composing processes. Smart reports on a study of discourse conventions influencing both the writers and their executive readers in a financial institution. From this study, Smart develops a theory on how a discourse community can invent the particular genres it needs to create written knowledge required by decision makers in that community. He hypothesizes that four major contextual influences can shape executives' reading practices and consequent expectations. In the final chapter, Cross reports on a case study that considers the interrelation of genre, context, and process in the group production of an executive letter and report. Using the language theory of Bakhtin (1981) to provide a conceptual framework, Cross analyzes in this case the social, generic, and dynamic features of language production. He argues that since the combination of the type of corporate culture and the type of genre can influence composing decisions and behavior, the influence of generic constraints should be considered along with their interaction with social forces in the context of document writing.

1 | Barbara Couture and Jone Rymer

Situational Exigence | Composing Processes on the Job by Writer's Role and Task Value

In their text on research methods in composition studies, Lauer and Asher (1988) claim that composition research has two focuses: rhetorical studies that develop theories about how discourse is produced and interpreted, and empirical investigations that report data validating the rhetorical theories (pp. 3–15). Our study combines the strategies of rhetorical and empirical research and offers a new approach to explore the influence of social context on professional writing.

Our goal was to identify some situational exigencies, or key contextual elements, that shape the process of workplace communication. Our rhetorical theory is based on two aspects of writers' composing situations: the relationship between the task and the writer's profession, and the value of the composing task. We assumed that professional writers' procedures differ from those of members of professions in which writing is not their primary responsibility. We also assumed that writers' procedures for producing texts differ depending upon whether the assignment is routine or significant.

Our empirical investigation of the validity of this theory consisted of a survey of over four hundred professionals employed in a variety of occupations by thirty-one organizations. For this study, we developed a special instrument, the Writers' Survey. Answers to this questionnaire provided information about practices of expert writers common across many workplace genres and professions.

In interpreting the survey data, we devised a new method for categorizing discourse communities and types by the nature of the context in which the writing is produced. Instead of grouping responses by the discourse communities traditionally defined by profession (e.g., Barnum & Fischer, 1984; DiSalvo & Larsen, 1987; Smeltzer & Gebert, 1986), we postulated two rhetorical communities that reflect a motivated relationship between the writing task and the writer's functional role: *professionals who write*, those for whom writing demonstrates their competence in another profession (for example, engineering); and *career writers*, those for whom writing is their profession (for example, technical communication) and hence a direct demonstration of their professional/technical competence. Further, rather than examining the distribution of professional texts in memos, letters, and reports (e.g., Anderson, 1985; Kirtz & Reep, 1991; Pinelli, Glassman, Barclay, & Oliu, 1989), we established two categories that identify a dominant functional relationship between writing and its context: *routine tasks*, for which speed of completion is more important than product quality; and *special tasks*, for which quality is as or more important than efficiency.

Our four rhetorical categories reflect some earlier research about the influence of context on workplace writing. Some researchers have noted that writers change procedures to correspond with their focus on a technical or rhetorical problem (Mathes & Stevenson, 1976). These scholars' observations parallel our distinctions between the professional who writes primarily to demonstrate technical or administrative competence and the career writer who writes primarily to demonstrate rhetorical expertise. Further, several researchers (e.g., Broadhead & Freed, 1986; Couture & Rymer, 1989; Odell & Goswami, 1984) have shown that writers on the job adjust their practices according to the importance of the task or the efficiency with which it must be completed. However, previous research has not elaborated on how these distinctions contribute to a theory of professional writing, nor has it verified empirically that these categories are situationally based. Specifically, research has not yet linked composing strategies to writers' investment in the task, contrasting professionals who simply write as part of their jobs with career writers' investment in writing as professional identification, nor has it linked writing behaviors to the situational exigence of routine versus nonroutine tasks.

This chapter presents findings that verify that the planning and revising procedures of professionals who write as part of their jobs differ less among this broad group than they differ from the writing practices of career writers, and that members of all surveyed professions recognize the task distinction between routine and special writing. In presenting these results, we discuss our rhetorical theories, which define composing strategies by the writer's role (professional who writes/career writer) and define genres by task value (routine or special). In this chapter, we describe our methodology, elaborate the discourse categories, present and discuss our survey results, and suggest implications for future research.

Empirical Method: The Writers' Survey

The Writers' Survey, a five-part questionnaire on workplace writing, focuses on writers' composing strategies for two categories of writing, routine and special. In exploring composing processes in context, our research expands on past surveys that have focused on varieties of workplace writing, time spent communicating, and conventional purposes and constraints (e.g., Anderson 1985; DiSalvo & Larsen, 1987; Keeler, 1990; Northey, 1990; Pinelli et al., 1989). Respondents indicated on a 5-point Likert scale (None to Very Much) how much time they spend writing each of ten common documents and identified their most typical routine and special writing tasks. For composing a specific document in each of these categories, subjects responded to questions asking how frequently (Never to Very Often) they practice fifty-five specific procedures, such as outlining or taking notes.

The survey population is an expert sample of 431 subjects experienced in occupations that involve writing and that are predicted to offer employment for future college graduates ("Job Outlook in Brief," 1982). The subjects hold thirty-three different jobs distributed among eight categories: administrators (30%), writers and technologists (19%), engineers and architects (19%), scientists (10%), health professionals (6%), marketing professionals (4%), police and corrections officers (4%), social workers (3%), and others (5%). Managers representing thirty-one Detroit-area organizations selected the subjects from among experienced employees they considered to be expert writers (see Couture, Goldstein, Malone, Nelson, & Quiroz, 1985). In asking managers with communications responsibilities to select effective writers in their companies as our survey subjects, we were proceeding on two assumptions: First, writing competence is determined by members of the discourse community itself, not outsiders (this premise reflects the theory that defining the value and truth of a text is a function of the interpretive community for whom the writer writes [e.g., Clark, 1990; Cooper & Holzman, 1989; Rafoth & Rubin, 1988]); and second, composing methods of expert writers in the workplace would differ from those of novices and those less skilled (e.g., Anson & Forsberg, 1990; Beach & Anson, 1988) and would provide a sharper view of the influence of context on composing. (Our subjects, averaging seven years of experience with their current employers, could not be unaware of the specific contexts in which they write.)

This social constructionist approach characterizes not only rhetorical scholarship but also management studies of expertise in organizations. Organizational expertise of any type cannot be defined by academics or others outside a firm because effectiveness is an elusive concept that differs in every context and varies over time; even the members of the organization itself can define it only imperfectly (Cameron, 1986; Cameron & Whetten, 1981). Conventionally in business, of course, it is not the performance of an employee that counts, but rather managers' perceptions of that performance, further reinforcing our choice of organizational insiders to identify our survey subjects. Moreover, research shows that supervisory evaluations of communication skills correlate well with employees' overall competence within the organization (Scudder & Guinan, 1989); effective writing is not an atypical measure of performance.

Rhetorical Theory: Categorizing Situational Exigence

In analyzing professionals' composing strategies for this study, we adopted a social perspective. Assuming that writing is socially constructed, we acknowledge the challenge of documenting the influence of context on professional discourse, including data on "all familiar aspects of the composing process" and data on how the text is disseminated, who reads it, how it is read, and how it shapes other texts (Faigley, 1985, p. 242). Scholars participating in this research effort are faced with the theoretical problem of speculating about how multifaceted social contexts motivate writers to think and act, and then with the empirical problem of conducting studies of writers' situations in a wide variety of organizations. This is a very ambitious agenda, and despite a growing number of case studies exploring hypotheses with a limited number of subjects, a gap still exists between rhetorical theory and empirically verified findings about the social construction of discourse.

As one means to help traverse the gap between rhetorical theory and empirical research on the social contexts for writing, we propose theoretically that situational exigency represents a primary motivation for writing behaviors in the workplace. Situational exigency refers to the environmental factor in a social situation that is interpreted as a dominant demand by the writer. Our concept of situational exigence has its roots in both rhetorical and linguistic theory. Bitzer (1968, 1980) notes that rhetorical discourse reflects its situation, responding to audience, constraints, and "exigence"— that is, a specific combination of persons, events, and instruments that creates a need for communication. Vatz (1973) supports a modification of Bitzer's view, holding that rhetorical exigence—while admittedly linked to situation—is specifically a function of an author's or audience's particular interpretation of what a situation means. From this rhetorical tradition, we have developed the broader concept of situational exigence, which names the phenomenon of rhetorical response linked to a kind of situation. In linguistics, Halliday (1978, 1985) has most thoroughly developed a theory of social meaning as it is linked to grammatical function. From this linguistic tradition, we have adopted the convention of viewing the social context for communication as a system of conditions in which writers make a series of choices that guide their communicative responses.

We have postulated two conditions of situational exigence that define an oppositional choice. The first condition is the focus of the writer's functional role: Is it solving technical or managerial problems, as for professionals such as engineers, scientists, and marketing managers? Or is it solving communication problems, as for career writers who may work in a variety of occupations (such as public relations officer, technical writer, or editor) but whose profession is "writer"? The second condition is the importance of the writing task: Is it routine, concerning business as usual, therefore dictating the writer's conventional, efficient response? Or rather, is it special, concerning what is nonroutine, addressing, for instance, an exceptional problem, a significant audience, a sensitive issue, therefore demanding the writer's considered response, one that is as effective as possible?

The Writer's Functional Role: Professional or Career Writer

We speculated that a dominant situational exigency might distinguish the composing strategies of the professional who writes from those of the career writer. Those whose professional affiliation is writer, whose role focuses on rhetorical problems rather than on technical or other functional problems, will likely conceive of composing tasks differently from engineers, architects, or administrators—professionals who must write as only part of their responsibilities. In making this distinction, we do not mean to imply that these categories are static or discrete. Many engineers, for example, become managers and move from technical to administrative problems; many career writers become managers and no longer function primarily as rhetorical problem solvers.

Harrison and Debs (1988) make clear how technical professionals conventionally view writing and writers:

> Traditionally, scientists and engineers have considered documents to be secondary to the "real" work at hand: developing a product or solution to a problem. . . . The product is independent of the documentation, while any writing is dependent on the product. . . . Denying co-product status to writing seems to relegate the technical communicator to a secondary support role. (p. 16)

8

This limited view of the career writer's function is based on the classical separation of rhetoric from scientific discourse—a logical description of the facts, with invention playing no part in the enterprise (Miller, C. R., 1985). Although we now acknowledge that science is rhetorical and that technical writing involves invention, the scope of many career writers' involvement in nonrhetorical matters may be more limited than is suggested by some models of the writing process in technical communication (Anderson, 1984; Keeler, 1990).

The context for the activities of career writers is typically very different from that of professionals who write. In fact, our demographic data linking genres with these two groups reveal a dramatic difference in their typical writing tasks. Confirming previous research (e.g., Anderson, 1985), most of the professionals who write spend their time (Some, Much, or Very Much) on four document types: memos (69%), short reports (59%), letters (56%), and procedures (53%). Despite a few exceptions (for example, social workers designate minutes among their most common documents), members of many different professions typically do the same kinds of writing. Most career writers, in contrast, spend their time writing manuals (76%), and nearly as many spend that much time on procedures (67%). Further, nearly half of the career writers (47%) spend at least some time each month writing bulletins, a document type professionals do not even mention.

These results strongly support our argument that the writing tasks of career writers and professionals differ in major ways and that this difference constitutes a dominant situational exigency, one that potentially differentiates their composing strategies. Career writers, like professionals, produce documents that help conduct business—memos to superiors and co-workers and letters to clients, for instance. But unlike professionals, their major task is to write specialized documents directing or reporting the activities of others, such as user manuals for computer software or bulletins recording corporate activity (e.g., Feinberg & Goldman, 1985; Kalmbach, Jobst, & Meese, 1986; Little & McLaren, 1987). Furthermore, career writers are typically affiliated with these tasks in ways quite different from professionals who write. Engineers, for example, do write procedures (career writers' most common task), but they tend to have developed the information themselves, whereas career writers typically prepare procedures originated by others (e.g., Harrison & Debs, 1988, p. 6). Although career writers may know a great deal about technical subjects and contribute to making meaning, their area of perceived expertise is not technical; typically, they are not "subject matter" experts (Little & McLaren, 1987). In short, career writers tend to document others' activities without having the central responsibility for invention or the personal stake in constructing meaning that is characteristic of professionals who write.

The Task Value: Routine or Special Writing

Our classification of writing into routine and special tasks is intuitive, but it is based on a wide variety of reported practice and research (e.g., Suchan & Dulek's distinction between sensitive and nonsensitive texts, 1988). Further, it is grounded in our own experience as writers: Some of our composing tasks seemed routine—our primary goal was efficient completion; for other writing tasks, our goal was the most effective product possible. The importance of the situation influenced our strategies throughout composing, so much so that our procedures for routine and nonroutine tasks defined two quite different methods of writing.

The distinction between routine and nonroutine appears universal in the business environment. Routine work involves known, structured problems with repetitive tasks; nonroutine work, by contrast, focuses on unstructured problems and uncertain tasks. In fact, the rhetorical conception of "writing as problem solving" has tended to emphasize nonroutine writing (for example, formal reports that require numerous revisions) at the expense of routine writing (conventional memos that rely on scripts or standard solutions). Our model of task value is a step toward correcting this bias that neglects routine communication, the more common task in the workplace (DiSalvo & Larsen, 1987).

Distinguishing routine from nonroutine business writing has long been a significant way to classify texts, though the distinction typically emphasizes the product and its reception, not writers' procedures (for example, internal versus external correspondence; informative versus persuasive messages). In fact, historical studies suggest that the concepts of routine and nonroutine work influenced the development of business genres. Yates (1989) notes that at the turn of the century, reports to upper management consisted of "routine or periodic reports, which were issued at regular intervals to provide information on normal operations; and special reports, which analyzed (usually in response to a special request) a specific problem, opportunity, idea, or physical entity" (p. 77). Moreover, the memorandum developed as an efficient counterpart to the formal, external letter as a means of conducting routine business between internal units and departments (pp. 95–100).

Some case studies have shown that workplace writers do distinguish their composing procedures according to what they perceive to be routine and nonroutine (e.g., Odell & Goswami, 1984). Some studies report that employees make their first draft "the final one with only a few minor revisions, if any" when they write "routine business memoranda and correspondence," but compose important documents in multiple drafts, often collaboratively (Van Dyck, 1980, p. 8; see Broadhead & Freed, 1986). In fact, writers may make distinctions that cut across document types, perceiving that one memo is simply a routine matter, reflecting what they would do if they "were in a hurry," while another is quite significant, reflecting what they would do if they "wanted highest quality" (Gould, 1980, pp. 106–107).

The contrast between what is routine and what is nonroutine assumes a dichotomy rather than a continuum from the mundane to the truly exceptional. Like any model, this one glosses over differences and classifies things identically when they may only be similar. Moreover, some factors may characterize either category. Certainly some standard of quality may govern even the most routine document, and the necessity for urgency frequently characterizes highly important matters. Thus, either the routine or nonroutine task may be governed by conflicting goals for meeting an imminent deadline and achieving excellence in the product. In addition, many characteristics of the individual writer and attributes of his or her organizational role will surely impact these basic distinctions.

However, such a dichotomous classification of task value does reflect the nature of human choice—"not one, but the other"—in linguistic and other social behaviors (Halliday, 1985), and it reflects the presentation of such choice in many textbooks. For example, one text contrasts the formulaic, fill-in-the-blanks nature of routine communication with the creativity and unique character of special documents (Andrews & Andrews, 1988, p. 343). The almost universal recognition of a distinction between routine and special writing tasks warranted our investigation of this phenomenon to determine whether writers respond to these situational exigencies with distinctly different composing strategies.

Results: Composing Processes by Writer's Role and Task Value

Researchers have begun to describe the composing strategies of professionals in the workplace, but most have studied either individual members of a specific profession (e.g., Winsor, 1989) or small work groups in a single organization (e.g., Doheny-Farina, 1986). Although such qualitative research permits building generalizations across several studies, results of specific case studies sometimes contradict one another and contrast with results from quantitative research. Therefore, in discussing our findings, we have not reported exceptions in individuals' practices as contrary evidence.

In presenting our results, we have developed a characterization of the writing behaviors of professionals who write and career writers through grouping the aggregated responses of subjects by these categories; this approach responsibly reflects the manner in which data were collected. In responding to our survey, subjects first defined their role in an organization and typical writing tasks and then were invited to make distinctions, if any, between routine and special writing. Further, we have characterized how writing behaviors during planning and revising are linked to specific social values, situationally based in workplace communications. We believe that this is a valid starting point for developing and testing a rhetorical theory about a writer's role and task.

For all comparisons of responses of professionals and career writers, significance was determined on the 5-point Likert scale by a chi-square test. For comparisons of responses reported for routine and special writing, a Z test of the equality of two proportions was conducted and all differences were found to be significant at the level of $p < .001$ (therefore, we will not report the statistical significance within the text). In discussing the results, we have combined the Often (O) and Very Often (VO) or the Never (N) and Rarely (R) responses.

Composing Processes of Professionals Who Write

Professionals who write, no matter what their field, take strikingly different approaches to routine and special writing tasks. They devote more time and attention to their nonroutine tasks, both in planning and revising.

Although our respondents claim to plan much of their writing, including routine work, they do so more for special assignments. Nearly all professionals (90% O & VO) mentally plan before drafting special writing. In fact, whereas nearly a third (32% O & VO) do not plan routine tasks, only 13% (O &VO) regularly omit planning for nonroutine work (table 1.1). Most professionals (86% O & VO) jot down notes or lists before drafting special writing, but only 55% (O & VO) plan on paper when doing routine tasks. Furthermore, a majority (60% O & VO) claim to outline their special documents, whereas less than a quarter (22% O & VO) typically outline routine writing.

Professionals also revise their special writing far more often than their routine, preferring to revise after drafting more often than during it (table 1.2). While drafting, 25% (O & VO) of those surveyed revise special documents in major ways, but only 15% (O & VO) revise routine assignments. After drafting, however, 39% (O & VO) of these professionals make major revisions of their special writing, with only 21% (O & VO) revising their routine writing in major ways. Professionals give particular attention to nonroutine writing: The majority (69% N & R) do not regard a first draft

Table 1.1. Planning Before Drafting by Professionals (*N*=351)

	Never/Rarely	*Some*	*Often/Very Often*
I mentally plan a lot			
Routine (NA[a] 3%)[b]	9%	17%	72%
Special (NA 1%)	1%	8%	90%
I mentally plan very little			
Routine (NA 2%)	45%	21%	32%
Special (NA 1%)	72%	14%	13%
I write notes and lists			
Routine (NA 3%)	19%	24%	55%
Special (NA 1%)	4%	10%	86%
I outline			
Routine (NA 5%)	52%	21%	22%
Special (NA 1%)	21%	19%	60%

[a]NA = "No answer" in this and subsequent tables.
[b]Rows in this and subsequent tables may not add up to 100% because of rounding.

as the final draft for special assignments. However, when doing routine writing, many (44% O & VO) simply prepare a single draft.

Additional analysis of the data on planning reveals that professionals focus more on planning their nonroutine documents than on revising them. Of those professionals (61%) who claim a difference in their tendency to mentally plan beforehand as opposed to revising afterward, almost all (92% O & VO) claim to do more mental planning. Of those (58%) who claim a difference between taking notes beforehand and revising after, almost all (98% O & VO) claim to take notes beforehand more frequently. And of those (59%) who claim a difference between their outlining beforehand and revising after, a majority (66% O & VO) claim to outline before more often. In short, planning is a significant characteristic of professionals' composing procedures.

This profile of professionals' planning and revising is clearly different from writers' procedures for routine and special tasks, regardless of the kind of document. These professionals approach routine writing expeditiously, moving quite spontaneously to drafting and completing the task without looking back. In fact, over a third claim to plan and draft at the same time, especially for routine tasks (35% O & VO compared with 23% for special

Table 1.2. Revision in Major Ways by Professionals (*N*=347)

	Never/Rarely	*Some*	*Often/Very Often*
I revise while drafting			
Routine (NA 6%)	52%	28%	15%
Special (NA 1%)	42%	32%	25%
I revise after drafting			
Routine (NA 2%)	40%	37%	21%
Special (NA 1%)	23%	36%	39%
I tend to make the first draft the final one			
Routine (NA 1%)	38%	17%	44%
Special	69%	15%	15%

writing). By contrast, they approach most special writing assignments with care, both planning and revising extensively.

The writer's identification of routine or special tasks represents a strategic choice between efficiency and issues of quality and effectiveness, based on an assessment of the situation (see Shelby, 1988). Routine work involves structured, known problems; routine tasks tend to be repetitive and characterized by sequential, efficient procedures. Nonroutine work, however, focuses on unstructured or semistructured problems, so the task tends to be characterized by deliberation and reflection. In classifying numerous managerial communications on a continuum of routine to nonroutine, researchers have identified that the key factor differentiating routine and nonroutine tasks is the "uncertainty" of the situation (Lengel & Daft, 1988). Effective nonroutine communication must reduce the ambiguous nature of problems and deal with the stakeholders' uncertainties (Daft & Lengel, 1986; Driskill & Goldstein, 1986).

Because dealing in writing with such novel or complex problems is so difficult, managers tend to select face-to-face communication for nonroutine situations (Lengel & Daft, 1988). Thus, it is not surprising that our subjects conduct frequent discourse interaction with peers or supervisors throughout the planning, drafting, and reviewing of their special writing. Through this oral interaction, they get rapid feedback and can adjust their writing to the concerns of various stakeholders (Couture & Rymer, 1991; Spilka, 1990b). In effect, special writing procedures embrace some of the advantages of oral communication in nonroutine contexts.

Situational Exigence

The tendency of professionals to plan special writing more extensively than they revise points to many possible causes. For example, writers may simply truncate revision because of imminent deadlines; or, when writers are familiar with the task, they may make revisions during the planning stage so that rewriting after drafting becomes less necessary (Witte, 1985). We believe, however, that professionals may focus on planning because their functional role dictates it. An engineer or architect, for example, may narrowly define the composing process as "writing up results," a process that begins after the "real work" of technical or managerial problem solving is completed. This limited conception of writing emphasizes working out all the answers prior to drafting as a professional activity and de-emphasizes both writing and revision as workaday transcription. Conventional wisdom about professional practice advocates logical, linear procedures, beginning with extensive planning ahead; some researchers have claimed that technical professionals tend to practice linear, deliberate composing with an emphasis on outlining (Broadhead & Freed, 1986; Roundy & Mair, 1982; Spretnak, 1982). Certainly, Selzer's (1983) much cited case study of an engineer appears less anomalous when analyzed from this perspective. The engineer's reported strategy of extensively planning and outlining before drafting, spending less than 5% of his time on revision, may be an extreme case but not out of character for his profession. Not only may some technical professionals perceive writing to be merely an instrument for reporting solutions, but they may regard revision as an inherently negative behavior, inconsistent with their professional ethos that emphasizes efficiency and doing the job right the first time. In fact, the major revising that our subjects claim to do may not represent the individual's choice so much as the organization's requirements for document review and approval (Couture & Rymer, 1989; Paradis, Dobrin, & Miller, 1985).

Professionals' tendency to regard writing as a subordinate activity is confirmed by the rhetorical theories that attempt to counter this view by separating technical and rhetorical problem solving. In their classic statement, Mathes and Stevenson (1976) caution that the writing of reports in the workplace involves the recursive consideration of both technical and rhetorical problem solving; the task of addressing a technical problem must look toward the rhetorical explanation of its solution. Yet, by nature, the focus of the professional who writes is on the task defined by his or her discipline; writing is a vehicle for achieving this primary goal more than it is an end in and of itself. (This does not mean that professionals are rhetorically naive; many are obviously highly skilled writers who focus on rhetorical problems and use rhetorical strategies to further their professional goals [e.g., Rymer, 1988; Spilka, 1990b].) Professionals who write may tend to regard writing as a demonstration of professional expertise, as Brown and Herndl (1986) explained in reporting professionals' preference for narrative structure as opposed to organizational patterns highlighting solutions. Narrative structure "allows writers to take roles which match their sense of themselves and their favored functions in the corporate environment: task centered, impartial, orderly, nondirective" (p. 23). For many professionals who write, the impetus to persuade may not be professionally motivated, nor for some, we would speculate, is the impetus to revise.

Composing Processes of Career Writers

Career writers in our survey also make a distinction between routine and special writing tasks, but unlike the professionals who write, career writers attend meticulously to all aspects of the composing process, giving more time overall to planning and revising a draft. Nearly all career writers mentally plan both routine (82% O & VO) and special writing (98% O & VO) extensively (table 1.3). Unlike professionals, career writers rarely omit planning even for routine writing; a third of the professionals (32% O & VO) omit planning routine tasks compared with only 10% (O & VO) of the career writers.

Planning on paper is always highly prevalent for career writers (table 1.3). Nearly all respondents (95% O & VO) make notes or lists before

Table 1.3. Planning Before Drafting by Career Writers (*N*=62)

	Never/Rarely	*Some*	*Often/Very Often*
I mentally plan a lot			
Routine (NA 2%)	3%	13%	82%
Special	0%	2%	98%
I mentally plan very little			
Routine (NA 0%)	69%	21%	10%
Special	79%	8%	13%
I write notes and lists			
Routine (NA 5%)	10%	21%	65%
Special	2%	3%	95%
I outline			
Routine (NA 3%)	45%	11%	40%
Special	15%	13%	73%

drafting special writing, with well over half (65% O & VO) doing so for even routine tasks. Outlining of special writing is frequent for three-quarters of the group (73% O & VO), and almost half (40% O & VO) outline routine work. Additional analysis of the survey data reveals that career writers often plan during drafting, but do so for routine writing far more often than for special writing: Nearly half (44% O & VO) plan while they draft routine writing, whereas a third (31% O & VO) plan while they draft special writing.

Career writers surveyed attend to revision with much the same care they give to planning. Approximately half (58% N & R) do not make the first draft final for routine writing, while most (86% N & R) do not do so for special writing (table 1.4). A comparison of the responses of career writers (table 1.4) with those of professionals who write (table 1.2) reveals that the latter have a greater tendency to make the first draft final for both routine and special writing ($p < .05$ by a chi-square test).

The career writers we surveyed have a greater tendency than other professionals to revise all their writing in major ways. A majority (56% O & VO) revise special writing substantially after drafting, with 36% (O & VO) even revising routine writing. Like other professionals, career writers tend to revise their writing more often after completing a draft than while drafting (table 1.4).

Although career writers we surveyed tend to do more planning than revising, their planning, in contrast to professionals, is more equally balanced by revision. For special writing, a comparison of career writers'

Table 1.4. Revision in Major Ways by Career Writers (N=62)

	Never/Rarely	Some	Often/Very Often
I revise while drafting			
Routine (NA 5%)	45%	27%	23%
Special	36%	34%	31%
I revise after drafting			
Routine (NA 2%)	29%	34%	36%
Special (NA 0%)	13%	31%	56%
I tend to make the first draft the final one			
Routine (NA 2%)	58%	10%	31%
Special (NA 2%)	86%	8%	5%

tendencies to make notes or lists or to outline with their tendency to revise shows no significant difference. However, a further analysis of the data reveals that of those who perceive a difference in these pre- and postdrafting activities (42%), all tend to do more planning beforehand ($p < .001$ by a Z test of the equality of two proportions). Similarly, career writers claim no significant difference in their tendency to outline routine writing as opposed to revising it. But of those who perceive a difference in pre- and postdrafting activities (49%), well over three-quarters (83%) claim to write notes and lists beforehand significantly more often than to revise later ($p < .001$ by a Z test of the equality of two proportions).

Career writers distinguish their composing procedures for routine and special tasks across document types, but they attend more diligently than professionals who write to every aspect of composing both their routine and special documents—from planning through revision. Their attention to revision may reflect a requirement of their profession (writers often revising others' drafts, serving as "translators" between various units, and managing document cycling, an integral part of communications production). Research confirms that career writers designate separate stages of the composing process, including researching, planning, drafting, and editing, as definable and necessary for their profession (Green & Nolan, 1984; Kalmbach, Jobst, & Meese, 1986).

Two other factors may account for the career writer's tendency to emphasize revision as much as planning. First, the career writer attends to the quality of the writing by virtue of his or her professional identification as "writer." When given a choice of two alternative versions of a sentence, career writers tend to prefer the version written according to readability guidelines far more consistently than other professionals (Couture, 1992). Because achieving readability often means countering natural tendencies (for example, to bury important points in narrative or to disguise agency [Brown & Herndl, 1986]), career writers' commitment to style presents one plausible explanation for their extensive revision.

Second, revision may be significant because the career writer's primary professional function is to accommodate the needs of someone else through communication. The career writer provides a communicative mechanism through which someone else accesses a goal or a product. In drafting documents on behalf of technical professionals or administrators, career writers must accommodate their own views to the expectations of those others for whom they speak. For some career writers, accommodation requires learning the conventions of a different discourse community, as well as adjusting their conceptual perspectives to those whose ideas they must represent, often at a distance, which increases the need for both extensive planning and revising (see Cross, 1990). For others, it is a matter of accommodating technology to the user, which requires intense attention both to language and to its situation and implies that writing must play a "self-effacing" and deferential role (Dobrin, 1983).

The instrumental function of the career writer as a mediator dictates an active investment in every aspect of the communication process that achieves that accommodation. This motivation sharply distinguishes the functional role in composing of the professional who writes from that of the career writer.

Conclusion

In the rhetorical tradition of developing a theory to define communicative practice as it is motivated situationally, we have examined the contexts of the writer's functional role and task value as they influence writing in the workplace. We have attempted to characterize professional writing both empirically and rhetorically through surveying the practices of writers on the job and interpreting them as they are shaped both by the writer's investment in a writing task and the value of that task.

We found that composing practices are not so much influenced by a writer's professional discipline and occupation as by a writer's functional relationship to writing. We found further that the importance of the writing task has far greater impact than the genre of a document. These global situational exigencies, in fact, are dominant factors which account for and explain how writers approach communication tasks in the workplace.

The compelling distinctions drawn from our findings suggest more research is needed to define composing practices in the workplace both generally and in detail. Future case studies may uncover the specific situational exigencies that motivate writers to employ certain writing strategies. And more detailed description can show how composing behavior integrates with other managerial/technical tasks. Such investigations will reveal situational exigencies that may be affirmed as contextual universals through broad surveys of writing practice, such as the one we conducted. Studies of both specific and global situational influences on communities of writers will further our understanding of the constraints on writing in the workplace, and they will contribute to breaching the gap between empirical research and rhetorical theory in studies of professional writing.

Acknowledgments

The survey discussed in this chapter was an outcome of the Professional Writing Project (co-directors, Barbara Couture and John Brereton), sponsored by Wayne State University's Department of English and supported by the Fund for the Improvement of Postsecondary Education (U. S. Department of Education).

We wish to thank Richard T. Brengle, formerly of the English Composition Board, The University of Michigan, and Kenneth Guire, Department of Biostatistics, School of Public Health, The University of Michigan, for their help in preparing statistical data.

2 | Barbara Mirel

Beyond the Monkey House | Audience Analyses in Computerized Workplaces

Analyzing software documentation through the lens of rhetoric in the workplace means relating both the production and use of instructional materials to contextual constraints and opportunities. At present, technical communications research generally focuses more on the relationship between context and the production of texts than on the situational dynamics in readers' workplaces affecting the functionality (uses) of texts. Studies on producing documents, for example, examine the ways in which writers' choices are shaped by such situational demands as corporate image, consistency across documents, managerial expectations, or interdepartmental politics. Findings from such studies explain what factors converge in the complex process of writing and why writers choose the content and design that they do, but they do not answer the question of whether a final product fulfills its purposes with actual readers at work.

For software documentation, knowing whether written instructions succeed with users—that is, knowing whether people value and actually use their manuals—is essential. Such documentation does not achieve its purpose unless people use it to improve their performance of computerized tasks. Just as writers' processes of document development are shaped by the dynamics of their production environments, so are readers' uses of their documentation and their perception of its effectiveness tied to the dynamics of their computerized workplaces.

This essay argues that, for computer users at work, manuals do not need just to satisfy textual issues of readability, accuracy, and accessibility of information. Nor must they only pass usability tests showing that users can perform the tasks documented in a manual. Documentation also needs to accommodate the effects of computerization on users' worklives, effects such as people's need to maintain job satisfaction by engaging in intellectually challenging computerized work and their need to contribute to their organizations by discovering ways of using computers to improve business practices and communications. Contextual usability tests must assess users' abilities to perform tasks that they define for themselves as they strive to enhance the quality of their work and the productivity of their company.

Unfortunately, documentation specialists currently lack a clear sense of the content and design that manuals must have if they are to satisfy effectively users' contextually based needs and goals. Researchers know too little about the tasks that users set for themselves in response to computerization or the professional modes of learning and doing that they adapt to suit the practices, expectations, and goals of their workplaces. Researchers must begin to analyze audience needs in light of contextual influences.

Findings from such analyses can aid greatly in the process of document production, providing writers with sound conceptions of users' actual definitions of their tasks, their mappings of these tasks to computing capabilities, and their criteria for judging if instructions are effective. Contextually grounded audience analyses can unite the two worlds of document production and document use, with factors from users' computerized environments shaping writers' textual choices in equal measure to factors in their own production environment.

This study analyzes documentation audiences in context. Through surveys, I examine the relationship between users' instructional needs for complex data processing tasks and users' job positions and responsibilities, flexibility in work arrangements, and professional modes of learning and performing job-related work. I interviewed twenty-five users of a popular data base program who work in a variety of positions in different types of companies. I asked them about the tasks that require them to engage in complex data retrieval and analysis, the instructional information that is most helpful for these tasks, and the job-related goals and professional strategies and methods that direct their specific uses of a program.

Perhaps the most consistent and important finding from my surveys is users' need for documentation to help make automated work meaningful, a finding that reinforces Zuboff's argument (1984) that people need training in "informated," not just automated, uses of computers. One respondent in my survey, for example, sharply criticized her current manual for telling her what each program function can do but not how to manipulate the software advantageously for her business purposes. "My manual turns me into a monkey," she said. "It tells me what to do but not why to do it for the job I want to do." The challenge here for audience analysts is to find out what this user's job is, what tasks she performs at work, and how she conceives of doing her task with the data base program so that her office is something more than a monkey house. By looking at these issues, my study draws a connection between the content offered in documentation and the quality of users' worklives in computerized settings. If improvements in documentation do not deal with users' needs for quality interactions with their computers, these improvements risk doing no more than dressing up old formats and content. To paraphrase a Spanish saying, a monkey in a silk shirt is still a monkey.

My discussion starts by reviewing trends in audience analysis for software documentation. I then present the methods and results of my survey, showing that respondents' job positions, responsibilities, flexibility in work arrangements, and modes of workplace learning play a crucial role in their tasks and program interactions. Finally, I suggest directions for future research on audience needs in context for software documentation.

Audience Analysis for Software Manuals

Unlike most documents, software manuals combine the two functions of texts, reading-to-learn and reading-to-do. As Redish (1988) argues, they are reading-to-learn-to-do documents. Two types of inquiry, therefore, are required for analyzing the needs, goals, and expectations of software manual audiences. On one hand, analysts must assess "learning" by focusing on the reading and cognitive processing strategies that users have for accessing and comprehending instructional information relevant to their tasks. On the other hand, analysts must also examine "doing" by inquiring into the tasks users perform and want to perform and their conceptions of those tasks. The goal of such "doing" analyses is to discover the accuracy in informational content and the completeness (depth) of coverage that will help users perform their tasks effectively and efficiently. For both of these types of inquiry, task is the unifying theme. Task purposes structure users' instructional needs and goals for learning about and doing computerized work.

The definitions of users' tasks that analysts employ shape what they will find about users' needs. Earlier research into audience analysis for software manuals has arrived at very different findings about users' instructional needs based on different definitions of task as either "computing tasks" or "real-world tasks" (Duffy, Mehlenbacher, & Palmer, 1989). When analysts define tasks as computing tasks, they assume that programmers' models of task in the software aptly represent the work that users want to do. For example, the logic of an edit function in a word processing program is assumed to correspond in one-to-one fashion with the activities that users engage in when they actually edit a document. From a computing task point of view, audience analysis needs to focus just on what users have to learn to execute the functions and commands associated with program models of tasks.

By contrast, analysts who define tasks as real-world tasks believe that users have conceptual models of job-related tasks that may not correspond with program models. For any one activity, such as retrieving messages from electronic mail, users may envision interwoven, concurrent means for handling this activity that entail picking and choosing commands from numerous program functions in order to achieve the job purpose (Cypher, 1986). Audience analyses for real-world tasks seek to discover the strategies and skills that users need to learn in order to adapt program operations to their conceptual models of their job-related tasks.

Traditionally, most analyses of users' needs focus on computing tasks, with investigators equating program models of tasks with the tasks users need to perform. Card, Moran, and Newell (1980) lay the groundwork for such inquiries in their assessments of what users need to know and do to make their cognitive strategies correspond to the Goals-Operations-Methods-Selection (GOMS) logic of a program design for a task. More recently, documentation specialists have analyzed the informational content and sequencing that can best help users develop the production rules that are represented in program task models (Anderson, 1981, 1987; Kieras & Bovair, 1985; Kieras & Polson, 1985). Other inquiries into users' instructional needs based on learning-to-do approaches seek to discover the analogies, examples, operational explanations, or instructional packages that can help users understand and perform computing tasks (Charney, Reder, & Wells, 1988; Foss, Smith-Kerker, & Rosson, 1987; Rosenbaum & Walters, 1986).

All these analyses of users' needs are based on tasks defined as computing tasks. For example, analysts examine the knowledge and skills required for performing such program-designed tasks as moving cells in spreadsheets or writing query commands from prompt questions whose phrasing directly matches the underlying logic of the query command syntax (Charney et al., 1988; Ray, 1985). From these analyses of users' needs, documentation specialists develop the content and designs that they believe will facilitate human-computer interactions. This testing, however, is somewhat circular. In controlled settings, investigators set tasks for users to do with the help of a manual and measure the effect of the manual on users' accuracy and efficiency. But the targeted tasks are tasks defined by a program. These controlled testing situations can gauge the effectiveness of manuals in meeting users' instructional needs for such predefined, program-based tasks. Yet, in actual work settings, users may define their own tasks and task needs according to situational demands, not program design.

During the past decade, audience analyses have taken a new turn, examining users' actual styles of learning as they use software for task purposes. Early in the 1980s, Carroll and his colleagues at IBM Watson Research Center showed that people do not rely solely on written instructions for task performance, but instead actively explore a program through trial and error, referring to written information only at particular times, for example, for resolving errors or verifying actions. Such notions of users as "active learners" ushered in new focuses in audience analysis. Now many analysts seek to identify the content and design of written information that is most relevant to active learning-and-doing. Necessarily, such analyses of users' instructional needs have a wide scope. They look at relationships among readers, text, tasks, interface designs, and exploratory types of problem-solving strategies (Carroll, Smith-Kerker, Ford, & Mazur-Rimetz, 1986; Charney et al., 1988; Mirel, Feinberg, & Allmendinger, 1991).

Unfortunately, even when audience analysts focus on users' needs for active styles of learning and doing, the concept of task remains centered on computing tasks. Analysts still assume that the tasks users want to conduct and the way they conduct them in an exploratory fashion are equivalent to the tasks and logic built into a program. In testing the effectiveness of manuals for active learners, investigators still define the tasks that they ask users to perform according to program design.

Recently, documentation and software specialists have begun to raise questions about the efficacy of defining tasks as computing tasks. As early as 1986, Partridge argued that "defining tasks performed by each command . . . is not really task orientation from the user's point of view. Rather it is task-orientation from the computer's point of view" (p. 30). Today, many industries and researchers are observing users at work to identify what their learning-and-doing needs are for the tasks they perform in natural work environments (Johnson, 1990; Simpson, 1990; Troolin & Sahlin, 1990).

Complementing this current research in interface and document design is an increasing number of studies in situational cognition and workplace learning (Lave, 1988; Linde, 1989; Schon, 1987; Suchman, 1987). Findings from these studies show that strategies and procedures for computerized tasks are primarily driven by people's job situations, not by technological functions or some context-free vision of mental processes. For example, people interact with programs differently at various times, depending on their job tasks, their professional approaches to these tasks, and the problems or breakdowns that they encounter during a task. From the perspective of situational cognition, documented instructions are not rote actions but are interpreted in use, succeeding only so far as that interpretation leads to improved intellective skills, coordination of social interactions and team efforts, and innovative approaches to business processes.

Documentation analysts are beginning to inquire into users' conceptions of their work with computers, seeking to determine if program models of tasks correspond with users' models of tasks. Duffy et al. (1989), for example, propose that users' concepts of a task may be more synergistic than computer representations of tasks. In other words, to stay true to their professional approaches to work, users may want to combine functions and commands from different parts of a program or sequence software operations in new ways.

Some users in workplaces may, indeed, adapt their job-related tasks to the logic and structure of a given program. Others, however, may be unwilling to change their approaches to their work, perhaps due to pressures from managers or desires for greater job satisfaction (Eason, 1977). In such cases, users seek to modify a program for their work purposes, finding compensatory activities that may never have been intended by system designers. As Norman (1986) argues, finding effective means to bridge this gulf between users' goals and system capabilities is one of the greatest challenges faced by anyone seeking to improve the quality of human-computer interactions.

One way to begin to bridge this gulf, according to Duffy et al. (1989), is for documentation specialists to define users' goals and tasks as real-world tasks and to inquire into the range of prototypical job tasks that characterize workers' uses of software products. A study on engineers using a CAD program to design a television monitor illustrates the complex knowledge and strategies entailed in users' conceptions of this task. Whitefield (1989) found that the ways in which engineers defined and executed their design task differed dramatically from the logic and structure of the task models in the CAD program.

To assess users' instructional needs, analysts need a better understanding of the categories of job tasks that users perform and the ways in which users' job-related needs and purposes prompt them to manipulate program-defined tasks in inventive ways. In order to obtain a better idea of these categories, I designed a survey to discover the tasks at work that prompt people to use their data base programs and the ways in which these programs serve as tools for these tasks.

Survey Method

Questionnaire. To discover users' contextual orientations to complex tasks involving data processing, I conducted twenty-five structured telephone interviews. I used close- and open-ended questions to gather the following information:

- respondents' job roles, responsibilities, formal education, age, and data base experience
- factors influencing their satisfaction or dissatisfaction with their data base work
- job tasks that call for on-line data retrieval, analysis, and reporting
- respondents' competencies with various program functions and commands and their uses of these functions and commands for specific job tasks
- respondents' strategies and methods for achieving task goals and resolving problems
- the instructional information that respondents believe would help them use their data base program even more effectively.

Respondents. I selected respondents from a list of three hundred members who belong to the dBASE users group of the Chicago Computer Society. Using this list for my sample ensured that respondents would satisfy three criteria. First, I sought respondents who worked in a wide range of workplaces and represented diverse professions and hierarchical positions. Such diversity is essential for discovering boundaries between universal and situation-specific job tasks and activities. My twenty-five respondents represent seventeen different companies and such varied occupations as bankers, dentists, university administrators, television producers, independent consultants, and civil, electrical, and nuclear engineers. The respondents include people who are project engineers, upper and middle managers, office administrators and clericals, and self-employed.

Second, I sought respondents with some data base experience, a criterion that would increase the chances of individuals engaging in difficult program interactions as well as complex job tasks. Respondents ranged from two months' to eight years' experience.

My third criterion was the use of a common data base package, dBASE II, III, III+, or IV. Maintaining a focus on a single program ensured that responses about data base interactions share a uniform frame of reference. I chose dBASE because it is one of the most widely used PC programs in businesses today.

Method of analysis. In order to construct a typology of tasks that would reflect the ways in which respondents talked about their computerized work,

I analyzed their responses to see if they discussed their data base work in terms of program-defined or job-defined tasks. Using this analysis, I categorized task activities, organizing them by associated job responsibilities and goals and by conceptual complexity.

To determine the factors underlying respondents' uses of their data base program for particular types of job-related work, I cross-tabulated the following four variables: respondents' positions in their organizational hierarchy; the activities that they perform or want to perform as part of their jobs; their reported mastery and use of various complex program functions and commands; and their years of experience with dBASE.

In assessing the relationships between these variables, I examined the effects of job position and job-related activities on the uses that individuals make of their data base technology. If users' tasks correspond in one-to-one fashion with program definitions of tasks, users should linearly build their competence in task performance as they accumulate computing experience and knowledge. If tasks, as real-world tasks, do not directly map onto program designs, then a dynamic relation should exist between users' self-defined goals and work activities and their computing experience and expertise. To gain insight into this dynamic relationship, I analyzed the influence of job position and job-related activities on respondents' data base interactions, looking at the role that job goals play in people's uses and combinations of program functions and commands. I also examined the ways in which evolving technical knowledge and experience affect people's views of their job goals, that is, how technical understanding incites people to think about and execute their work in new ways.

Survey Results

One of the most striking findings from this survey is that instructions that assume a one-to-one correspondence between users' tasks and program-designed tasks are rarely sufficient, even for the most inexperienced users. After a small amount of experience, users quickly move beyond the routine activities that they can perform with discrete program commands and functions, and they attempt to use the program for more complex job-related tasks. For these software interactions, users desire instructions that help them integrate various program capabilities and help them infer the combinations and sequences of commands that work best for diverse situations and goals. To develop such instructions, writers need to understand users' tendencies to conceive of tasks in job-related terms and the link between job flexibility and users' evolving computing knowledge and experience, on one hand, and users' pursuits of challenging job goals through electronic means, on the other hand. This section describes my findings in these two areas, moving from the general ways in which respondents define tasks to the specific factors influencing task performance and computer interactions.

Users' conceptions of tasks. My findings support the recent trend in documentation and human-computer interactions to describe tasks as real-world tasks. All respondents defined particular data retrieval and analysis tasks in terms of their job responsibilities, not the names of program options (tasks). A manager, for example, describes one of his tasks as assigning engineers to new project teams. To carry out this task, he assesses employees according to availability, specialization, and prior experience. The query option in dBASE (a function for selecting records with designated characteristics) helps him retrieve and analyze the records of employees with the right qualifications, but he did not call this task a querying task.

Across the board, respondents mirrored this manager's tendency to describe their computerized activities according to such job-related work as assigning team members. When I asked respondents to detail a given task, they all broke the task into subtasks. These subtasks reflect respondents' methods for conducting their work and for figuring out ways to adapt program capabilities that support these methods. In some cases, professional approaches to subtasks correspond directly to program-defined tasks or functions. For example, in assigning team members, the manager followed the sequential logic of the query function in dBASE.

In other cases, however, the subtasks of a job-related activity did not necessarily translate directly into the logic of a program-designed task. For example, an engineer and an administrator both described one of their tasks as producing action lists for projects, but only the administrator's methods coincide with the set logic of the program and its predefined subtasks. The administrator's action lists are boilerplate so that she can generate them solely by using predefined commands in the report generation function. The engineer, by contrast, generates action lists by jumping around in the program and combining functions in unique ways. He first calculates dates by writing macros and using the calculation functions to find where slack time exists. Then he merges the results with the operations he conducts in the report generation function.

This study suggests that the more complex a job-related task is, the more likely it is that users will deviate from the subtask sequences designed in a program. Users invent combinations and sequences to suit the complexities of their job needs. One administrator who coordinates the inventory demands of many offices developed her own approach to this task that does not conform to the logic of any one of the computing tasks displayed in the menus. She skips around in the program, relating multiple data bases, copying values into memory variables, and using these variables to update yet another data base. Most respondents who use inventive combinations of program functions said that they discovered these approaches on their own, wanting but not finding help in their manuals. Their manuals describe only procedures for executing discrete program functions (computing tasks). What these respondents want, however, is instruction in "program management" to help them manipulate data base capabilities for their needs. Survey results suggest that users' self-defined tasks or subtasks are not necessarily congruent with predefined computing tasks. Instead, they are shaped by users' goals and the methods they value for performing their jobs.

Users think in terms of job activities. They have preconceived notions about how to perform their jobs, and when computerization enters the picture, they adapt program capabilities to their approaches to their work. Table 2.1 lists the variety of tasks that respondents in different job roles perform with the help of their data bases. Included in table 2.1 are users' constituent program interactions for these tasks, with tasks ordered by frequency.

The existence of such wide-ranging job tasks across organizational roles implicitly raises questions about the forces that influence users to perform particular tasks in specific computerized ways.

The effects of job goal, computing knowledge, and job flexibility on the uses of data bases. Even though data base programs do not determine how people define their workday tasks, the technology does affect people's notions of the activities they can and will perform at work. As supported by tables 2.2, 2.3, and 2.4, respondents' uses of data bases vary with their job roles and responsibilities, amount of dBASE experience, and level of technical competence.

According to this study, job role and its flexibility, experience, and technical competence can affect respondents' uses of their data base for job purposes in four ways:

Highly experienced users master the greatest number of functions and perform the most complex tasks.

Three respondents worked with dBASE the longest, six to eight years, and all of them had mastered the nine complex program functions that I asked about. Four other respondents with only three and a half to five years' experience also mastered all program functions. But these respondents do not combine functions as regularly as do the users with six to eight years' experience. The job roles of the three highly experienced respondents vary (manager, project engineer, and self-employed consultant) as does the range of their complex job activities (project management, inventory tracking, accounting, and so on). For all these activities, respondents use multiple

Table 2.1. Job Tasks and Percent of Respondents in Each Role Who Perform Them

Managers	Project Engineers	Administrators and Clericals	Self-Employed
87% Making decisions by generating and analyzing reports	50% Tracking milestones	100% Helping managers make decisions by generating reports	100% Expediting others' work by developing custom programs
50% Keeping project data current through automatic updates	Generating action lists	62% Generating action lists	40% Making decisions by generating and analyzing reports
37% Scheduling and tracing material orders/deliveries	Monitoring computing costs by maintaining time counts on-line	37% Maintaining office accounts by calculating statistics	20% Scheduling and tracking material orders/deliveries
25% Expediting others' work by developing custom programs	Expediting one's own work by developing custom programs	25% Expediting one's own work by developing custom programs	Distributing reports by printing labels
Setting priorities by relating data from multiple data bases	25% Expediting others' work by developing custom programs	12% Tracking milestones	Enhancing dBASE speed
Analyzing finances, budgets, and costs with calculating functions	Tracking projects by relating data from multiple data bases	Analyzing duplicated efforts	
	Making decisions by generating and analyzing reports	Improving communications between offices with networks	

Table 2.1. (Continued)

	Managers	Project Engineers	Administrators and Clericals	Self-Employed
12%	Tracking milestones	Scheduling and tracking material orders/deliveries		
	Scheduling and tracking responsibilities	Calculating costs		
	Generating action lists	Increasing efficiency by enhancing the speed of dBASE		
	Distributing reports by printing labels			
	Assessing productivity by calculating statistics			
	Evaluating salaries by querying for data on performance reviews			
	Increasing efficiency by enhancing the speed of dBASE			
	Total number tasks = 13	Total number tasks = 10	Total number tasks = 7	Total number tasks = 5

Table 2.2. Distribution of Respondents by Job Role (*N*=25)

Managers	Project Engineers	Administrator and Clericals	Self-Employed
32%	16%	32%	20%

Table 2.3. Distribution of Respondents by dBASE Experience (*N*=25)

High (6–8 years)	Intermediate (2–5 years)	Low (2 months–1 year)
12%	64%	24%

Table 2.4. Distribution of Respondents by Technical Competence (*N*=25)

Mastered all 9 functions	Mastered 6–8 functions
28%	48%
Mastered 3–5 functions	Mastered 1 function
20%	4%

Note: The nine program functions are: querying, writing command files, setting up indexes, customizing report formats, interfacing programs, calculating dates, relating data bases, calculating numerical values, and updating values.

program commands and functions, often in unique combinations, and almost always make some use of the command file function to write small programs to expedite their work. Some of these respondents even use programming to connect their PC data base activities with mainframe interactions for the purposes of product design or design tracking. These respondents expressed a desire to have manuals that would teach them an even greater range of technically and professionally challenging tasks.

Programming knowledge has been cited as a key characteristic of expert users (Schriver et al., 1986). In my study, the three respondents with the most experience and greatest technical proficiency all demonstrated programming abilities. Yet, twenty other respondents also reported expertise in the command file function. Not all of the other twenty, however, perform job activities as complex as do the three most expert respondents. Many of these other respondents acknowledge that, though they know how to program with the command file function, they do not understand fully how to use that function in conjunction with other commands and functions to perform their job-related tasks. Programming knowledge, therefore, is not so much the key characteristic of expertise as is strategic knowledge about how to integrate programming with other program interactions.

Inexperienced users are not necessarily low in technical competence nor in task complexity.

Finding a direct relation between high experience and high competence is not surprising. Yet, my findings do not conversely show that low experience correlates with low technical competence or routine job activities. Audience analysts cannot assume that relatively inexperienced users make only routine uses of a limited number of preset function and command sequences. One respondent with only three months' experience does indeed only know and use one program function. But three of the eleven respondents who have mastered six to eight of the program functions have little dBASE experience (two months to a year). One of these respondents, a clerk with two months' experience, uses her knowledge of six program functions to conduct complex job tasks. She devises means to link the communications between offices in her organization. The data base program offers her new methods for integrating, analyzing, and reporting information on equipment tests from various sections of her division. She develops new reports and reporting formats and disseminates these documents to various project teams concerned with common projects.

Job role strongly influences how users apply technical knowledge to their tasks and methods.

Technical knowledge and skills alone neither determine the types of tasks users perform nor the uses they make of computers for these tasks. Respondents' competencies in various program functions differ according to job role (see table 2.5).

To a large extent, individuals use their knowledge of a program differently according to job responsibilities. For example, proficiency in writing small programs with the command file function is no guarantee that individuals will apply this expertise to the same types of tasks, or even that they will apply this knowledge at all. All the self-employed respondents mastered writing small programs with the command file function, and all use that knowledge to help other people expedite their computerized work by developing custom applications for them. All of the project engineers similarly mastered command files, yet only a quarter of them help others by devel-

Table 2.5. Percent of Respondents in Each Job Position Mastering Specific Program Functions

Managers		Project Engineers		Administrators and Clericals		Self-Employed	
100%	Query*	100%	Query*	87%	Query	100%	Query
87%	Command files*		Command files		Indexing		Command files
75%	Indexing		Indexing*	75%	Command files*		Indexing
	Customizing formats*		Interfacing with other programs	62%	Customizing formats		Calculating dates
	Merging 2+ data bases*		Calculating dates	50%	Merging 2+ data bases		Merging 2+ data bases*
	Updating values		Updating values		Updating values	60%	Customizing formats
62%	Calculating dates	75%	Customizing formats	37%	Calculating dates		Interfacing with other programs
50%	Calculating numbers		Merging 2+ data bases	25%	Calculating numbers		Updating values*
37%	Interfacing with other programs	50%	Calculating numbers		Interfacing with other programs	40%	Calculating numbers

Note: * indicates that the function still causes occasional errors.

oping custom programs for them. Managers, too, were highly proficient in the command file function (87%), but, like project engineers, only 25% use this knowledge to expedite the work of others. Finally, three-fourths of the administrators and clericals know how to write command files, but none of them consult with others for improved approaches to work.

Even when respondents in different job positions share general types of job tasks, the program interactions on which people rely for these tasks are not always the same. For example, a manager and project engineer both use dBASE to schedule and track material orders. Both individuals work in the same civil engineering consulting firm, both have at least five years' computing experience, and both have mastered all the program functions. Yet, they use very different data base means for conducting this task because of the goals related to their job roles. The manager tracks materials in order to manage accounts and judiciously order supplies. He downloads CAD data to dBASE and uses dBASE to count a specific design element, such as a steel beam, merging this count with supplier data and creating an order for only the required material. The engineer, by contrast, tracks materials to keep abreast with other engineers and gauge that his use of materials does not exceed the average. He tracks materials by retrieving information from the data bases of other functional groups and comparing his and other engineers' use of resources.

Users with flexible job responsibilities and high job satisfaction are motivated to use data base programs inventively.

Job responsibility determines the work that individuals do in their organizations. Yet, it is too simplistic to say that people perform only the complex tasks that are "written into" the general job descriptions of their roles. In the survey, respondents explore new ways of using available data to improve business processes when they have a good deal of leeway and autonomy in their work.

One administrator, whose open work environment encourages her to define new responsibilities as long as they do not overlap with the work of others, has developed new networks between offices for data communications, enhancing her status as the "resident technical expert." Another administrator, however, whose office demands strict adherence to assigned responsibilities, uses dBASE only to put together mailings, the fixed responsibility of her job.

Desires for greater job satisfaction also prompt users to learn new approaches to their computerized work. Of the eleven respondents who offered explanations for why they want to learn new applications of the program for their work purposes, all said that they were motivated by the aim of gaining greater challenge and satisfaction with their work. None of these respondents were given specific incentives by their workplace to pursue new work practices or technical competencies. Seven of these respondents, however, were motivated to learn new computerized approaches to work because recently they had been given new responsibilities in their job roles.

Implications of Results

These survey results suggest that it is not enough to trace program competencies simply to years of computing experience. Job position markedly influences that competence. Individuals in the same job role often attain similar competencies despite different amounts of experience; alternately, people in different positions with comparable experience may vary in program proficiency. Users' job responsibilities may be the critical factor motivating them to shift from asking, "What can a command do?" to, "What can sets of combined commands do?" or even, "What routines can I generate to do my job?" This shift represents the move from an automated to an informated stance toward their computerized work. In addition, neither program competence nor experience fully explain what job-related tasks users are apt to pursue. Job role, more than anything else, shapes users' range and types of real-world tasks. These tasks, however, are affected by users' technical expertise and experience. People with greater expertise and experience are more likely than others to attempt tasks outside their conventional role responsibilities, tasks that are at once more sophisticated and more informated.

It is not sufficient, therefore, to categorize real-world tasks solely according to job role. In constructing a typology of complex, real-world tasks, I arranged tasks according to the levels of conceptual sophistication required for performing them. These levels of sophistication are a function of the combined effects of job role, professional expertise, technical expertise, and computing experience. The Appendix presents the typology of tasks that I devised from the survey responses.

What are users' learning needs for the tasks in this typology? Since the scope of this study aimed at gaining a broad understanding of the types of complex tasks and task approaches that users perform at work, my findings do not provide details on the instructional information that would best accommodate respondents' specific approaches to particular types of tasks. My findings, however, do highlight that audience analysts must assume that users' instructional needs have a social and organizational base, not just a cognitive one. Users' learning needs and their actual computing activities are driven by job-related goals; conceptions of tasks as real-work tasks; and intentions, plans, and problem-solving strategies that accord with workplace practices, expectations, and opportunities. The goal, therefore, is to redefine workplace tasks and their composite computer interactions from an acting-in-situation, not from an acting-with-program, perspective.

Directions for Future Research

Increasingly, many researchers are examining the effects of workplace contexts on the development and production of written texts (Brown & Herndl, 1986; Doheny-Farina, 1986; Harrison, 1988; Spencer, 1988). Yet, descriptions of document development in context are incomplete without evaluating whether the final written products are effective for readers' needs and purposes. This study highlights document effectiveness in context, analyzing audience needs and purposes in business environments. I find that unless audience analyses include assessments of users' job roles, flexibility in work arrangements, and practices for greater job satisfaction, these analyses will miss the mark in identifying audience needs and purposes in computerized workplaces. In 1986, Schriver et al. noted that "research has not provided designers with consistent definitions of user groups nor of the needs and proficiencies of particular users" and that "further research on user groups and their information needs is essential" (p. 55). Seven years later, such further research is still essential.

Results from this study suggest new directions for research into audience needs, complementing current inquiries into users' technical proficiency, computing experience, task-domain expertise, problem-solving styles and strategies, and reading and comprehension processes. Situational demands and interactions also strongly influence users' tasks and task needs. Many more studies need to be designed to discover the concrete approaches that users at work actually employ or want to employ for specific types of tasks.

Admittedly, it is impossible for documentation designers to address the infinite range and diversity of users' actual tasks and methods in different work settings. Yet, designing documentation for specific *types* of tasks may be a manageable goal. Researchers, therefore, need to pursue the following questions:

- To what extent do users' activities in different work settings fall into a reasonable number of real-world task types, with certain patterns of performance characterizing each type?
- What specific procedural and conceptual information do users need for various types of tasks?
- What instructional design and media are best, given workplace users' demonstrated means for acquiring help?

- How do users represent the goals and methods of their real-world tasks, and what instructional content and organization correspond to users' ways of thinking about their work?
- What is the relation between the tasks designed into a program and users' definitions of their tasks, and how can manuals address users' preconceived notions of a program and its potential for their work purposes?

Such research will explore new possibilities in form and content to meet the actual demands of real world goals and tasks. It also will uncover practical problems that prohibit documentation from answering many of the situation-specific needs of users. Findings from documentation studies on users' real-world rather than computing tasks can also affect what students learn in technical communication classes about audience analysis and applying findings to texts.

More generally, the need to assess the ways in which contextual dynamics shape readers' responses to and uses of their documents applies to all types of business and technical communications. A growing number of studies focus on how writers' work environments influence the documents they produce. The same contextual assessment needs to be applied to readers. After writers produce a document amid contextual influences, how effective is it with readers, given their own sets of situational factors? More use-oriented analyses would provide insights into the specific organizational conditions, opportunities, and constraints that underlie readers' actual reactions to and uses of the texts they receive. Contextual analyses of reading are a necessary corollary to contextual analyses of writing. Combined, the two analyses can provide a strong basis for distinguishing the textual choices that lead to effective communications between readers, writers, texts, and multiple contexts.

Acknowledgments

I want to thank my research assistant, Roger Theodos, for the invaluable help that he provided throughout this study. I'm also grateful to John Root for working with me to develop the proposal to the Spencer Foundation that resulted in funding for this research project.

Appendix. Typology of Job Tasks and Associated Program Interactions Categorized by Levels of Conceptual Sophistication

Regularly conducted project management tasks using records and files from one data base and preset program commands and functions

Conceptual demand: Linking command statements into chains to accomplish entire tasks

- single-step scheduling and tracking, personnel evaluations and decisions, report generation, and inventory control

Regularly conducted project management tasks using two or more data bases and combined sets of commands or functions

Conceptual demand: Integrating knowledge of command chains with more generalized procedures to accomplish wide-reaching task goals

- multi-step scheduling and tracking, personnel reviews and evaluations, report generation, inventory control, and billing
- calculating productivity

Inventive and strategic approaches to business by uploading or downloading data

Conceptual demand: Using complex technical operations to invent new, global approaches to job processes and practices

- research and development/design
- program development for others

Strategies for improving the efficiency of job tasks by enhancing program capabilities

Conceptual demand: Creating new syntactic elements within the system to transform the program's capabilities for one's job needs

- enhanced speed, storage, and/or accuracy

Adapted from the User Sophistication Taxonomy proposed by M. L. Schneider, 1984

3 | Jamie MacKinnon

Becoming a Rhetor

Developing Writing Ability
in a Mature,
Writing-Intensive Organization

While a good deal of research has been done on the development of writing ability in schoolchildren (e.g., Bereiter, 1980; Britton, Burgess, Martin, & Rosen, 1975), little is known about the development of writing ability in educated, working adults. Research indicates that on-the-job writers believe that they do develop significantly through on-the-job writing experience (Bataille, 1982; Brown, 1988) and that this experience is valued more highly than other factors such as writing courses or training in school (Paradis, Dobrin, & Bower, 1984). The nature of this development, however, has not been closely examined.

Indeed, research on the what, the how, and the why of development of on-the-job writing ability has hardly begun. As a result, we have an incomplete picture of writing development, one that implies that development is primarily school-based and thus conceived as "whatever the schools make it to be" (Bereiter, 1980, p. 88). The result is also a limited perspective on nonacademic writing, one that lacks an understanding of the intellectual abilities that nonacademic writing "demands and fosters" (Scribner & Cole, 1981, p. 76).

While interest has grown recently in writing as a "local" phenomenon, with context-dependent aims and characteristics (e.g., Bazerman, 1988), we are still far from understanding the relationship between the development of writing ability and the contexts in which it occurs. Britton was perhaps one of the first empirical researchers to underline the importance of context to development, especially to the significant audience- and function-related aspects of development (Britton et al., 1975). And Britton has warned repeatedly against "mistakenly treat[ing] writing as a single kind of ability, regardless of the reader for whom it is intended and the purpose it attempts to serve" (Britton, 1978, p. 13). Of course once the idea of development in context is accepted, the more difficult and problematic it is to conceive of a satisfactory *general* model of development, or even, perhaps, of "rhetorical maturity" (Miller, 1980), except in a local and contingent sense.

These very difficulties, however, point to the kind of theoretical contribution that might be made by research on the development of writing ability in various workplaces, especially in university-educated adults. In contrast to children, whose writing development intertwines with rapid growth in the mechanical and linguistic abilities needed to produce written text, educated adults who develop on-the-job writing ability should theoretically develop in a more purely rhetorical fashion, that is, in their ability to move the world through written language. And theoretically, growth in the writing ability of educated adults should be determined largely by the specific characteristics and demands of the work context in which it occurs. A better understanding of how and why educated adults develop on-the-job writing ability would therefore extend development theory by suggesting elements of a theory for rhetorical development in context.

Such an understanding, even a provisional one, should also widen the perspective on nonacademic writing in two different ways. First, it would add a dynamic, diachronic dimension to the picture, a dimension that has been largely ignored. Writers move the world through writing, but they too move, even as they write. Second, if development is shaped by the demands of the context in which it occurs, knowledge of this growth should also help us understand some of the determining features of various workplaces as discourse communities.

These issues provided a theoretical context for a naturalistic, longitudinal investigation of writing-related change in ten newly employed, highly educated adult "knowledge workers." The investigation was an attempt to discover some early, provisional answers to two complex questions. First, what writing-related knowledge do university graduates acquire in their first one to two years on the job in a writing-intensive, mature organization? Second, how do they learn what they learn? These questions in turn suggested a number of lower-level questions about the role of attitudes and beliefs in developing on-the-job writing ability, the effect a growing understanding of the socio-organizational context might have on writing, and possible changes in the writing process and written products. The investigation was also an attempt to provide a tentative answer to a third, higher-level question: How best to characterize writing-related knowledge acquired on-the-job?

Setting

I am a writing instructor at the Bank of Canada, Canada's central bank. The Bank's major activities include financial and monetary analysis, securities analysis, and econometric modeling. These activities are largely enabled by and carried out through writing. The Bank could be characterized as "writing-intensive": Writing is one of the most pervasive and important value-adding activities in the organization.

The Bank of Canada is large, employing hundreds of analysts and economists; it is stable and mature, being more than fifty years old; and it is organized into a fairly rigid hierarchy. These characteristics help distinguish the Bank as a unique and partly self-regulating discourse community. Other aspects of the Bank that are relevant to its functioning as a discourse community include the importance of writing to the carrying out of virtually all of the Bank's business functions, and the high regard given good writing, especially by members of senior management; a high degree of caution and care in decision making; the research orientation and academic background of its economists and analysts; and the predominance of "document cycling" (Paradis, Dobrin, & Miller, 1985) as a vehicle for "massaging" texts and managing the documentation process.

The writing done by analysts and economists responds to the information needs of various senior decision makers in the organization. These information needs are not readily apparent to new employees, and senior decision makers are often many levels removed in the hierarchy from junior employees. New employees typically write analytic reports dealing with ad hoc issues, as well as regularly scheduled, more generic texts such as "weekly notes," "updates," and "monthlies." Most of this writing involves research, analysis, and evaluation, and often in the case of the analytic reports, the development of a tightly reasoned argument.

The size and maturity of the Bank mean that newcomers accommodate and adapt themselves much more to the organization than in a small or "emergent" organization (Doheny-Farina, 1986). The strength and singularity of the Bank's culture are hinted at when employees speak of the "Bank culture," the "Bank point of view" on economic events, and the "Bank style" in writing. The Bank has its own style guide and in-house editors to review many of its most prestigious and important public documents.

Method

To maintain the required level of professional staff, the Bank regularly recruits newly graduated economists and financial analysts. This study involved investigating changes in the writing and writing-related knowledge of ten of these newly-arrived professional employees. The participants were the first ten economists and analysts to be hired following Bank approval to conduct this research. All of the participants were recent university graduates; several had masters' degrees. None of the participants, save one, perhaps, had ever written much outside of school. All of the participants, eight men and two women, were under the age of thirty.

Most of the data came from intensive two-hour interviews. The participants were interviewed twice. The first interview immediately followed the final draft of their first major paper (on average, about three months after joining the Bank) after they had revised on the basis of the final round of feedback. The second interview, ten to twenty months later, immediately followed the final draft of another major paper. Following the second interview, in-depth interviews were conducted with six managers (those who consented) of the participants. In addition to supervising the participants, these managers act as reviewers in the document-cycling process.

The interviews with the participants and the managers were document based. That is, the interviews took place immediately following the production of a large document and focused largely on the concrete and discrete experience of writing the single document at hand. Because of the variation in document types and because of the effects of managerial intervention in the document cycling process, discourse analysis was not practicable. The first interview had participants respond to identical, open-ended questions and dealt with four areas: attitudes and beliefs regarding writing; knowledge of the social and organizational context of writing; the writing process; and the written product.

The second interview asked participants first to describe any possible global changes of significance in their writing, and then the four areas were probed both generally and with participant-specific prompts, such as quotations of salient comments made by the participant in the first interview. Participants were asked to refer to aspects of the document at hand to illustrate statements regarding possible change since the first interview. The interview concluded by asking participants about differences between writing at a university and the Bank, advice they would give an incoming employee about writing, and whether they thought their writing would continue to develop in the following year.

As preparation for their interviews, the managers were asked to review the first-stage and second-stage documents. The first part of this interview involved asking the manager about possible changes in the employee's writing, both generally and in the four areas investigated. The second part had the manager react to interesting or salient participant statements regarding change from the participant's second-stage interview. Immediately following the interview, the manager was asked to fill in a reaction sheet that posited possible writing-related changes in the employee. The manager checked changes that were seen as true and then ranked the changes in terms of significance.

In general, the methodology was naturalistic and qualitative in orientation and both emic and etic in data production. The largely retrospective data from the participants' reports were triangulated through reference to the documents (by the participant, manager, and researcher), through comparing the managers' general remarks with the participants', and through having the managers comment specifically on some of the participants' salient statements. The personal and collaborative nature of the writer-manager relationship meant that more "process-based" investigative methods would have been seen as intrusive.

Findings

All participants appeared to acquire a wealth of writing-related knowledge over the ten to twenty month research time frame. It should be noted that the participants spent a good deal of time writing in this period. Seven of the participants reported spending 60% or more of their work time writing; one spent about 50%, one about 40%, and another about 35%. Many of the document types written over the research period were new to the participants.

The participants, managers, and researcher tended to have similar and corroborating perceptions regarding changes in the participants' writing and writing-related knowledge. The writers developed in the four areas examined, although many changes or developments did not fit neatly into a single area. Many of the findings show a complex, dynamic relationship between learning more about (and through) writing and learning more about the place of work, its employees, its culture and business functions, and the individual's job.[1]

Understanding of the social and organizational context. A critical aspect of the participants' development appeared to be learning a good deal about the social and organizational context in which they wrote: the business functions performed by their departments, the jobs performed by their readers (and thus their readers' needs for information), and the values and beliefs implicit in the organization's activities (more than one participant mentioned the "Bank view of the world").

Most participants said that increased knowledge of the social and organizational context had significant effects on their writing. "Understanding the power structure . . . knowing . . . my readers personally and how they fit into the workflow . . . helps me know how to convince my readers," said one participant. Another said, "You have to know what people know and don't know and that takes time." One participant who, according to his manager, had gained in several important ways as a writer over the course of his first year and a half, did not "put much value on knowing the organizational context" in the second interview. His manager, however, believed that he had acquired a good deal of knowledge in this area and thought this knowledge critical to his improved writing. The manager cited better understanding of the department's business functions, the participant's audience, and the participant's own job requirements as being the most important factors in helping the participant to write more useful papers. All managers interviewed confirmed the importance of this contextual knowledge for writers: "You want to understand what your reader is going to be doing with the information you're giving him in order to give it to him in a useful way," said one.

Another manager, in commenting on how useful it was for a writer to "know who's deciding what, and who needs what information" noted that in a large, hierarchic organization, this learning took time, typically more than a year. On the other hand, one participant noted that at the higher levels of a university, "you can go a long time without seeing your professor" while "here you see your boss every day."

In the first interview, most participants were confident in their knowledge of the audience and the underlying purpose of the document just written. Interestingly, ten to twenty months later, most participants looked back on these earlier certainties with disbelief. "I definitely wasn't clear [when I started working here] about the readership and how readers used the documents. . . . Sometimes you're wrong," was one representative comment. All managers confirmed the participants' beliefs that they had developed a much better sense of audience and purpose over the research period; most managers also predicted that this knowledge would continue to grow.

Another significant, though largely unconscious, aspect of the writers' development was in how they learned to use and manipulate a social/organizational process—document cycling and complex feedback—in order to help them produce satisfactory documents. As they learned how to deal with feedback and document cycling, which all participants found enormously frustrating at times, they were also learning more about their readers as individuals as well as their information needs, more about Bank discourse conventions, and more about the business functions enabled by or related to the documents they were writing. This increased acuity appeared to prompt consequent changes in the "macro" aspects of their writing processes, as suggested below.

The writing process. The participants reported more change in their writing process than the researcher had expected. Eight of the ten participants volunteered in the unguided, global part of the second interview that there had been major changes in their writing processes. These changes tended to be "high-level" or "macro" in nature, reflecting an accommodation to the larger dynamics of organizational life as well as an improved understanding of audiences, purposes, and writing-related business functions.

The following developments appeared to be the most common. In the second interview, the participants reported being more apt to:

- initiate ad hoc documents;
- clarify assigned papers orally to a greater degree when they were assigned and later while planning;
- be clearer before starting to draft about the "story" they would write, a story that economic or financial numbers would support;
- discuss writing with colleagues, especially in the early stages of writing;
- keep their readers in mind as they wrote ("On the last paper I went through so many drafting changes as a result of suggestions," said one participant, "that I began to think that there must be an easier way of making the paper acceptable to the reader earlier in the process. So, 'Would he [the manager] consider this acceptable' became my standard, my benchmark.");
- react to feedback effectively. Usually this meant better affective reaction as well as better instrumental strategies for using feedback. Virtually all of the participants felt less personally threatened and less depressed about feedback as time wore on: "A million red marks doesn't mean you aren't a good writer," said one participant. By the second interview, participants tended to take a more active role in the feedback sessions, understand more of the feedback, and revise on the basis of this understanding more effectively. Some participants had started asking colleagues for feedback. Participants said that "learning to use feedback" had been critical in making gains in writing; they also said that "feedback was the main [vehicle] for learning" about the Bank and its activities, readers' needs, and standards and expectations for documents.

Several participants obtained their own microcomputers during the study period. While the participants did not attribute significant changes in process or product to the use of word processing, more than one participant commented on increased speed and on not having to wait while a draft was tied up with a secretary.

Some participants reported an increase in efficiency and automatization in writing short, formulaic document types.

The written product. The participants' written products changed considerably over the research period to match more closely busy readers' narrow needs for information and analysis. Documents tended to be more focused, more visibly and hierarchically structured, more analytic, and less descriptive. Following are some representative comments from managers about changes in the participants' written products. The managers' interventions have a large effect on each draft; these comments therefore refer to changes in first or early drafts.

- "An improvement in making sure he's addressing the right audience."
- "Doesn't overburden the readers with details so much."
- "He [knows] the need to get a *story* out."
- "The structure and the purpose [are more] obvious [now]."
- "The content improved. . . . After a year he knew . . . what information would help his readers."
- "An improvement in first drafts. . . . [Better at] getting at the bottom line."

Attitudes and beliefs about writing. The participants' attitudes and beliefs about writing changed in various ways. Belief in the possibility of development was one important change. Few participants, when first interviewed, believed they would develop significantly as writers in their first year or two at the Bank. When asked about possible changes in their writing over the coming year, a few participants predicted no change ("Quite frankly, [I have] the same writing skills I've had since grade school," said one); several predicted possible change in rather narrow aspects of writing such as "better terminology" or "improved style"; a few were open to the idea that there would be broad change but had trouble making concrete the abstraction "something will change in relation to changing readerships."

By the second interview, ten to twenty months later, eight of the ten participants believed they had developed significantly as writers. In one revealing comment, a participant said: "Before I started . . . I would have definitely said that my writing wouldn't and needn't change all that much. But there have been significant changes and there need to be more changes. . . . I see there is a lot of learning to be done and a lot of improvement to be made. . . . I guess I was being conceited." While few participants predicted they would develop as writers when they were new employees, in the second-stage interviews, most predicted further development.

Self-confidence in writing ability increased generally among the participants, although earlier self-confidence was seen later as unjustified, too "naive" or "too high."[2] More than one manager made explicit reference to the relationship between attitude and writing development. One said, "Because he sees it [learning yet to be done and improvement yet to be made] he's making progress and he'll continue to make progress. It's the fellow who comes in saying, 'Hey, look. I did very well in English in university and I write poetry. You can't teach me: What are you, some bureaucrat?' Those guys don't do so well."

Participants' notions about the functions of writing broadened considerably. For many participants, this was reflected in a change from viewing the major function of writing as "to inform people about events and ideas" to the more dialogic sense of getting "reaction to ideas in hope of producing more research." Some participants developed a deeper understanding of the epistemic possibilities of writing as well. One participant said in her first interview that the role of writing was "to let other people know what you were doing and to get comments on your research." Eighteen months later, she added these three functions: "to answer questions" (analytic function); "to help people who come after us" (archival function); and "to clarify points of uncertainty . . . for ourselves" (exploratory or learning function). Significantly, most of the participants developed a powerful understanding over the research period that their writing needed to address the concrete information needs of their audience and not simply express what they, the writers, knew on a given topic.

Interestingly, many of the participants came to appreciate the "local" nature of writing in the Bank, and perhaps that "good" writing is not a fully generalizable notion: "If you don't know the culture, if you don't know the people you're working with, then you don't know your 'clients,'" said one participant. "It's a marketing strategy: if you don't know your readers, then your paper is not marketable. . . . You have to write taking into account the environment in which you are working. This is definitely a change in the last year. . . . You have to adapt to new environments and change your behavior."

How the participants learned. The developments outlined above appeared to be triggered by a variety of experiences, but two elements seemed critical: the new demands placed upon the participants as writers, and the feedback they received on their writing. The learning appeared to occur through various activities and media: through writing itself; through thinking about feedback, especially substantive, questioning feedback (from reviewers primarily, but also from colleagues, both in writing and orally); through reading, talking, listening, and observing; through developing subject-matter expertise; and through being directed, admonished, questioned, and encouraged as an employee. All participants emphasized the importance of feedback for their development as writers. The document cycling process appeared to be a vehicle for building consensus and sharing and making knowledge, as well as for "massaging" texts. Most participants emphasized the importance of learning more about their readers, both personally and as consumers of specific information to perform specific business functions. Several managers stressed the importance of good listening and interpersonal skills to writing development. One manager said "she had a very good network of peers with whom she could talk and learn a lot that way. I think that's perhaps the major route through which people learn about this organization." Two managers mentioned "shyness," being "passive," and not being "challenging" in the feedback sessions as factors that would limit an employee's development of writing ability.

The participants' consciousness of the learning varied. A few participants appeared to develop much more than they were aware, perhaps because they had narrow, restricting notions of the nature and domain of writing. Some managers were "quite surprised" to hear that their employees had attributed a great deal of importance to the feedback they had received for their development as writers. One of these managers was "quite mystified" about how his employee had learned as much as he had. Other managers were more aware of their role in this regard.

Managers confirmed most of their employees' quoted comments on aspects of their learning. There were no major differences between participants' and managers' perceptions, save that the manager sometimes saw a less "dramatic" change than the writer. Interestingly, more than one manager seemed to think of their employees as still developing and predicted further rhetorical growth: "This is going to be the next stage of his development if he stays here," said one manager. "He sees himself as someone paid to answer questions. Well, you know, as he moves up, he's going to be paid to *ask* questions."

Discussion

Overall, the writing-related changes were considerable, consequential, and a shock for some participants: "It's like going to China," said one. For most of the ten participants, the complex totality of the writing-related changes they experienced added up to a "sea change": a major shift in their understanding of what writing is and does in an organization, a revised understanding of the roles they saw for themselves as writing workers and as working writers, and often major changes in various aspects of the macro writing process.

▌ Becoming a Rhetor

The findings strongly support the idea that educated employees can develop writing ability on the job (Brown, 1988) as well as the notion that on-the-job experience is the major source of this learning (Paradis, Dobrin, & Bower, 1984), although the nature of this experience is complex and begs explanation. Interpreting development is always difficult—and usually needs explanation at some level—but perhaps it is useful to distinguish here between the developmental process and the developmental outcome.

The developmental process appears to have been instigated and informed by the new rhetorical demands of a new social-organizational context. If expertise in writing is "not categorical" but relatively domain-specific (Freedman, 1987; Nystrand, 1989) and cognitive strategies are less "portable" than previously assumed (e.g., Lave, 1985; Rogoff, 1984), then novel rhetorical demands are likely first to elicit inappropriate responses and then to spark new cognitive and social response strategies. In the Bank, the writing process is intertwined with a number of social processes, in particular, document cycling. It is through engagement in these social processes that newcomers to the Bank seem to acquire higher-level contextualizing knowledge, which in turn promotes gains in writing.

Over the research period, most participants acquired a wealth of knowledge that allowed them to function more effectively as writers. The most important knowledge gained, because of its catalytic nature, appeared to be contextualizing knowledge. Listed (roughly) from high-level, perhaps abstract and distant forms of context to lower-level, more immediate forms of context, the important elements of this knowledge included:

- aspects of the Bank as a discourse community that accomplishes specific (and at times unique) business functions through the specific discourse practices of a specific culture with its own distinct point of view;
- the information needs of senior, often remote, readers;
- the business functions enabled through writing and the relationship of written texts to various larger institutional "value-adding" processes;
- the forms of argument and informal reasoning conventional to, and found persuasive in, the Bank;
- the participant's role as an employee and writer in the larger, ambient, business-function processes;
- the rationale for and the mechanics of the document cycling process;
- the participant's growing, job-specific professional knowledge.

As recent university graduates working in their first major jobs, the participants were writing, perhaps for the first time in their lives, to an audience with real needs-to-know and in order to make things happen. Instead of writing to display mastery of knowledge as they had done in

▌ 51

school, they were writing, as they came to understand over time, to promote action and to inform decision making.

A key to the participants' development appeared to be a much greater awareness of, and sensitivity and adaptiveness to, the particular demands placed on writing by the Bank. Their growing awareness of these unique demands came as a surprise to some of the participants and appeared to be the precursor to writing more audience-sensitive text. In other words, the participants were not merely developing on some abstract continuum of "social decentration." Rather, some participants seemed to have come to an explicit understanding, perhaps for the first time in their lives, that audience counts. Indeed, some participants came to understand that meeting their readers' specific needs was the key determinant of success of written communication in the Bank. This growing realization appeared to precede later gains in audience sensitivity and adaptiveness.

Researchers have suggested that social cognitive ability—the ability to effectively represent one's social environment—may play an important role in the development of writing ability (e.g., Piché & Roen, 1987) and that "social cognition" may best be seen as a multidimensional ability that interacts in a complex manner with the composing process (Rubin, 1984b). These two notions cast light on the nature of a significant part of the participants' development: that of audience sensitivity and adaptiveness. Development occurred as the writers grew to understand some of the complexities and demands of the social structure in which they were writing.

Most of the participants contrasted their on-the-job writing with university writing by referring to the specificities of audience requirements in the Bank. It is tempting to speculate that in academia, a gradual, perhaps instrumentally motivated increase in "decentration" occurs, while initiation into an adult knowledge-working community might provoke a more sudden increase in social cognition, integratively as well as instrumentally motivated. Perhaps one needs to write to real, variegated audiences with real and divergent information needs to develop one's social cognition.

While social cognition and the demands of a new context account in part for the developmental process, a rhetorical perspective can help characterize the outcome of the participants' development. The participants were developing not only as writers, but also as members of a community they were still struggling to understand. In accepting and initiating writing assignments, submitting drafts at various stages of development to their reviewers, voluntarily seeking formal or informal feedback from colleagues, testing assumptions about their authority to make interpretive claims, responding in various fashions to feedback, and a plethora of other actions, the participants were assuming and adjusting writing-related roles for themselves and learning and conceptualizing the writing-related roles of others. The wide-ranging, role-related, and epistemic character of the writing-related changes, viewed as a totality, suggests that at least some participants experienced significant *rhetorical* development.

That is, over the research period, the participants enhanced their ability to engage the work community and carry out various tasks through discourse. As McCloskey (1985) and others have pointed out, writing in economics is highly rhetorical. In the Bank, most writing is analytic and argues a case. Writers pose and defend contestable ideas; they analyze and evaluate other people's ideas, all within an institutional forum. Senior managers have a pejorative term to describe merely descriptive writing: "elevator economics" (for example, housing starts are up; productivity is down). Young analysts and economists are often told that senior readers want analysis, evaluation, arguments, and "stories," but this must mystify the new employees at times. The making of persuasive stories in a community requires an understanding of the community's shared assumptions, beliefs, and values, as well as the forms of argument seen as legitimate in that community.

The participants in this study started to develop this knowledge by jumping into the fray, by joining the conversation, by making their own arguments. When their arguments failed to persuade, they knew so immediately, concretely and consequentially. When their arguments succeeded, it meant that they had succeeded in understanding the rhetorical dynamics of the Bank and the demands of their own rhetorical situation.

The growth of the economist/analyst as a writer can be viewed as the apprenticeship of a rhetor. The participants developed an effective, though largely tacit, understanding of the organization as a rhetorical domain. In acting rhetorically—in speaking, writing, talking, and listening—they were discovering what knowledge was socially significant and which forms of reasoned argument readers found persuasive. In so doing, the participants found a voice and conceptualized and assumed roles for themselves in a rhetorically bound, rhetorically functioning community. They joined in making and testing the community's knowledge and thus engaged more fully in the community's practices. In becoming rhetors, they became active participants in the community's business.

Implications of the Study

This study underscores the inadequacy of development theories based on the writing of children and adolescents in school settings to explain and interpret the development of educated adult writers in a work setting. If context is as important as it appears to be in determining the development of adult working writers, then an adequate *general* developmental theory may prove elusive. Developing domain-specific theory may be a more realistic, if more modest, goal.

Context would appear to be a critical element in any speculative model of rhetorical development of on-the-job writing ability. While theoreticians are starting to understand just how complex and multidimensional context can be (e.g., Piazza, 1987), it is useful to remember that writers and employees always start with the context at hand. In a large, hierarchic organization, "high-level context" (for example, the decision making of senior executives) is likely to be unknown and largely invisible to new employees. And yet in a large organization where knowledge is both the "raw material" and the goal of writing (cf. Gage, 1984), an understanding of this context will be critical to rhetorical growth. Development may occur as the employee engages and is engaged by a more immediate "mid-level context," the local organizational structure and forms of social interaction. Depending on the individual's ability to perceive, manipulate, and interpret that more immediate context, and depending on the supportive and inhibiting features of that context, the writer will over time gain a sense of the less immediate, though rhetorically important, high-level context. That is, the developing writer interacts primarily with an immediate context that intermediates information about and from higher-level contexts.

For on-the-job writing trainers, knowing that important aspects of writing development may naturally follow an increased understanding of business functions, audience, and corporate culture will have implications for, among other things, the timing of training. In addition, if writers' managers are as important as they appear in developing new employees' writing, training these managers in the effective management of writing may be warranted.

For writing teachers in colleges and universities, one obvious implication of this research is that they need not expect students to "master" writing before they graduate. Writing development is likely to continue after students leave school, it would seem, if their writing situation demands the kind of changes that prompt rhetorical growth. For students in professional programs, being told the simple (but perhaps counterintuitive) fact that their writing will likely develop in important ways "even" after graduation may be the most important lesson of all.

This study examined development in newly hired, recently graduated employees only, and in just one workplace. Future research on the development of nonacademic writing ability might examine a variety of local, situationally specific development patterns. Research on highly educated adults shows particular promise and should be pursued.

Just as studies of the development of academic writing ability sometimes tell us more about the school system than the children (Bereiter, 1980), the study of the development of nonacademic writing ability is likely to tell us as much about the worlds of work as about writing and development. And it will always be difficult for the researcher to separate learning to write from learning the job. But if we view writing as a way of doing work, the study of these twin developmental processes will afford a strategic opportunity: the chance to further integrate research on development and nonacademic writing with rhetorical theory. Such an integrated approach is likely to generate additional elements of a theory for rhetorical development in context.

Notes

1. A summary of the findings of a naturalistic study is problematic in that the methodological and persuasive benefits of "thick description" are absent, and a rather "thin," decontextualized list of assertions is the apparent result. The findings presented here are the synthetic outcome of two earlier, "lower-level" rounds of classification and analysis. First, portraits of individual participants' writing-related changes were sketched. Second, thematically organized, generalizable changes were drawn from these portraits. The findings presented here, then, "hide their tracks," and represent only a few of the most important writing-related changes, those that suggest significant development of writing ability.

2. See Myers (1980) for a look at how "bounded rationality" and the "self-serving bias in the way we perceive ourselves" (p. 49) are powerful forces in shaping self-image.

4 | Susan Kleimann

The Reciprocal Relationship of Workplace Culture and Review

Writing in the workplace is a collaborative act required frequently by organizations; it is, as Ede and Lunsford state, "a fact of life" (1990, p. 72). Their extensive survey established that in the workplace, collaborative writing is both horizontal and vertical, horizontal among peers and vertical among unequals within the hierarchy. Moreover, they find that vertical collaboration is "a widespread means of producing texts" (p. 133). Within workplace settings, organizations often distinguish between revision, the individual's process, and review, the organization's process. Most current research, however, has focused on the individual's revision with little work on the organization's review. For example, in Broadhead and Freed's study (1986) of process and product in a business setting, they consider second author, nonvoluntary changes but do not focus on them.

As only a few studies have shown, review can and does occur frequently in business settings. Kelton's study (1984) suggests that staff members produce twenty-one or more drafts for a single report, and Paradis, Dobrin, and Miller (1985) establish the first widespread acknowledgment of document cycling—the moving of a document between writer, supervisor, and manager—as a pervasive, iterative, and common organizational process. Moreover, their interviews catalog strong feelings about review's function, utility, and methods. Spilka's study (1988a), like Broadhead and Freed's (1986), focuses on the composing process of individual writers but establishes that a writer's success is related to managing the input of others.

Not only is review an important workplace process about which we know too little, but also the need to situate it in a particular setting is important. Even as surveys by Anderson (1985), Faigley and Miller (1982), and Couture and Rymer (1989) have documented the existence of collaborative and group writing, so has other research emphasized the need to regard the organization as a dominant influence on its staff who write (Faigley, 1985; Harrison, 1987; Nystrand, 1986; Odell, 1985; Piazza, 1987). More specifically, researchers have established that staff reflect the values of their environment (Brown & Herndl, 1986; Freed & Broadhead, 1987; Knoblauch, 1980); staff members' jobs can shape their way of thinking (Odell, 1985; Rutter, 1982); and the act of writing in an organization can have a symbiotic relationship with the organization (Dautermann, this volume; Doheny-Farina, 1986; McKinnon, this volume). None of these studies, however, focus closely on the culture within which writers play out their individual preferences or on cultural influence on what researchers observe in these settings. Without a close assessment of the cultural influence, we may make false assumptions and reach false conclusions about writing in the workplace. (See Winsor, 1990a, who discusses one such instance.)

In October 1987, I began an eighteen-month descriptive, qualitative study of the review process at a federal agency to identify and investigate in some depth the review process for reports, the organizational influence on review, and the interactions among the staff involved. Specifically, the questions for the study asked, (1) How do organizational and divisional cultures affect the nature of review comments?, and (2) In what ways do reviewers reflect the organization's culture in the style and content of their comments? This study demonstrates how the different cultures of individual divisions in a federal agency affect every aspect of the review process, from the structure of the process to the way reviewers frame their written comments to the number of written comments. In addition, from this study emerges a delineation of the dynamic relationship between the organization and review.

Research Methods

The Setting

This study is set at the United States General Accounting Office (GAO) in Washington, DC. (At GAO's request, the organization's name is not changed.) GAO is a midsized organization providing research reports requested by members of Congress to help them formulate policy, allocate funding, and initiate or revise legislation. In 1990, GAO produced over twelve hundred written reports for Congress and federal agencies, provided testimony, offered legal opinions, and resolved contractual disputes. Its report topics are wide-ranging (from logistical support for the B–1 bomber to reduction of the federal deficit), and its professional staff are well educated, often holding advanced degrees in public administration, social sciences, economics, or accounting.

GAO employs about five thousand staff members in fourteen regional and two overseas offices, with the largest concentration of personnel at Washington headquarters. Within headquarters, the staff is divided into four program divisions and three technical divisions, depending on the focus of the work. The assignment team, GAO's basic work unit, generally includes a primary writer and two levels of supervisors, with the primary writer being a professional who writes (Couture & Rymer, 1989).

Two major influences shape aspects of GAO's culture. First, GAO reports often result in changes to national policy, legislation, and funding; second, until recently, most GAO employees were educated as accountants, valuing minutiae and accuracy. Consequently, the agency has a cautious culture that demands maintaining detailed and extensive workpapers, referencing all facts to these workpapers, wanting both accuracy and objectivity and requiring an extensive review process. Moreover, because of the reports' potential impact, review is used to ensure that reports are correct from several perspectives. A bureaucracy tends to divide responsibilities among several employees and to fragment expertise, using specialists to perform specific jobs (Pace, 1983); thus, in GAO, many people read report drafts to ensure that all aspects, all views, and all expertise in the organization are represented. For example, a typical review chain might include the primary writer (who knows the most about the assignment), a supervisor (who has broad knowledge of GAO's mission, standards, and policies), an editor (whose expertise is with language and editing), a subject matter expert, a lawyer, and managers (who have even broader knowledge of GAO and its work environment). The goal of review is to produce an institutional product that speaks with the voice of the agency, not of an individual or an individual group. More than a mere anthropomorphism of the agency, the agency is granted a voice and an existence beyond its constituent staff. As a result, reviewers read for balance, objectivity, tone, adherence to organizational priorities, consistency with image and values, and a range of other complex and subtle points.

Research Design

As a participant in GAO's Doctoral Research Program, I had access to seven reports in three divisions as the reports moved through review to publication. GAO selected the three divisions to represent differences in

GAO's work, division size, and the number of reports issued by each division. Divisions chose report teams who agreed to participate and predicted that their reports would be issued within six months, the study's proposed time frame. I followed each report through the thirteen to twenty-four drafts each team produced. Four changes to the original design occurred: (1) Early steps in the research generated so much data that I did not consider the quality of the changes or the reports; (2) case attrition narrowed the seven assignments to five and reduced the number of primary participants from fifty-six to forty; (3) I collected data for twelve months because only one of the five reports was published within the study's original six-month time frame; (4) although I collected data on five assignments, time constraints meant that I analyzed data on three assignments in two divisions.

Data Collection

Because the study involved qualitative research, data collection combined different methods to allow for methodological triangulation, building reliability by accretion. I collected information about the context of GAO, the division, and the assignment, as well as details about each staff member to capture the many subtle influences that comprise a culture.

Context. I collected contextual information about GAO and the divisions in two ways. In one, I reviewed GAO's history, written guidance, policies and procedures, performance appraisal standards, and the content of its training classes. In the other, I conducted structured and open-ended interviews with primary participants about their backgrounds, experiences, and agreement with the official stance toward review.

Assignment details. I collected three types of information about the assignment: background information, details of the process, and details about the drafts and review comments. For each assignment, I collected background data through open-ended interviews and examination of documents about the history, request, and negotiations with the congressional staff. Details about the review process for each assignment were collected in the following ways: attending formal and informal meetings to observe discussions about a draft; conducting open-ended interviews after meetings to confirm my observations and to allow participants to explain occurrences or responses to the meetings; conducting structured interviews with staff to record differences in perceptions about the same events; collecting communication logs, sheets that required participants to record discussions, meetings, and phone calls pertaining to the assignment when I was not present; collecting copies of all drafts with written comments of reviewers; conducting discourse-based interviews that probed writers or reviewers about the reasoning process behind specific changes; conducting informal and often unplanned interviews with participants who wanted to talk about the process; and conducting open-ended interviews with staff as each report was completed about their perception of the assignment's success and reasons for the report's process.

To organize written comments (that is, any reviewer's mark made on a draft), I modified a GAO computer program. When defining "comment," I included spelling changes as well as requests to insert additional information. Data were entered identifying each comment by number, the draft number, the reviewer, the reviewer's position in the hierarchy, the comment's mode (such as, question, statement, or direct change), and the type of change, based on one of Broadhead and Freed's variables (1986).

Data Analysis

Data analysis included four techniques. First, for analysis of details about the comments, SPSS (a statistical software package) was used to create cross-indexing of various measures, such as the number of comments made by each reviewer or the number of comments phrased as questions or direct changes. Second, to provide a picture of the entire review process for each report, I developed a visual analytic tool, the complexity chart. Each chart illustrated a report's review process, including the number of drafts, the reviewers, the order of review, the date each draft went to and was returned by a reviewer, and the total time needed from first draft to publication (Kleimann, 1991). Third, to analyze details about the review process, I categorized data from the interviews, observations, and field notes. Some categories that evolved were goals of review, methods of review, or problems with review. From these categories, themes emerged, such as attitudes toward review or management philosophy. Fourth, as is typical in qualitative research, I asked participants frequently, at the end of meetings or interviews, to verify observations, and adjusted the data for accuracy. Furthermore, during a variation of discourse-based interviews, the primary participants reviewed the complexity charts, verified their accuracy and typicality, and discussed the implications for review suggested by the charts.

Results And Discussion

Differences in the Divisions' Cultures

Both divisions in this study share similar goals for review: to ensure that no errors are made in the details or in the interpretation of details and that the report is an institutional report, balancing and representing the various GAO perspectives. These shared goals dictate that review will be meticulous, and many individuals will review each report. Beyond these broad consistencies, the different characteristics of each division's culture produce two different review processes.

Division 1 is Based on Collaboration.

Staff at every level in Division 1 perceive review as a collaborative, negotiation process. For example, a top manager says, "I have always taken the position that just because we make a comment, you [the work team] may come back and say, 'Hey, we don't think we can do this, and here's why. . . . ' And we will back off or we will change and all that." The technical reviewer cites necessary collaboration when she says, "There are no soloists in GAO; there is only chorus." The primary writer, the lowest ranking team member on this report, captures the essence of the collaborative spirit as she discusses her willingness to make changes in response to review comments: "They've seen something that I've missed. Even if they're only one reader, I need to decide how general their response was."

Division 1 sees both its work and its staff holistically. Staff at all division levels consider thinking and writing as intimately related. The technical reviewer expresses a sentiment nearly every divisional participant shared: "I don't distinguish so well between good writers and good auditors. I think their writing is very often an honest reflection of the thought process, and the ones who write well, they audit well. They thought well."

Four beliefs form the cornerstone of Division 1's collaborative culture: writing and thinking are related processes, review in organizations produces institutional products, review is a negotiation process, and reviewers and writers can learn from each other. As a result, Division 1 management intervenes during review to smooth the review process for staff: It looks for opportunities to encourage thinking; it structures review to encourage multiple perspectives; it allows many review points to be open for discussion; and it establishes that reviewer and writer perspectives are equally valid and important.

Division 2 is Based on the Hierarchy.

Division 2 accepts the hierarchy's value and the consequent fragmentation of responsibilities and duties. Few staff members overtly support review. Most separate writing and their work of auditing, valuing auditing more than writing. For one primary writer and for many Division 2 staff, writing is not considered a way of knowing or coming to know. One primary writer characterizes his having to write the report as "not worth the investment for GAO." Writing is seen simply as the act of recording existing thoughts. Review is not seen by some staff as a valuable means to create an institutional product but as a hierarchical requirement of those who "have to see the report." The emphasis is on processing the report through the hierarchy rather than incorporating another perspective. When special reviewers in the division make few comments, staff perceive that reviewers add little substance and take up time; however, if reviewers make many comments, staff complain about personal preferences and reviewers who try to "do more" than their jobs.

Moreover, the high value placed on the hierarchy discourages negotiation and minimizes the sense that writers learn from each other. For example, if the reviewers and the team in Division 2 disagree about suggested revisions, the team can appeal to the next review level. In such cases, the reviewers cite their concerns in a memo (informally called a "nastygram"). The team, which includes higher-paid and higher-grade staff than the reviewers, and the next level of review resolve the disagreement without involving the original reviewers or even informing them of the resolution, even if the reviewers' suggestions are accepted.

Three beliefs form the cornerstone of Division 2's hierarchical culture: Thinking and writing are distinct activities; review is necessary as a bureaucratic stamp of approval that the report is correct; and expertise is based on one's location in the hierarchy, that is, the nearer the top, the greater the expertise and value to GAO. Division 2's hierarchical culture emphasizes the product and the need to monitor more junior staff. Staff perceive review within a traditional paradigm of organizations, as a mechanical process that requires a start-up and eventually stops (Morgan, 1986). Review is managed and structured so that each item in the checklist of necessary steps can be completed; the focus is on the steps in the process, not on how the process can help the team incorporate and understand the comments.

How the Divisions' Cultures Affect the Review Process

These two cultures result in review processes that differ in the written information available about review, the sequence of review, the use of meetings, the mode of the comments, and even the number of comments.

Hierarchical and Collaborative Cultures Place Different
Emphasis on Written Guidance.

Since information is power in an organization, a decision to place and disseminate information in writing suggests a willingness to share both information and power. Conversely, a reliance on unwritten guidance maintains a separation between the "haves" and the "have nots." Written information about review (if used and referred to) creates a context for individual review comments and thus allows staff to "de-particularize" or distance themselves emotionally from those comments.

Division 2 has (at the time of this study) no written guidance about functions, procedures, or rationale of review. Information about review is oral; written guidance consists of instructions on the sequential routing of reports. Supervisors are considered to have more information about GAO and divisional processes than those lower in the hierarchy, and the flow of information is restricted. A team member needing information may ask a supervisor, or a supervisor may decide a staff member is ready to have specific information. Furthermore, the lack of written guidance means comments are not perceived within a context; thus staff may particularize review comments and focus on the isolated instance. A word change, for example, may be seen as reflecting personal preference, not divisional knowledge. Consequently, staff members see review as a time-consuming barrier to their completing the report or as "not making any real difference." By not placing its goals in writing, therefore, Division 2 values the hierarchy, limits access to information, narrows staff's interpretation of review comments, and minimizes the importance of collaboration.

Division 1, on the other hand, has distributed to all staff written guidelines explaining the purpose of review and the reasons for some procedures. In interviews, staff and the head of report review refer to this guidance to support, explain, and predict what they do. Furthermore, the written guidance provides coherence to group perceptions of review. Staff members say that they use review comments to understand how "management" thinks or the context of the report topic. In sharing its goals in writing, the division has flattened the hierarchy within the division, provided a context for review comments, and established a sense of collaboration.

Hierarchical and Collaborative Cultures Structure Review Differently.

Review attempts to bring multiple perspectives into the draft. At GAO, in sequential review, only one reviewer at a time sees a draft. In concurrent review, staff send copies of the same draft to several readers at the same time. A natural outgrowth of concurrent review is consolidating comments to set revision priorities for the team.

Sequential review. Division 2 often relies on sequential review. Each level of the hierarchy is expected to produce a "perfect" draft before the draft ratchets to the next review level. Sequential review allows the team to incorporate the latest review comments before passing the draft to the next level of review; thus, the current reviewer always receives the most current thinking on the most current version of the draft.

But sequential review has liabilities. Although reviewers return comments quickly and the team incorporates comments quickly, sequential review lengthens the time frame. For example, in one report, three drafts were completed and reviewed by three reviewers over an eight day period. Draft #7 was sent to an immediate supervisor on Wednesday and returned on Friday. Immediately incorporating those comments, the staff sent the draft to the next level; it was returned on Monday. On the same Monday, Draft #9 went to the next reviewer and was returned on Wednesday. Staff and reviewers responded promptly to their tasks, but the review still took eight days. In sequential review, expertise and thinking are compartmentalized, reflecting the fragmentation of duties typical of bureaucracies.

Concurrent review. Division 1's concurrent review grows out of three givens: review requires multiple perspectives; review should be as speedy as possible; and the team should get help to work faster and more effectively. For example, in contrast to Division 2, one draft is completed and reviewed by four reviewers in four days. Staff send a draft to two report reviewers, the technical reviewer, and a division manager on one day and receive all comments four days later. The team then produces one new draft based on the reviewers' multiple perspectives, instead of the four separate drafts that sequential review would yield. Concurrent review flattens the hierarchy, because it suggests that reviewers have different but equally important information. Concurrency allows the team to judge revision suggestions against its knowledge of the topic; however, contradictions or the number of comments can make this task overwhelming.

Consolidated comments. To focus the team on important revisions and thus to speed revisions, Division 1 incorporates consolidated comments into its review structure. Different reviewers can give conflicting advice for various reasons (Kleimann, 1989), and the team, because GAO is a hierarchy, may feel awkward forcing the needed resolution. Division 1's head of report review, because of greater access to management, resolves all conflicting comments before the team receives the comments, sets revision priorities, and then allows the team to judge the suggestions against its knowledge of the topic.

Without revision priorities, the team responds to the first written comment and then moves on to the next one. With consolidated comments, the head of report review can say, "You need to get this title straight, but we've got a big problem here with this terminology. [The technical reviewer] said that you need to distinguish here between bands and frequencies." The team knows where to focus its efforts and tends to act more quickly. Moreover, sorting comments and setting priorities must be done by someone. For example, one Division 2 team leader waits for the return of all drafts before incorporating any comments. When asked why he waits, he responds, "There's no point in making changes until I have them all. I want to see what they agreed and disagreed on." Thus, the team leader in Division 2 does his own consolidating and comparing of comments, sometimes missing the point a reviewer was trying to make.

To reduce review time, however, management must set due dates for returning comments. Without stipulated return dates, reviewers set their own time frames and priorities. In one instance, a team sent concurrent review copies to three reviewers on 30 October with no return date stipulated by management; one reviewer returned comments on 31 October, another on 3 November, and the third on 15 November for a total of two weeks before the team could incorporate all comments. In addition, the team still had to allow time to resolve conflicting advice from reviewers.

In sum, Division 1 actively facilitates the review process by its structural management. Concurrent review, consolidated comments, and management deadlines serve to ensure that all views have been elicited, identify any conflicts in an early draft, set priorities for the team, and decrease review time.

Hierarchical and Collaborative Cultures Determine
the Nature and Frequency of Meetings.

Although Division 2 relies on oral culture to share the nuts and bolts of review, it requires no formal meetings about review comments. The team decides independently whether to meet with reviewers, unless someone higher in the hierarchy calls the meeting. Without meetings and discussions to help the team set priorities and understand the reasons behind the comments, staff make their own assessments with two results. First, they sometimes fail to expand their knowledge of the organization and tone. For example, what appears to be a simple, arbitrary word change often is charged with organizational implications; one primary writer perceived a review comment to alter the phrase "inadequate justifications" to "unreasonable justifications" as a superficial word change suggestion. Second, without meetings and discussion, staff members retain a false sense of power, because they make initial decisions about which comments to incorporate or ignore. However, when later revisions overrule these initial decisions, staff complain that their work is ignored or that the organization gives them no control. Meetings force them to negotiate with others and, thus, expand their organizational knowledge and increase their actual control over the report.

In contrast, Division 1 requires face-to-face meetings whenever consolidated comments are returned. During this team meeting, the head of report review sets priorities, explains the logic behind some requested changes, and clarifies any misunderstanding. The team asks for clarification of some points ("Do you mean we should eliminate this section?"), revises some sections with the reviewer ("What if we say it this way?"), and explains why a suggested change will not work ("If I say it that way, I'll have to put in too much additional information to explain why we changed the original due date"). As a result, these exchanges reduce the number of further iterations. Since much review involves honing the thinking and the presentation of the report from multiple perspectives, meetings allow staff to negotiate nuances and clarify meaning immediately. Meetings also create ownership of the report; one team leader says, "I want buy-in, but I also want them to feel like they're part of the process." Since the exchange is fluid, with the team refusing changes almost as often as they incorporate them, the meetings encourage collaboration.

Hierarchical and Collaborative Divisions Have Different
Modes and Frequency of Commenting.

For both divisions, I classified the way reviewers made comments into four modes: statements, questions, direct changes, and nonword symbols, such as marginal exclamation points. The proportion of one type to another seems to correspond to the division's culture and its assumptions about writing and reviewing. Statements and questions tend to deal with larger, less tangible issues of logic, additional needed information, or support for a point; their use adds complexity to the process because responding to either statements or questions requires the team's involvement in the problem-solving process. Nonword symbols serve more as markers for the reviewer than information for the team. Direct changes are the most explicit in terms of task, but the most ambiguous in terms of implied relationship. Direct changes are linked to surface features, such as word choice, spelling, and layout changes. In some cases, the changes set up a hierarchical relationship of "I know and you don't" or "I noticed and you didn't" between the reviewers and the team. In other instances, the direct changes are a part of the collaborative effort of the reviewers and the team to create a best product. The division's culture seems to determine which interpretation dominates.

In Division 2, reviewers made nearly twice as many comments (over four thousand) on a series of drafts than Division 1, and one reviewer made nearly fourteen hundred comments on a single draft. Of those comments, 75% were direct changes and 20% were statements and questions, although many statements were indirect requests for changes. This proportion is true at each level of the hierarchy. The high percentage of direct changes reinforces the hierarchy and the assumption that those nearer the top know more. The large number of changes reduces team members to mere clerks for incorporating change with little ownership of or responsibility for the report.

On the other hand, Division 1 reviewers made fewer than fifteen hundred comments on a series of drafts. Of those comments, 48% were statements and questions; this relatively high proportion suggests that reviewers return the final decision-making about changes to the team. Reviewers nearer the top of the hierarchy rely on questions and statements even more than reviewers closer to the team. Although some Division 1 statements request changes, others return responsibility to the team by suggesting general strategies ("I'd like this intro to be condensed") or by having the team double-check a point ("I thought you had verified this number"). When asked why he relies on questions, one reviewer responds, "I don't know this information as well as the team does. I don't see that I have any choice but to ask them if they can make a change or if they've considered this possibility." Division 1 acknowledges the team's expertise about report details and values them for that expertise.

Widespread use of questions and statements reinforces the idea that review is a negotiation process and that institutional products require balancing organizational values, knowledge bases, and perceptions. The team's engagement in the task of producing a well-supported message becomes the root of its ownership and responsibility for the report.

Conclusions

Writing in the workplace is always situated in a context. This study confirms that both the organization as a whole and the subunits within the organization can affect nearly every aspect of writing. Although GAO has a documented dominant culture, divisions establish their own cultures that result in different review processes. This study shows that although the purpose of review can be consistent, culture can affect even subtle aspects of the review process and hence the way staff perceive that process. As Knoblauch (1980) suggests, writers in the workplace want to accomplish organization goals, and their problems may be linked more to a weakness in understanding the organization than to a weakness in writing skill.

In any organization, the review process is designed to create an institutional product. As such, it deals not only with content but also with organizational values. Writers work not merely to convey information but also to clarify ambiguity about the dominance of certain values and constraints over others. This kind of ambiguity is inherent in each writing situation, especially if the written document is complicated, controversial, or influential. Workplace staff and reviewers look for a delicate balance among audience, task, document use, politics, and conflicting values in a piece of writing before they judge that piece good or effective. Since review is aimed at producing an institutional product, the task of reviewing is to articulate values and decide which ones will dominate in a given situation.

Because review involves negotiating a balance of values and constraints, oral exchanges are central to the success of a review process. Frequent exchanges help staff members navigate the political waters of any organization; they help staff members learn the organization and secure agreement on an approach to a report long before they have committed a great deal of time and effort to writing; they help staff members achieve buy-in to their institutional product. Frequent oral exchanges increase the chance that people communicate with, rather than past, each other.

Two additional conclusions about effective review grow out of this study.

Contributory Expertise and Institutional Products

In its simplest form, the review process merges the perspectives of the work team and divisional management. The work team perspective is rooted in the task's details, that is, knowledge of the facts and rhetorical constraints, such as the level of cooperation from the audited agency. Work team members are experts in the specifics of the assignment; they have a sense of how the pieces "hang together," of the fit of the facts. This assignment information, inherently short-term and narrowly focused, is essential to the report.

In contrast, the divisional management perspective is both long-term and broader. It is rooted in the individual managers' experiential knowledge of where the organization has been and their cultural knowledge of where the organization wants to go. By virtue of their time in the organization, managers have a store of knowledge about and experience with other assignments and other people that they bring to current assignments.

Since both "work team knowledge" and "management perspective" have constituent parts, we can create a model (see figure 4.1) of the different expertise brought to bear on a final report, with additional types of expertise layered on ad infinitum. The model illustrates the concept of contributory expertise, that is, a strand of expertise that shapes the final report. Each strand of contributory expertise modifies the report (as seen by the intersection of the sets) to meet the exact constraints of the assignment and to build a good report.

Organizational writers have responsibility, but rarely have autonomy, a distinction blurred by many. Responsibility is tied to the individual's contributory expertise—the individual's knowledge of some aspect of the assignment, whether very particular to the assignment or broader and based on previous experiences. To produce a "good report," in many cases, the contributory expertise of the team, management, technical experts, writer/editors, graphics designers, and so on must be tapped; these individuals have the re-

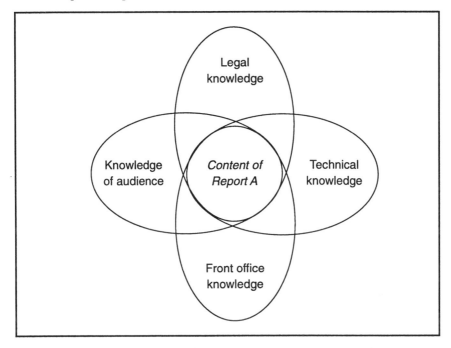

Figure 4.1. Contributory Expertise for Report A

sponsibility to bring the best of their expertise to the report. In a large organization, however, a report often needs to reflect multiple perspectives, and no one person holds all of these. Since a goal is an institutional product, built from the expertise of many, not one, autonomy often is simply not possible.

Advantages of Collaborative Review

A collaborative culture, which may exist within a hierarchical structure, emphasizes contributory expertise and thus produces a sense of ownership and responsibility. In contrast, a culture that devalues the contributions of some writers by emphasizing position undermines the responsibility of the individual writer and diffuses the power of collaboration. Yet, the lack of autonomy need not strip the work team of ownership or pride. The culture within which a team acts will determine the impact of responsibility without autonomy.

Producing a report that carries both the team and management perspectives requires something more complicated than adding decorative embroidery to a garment. Contributory expertise must be woven into the fabric of the report, which requires loosening the strands of one perspective in order to interweave the strands of another.

To accomplish this "weaving," staff negotiate with each other and management to know the other perspective in order to create meaning. There is no formula for developing each report. Sets of expertise for assignments will vary, but the concept of contributory expertise is basic to the concept of collaboration. Since each expertise contributes to the shaping of the report, review becomes a collaboration among "equal" experts. With this view, the hierarchy of the organization is collapsed, because an individual's position in the hierarchy is indicative of the particular kind of knowledge or contributory expertise he or she is likely to have, not of the relative importance of that person's comments; all types of expertise become necessary and valued.

Implications for Further Research

Despite the information provided by this study, much more research needs to be done. Two particular aspects for further research are suggested by this work: Additional descriptive studies that focus on workplace processes in organizations could broaden our understanding of document cycling in other types of organizations; and studies that focus on individual processes within organizations could broaden our understanding of what prompts the changes initiated by primary writers.

The issue of quality needs to be addressed, but such studies must use the complex definition of quality operative in the workplace. Given that definition, which changes were valuable? Who made them? Which changes were ignored? Which changes affected the quality of the document as an institutional piece of thinking and writing? Which changes could not be ignored, but harmed the quality of the final document? We need more intensive analysis of written comments using Broadhead and Freed's variables (1986) to determine what motivated subsequent changes. We need longitudinal studies that track a document from beginning to end; starting observations with the initial assignment, rather than when the report is being written, would provide a deeper understanding of the context, quality, and constraints of writing in organizations, which, in turn, could lead to persuasive and realistic recommendations for streamlining review or modifying other aspects of the workplace.

Reviewing in the workplace can be either a burden and a strain, or an arduous but exciting task that produces an institutional product incorporating both subject knowledge and the organization's broader expertise and values. But accomplishing the latter requires review to be seen not as a series of discrete skills, but as a systematic bringing together of webs of knowledge and skills to negotiate a balance among conflicting values and contributory expertise.

5 | **Rachel Spilka**

Moving Between Oral and Written Discourse to Fulfill Rhetorical and Social Goals

Is it possible to understand written discourse in the workplace adequately without appreciating how it relates to oral discourse? Recent research suggests it is not. Qualitative studies conducted during the 1980s suggest that any analysis of the composing process in the workplace needs to account for both oral and written discourse. Studies in the early and middle 1980s suggest that, in nonacademic settings, both oral discourse (for example, speech; informal and formal social interaction; writing resembling speech, such as comments written in margins or the minutes of meetings) and written discourse (for example, writing in isolation; written products) can be highly influential in fulfilling important rhetorical goals. Selzer (1983), who observed one engineer's composing processes, found that this engineer devoted much composing time to invention and did so not just silently, but also orally. Selzer hypothesizes that the more experienced writers become in a corporation, the more they recognize the value of talking to others during the composing process. Paradis, Dobrin, and Miller (1985) noted that new corporate writers at Exxon, by talking to supervisors during the planning process, can specify the purpose, audience, and ideal organizational scheme of a document and thereby circumvent quite a few problems the writers would otherwise have difficulty detecting or resolving on their own.

More recent qualitative studies suggest that oral discourse contributes even more than written discourse to such rhetorical and social functions as analyzing and adapting discourse to a multiple audience (Bocchi, 1991;

| 71

Spilka, 1988a), adapting to the review process (Kleimann, 1989), and fulfilling social goals for individual projects (Debs, 1986; Kleimann, 1989; Spilka, 1988a). (In this chapter, "social goals" are defined as those objectives an organization, its internal social groups, or its individual members perceive as being important to fulfill for the organization's perpetuation or advancement. Social goals can be as specific as needing to increase an organization's net worth by a certain percentage during a certain time span or as general as needing to overcome external prejudice against an organization's modes of behavior.) On a larger scale, oral discourse can be more instrumental than written discourse in building, shaping, and reshaping a corporate culture (Spilka, 1990b).

Although the profession has learned much about oral discourse in the workplace in the past decade, a number of significant gaps in knowledge remain. First, given that oral discourse can be more powerful than written discourse in serving rhetorical functions and fulfilling social goals in the workplace, why do writers in the workplace still rely so heavily on written discourse as well? Why do professionals seem dependent on not one, but both modes of expression during the composing process?

Also, studies to date have yet to explore in sufficient depth and detail how oral and written discourse function together to help professionals fulfill various rhetorical and social goals. Gaining this perspective seems especially important, because in the workplace, professionals repeatedly move back and forth between oral and written discourse while working on documents. More and more, the profession is recognizing that writing in the workplace is a process consisting of a chain of verbal and written interactions functioning together over time to enable professionals to fulfill various project goals and to contribute to an organizational culture (Debs, 1986; Spilka, 1988a).

Odell (1985) and Faigley (1985) argue that in the workplace, a reciprocal relationship exists between social contexts and the composing process. This theory suggests that just as social contexts can influence rhetorical choices, so can rhetorical choices influence social contexts. In the workplace, could the process of repeatedly moving back and forth between oral and written discourse serve as a means of modifying social contexts? Could movement between oral and written discourse help rhetors in the workplace fulfill social goals? If so, in what ways?

Methods of Data Collection and Analysis

To investigate these research questions, I conducted a multiple case study of professionals writing in two bureaus of a state Department of Environmental Protection (DEP) between August 1989 and May 1990. One bureau specialized in protecting state waterways, the other in protecting the environment from problems associated with oil contamination and hazardous waste. I conducted six case studies simultaneously, three in each of the two bureaus. The focus of each study was on the oral and written interactions taking place during the evolution of a major document. Most observations, however, centered on the composing and social behavior of the professional in charge of managing the project and assembling the major document associated with it. In this study, these professionals were all managers or coordinators, either by title or by their social role in the particular project observed in the study.

Research observations focused on the evolution of six major documents: a sewer license, a pollution report, a water system contract, an oil system contract, a request for proposal (RFP), and a series of newsletters aimed at both an internal and external (statewide) audience. In each case, I used methodological triangulation for data collection, which facilitated later detection of significant rhetorical and social patterns (that is, regularities of rhetorical and social behavior) occurring both within each case and across multiple cases. In addition, by using a wide variety of diverse research methods throughout the composing process, all chosen to help answer the original research questions, I hoped to compensate for the weakness of individual methods while also increasing opportunities for observing how movement between oral and written discourse might contribute to the fulfillment of social goals. Although not all subjects permitted use of all desired research methods, I was able to use most of the following measures in each case of the study:

Phase 1: Preliminary Data Collection

   structured interviews of the bureau directors, DEP communication specialists, and the six major subjects (about communication habits and patterns at the two bureaus and DEP, the unique social and cultural features of the settings, the history of each case, and predictions of interaction and document cycling patterns)

   collection of previous and ongoing documents associated with each case, including all plans, outlines, and drafts of major documents, as well as such other documents as memoranda, notes, letters, minutes of meetings, preliminary reports, and previous contracts consulted or produced by the subjects

Phase 2: Observation of the Composing Process

   observation of social interactions on-site

   log books about social interactions taking place while I was unable to be on-site (subjects recorded information about those interactions concerning the project)

   structured interviews conducted with each subject every two weeks to learn as much as possible about interactions that had taken place while I could not be on-site

open-ended interviews, both in person and on the telephone, with each subject as soon as possible following a major meeting or critical milestone in the project to inquire about its effects on subsequent social interactions, documents, and rhetorical/social plans and activities

discourse-based interviews, as soon as possible after a draft was completed, to discover any social or cultural influences on text-based decisions made in that draft

process-based interviews, approximately every few weeks, to determine personal, rhetorical, social, or cultural reasons for moving from oral to written discourse, or vice versa, at that juncture; during these interviews, subjects were asked to justify their composing process patterns, to date, of moving between oral and written discourse, similar to the way writers might justify text-based choices during a discourse-based interview

Phase 3: Postcomposing Process Measures and Analysis

retrospective open-ended interviews with subjects concerning social and cultural constraints that may have affected their perceptions, decisions, reactions, and interactions during the document's evolution to that point

discourse-based interviews of the latest draft

process-based interviews with subjects about the patterns of verbal and written interactions unique to that project and how those patterns might relate to rhetorical and social goals

Also, to achieve methodological triangulation for data analysis, I asked subjects, as often as possible, to validate my interpretations of rhetorical, social, and cultural patterns detected to date and made adjustments to these interpretations, as needed, to ensure accuracy. After the study, my central aim was to determine if and why the rhetorical participants in all six cases had relied on the back-and-forth movement between oral and written discourse to fulfill common rhetorical and social goals. To this end, I identified rhetorical and social goals all cases had in common, identified (in each case) back-and-forth movement between oral and written discourse over time, and then (in each case) matched patterns of movement between oral and written discourse with rhetorical and social goals shared by participants of all six cases.

Research Findings

Data analysis suggests that in all six case studies, moving between oral and written discourse, over time, contributed to fulfilling important rhetorical, social and cultural goals, and thereby contributed to the perpetuation and reshaping of the workplace culture. Several reasons might account for this finding: First, in all six cases, both oral and written discourse served the same rhetorical functions and contributed to the same social goals. As a result, DEP professionals seem to move closer to fulfilling social goals by relying on both oral and written discourse during the composing process rather than relying on just one of the two. Also, in all six cases, oral and written discourse had an interdependent relationship that encouraged and facilitated the back-and-forth movement between oral and written modes of expression throughout the composing process. Research results suggest that this interdependent relationship serves rhetorical functions that help fulfull social goals critical to the short-term success of individual projects and to both social acculturation and social change over the long term. The following sections discuss in more detail these possible contributing factors to the back-and-forth movement between oral and written discourse during the composing process at the DEP.

At the DEP, both oral and written discourse contribute to the same social goals.

In all six cases, the rhetorical participants were concerned about the same social goals, a finding that suggests the DEP culture is firmly and deeply entrenched in the consciousness of those who work there. For example, all rhetorical participants interviewed in all six cases agreed that, by far, the major social goal of the DEP is establishing and building its credibility. DEP employees were equally certain, in all six cases, that to establish and build credibility, it is critically important for them to help fulfill more minor social subgoals. For example, to establish credibility, DEP employees agree they need to attain public cooperation, and that to accomplish this, they need to build trust, reassure people, clarify doubts, minimize people's sense of threat, and establish the reasonableness of DEP regulations and activities. Likewise, DEP employees agree they need to achieve consistency in what is communciated and accomplished at DEP bureaus, a consensus perspective with outsiders about DEP regulations and practices, and enfranchisement of outsiders in decision-making processes.

One reason DEP employees all seem to recognize the same goals and subgoals is that almost daily they all confront anti-DEP bias. In all six cases, I observed anti-DEP bias directly (for example, in both social interaction and documents) and listened to people discuss the problem with me, individually, and among themselves at informal and formal meetings.

Anti-DEP bias is by no means a new problem for the DEP. Since its inception in the 1960s, the DEP has had a negative reputation throughout the state for several reasons. First, much of the state population resents government interference of any kind in what have been, so far, private affairs. Many fear government regulations will ultimately destroy a way of life they cherish and hope to protect. In addition, as a relatively new and ever-expanding government department, the DEP has yet to achieve consistency in what it communicates and in its operations. As a result, the public tends to be highly critical of the DEP's seeming inability to provide consistent and trustworthy information or responses to questions. This situation has had an adverse domino effect on DEP's ability to fulfill social subgoals, such as gaining cooperation for its regulations, programs, and activities. In the absence of cooperation from state, industrial, environmental, and other interest groups and the general public, DEP regulations tend to be unheeded, a situation making enforcement actions necessary and signaling DEP failure to achieve goals through less costly means, such as negotiation and volunteerism.

In response to almost daily exposure to anti-DEP prejudice, DEP managers attempt to build a strong internal cultural allegiance by focusing on social goals both at weekly meetings and in regular written correspondence with staff. In both bureaus observed, the directors realized from weekly meetings with the commissioner that he considers the goals of credibility, consistency, and consensus paramount in importance. These directors would discuss these goals (and ways to achieve them) at weekly management meetings, and department heads, in turn, would convey the same goals in weekly staff meetings and in informal notes and memoranda to their staff. Therefore, at the DEP, both the strong social hierarchy (of who exercises authority and power) and rhetorical channels (consisting of both oral and written modes of communication) seem to contribute to successful cultural indoctrination.

Because the culture of the state conflicts so dramatically with the DEP culture, many DEP employees believe it close to impossible, at least in the near future, to overcome completely the problem of poor credibility. Even so, many believe it possible to fulfill social subgoals and consider such attempts a social investment in the future. At the DEP, accomplishing social subgoals typically is seen as part of a long-term process of acculturation and change, already taking place, which eventually will establish and build DEP credibility throughout the state and reshape both the DEP culture and other cultures in the state. As one DEP writer put it, "I see our project as part of a twenty-year process of cultural change in the state; this will involve not just remediation, but behavior modification as well."

To fulfill social subgoals, DEP rhetors in all six cases found it more expedient and effective to rely on both oral and written discourse than on just one mode of expression or the other throughout the composing process. For example, to establish trust among members of a project committee, the rhetors in one case decided to establish a positive rapport with them during formal meetings, informal conversations in person or on the phone, and collaborative writing sessions. However, these rhetors also relied on informal notes, formal letters, and contract drafts to demonstrate their acknowledgment and acceptance of some committee ideas and preferences, thereby enfranchising committee members into the decision-making process.

At the DEP, oral and written discourse have an interdependent relationship that serves critical rhetorical functions, which, in turn, help fulfill social goals.

In all six cases, oral and written discourse had an interdependent relationship, which helps explain why both modes of expression are used to fulfill goals at the DEP. For example, as later sections will detail, oral modes of expression at the DEP seem to facilitate or reinforce written modes of expression, and vice versa, thereby adding strength to both. In addition, moving back and forth, continuously, between the two modes seems to increase opportunities to benefit from the inherent strengths of both modes, a situation that seems to add leverage in overcoming significant rhetorical and social barriers to project success and goal fulfillment.

In all six cases in this study, interdependency between oral and written discourse at the DEP served the following critical rhetorical functions, which, in turn, contributed to fulfilling social goals and long-term acculturation and change:

- facilitating progress in the composing process
- facilitating idea development, planning, and problem resolution
- encouraging cooperative dialogue between rhetors and their audience
- increasing opportunities to exercise power.

Facilitating Progress in the Composing Process

At the DEP, rhetors often choose to move between oral and written discourse to facilitate progress in the composing process. One reason is that written discourse can instigate, or trigger, subsequent oral discourse, and vice versa. For example, in one case, reading the draft of a DEP contract for repair of a town water system typically triggered the town planner's decision to set up a meeting of a town subcommittee in order to reach a consensus perspective among subcommittee members as to how the contract should be revised. After this type of meeting, the town planner would invariably feel obligated to report this consensus perspective in a formal letter to the DEP. This letter, in turn, would typically compel the contract writer to phone the town planner in order to negotiate, verbally, how the contract might be revised, based on the new information. This type of continuous back-and-forth motion between written and oral modes of communication often kept up the momentum of a project, which, otherwise, could lie stagnant, without any progress (or verbal or written interaction) for months at a time. DEP rhetors, therefore, could consider moving between oral and written discourse a way to step up progress in the composing process or to keep it going at a reasonable pace to prevent stagnation and to contribute to the social goal of efficiency.

Another rhetorical function of moving continuously between oral and written discourse is to establish a point of agreement in an ongoing argument or discussion. This function not only promotes progress and efficiency in the composing process, but also helps DEP rhetors achieve a consensus perspective.

In one case, the two writers of a pollution report needed, periodically, to solicit the opinions of an agricultural subcommittee consisting of representatives of interest groups, individual farmers, and various government managers and staff people. This subcommittee's opinions were important to the report's success because the DEP needed to demonstrate to the EPA that it was enfranchising the agricultural community in its process of assembling a state pollution plan. Soliciting the subcommittee's opinions was relatively easy, since the subcommittee met regularly. However, soliciting a consensus perspective from the subcommittee was a challenge, since members' opinions varied radically from those of the DEP. To move the subcommittee closer to a consensus with the DEP, the writers needed, continuously, to establish a point of agreement as to what the committee had decided so far, how it felt at that point, which milestones had been met, and what it wanted to do next.

To establish points of agreement, movement between writing or reading documents and interacting with others proved essential. For example, the two writers typically needed to update previous documents to represent what they perceived as recent progress from ongoing discussions; they would then set up an informal meeting with their DEP bureau director to secure his agreement to what was said in the updated documents. The next step would be to send a formal letter about the DEP managerial perspective to the head of the agricultural subcommittee, another manager at the Department of Agriculture (DOA), who, in turn, would phone the writers' DEP manager with her response to the letter. The DEP manager would send a memo to the writers with this information along with his own response. With this combined perspective, the two writers would feel it necessary to call another short meeting, attended by both the DEP and DOA managers, with the aim of gaining their consensus perspective prior to the upcoming meeting of the agricultural subcommittee. The writers felt gaining managerial consensus before the formal meeting was important to ensure that the DOA subcommittee head would represent DEP as well as DOA interests at the meeting.

During the meeting, both oral and written sources of knowledge proved important for reaching a point of agreement among various subcommittee members and between them and DEP writers. Similarly, both oral and written markers of progress were required to reassure all rhetorical participants that they were being thorough in examining what had transpired to date and which goals various groups had for the future. Moving between oral and written discourse throughout the composing process helped demonstrate to the EPA that the entire process had been a collaborative effort.

Facilitating Idea Development, Planning, and Problem Resolution

Just as DEP rhetors were able to speed up the composing process by moving between oral and written discourse, they also found it useful to slow down the pace, at times, to accomplish social goals. This study suggests that action is not always desirable and that delays can be socially profitable in the workplace. Moving between oral and written discourse can enable rhetors to delay progress in order to facilitate idea development, encourage more planning, and resolve problems arising during the composing process.

In all six cases, rhetors were able to promote more thinking and idea development by moving between oral and written discourse. Moving from one mode to the other tended to increase opportunity for incubation, a term used by Young, Becker, and Pike (1970) to describe a state of inquiry, a "period of subconscious activity" (p. 73) that is brought to bear on a problem, for example, after a person has shifted attention to new matters. In this study, rhetors typically thought more extensively about a problem and came to new ideas more quickly after switching from an oral to a written mode of expression, or vice versa, as if moving to a new type of mental activity provided a necessary break from the old type, along with a chance to "incubate" about the problem. In one case, for example, two writers often found it easier to think through a problem by isolating themselves from one another, and from others, in order to jot down ideas or translate their ideas, to date, into sections of an upcoming document; yet, they also found that after writing awhile, it was equally important to switch back to oral discourse in the form of conversations with each other and various colleagues in order to develop their ideas further or to overcome a writer's block about how to express an idea. Oral discourse, therefore, can serve as an opportunity for incubation and idea generation, just as written discourse can.

Moving between oral and written discourse also proved useful in extending document planning. In one case, writers needed to ensure their reports would reflect a consensus perspective; by continuously moving between social interactions and writing in isolation, they were able to prolong planning, to give others as much time and opportunity as possible to participate in decision making processes. Typically, the writers would produce and send interim documents for subcommittee members to consider and respond to between informal and formal meetings. Formal meetings would sometimes be delayed to allow members of the DEP and of the subcommittee more time to discuss ideas among themselves, write their own responses to interim documents, and submit those responses to the subcommittee head. At the DEP, switching back and forth between oral and written discourse proved useful in ensuring shared knowledge among group members, as well as enfranchising as many people as possible in the important early stages of a project, when plans start to develop. Relying on both oral and written discourse during planning also promoted shared goals among rhetorical participants.

In this study, rhetorical participants tended to move between oral and written discourse more frequently during invention and planning than during writing and revision. This more rapid movement might reflect the desire to involve as many people as possible in the decision-making process but also seems to reflect the degree to which social and cultural compatibility is lacking or deficient among rhetorical participants. For example, in one case, the writer of a water system contract for a small town found it necessary to move quickly between oral and written modes of expression during invention and planning simply because of the radical differences in perspective between town representatives and himself concerning the problem and its scope. Town representatives believed the problem affected a larger residential area than did the DEP and asked for DEP assistance in establishing a water system much larger and costlier than the one the DEP had in mind, could afford, and considered legally necessary. The result was a flurry of movement during planning between writing and reading documents and interacting on the phone or in person in attempts to reconcile widely incompatible desires and goals. This study suggests that at the DEP, if little social compatibility exists between rhetorical participants, there is a tendency to move back and forth more frequently between oral and written discourse during invention and planning.

Besides promoting more invention and planning, moving between oral and written discourse also facilitated problem-solving activity. In all six cases, rhetors found it useful to move back and forth between writing down their ideas and consulting with others until they could reach a consensus about problem identification, definition, and resolution. In some cases, reaching this type of consensus proved time-consuming and difficult, since rhetorical participants had such wide-ranging notions about the problem and its resolution.

Encouraging Cooperative Dialogue Between Rhetors and Their Audiences

Moving between oral and written discourse may also encourage rhetors to negotiate more frequently with various audience segments and individuals, which can increase opportunities to exercise an ethical appeal and thereby move closer to fulfilling such subgoals as attaining cooperation, achieving a consensus perspective, and establishing a stance of reasonableness toward others. In one case, a DEP writer needed to secure the cooperation of small-town representatives who, up to that point, had resisted DEP intervention in their environmental affairs. To win over this audience, the DEP writer made a special effort to follow up a phone call with a meeting at the town hall, during which the writer elicited town representatives' suggestions about problem resolution. Later, during a tour of town facilities and the pollution site, the writer refrained from commenting on humorous or appalling sights and focused, instead, on issuing compliments and reassurances. In follow-up letters and visits, he continued to approach this audience with respect, courtesy, and a willingness to negotiate with the town toward a mutually satisfactory solution to the problem. The repetition of this approach to the audience in both oral and written modes of expression convinced townspeople that they could work well with the DEP.

Increasing Opportunities to Exercise Power

Within the DEP culture, gaining cooperation from others usually depends on whether those people respect the authority with which you make statements, decisions, or requests. By moving between oral and written discourse, DEP rhetors seem better able to establish or build upon their authority with all members of their target audience.

In one case, two writers of a pollution report, both DEP staff members at a rank considered relatively low in the organizational hierarchy, decided they needed to demonstrate more authority in negotiations with the head of the agricultural subcommittee for the report, who was a DOA bureau director. After months of tension and "backfighting" in the subcommittee, the writers asked their own bureau director to write a letter to the DOA bureau director to explain the DEP position on regulations and enforcement activities. This strategy worked well: The DOA bureau director asked for a meeting with the writers and bureau director to negotiate how the DEP and DOA might resolve their differences. Formal letters that preceded and followed this meeting further convinced the DOA bureau director that she finally was dealing with authority she could respect and rely upon. This study suggests, then, that to fulfill important social goals, it can become necessary, first, to "borrow" social power from those with more authority and then to take advantage of that new power while moving between oral and written discourse. The back-and-forth movement between oral and written discourse seems to add extra leverage to a rhetor's effectiveness in demonstrating authority. The result is increased personal and social ethos and power, which at the DEP is especially helpful in establishing and building credibility and in effecting social change.

Implications for Future Research

This study suggests that at the DEP, increased knowledge of how to manipulate the composing process can result in a special kind of social power. In turn, such cultural influences as the high degree of consensus within the DEP culture and the strong clashes between the DEP and other social contexts engaged in the same rhetorical situation (for example, the DEP and agricultural community of the state; the DEP and the DOA) can affect, first, the frequency of movement between oral and written discourse, especially during invention and planning, and second, reliance of DEP rhetors on both oral and written discourse throughout their composing process for increased effectiveness in fulfilling important project goals.

Clearly, though, the nature of this reciprocal relationship between social contexts and oral and written discourse at the DEP might differ radically from that found elsewhere, for example, in other government departments and in the private sector. However, findings from this study do open up new possibilities for future research. To confirm, challenge, revise, or expand upon the conclusions drawn from this study, researchers need to investigate the following questions:

- Which functions and effects typify oral-written discourse combinations in other types of rhetorical situations in other types of social contexts?
- To what extent, and in what ways, do back-and-forth patterns of oral and written discourse differ according to social context, or depend on social context?
- How might movement between oral and written discourse influence multiple social contexts over time? How might multiple social contexts influence interdependency between oral and written discourse over time?
- What distinguishes effective from ineffective combinations of oral and written discourse?
- What are some cues that signal the need for certain types of oral or written communication or both, or for types of movement between the two?

- Can patterns of oral-written interdependency be tied to gender?
- What are implications of the interdependent relationship between oral and written discourse for notions of intertextuality? How can the profession understand better the complexities and unique features of those types of texts that seem hybrids of written and oral modes, such as the minutes of meetings and e-mail? Also, what are some rhetorical and social roles of silence and delays?

By investigating these and similar questions, researchers can help the profession mature in two important ways: in its appreciation of the complex relationship between social contexts and the composing process, and, perhaps more importantly, in its understanding of what it takes to gain rhetorical and social empowerment while collaborating with others toward fulfillment of shared social goals.

Acknowledgments

I thank Janice Lauer, Barbara Mirel, James E. Porter, and Patricia Sullivan for reviewing earlier drafts of this chapter.

6 | Judy Z. Segal

Writing and Medicine | Text and Context

Much has been written in recent years to illuminate the nature of persuasive strategies in scientific texts (e.g., Bazerman, 1988; Gross, 1990; Myers, 1990b; Prelli, 1989). While some of the work has been discipline-specific (Myers writes about biology; Bazerman, about physics), its purpose is often to claim something about scientific texts in general. Myers, for example, says that he hopes his book will contribute to "a change in reading habits that would make us more active, critical readers of the scientific discourse that enters our lives" (p. 252).

Here I will examine the rhetoric of medicine. My intention is not to generalize from a discipline in order to make a broad claim about scientific texts, but to specify the nature of a professional rhetoric in order to make a deep claim about a particular discipline. In studies of a number of scientific and quasi-scientific disciplines, Bazerman (1988) has illustrated "how social situations structure communication events and how forms of communication restructure society" (pp. 128–129). The purpose of my own study is to gather into this understanding of texts and contexts the nature and conduct of Western medicine.

My study extends and further grounds a claim made recently by Anderson (1989), who argues that physicians are locked within scientific medicine's frame of reference because of the "nature of language itself and . . . the rhetorical processes by which it defines, shapes, and maintains the particular world or reality in which physicians (indeed all human beings) dwell" (p. 8). Focusing on the rhetoric of the physician-patient dialogue, Anderson describes traditional medical rhetoric as "vertical"; it is a rhetoric of persuasion that descends from the physician as actor to the patient as acted upon, a rhetoric that, he says, may deprive patients of their voices in "the healing dialogue" (p. 13). Anderson presents an alternative, "horizontal" rhetoric that he calls, after Burke (1969b), a "rhetoric of identification." In the "new" rhetoric, "power is not exercised to manipulate, but to induce attitudes and to bring about actions designed to achieve a state of cooperation out of which healing in the very broadest sense of the word can arise" (pp. 15–16). Anderson argues for a horizontal medical rhetoric, or rather "a balanced dynamic between the two [rhetorics] that at once allows the physician to have the benefits of medical science and to use those benefits in a humane manner" (pp. 18–19).

The rhetoric of the physician-patient relationship that Anderson describes is only one manifestation of a rhetoric of medicine that characterizes all its texts and both shapes and reflects the epistemology and the values of the profession. Anderson's analysis can be extended through a fuller description of the nature and consequences of medical rhetoric.

This chapter argues that because Western medicine and its texts operate in a somewhat closed and reciprocal system, the discipline of Western medicine is, overall, conservative, resistant to change. The characteristics of the Western medical paradigm are supported and perpetuated in features of discourse that are used largely unself-consciously by writers in the profession. As I point out in my conclusion, some breaks in the system are becoming evident. From a number of quarters, a different paradigm begins to be articulated. In general, however, we have underestimated the extent to which discourse strategies and genres themselves are implicated in the process and the rate of change in the theory and practice of medicine.

My argument is built in three parts. First, I describe the current Western medical paradigm, focusing on well-documented characteristics of paternalism, interventionism, and fragmentation. Then, referring to a selection of articles in major medical journals, I demonstrate the extent to which elements of the Western medical paradigm are supported and reinvented in the features of medical discourse. Finally, I present a case study: I examine a review article in a wide-circulation medical journal as an example of how the paradigm asserts and continues itself in text. The case study is especially revealing, because it describes some medical literature as epideictic rhetoric— rhetoric through which readers' prior knowledge is neither changed nor increased but restated and re-presented from an author's point of view.

Method

Although this chapter begins with a description of Western medicine, my investigations did not. They began, instead, with a curiosity about the rhetorical strategies medical authors use to make their cases in journal articles—how they convince peer reviewers and other readers of the value of their work and how they insinuate their research or observations into the conversation of their discipline. My procedure, then, within the constraints of the (largely classical) rhetorical theory that informed my searches, was inductive.[1]

The articles I examined for this study were all on the subject of functional headache.[2] All appeared in well-established medical journals *(Journal of the American Medical Association, American Family Physician, New England Journal of Medicine, Postgraduate Medicine, Lancet, Headache);* all appeared within the last ten years; and all were directed to an audience of family physicians, as opposed to neurologists, psychologists, or other specialists. The sample included over four hundred articles, although I restricted my attention to two hundred of the less technical pieces.

Most articles on functional headache treat one of three topics: diagnosis, origin, or treatment of headache conditions; the articles are, in general, reports on research, "original observations," or review articles. The two hundred articles I selected for the study were distributed among these topics and genres.

Reading within the sample served to immerse me in the field of headache studies: I read to discover current issues in the field and to glean some of the conventions of medical discourse. With this background reading done, I selected (essentially at random, but with some attempt to maintain a fair distribution among journals and among types of articles) thirty-five articles for closer examination. These I read closely to discover what kinds of rhetorical features and patterns recurred in the texts. Once I had discovered a number of features (common inventional strategies, structures of arrange-ment, elements of style), I was able to use these features heuristically to guide the analysis of any article in the sample. The case study I include here is an example of an analysis enabled by the heuristic.

Despite my immersion in the literature of medicine, I remain, of course, outside the professional conversation of medical researchers and physicians. While I did not elicit systematic reading protocols from informed readers, I did, in order to redress some of the problem of my own naïveté, consult two physicians who read and responded to selected articles; a pharmacologist at this university reviewed my analyses once they were drafted.

When the examination of texts was complete, recurring discourse characteristics began to suggest reciprocity with certain characteristics of the Western medical paradigm. I undertook historical and theoretical research to test the claim that my more empirical research had suggested.

The Western Medical Paradigm

Any description of the features of Western medicine might seem in this context to be also a criticism of them; this is the effect of dissociating from the paradigm and viewing it against, for example, the ideal of "a state of cooperation out of which healing in the very broadest sense of the word can arise." My intention, though, is not to criticize Western medicine but to explain, by looking at its texts, its tenacity.

Finding some consensus among several authors concerned with Western medicine, I identify three major features of the paradigm. The first is paternalism. Anderson's observation (1989) that physician–patient dialogue is vertical corroborates Stewart and Roter's observation (1989) that the traditional and most common physician–patient relationship is characterized by "high physician control and low patient control." According to Stewart and Roter, "The [traditional] physician will dominate, making decisions in what he or she perceives to be the patient's best interest. These decisions entail access to information and services. The patient's job is to cooperate with medical advice, that is, to do what he or she is told" (p. 20). Contrasting this traditional model to one characterized by "high patient control and low physician control," Stewart and Roter call the traditional model "paternalist." (They label the contrasting model "consumerist" and call for a balance between the two: a "mutualist" model.)

The second feature of the Western medical paradigm is atomism. Anderson (1989) discusses not only the tendency of Western physicians to separate body and mind, but also the tendency of the discipline to fragment the human body into discrete systems and parts. He discusses the centrality of dissection to medical education: "Students learn how the parts of the body fit together but cannot see how they work together with a human spirit to produce a living person" (p. 10). Anderson's view of the outcome of such education is confirmed by Young (1989) who, in exploring "enclaves of the self in the realm of medicine," finds that the traditional physician–patient interview invites the patient "to regard his body from outside instead of from inside, and . . . invites him to see it in parts instead of as a whole" (p. 155). The medical examination that follows the interview, Young says, "is the rendering in a physical medium of the estrangement of the self and the fragmentation of the body" (p. 159). Central to the practice of medicine as she describes it is the "disarticulation" of the whole into parts.

Interventionism is the third feature of the paradigm. Whereas "alternative" medical models—traditional Chinese medicine or current naturopathic practices—stress prevention of disease, the primary focus of Western medicine is intrusion upon disease processes already in progress. Eisenberg and Wright (1985) note that most Western medical research focuses on the intricacies of active disease and gives comparatively little attention to the effect that life-style, personal disposition, and thoughts have on its course (p. 235). Not surprisingly, the interventionist fix of the profession is closely related to its atomist bias. Stewart and Roter (1989) write, "The traditional method is strictly objective: it diagnoses diseases. It does not aim, in any systematic way, to understand the meaning of the illness for the patient or to place it in the context of his life story or culture" (p. 27).[3]

Paradigmatic Features of Medical Discourse

In mapping the rhetoric of medicine onto its practice, we may note the extent to which use of entrenched discourse features, virtually irrespective of what they are, contributes to the persuasiveness of journal articles. Ziman's insight (1968) that using the conventions of scientific writing embeds new information in the existing consensus provides one way of understanding the authority dynamic. Latour's discussion (1987) of the ways in which scientific articles use convention and citation to create a block of authority behind their assertions provides another: "Although it sounds counter-intuitive at first, the more technical and specialised a literature is, the more 'social' it becomes, since the *number of associations* necessary to drive readers out and force them into accepting a claim as a fact increase" (p. 62).

This intertextual appeal is essentially ethical. Authority accrues to the author not only as an individual speaker but also as the voice of the profession, which speaks *through* him or her. The ethos of individual articles, then, includes the character of Western medicine itself instantiated in particular authors. Conversely, one purpose of the articles collectively is to maintain the strength of that disciplinary ethos.

The appeal from ethos may, in fact, carry a medical journal article when the appeal from scientific logos fails. One study (Szekely et al., 1986), which assesses the effects of behavioral treatment on women suffering from paramenstrual headache, relies on the ethical argument advanced by the use of conventional methodology and conventional reporting to establish its value. The authors describe their study this way: "16 women with paramenstrual headaches self-monitored 4 times daily for a 2-cycle baseline, then were matched on pre-treatment pain levels into 8 pairs and randomly assigned to treatment. . . . Post-treatment group data analysis was by three-way analysis of variance with 2 repeated measures" (p. 86). The study, in other words, used two treatments on sixteen women suffering from four different headache conditions, then asked them how they felt. Yet the form of the article—more specifically, the authors' expertise at working within the constraints of scientific convention—argues that the research is bona fide science and the researchers bona fide scientists.[4]

Starr (1982) sheds further light on the radiant ethos of Western medicine. His account of the institutionalization of power in American medicine documents the process by which the distance between physician and patient grew as increasingly sophisticated instrumentation reduced the physician's dependence on subjective accounts of the patient, and distance among practitioners diminished as the profession organized to lay claim to a body of knowledge and a source of income. These changes in delivery of health care, Starr explains, were largely a result of the coming of science to medicine: "The less one could believe 'one's own eyes'—and the new world of science continually prompted that feeling—the more receptive one became to seeing the world through the eyes of those who claimed specialized, technical knowledge, validated by communities of their peers" (p. 19). The power of medical authority as a consequence of the scientization of medicine was so great that, according to Starr, it was not necessarily weakened when physicians' advice was "objectively incorrect."

In his account of the politics of cohesion within the medical profession, Starr not only confirms the notion that authority defines the culture of medicine, but also reveals the extent to which the authority of physicians is derived from the profession itself. It is not individual authority, but collective authority embodied in individuals.

Given the persuasiveness of collective authority in medical discourse, medical authors, not surprisingly, seem to work at purging individual ethos from their texts. The use of passive voice and nominalizations to obviate the need for first person speakers is part of this effort, as is the tendency in medical prose to use agencies as subjects in lieu of agents (for example, "the study demonstrates . . ."; "the data show . . ."). But the effort is necessarily in vain. Medical writers necessarily make implicit appeals of individual ethos. They attach their names to their work, along with their degrees, affiliations, and reputations; they note their sources of funding; they publish in journals whose ethos they borrow; they demonstrate their connection to the profession in their use of disciplinary conventions and well-chosen citations and acknowledgments; they argue as well as they can. Ironically, they also establish a presence by absence. Their claim to anonymity or insignificance itself embeds their work in the professional canon.[5]

Specific medical practice is to some extent mediation between texts and patients. Cicourel (1986) explains how the authority of medical writing becomes the authority of the physician who applies in the practice of medicine what he or she reads in texts. In what Cicourel describes, we can see how the authority of the physician then reinforces the authority of texts. Cicourel explains that medical diagnosis is a process by which professionals armed with "schematized knowledge," essentially the knowledge of texts, "convert the often idiomatic and sometimes ambiguous language . . . of the patient into unambiguous declarative knowledge using a systematic notation system" (p. 94). That is, physicians turn patients' accounts into acceptable or interpretable narratives; they do not revise their knowledge structure to accommodate the patients' accounts, and so original (textual) classifications are sustained. Young as well as Levenstein et al. (1989) explain how the medical interview is orchestrated to reveal just the information the physician seeks for differential diagnosis. So physicians at work conspire to reinforce the power and authority of texts.

Effectively, credible medical articles enhance the credibility of the profession. The collective constructs its character from the work of its members as the members construct their character from the work of the collective. It is from this interplay between medical text and context that medical prose and the medical profession derive their authority. Furthermore, that authority is the main feature of their ethos and the rationale for their structure of certainty.

The authority and certainty that characterize medicine and its texts suggest also the quality of "paternalism," a term chosen to reflect the masculine and parental attitude of science in general and medicine in particular. The designation is supported by feminist accounts of science (e.g., Harding, 1986; Keller, 1985) as well as by treatments of medical discourse (e.g., Stewart & Roter, 1989) and by popular literature. As an example of the last, one acclaimed book on pregnancy and childbirth asserts, "Some obstetricians are convinced that their patients should not know more than is 'good' for them and should simply give [the obstetricians] their trust" (Kitzinger, 1980, p. 6); that is, physicians (most often male) expect to be regarded by their patients (in this case, female) as fathers.

Textual correlates of paternalism in Western medicine include signs of certainty and dissociation established especially by rhetorical features of style. Particularly noteworthy are the judicious use of qualifying language and the use of passive voice and nominalizations.

In some cases, qualifiers are used simply to ensure precision of medical claims. While it may be accurate to say that an experimental drug "would appear to be superior to the alternative methods of therapy available" (Lane & Ross, 1985, p. 304), it may be less accurate to say that the drug *is* superior. That is, vague language protects authors from making inaccurate claims and facilitates reader adherence to the claims made by minimizing grounds for disagreement.

However, qualifiers not only allow for accuracy of reporting, they also give authors a way of handling, with confidence and without apology, matters that are hypothetical, theoretical, or controversial. One author distills research on diet and migraine by saying, "Foods or alcohol *can* provoke occasional attacks [of migraine] in *some* patients [my emphasis]" (Diamond & Blau, 1986, p. 184). Another reports that "the demands of child rearing *can* foster migraine attacks, and unresolved grief *may* play a role in *some* patients [my emphasis]" (Kirn, 1987, pp. 12–13). Interestingly, however, many of the qualifications raised implicitly by vague assertions are not raised explicitly. In the absence of explicit qualification, assertions may appear to be positive. Certainty, then, is not a necessary condition for the effect of certainty; some certainty seems inevitably to be a byproduct of textuality.

The absence of qualifiers is as telling in medical literature as their presence. One author writes, for example, that "all headaches should be initially viewed with concern" (Silberstein, 1984, p. 65). This statement, as a commonsense assertion, has some right to its sound of certainty. However, this statement from the same author is more troublesome: "All patients should be treated prophylactically for cluster headache" (p. 70). The second sentence has the same syntax, the same tone, and the same rhetorical effect as the first, yet it is not a commonsense assertion but a statement of opinion that would consign a patient to taking drugs indefinitely to prevent possible headache attacks.

Of all the features in scientific writing, passive voice has been written about the most (Campbell, 1975; Gopnick, 1973; Guinn, 1983; Rubens, 1981; Savory, 1958; Schindler, 1975). Certain questions concerning the use of the passive in medical writing, then, need not be addressed here. Must language be self-reflexive to be responsible? (Rubens); do scientific authors use the passive to protect themselves from charges of immodesty? (Schindler); can scientific writing be free of persona? (Campbell). Of concern here is the extent to which passive voice is part of a pattern of dissociation and objectification that interacts with a pattern of paternalism in medical practice.

Use of the passive voice in medical texts separates researchers from subjects and reinforces the sense in which, recalling Anderson's language (1989), one is "actor" and one is "acted upon"; it also argues that this attitude is usual and appropriate. The style manual of the *Journal of the American Medical Association* includes this guideline: "It is often said in books about writing that active voice is preferred. This is not always true, and it may be true less often in medical writing than in some types of narrative prose" (Barclay, Southgate, & Mayo, 1981, p. 9). A typical article reports that "patients were invited" to participate, their "informed consent was obtained," "the diagnosis of migraine was made," "the condition of each patient was evaluated," and so on (Solomon, Steele, & Spaccavento, 1983, p. 2500).

The appearance of the passive in medical journal articles is consistent with conventions of scientific writing. It fosters the impression that methodology accords with accepted scientific practice and that data made available through the methodology reflect phenomena that exist independently of the researcher-observer. That is, investigators are interchangeable; any one would have observed the same thing. Arguably, a secondary effect of passive voice among those who use it habitually is to encourage an artificial view of subjects, depriving subjects of a role in their own experience and turning subjects into objects.[6]

The other common device to circumvent the need for first-person agents is nominalization. That mode of suppressing agency is evident in this discussion of headache and marital stress: "Recognition of underlying family conflicts is of utmost importance. Intervention and correct diagnosis and treatment of family issues often result in amelioration or reduction of head pain" (Roy, 1986, p. 360).

Researchers are alienated from subjects (and possibly, by extension, physicians from patients) not only as a feature of style in medical writing, but also as a feature of rhetorical invention. A case in point is this appeal from pathos. One message implicit in the headache literature is that "they" (patients) get headaches and "we" (the author and the readers together) do not. The strategy recalls Burke's term "scapegoating" (1969b)—the "purest rhetorical pattern" in which "speaker and hearer [are] partners in partisan jokes made at the expense of another" (p. 38). One author (Edmeads, 1984) refers condescendingly to the "hard-core headache patient" as "our specialty albatross" (p. 342). He then expresses his puzzlement at the "peculiar" tendency of headache patients to be more concerned with having an explanation for their headaches than with getting relief from them. "Most of *us*" he says, ". . . would be far more interested in getting rid of our pain than in knowing why we had it [my emphasis]" (p. 343). Motivating this language of separation is the same kind of dissociative impulse responsible for the well-known medical synecdoche through which a patient and his or her ailment (or ailing organ) are made one, as in hospital parlance one speaks of "the pancreas in Room 252" (see Tiefel, 1978).

Textual features of medical journal articles are implicated not only in the paternalism of the profession, but also in its atomism and interventionism. The physician writing about the "hardcore headache patient" is implicitly focused on the patient's head (as opposed to the patient's whole self), and he sees his purpose as correctional, to come between the patient and the patient's pain. So novel is the idea that headache may be a disorder of the whole person that one author (Kirn, 1987), writing a review article on migraine, treats as newsworthy this quotation from a headache specialist: "From our experience with migraine, you are not really treating a headache, you are treating an individual" (p. 12).

An article by physician Gettis (1987) supplies further evidence of the proclivities of the profession. The article reports on the case of a patient whose chronic headaches disappeared in the course of his treatment for gastric ulcers. Readers of the case study are urged to agree it is "serendipity" that the restricted diet treatment for the ulcer removed the dietary triggers for the headaches. The article mentions, but fails to note the significance of, the fact that the patient's ulcers had been caused by his ingestion of thousands of aspirin tablets for his headaches. The "patient" is implicitly viewed as the locus of two disease processes rather than as a whole person whose health was undermined by the treatment for one of his symptoms and restored by the treatment for another.[7] The author implicitly perpetuates an interventionist approach to health care and a fragmented view of patients.

A traditional view of language, indeed, a scientific view of language, arguing that reality precedes its representation, would find that the language of medical journal articles has evolved to accommodate what the profession has to say. More recent language theory and theory in the sociology of knowledge, noting that representation itself gives rise to reality (e.g., Woolgar, 1988), makes clear the extent to which language and genre, in constructing the disciplinary discourse, construct the discipline itself. We may look more closely at the negotiation between text and context in medicine by use of a case study of a particular medical journal article.

A Case Study in Medical Writing

An interesting moment in the perpetuation of the knowledge structure and authority of the medical profession is the publication of the review article. The review or "update" article is a special case of the journal article. It does not purport to be original, only well informed, and it is often solicited by a journal editor to meet reader demand for a clinical review in a specific area. With a mandate to "identify, assess, and synthesize information" in a special area of inquiry (Mulrow, 1987), the review article is a view of a field from the vantage point of a particular author. Close reading of a review article demonstrates the extent to which the medical paradigm is not only reflected but also revitalized in the publication of texts.

Five review articles appeared among the two-hundred article sample that constituted the data for this study.[8] Gunderson's "Management of the

Migraine Patient" (1986) was chosen for discussion here as the most accessible to the uninitiated reader.

The article is in most ways typical of its genre. Unlike reports on research or "original articles," review pieces tend to display a rather flat organization. Parts are not organized with persuasive introduction and discussion sections flanking a more descriptive middle; rather, they are arranged according to topics, with headings and subheadings directing reader attention to particular areas of professional interest. Review articles, however, are not less persuasive because of this seemingly arhetorical organization. In fact, their apparent shapelessness contributes to their effect of being simply and directly reportorial. The Gunderson article begins by discussing identification of the migraine patient and ends with the statement that headaches associated with orgasm are "no longer believed to be a common presenting symptom of subarachnoid hemorrhage" (p. 143).

The apparent purpose of the Gunderson article is to keep the primary care physician apprised of recent advances in the diagnosis and treatment of migraine. However, two related observations about the article call that purpose into question: First, the article reproduces in basic content other recent review articles on headache; second, it (like its counterparts in other journals) largely rehearses what the practicing physician already knows.

Both observations are supported by the following summary. The five review articles examined say essentially this: Migraine must be distinguished from a symptom of organic disease on the one hand and from other forms of functional headache on the other. Following diagnosis, treatment should include behavior therapy and/or the prescription of one or more of the following kinds of drugs: analgesics and narcotics (to ease the pain of headache), ergotamines (to abort the headache), and certain drugs, notably beta-blockers and tricyclic antidepressants, used prophylactically against frequent, incapacitating headache.[9] These points, with only minor variation, also form the core of assumptions of most of the other articles, including reports on research, examined for the study. Review articles vary in their emphasis and in the points they add to this core.

The Gunderson article does not deviate from the common prescription, and because Gunderson writes essentially of what the physician already knows, his article has the effect of being not so much informative as affirmative. While the article seems to be an update, it is more realistically a declaration that little is new in the field of headache of consequence to primary care physicians. Its rhetorical agenda is to be "true" by reasserting what the physician already knows and to be influential by re-presenting information from the author's point of view.

Many of Gunderson's statements of what is already known constitute not only a starting place for argument, but also, to a large extent, the argument itself:

> The physician must distinguish migraine from muscle contraction (tension) headaches, headaches associated with serious intracranial disease, and other forms of vascular headache. (p. 138)

> A number of dietary factors have been associated with changes in headache frequency. The principal offender is probably alcohol. (p. 143)

> Aspirin's effectiveness in relieving migraine may be enhanced by the addition of either barbiturates or antihistamines for sedative and antinauseant effects. (p. 140)

Thus, the article is woven into the fabric of common knowledge. New bits of information, as well as personal views of the author, are added seamlessly:

> Unusual stress or depression is perhaps the most likely cause of a change in migraine pattern. (p. 142)

> [Antidepressants] are . . . of value, especially in patients whose headaches have a muscle-tension component or are triggered or exacerbated by depression. This is particularly true when increases in migraine frequency are associated with menopause or retirement. (p. 141)

> Simple analgesics, such as aspirin and acetaminophen, are probably more effective than most authors believe them to be. (p. 140)

Interestingly, Gunderson's article derives much of its persuasiveness from its ethical appeal, and in this case, as the article is not a report on research, the ethical appeal is largely individual. Gunderson uses the first person readily, although not to refer to himself as practitioner (in relation to patients) but to himself as authority (in relation to readers). He says, for example, "I agree with . . . [another author] that the dangers of the ergot preparation have been overstated" (p. 140), or "I have been most impressed with hydroxyzine pamoate . . . [administered] intramuscularly" (p. 141). In general, Gunderson develops his relationship with his readers by being authoritative but not authoritarian. While he sometimes advises readers directly ("Special attention should be given to the nervous system and the patient's blood pressure" [p. 139]), he is just as likely to make an assertion that simply has the indirect force of advising: "If a headache develops extremely rapidly . . . or is associated with neurologic findings . . . subarachnoid hemorrhage may have occurred" (p. 138). Gunderson finally has the ethos of the trusted physician: aloof but concerned, helpful but firm, calm but cautious. His photograph, which appears on the last page of the article, can have no purpose but to reinforce this ethos. Gunderson, chief of neurology at Walter Reed Army Medical Center, and consultant in neurology to the surgeon general of the army, appears in uniform.

Energized by the argument from ethos, review articles like Gunderson's function rhetorically as epideictic rhetoric. They are epideictic not formally, in the sense of being ceremonial, but functionally, in the sense of affirming and perpetuating the values of a community (see Perelman & Olbrechts-Tyteca [1969] on the subject of education as epideictic rhetoric). Gunderson's article does not, sentence for sentence, reiterate common knowledge, but it does, partially by virtue of its situatedness in common knowledge, affirm and perpetuate the community's higher values of paternalism, atomism, and interventionism. Note, for example, the title of the article: "*Management* of the Migraine Patient [my emphasis]."

Conclusion

Not everything that appears in headache literature is as conservative as the articles I describe in this study. Sacks (1985) has written a book-length treatment of migraine, which has none of the characteristics of paternalism, atomism, or interventionism I attribute to Western medicine. Indeed, the first long section of his book is on the *experience* of migraine. Creditor (1986) has written an unconventional case study describing his own headaches for the *New England Journal of Medicine*. Other work appearing in mainstream journals flouts the traditions of Western medicine as well. In a guest editorial in *Headache*, Graham (1986) puts forward a theory of migraine as cranial angina—"resulting from suffocation or throttling or overloading of the brain, and maybe, even of the soul" (p. 105). Articles appearing in the *American Journal of Chinese Medicine* explore the effectiveness of tai chi (Koh, 1982) and acupuncture (Chang, 1982) in medical treatment. In each case, certain habits of discourse are also put aside.

However, the texts I cite here as deviating from the paradigm appear in small numbers, and they remain noteworthy *because* they are deviant. Sacks is well known for challenging the common discourse styles of his profession; Creditor's article in the *New England Journal of Medicine* is the only one of two hundred articles surveyed that takes a *subject's* approach to headache; Graham's piece on cranial angina appears in the protected realm of editorial—not a "scientific" piece at all; and certainly, the *American Journal of Chinese Medicine* circulates less widely than the other journals that formed part of this study.

The existence of these texts does demonstrate that the dominant paradigm of Western medicine is not unassailable; it is only tenacious. This study suggests that its tenacity is bound to discourse conventions that themselves now deserve our attention. In her study of the writing of Luria and Sacks, Journet (1990) notes that both authors realized that neither exposition (the traditional form of scientific discourse) nor narrative (the form the two practitioners use to render the experience of their patients) is adequate for representing the complicated phenomena of neuropsychology (p. 179). As Journet's findings suggest, changes in the texts of medicine will not be simple and will not be the trading of one normative system for another. Whatever changes are realized, however, will be significant. They will both arise from and engender different values in medicine and different ways of knowing about health and healing.

In demonstrating the nature of the reciprocal relationship between text and context in a particular discipline, this study of the rhetoric of medical journal articles points to further research in the rhetoric of medicine, particularly for an audience of medical professionals, whose actions might support their insights, and also to research in the reciprocity of text and context in other disciplines.

Notes

1. Gross (1988) recommends a similar procedure.

2. Functional headaches are those that, unlike "organic" headaches, do not originate in a specific pathology. Migraine and tension headaches, for example, are functional, while headaches due to brain tumor or cranial inflammation are organic.

3. Compare Journet's (1990) account of the role of "life story" in a *non*-traditional approach to medicine.

4. Physicians I consulted on this did not question the value of the study. Asked to read the article as they would if they had encountered it in a journal, they responded that the piece was interesting but "too scientific." One physician suggested the study was "probably someone's dissertation research."

5. Burke (1969b) sheds some light on the process: "If, in the opinion of a given audience, a certain kind of conduct is admirable, then a speaker might persuade the audience by using signs and images that identify his cause with that kind of conduct" (p. 55).

6. In this regard, it is interesting to note that users of the medical system are called "patients" (according to the *Oxford English Dictionary* "patient," 1971), people who are suffering, sick, passive), rather than, for example, "clients," people who, for their own benefit, seek the advice or services of experts.

7. Since 1988, listings in the *Index Medicus* indicate an increased awareness of iatrogenic (treatment-induced) disorders.

8. The articles are by Caviness and O'Brien (1980); Diamond and Blau (1986); Gunderson (1986); Kirn (1987); and Silberstein (1984).

9. Because the sample stops at 1987, none of the articles mentions the antimigraine drug sumatriptan.

Negotiating Meaning in a Hospital Discourse Community

Composition theorists such as Bazerman (1983), Faigley (1985), and Purves and Purves (1986) have suggested that community discourse both influences and is influenced by the community in which it arises. Sociolinguists have also stressed the importance of "local knowledge" (Geertz, 1973) and the effects of speech communities on language use (Gumperz, 1982; Hymes, 1972).

Despite the growing emphasis on writing as a social act (Berlin, 1988; Bizzell, 1989; Bruffee, 1986; LeFevre, 1987) and surveys pointing to multiple authorship in a wide spectrum of professions (Anderson, 1985; Couture & Rymer, 1989; Ede & Lunsford, 1990), research on writing at its most visibly social—multiple authorship—has been surprisingly rare. Many of the studies that explore writing by collaborative groups focus on the captive subject pool of composition classrooms (Janda, 1989; Morgan, Allen, Moore, Atkinson, & Snow, 1987; Sperling, 1989). Even though serious ethnographic investigation of writing outside the classroom is beginning to come of age (Odell and Goswami's important collection was published in 1985), only a few investigations of nonacademic writing have focused on the effects of collaboration as a primary feature of composing (Debs, 1986; Doheny-Farina, 1986; Myers, 1985; Sullivan, 1990). Although other workplace research has touched on the less direct forms of collaboration, such as shared boilerplate (Selzer, 1983), supervisory influence (Barabas, 1990), and the roles of editors (Cross, 1990; Simpson, 1989), collaboration among writers holds the potential for revealing composing processes through natural inter-actions among writers. As Mirel (1989) and Dobrin (1983) suggest, writing can be thought of as mediation among the perspectives of those who gener-ate, regulate, and use the discourse produced. Such acts of mediation among conflicting social forces within a specific discourse community are the focus of this research.

The presence of a collaborative writing group, a variety of community interests requiring accommodation, and an open-ended collection of regula-tory texts made the Department of Nursing at Good Hope Community Hospital (not the hospital's real name) an apt site for observing a composition project in which discourse production both influenced and was influenced by the social fabric of the community. During the observations, the nursing division of Good Hope consisted of twenty patient care units supervised by head nurses, three nursing service directors, and a vice president for nursing services (herself a nurse). The hospital provided facilities for major surgery, maternity care, intensive care, general medical/surgical care, and many out-patient services.

The dimensions of the Good Hope writing project allowed for examin-ing group composition in a context where significant organizational change was attempted by writers with relatively little power within the hospital but who were directly involved in the activities regulated by the documents at stake. In this project, fourteen nurses came together to revise the hospital's nursing regulation system to make it more accessible to practicing nurses. Although some individual documents were revised directly by the group, their primary work focused on redesigning a plan for distribution, storage, and regular update of nursing policies and procedures throughout the divi-sion. Despite this primarily planning role, group members constantly were making language choices related to specific wording of index entries and category titles. They specifically wrote several document definitions, format specifications, and descriptions of the distribution plan. Since they expected specific documents to be revised by different nurses throughout the division, group members served as system designers, as writers, and as managers of writers. Composing community discourse in this setting required constant negotiation among the various specialty interests of the nursing community, as well as mediation among members of the writing group. Negotiation strategies employed here reveal some processes of social construction cen-tered around the acts of composition and illuminate the interaction between context, community, and composition. Questions that guided the research included: What strategies appear in collaborative writing on the job to address creative dissonances within a group and pressures from the commu-nity beyond the collaborators? What relationship do the acts of composition have, in return, on the social contexts of writers? What (if anything) changes in the social context?

Research Methods

Because workplace writing projects such as this one may extend over time measured in decades and document systems measured in volumes, investigators of collaboration in such settings must attend to the shifting dynamic of organization climates as well as to patterns of interchange among collaborators. Research into such matters does not fit easily into the paradigms of controlled and statistically validated research of the social science tradition but is accessed more appropriately through ethnographic tools that provide for observing the externalized composition processes in collaborative writing sessions and the social contexts in which they function.

Although my observations of the Good Hope writing project extended over a period of almost two years, the work of this writing project was neither initiated nor completed during this time. The task represented an ongoing problem for the nursing department where constant technological change, shifting personnel patterns, and advances in nursing practice continually stayed ahead of attempts to keep the materials current and accurate.

While consulting with the writing group and creating a small computer data base to house the materials, I collected observations from multiple community sources: audio tapes of writing sessions, field notes of normal community activity, and both formal and informal interviews with community members (both writing group members and others). System plans and texts-in-progress were collected and compared to currently circulating documents from nursing and the hospital administration. Influential texts from nursing literature used by the group were also consulted.

As patterns were observed in interviews with the nurses, in transcripts, or in texts, they became tentative hypotheses that guided the collection of additional material. During a period of reflection and analysis following the primary observation phases, comparisons of data between sources were made in order to adjust the emerging picture. The assumptions listed below emerged during the design and observation phases of the project. They were tested against the collected data during the analysis phases illustrated in figure 7.1.

1. Any writing is a social act influenced by contextual factors and holds the potential for influencing the social fabric of the environment, in return. The composing of community regulatory prose focuses on that potential as a primary goal.
2. The elements of audience, text, and writer are interrelated in intricate ways that complicate the acts of invention. Situations where writers are part of the

community addressed blur the distinction between these elements and lead to richer ways of thinking about the ways language operates as an instrument of social change.

3. Collaborative writing makes composition forces visible by exposing dissonances and resolutions as verbal exchange among group members. Strategies seen in collaborative writing sessions may also be present in the work of individual writers whose responses to the social dynamic of writing are often inaccessible, internalized, and silent.

Contexts for Writing at Good Hope Hospital

Despite the nurses' mission that focuses on clinical activity and the acts of healing, written documents hold considerable power over the nurses in this community. From the daily charts at the patients' bedside to the formal annual reports, nurses constantly are required to record and justify their practices through written products that are examined by their immediate supervisors, hospital administrators, funding agencies, boards of health, and legal experts. In addition, few nursing acts are permitted without express written directives from hospital authorities or physicians.

Nurses and administrators at Good Hope assumed that their local nursing regulations would have that kind of power, as well. Written documents were expected to accomplish managerial tasks, keep priorities in order, and standardize procedures throughout the nursing division. But despite these clear expectations for written material, actual practice among nurses at Good Hope often failed to fulfill these expectations. Staff members consulted written documents only rarely. As in Mirel's 1989 study of computer information manual use, this community tended to rely in practice more on oral

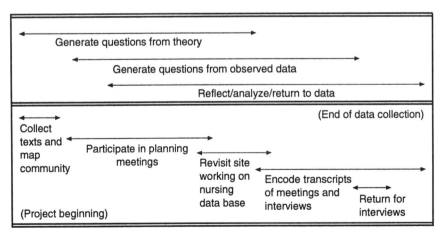

Figure 7.1. Time Line of Analysis and Data Collection

information transfer than on written documentation. Mirel suggests that the social benefits from oral exchange contribute to the neglect of written documentation. However, the condition of the Good Hope documents was also a possible deterrent to their use. The system contained over two thousand individual titles, ranging from one to fifteen pages in length. This mosaic of hospital-approved procedures, divisional directives, and unit-specific documents was housed in loose-leaf binders throughout the units, where the materials were poorly organized, full of redundant and obsolete material, and practically inaccessible to most potential users.

Negotiated Composition

The nurses who worked on this project had volunteered to reorganize current materials for improved accessibility and to propose changes that would facilitate future additions. Their work primarily consisted of weekly planning meetings in which they worked out plans for assembling a master file to be housed in the central nursing office. Department heads would be expected to select appropriate items from this file for their own unit manuals. Table 7.1 points to the various project functions that were necessary to the project and the negotiation acts that those functions entailed. It should be noted that the work of the group extended well beyond drafting and revising individual texts. As the group addressed each project function, negotiations operated in three primary arenas. First, group members had to negotiate among themselves to reach group consensus. Achieving an adequate com-

Table 7.1. Project Negotiation Areas

Project Function	*Negotiation Acts Required*
Project Management	Mediating diverse project goals
System Design	Accommodating multiple use and centralization of macrostructures
Drafting Text	Establishing community discourse standards Creating an implementation language
Evaluation	Reflecting actual hospital practice Assessing community acceptability of plans
Implementation	Publishing the system Selling the ideas to the community
Maintenance	Coordinating update and revision procedures

munity response to professional regulators was a second important arena of negotiation, although the influence of those regulators appeared primarily in the form of directives and models rather than in face-to-face contact. A third important arena centered on attempts by the writing group to secure acceptance of their plans in the various units of their division. These three arenas of negotation will be discussed in the sections below.

Creating Consensus Within the Writing Group

Since within the writing group, each writer represented a unit, a specialty, a hospital role, or a level of commitment to the hierarchy at different moments in the discussion, achieving group consensus was the first major arena for negotiation. Five principal members were usually in attendance, but nine other head nurses and specialty representatives functioned as regular group members, although their attendance at writing sessions was inconsistent. Three of these intermittent group members were nursing administrators whose influence on the discussion sometimes altered the power structure of the negotiations.

Group meetings often consisted of a series of interconnected persuasion episodes in which different group members argued for particular system features, language features, or ways of implementing the system. At times, group consensus seemed a more important goal than examining actual documents. When consensus appeared threatened, unresolved issues were tabled, deferred, or even resolved tentatively with an agreement to return to the discussion at a later time. Because of the strength of the chain of command in this organization, many dissonances eventually were resolved simply by accepting the opinions of the hospital hierarchy or by direct adoption of regulatory language, but the group also began to find ways to name their own project goals and establish a sense of their own autonomy.

The ability to dream, create, laugh, and share frustrations together enabled the five core group members to build a sense of community among themselves. Direct confrontations among them became rare, and a spirit of respect for different points of view grew as various perspectives were voiced by different members. Individual roles constantly shifted as individuals spoke up for groups to which they did not directly belong. It also became easier for the writing group to criticize others from service areas, such as surgery and adult intensive care, whose reluctance to be involved was clear. The head nurses from those units never attended writing sessions, nor did they send any representatives, even though their involvement was directly sought.

Much session time was spent in devising a taxonomy of existing documents by title, a process that allowed activities listed in table 7.1 to occur without the documents actually being in the room. Some episodes centered on writing document definitions or descriptions of their plans, but often texts produced in one meeting were not present at the next. Despite the institutional emphasis on written products, the acts of composition in this group often were quite separated from written text, leading to (or perhaps growing from) a dependence on group memory and shared understanding.

Joint classification episodes, in which several members worked together to sort a list of titles into categories, occurred both inside and outside group meetings. Sometimes members would meet in the mornings to work on these lists before their clinical day began. They all reported that it was easier to sort documents with others than alone. Episodes of such sorting that occurred during recorded meetings also illustrate a dependence on group agreement.

The act of choosing categories for documents that defied placement illustrates both the leakiness of categories in the emerging system and the tendency of the group to preserve certain unfilled categories. Geographical divisions, specialties, and administrative categories already functioning in the community organizational chart appeared in the classification scheme early and persisted, despite their containing no documents. Thus certain visible organization structures were preserved in the system.

However, the group also struggled to retain certain departures from the usual organization patterns operating in the hospital. One particularly important set of categories grew out of the current trend in nursing education to describe clinical activity in terms of "nursing diagnoses" rather than "medical diagnoses."

Current nursing education encourages the use of nursing diagnoses such as "immobility," "pain," and "skin integrity" in nursing regulations (Gordon, 1985) rather than the descriptions derived from physicians' diagnoses of specific diseases. The group kept open the possibility of using nursing diagnoses even though they acknowledged that most practicing nurses at Good Hope continued to use descriptions based on diseases rather than on nursing diagnoses. Although "the gall bladder in 3-B" was being replaced by a patient's name, many staff members at Good Hope lacked training, experience, or the will to resist predominant medical language in their daily work. Thus, the categories for nursing definitions such as "immobility" and "skin integrity" remained in the classification system primarily as possibilities for the future.

Social construction theories of composition warn against the dangers of group pressures in collaborative writing that allow a group to silence certain members (Beade, 1987; Bizzell, 1989; Foster, 1987; Johnson, 1986). That, indeed, is one of the dangers of group collaboration inside or outside of classrooms, and this group fell prey to the tactics of group pressure on several occasions. But as Trimbur (1989) notes, "A rehabilitated notion of consensus in collaborative learning can provide . . . exemplary motives to imagine alternative worlds and transformations of social life and labor" (p. 615). For Trimbur, "dissensus" in collaborative groups creates the opportunity for tolerance of diversity and the recognition of the rights of marginalized voices inside and outside collaborative groups. In the case of this nursing writing group, both the danger and the promise appeared.

While balancing the tensions between inclusion and exclusion, autonomy and accommodation, the writing group at Good Hope worked in an environment where hierarchical forces are easier to accommodate than to challenge, but where diversity is a fact of life, as well. Primary exclusion strategies appeared in attempts of the group to establish their own authority over the emerging document system. Some of those exclusion strategies were to earn and exert managerial authority, to claim the rights of professional standing, to plan for centralization and standardization, to become a clearing house or an editorial force, and to take on responsibility for community choices.

Inclusion of diverse voices was also a necessity in a community where nursing practices in areas such as surgery and intensive care vary considerably from those of maternal/child health and general medical/surgical units. Verbalizing community standards that would be acceptable to these diverse interests required the group to work to accommodate those voices. Some strategies of inclusion seen in this community were recognizing and speaking for the interests of units, specialists, and/or managers; involving diverse personnel in drafting, planning, and testing; reaching out to hesitant outsiders; and influencing colleagues by request, persuasion, and example.

Accommodating External Demands on the Project

The influence of powerful medical hierarchical authorities represented a second major arena where conflicting discourses required negotiation. Both the State Board of Health and the Joint Commission on Accreditation of Hospitals issue formal requirements for nursing documentation and make spot checks of nursing documentation on the units during their regular inspections.

The group looked first to those authorities for samples they could incorporate directly into their own system, but as they searched nursing textbooks and regulators' models for statements that would clarify their work, they found regulators' language contradictory, ambiguous, and confusing. For some time, the nursing division had been attempting to adopt the model of a nurse/management consultant who sells a nursing document system model to hospitals nationwide (Marker, 1988). But when neither authority texts nor the Marker model provided satisfactory direction, the group gradually began to define the limits of their project in terms of their own needs. Debates on the virtues of system features in various models began to end with, "But we need a system that works in THIS hospital."

A document definition problem illustrates the process of localizing document goals. The group found themselves frequently debating the practical meaning of policy, procedure, guideline, protocol, and standing order, terms recommended by regulators but used throughout the hospital without much consistency. Binding policy written by physicians might be called a guideline, while step-by-step procedures might appear in the text of a document called "Policy on Administration of IV Medications." This confusion was exaggerated by Marker's hierarchy of nine functional document types.

The need to find ways to bring their document system closer to their own ideals led the nurse writers to take a more ambitious role in defining their own discourse niche in the organization. Choosing among elements from models to serve their own needs, the group locally redefined document types in three ways: They rewrote standard definitions of the terms for their own use; they redefined at least one category from the Marker model and limited it to a far more specific purpose; and they collapsed several categories into one after it proved impossible for them to discriminate satisfactorily among terms used by authorities. Such changes became instruments of solidarity among group members, even though they proved difficult to transfer to the larger community.

The process of claiming their own right to speak was not complete, uniform, or without retreat. The group often used cumbersome language and awkward classifications in direct response to administrative or regulatory edicts, but the act of composition enabled them to find ways to begin to use their own voices. In some cases they developed strategies of language formation to resolve dissonances in source language. They revised received language by redefining terms from regulators and models, retelling history, and rejecting terms they considered inappropriate for local use. In addition, they created new community language by inventing new system dimensions, by establishing new conventions and formats, and by naming, sorting, labeling and categorizing community acts.

Composition researchers have pointed to the need for writers to set their own writing goals (Flower, 1981; Lauer, Montague, Lunsford, & Emig, 1985; Young, Becker, & Pike, 1970). Writing at Good Hope required localizing goals because of the confusion embedded in the "assignments," which were vague and conflicting regulatory edicts. Certainly, this writing task was imposed from outside before it was accepted and redefined by these writers, but confidence in their own right to affect community discourse eventually became a primary motivator for them.

Translating Group Decisions into Community Action

Writing in this group required constant negotiation among forces which in composition terms might be called "audiences." But in contrast to views of audience as external to the writer, audiences in this case often were represented internally by group members themselves. The writers served as both audience and authors of the community discourse. As the project approached publication and implementation, this ambiguity was realized in encounters between the group and the larger nursing community. Audience analysis in the forms proposed by Lauer et al. (1985), Mathes and Stevenson (1976), and Porter (1986) suggest a sense of otherness in the idea of audience. But when distinctions between writers and their audiences are blurred in projects such as this one, collaborators in the creation of community discourse are at once fictional and real, assumed and named, self and other.

Thus, a third arena for negotiation in the Good Hope writing project concerned the transfer of their plans to the nursing community, of which the group was a part. Although the process of distribution and implementation of the documentation system was not completed during my observations, concern for community transfer appeared from the beginning of the sessions. Throughout the project, the writing group made plans to secure the cooperation of floor personnel, other unit heads, administrators, and writers.

When the group consciously invented new language or redefined old terms, those changes competed with general definitions that were circulating in the community and sometimes met direct resistance both within the group and from others. A particularly hard-won description of standing orders composed in one session was abandoned the next week when an administrator criticized it.

Securing agreement from peers outside the group proved difficult as well. The elimination of the category "protocol" met resistance from people who had written copious protocols according to their understanding of the Marker definition. The head of the postpartum unit, for instance, was reluctant to give up the term, assuming that the information her unit had created in that category would have to be abandoned as well. Unable to recreate the complete discussion that had led to their abandoning of the term, group members presented their action to this nurse as an accomplished fact, and she saw no value in their idea. This instance of "group-centered" argument resembling Flower's (1979) writer-based prose caused considerable stress for the postpartum nurse and puzzled group members who found themselves resorting to strenuous persuasion to get the nurse to agree.

In this instance, the comfortable compromise achieved inside the group may have blinded group members to the need to recreate those compromises with community members who had been represented, but not present, in the deliberations. Neither the language nor the decision made sense to the postpartum head nurse who lacked sufficient contextual information to cooperate in the choice that had been made.

Expecting misunderstandings from contributors, the group spent considerable time attempting to "define out" what they had in mind for specific document features. Elaborate training sessions were planned, and assignments were given to other community members. But few nongroup writers had developed the same personal commitment to the division-wide system as had the group members, whose hours of work represented a significant investment in the project. Rather, most other writers composed documents reflective of the interests of their own unit or specialty needs, without much consideration of how they fit into the general system. Thus, translation of the group's intentions to nongroup writers remained a subject of further negotiation.

As group members struggled to convey their ideas to the community, they used accommodation, active persuasion, and even direct edict with mixed success. In persuasive episodes both inside and outside the group, the emerging document system constantly was exposed to community forces that challenged its practical features, its conformity to department values, and its relationship to outside regulations. Features of the system were adjusted in response to opinions expressed both inside and outside the group.

Despite the problems of translating group intentions to outside contributors, the cooperative atmosphere within the group did have a beneficial effect on the ability of the head nurses to predict some of the responses they would encounter when their system was introduced to the community. Awareness of issues raised in group discussions led to a better understanding of the concerns of the greater nursing community and enabled the writers to employ persuasive appeals derived from the original discussions.

Persuasive strategies developed within the group that were of primary concern in translating the system to the general community. The group worked to align their intentions with influential authorities by quoting them, enlisting the support of powerful members of the hierarchy, and protecting the hospital's mission and interests. They also worked to accommodate diverse community interests by allowing for unit variations, including unit language in the index system, making concessions for varied users, and using the techniques of example and indirection.

Composition as Social Construction

Throughout the processes of claiming the task, group formation, system design, and testing and implementing this project, discourse strategies appeared for responding to community diversity in this hierarchical organization. Writers at Good Hope had some success with balancing input from throughout the division, agreeing among themselves, and working toward implementing a system of their own design. Their eventual product reflected many existing community organizational structures but preserved the promise of change, as well. While accommodating their own local constituencies, writers at Good Hope responded to influence from hospital management, state laws, and national regulators but retained a belief in their own ability to achieve community results through the use of language.

As group negotiations became a microcosm of the subsequent negotiation required outside in the larger nursing community, the group began to predict reactions they would encounter as they transferred their ideas to others. Thus, negotiated solutions achieved by the small group sometimes enabled group members to enhance their persuasion of the larger community. Yet, at other times, those hard-won solutions created a sense of closure that made external persuasion seem unnecessary.

Belief in the ability of language to change the community promised more accessible documentation, greater adherence to nursing standards hospital-wide, and increased respect for nursing ideas throughout the hospital. The writers expected to see other specialty areas such as Laboratory and Pharmacy take the nursing project as a model and revise their own information systems in similar ways. Such a development would overturn the traditional hierarchical position of nursing by making nurses leaders in an activity they considered particularly important to their status as hospital professionals. In interviews near the end of my involvement with the group, several community members expressed confidence that professionalism is tied directly to the ability to articulate ideas in written form. Given this assumption and the opportunity to redefine their own experience in written terms, writing group members occasionally expressed a sense of power in the activity they were pursuing.

At the completion of the study, some other departments did seem curious about the project, but concrete results in this area await a more complete version of the nurses' own work. Yet, even though their expectations may not be achieved completely, composing together enabled these nurses to mediate their own experience through language, to recognize the discourses of others, and to begin to carve out a place for their own voices in the community.

Composition theories that name social context as *one* of many elements writers consider as they write reduce the production of community discourse to a rhetoric of manipulation or, at best, mutual exchange. But at the same time, theories that would reduce the interplay of voices in context to a cacophony of unintelligible and unknowable subtleties beyond the consciousness or control of writers deny the possibility for language users to have any effect on that context. This research suggests an intricate social balance is at work in the production of community discourse. Grounding composition theory in studies of actual practice is essential to the development of theories that can account adequately for the ways this balance is achieved. Studies such as this one and others to come must inform a rhetoric of social responsibility that reflects the interdependence of all members of a discourse community—a rhetoric that sees language as a useful, if fallible, tool for influencing the worlds where it appears and for changing the perspectives of those who would use it.

| **Anthony Paré**

Discourse Regulations and the Production of Knowledge

The current social perspective on writing, and especially the concept of discourse community, has allowed writing teachers and researchers to draw convenient boundaries in a complex world of writing. Within those boundaries, groups of people create and use written discourse in particular ways for particular ends. Unfortunately, a rosy view of this phenomenon is prevalent, a view in which "community" suggests togetherness, mutual support, identification, and a group effort. This benign interpretation obscures the dynamics of restriction and regulation, the means whereby a community enforces its discourse conventions and its methods of producing knowledge. My aim in this chapter is to describe the relationship between discourse regulations and knowledge by drawing on the writing experiences of a team of social workers attached to the juvenile court system in Quebec.

Following Williams (1976), who calls community a "warmly persuasive word" (p. 66), a number of writers have commented on the largely positive connotations associated with the idea of community. Harris (1989), for example, warns against uncritical acceptance of the concept, which he says is "vague and suggestive . . . seductive and powerful" but also, potentially, "empty and sentimental" (pp. 12–13). Cooper (1989), too, notes that community, although "an attractive notion" (p. 203), is in need of careful definition. A major problem with the rosy view is its emphasis on the ways in which communities provide opportunities for discourse. As Faigley (1986) puts it, "Commentators on writing processes from a social viewpoint have neglected the issue of what *cannot* be discussed in a particular community" (p. 539). In other words, only one side of community generally has been exposed, the side that encourages, includes, and protects.

However, some writers have balanced the view. Russell (1990), for example, points in two directions: "First, community implies unity, identity, shared responsibility. Second, it implies exclusion, restriction, admission or non-admission" (p. 53). Freed and Broadhead (1987) indicate a similar division when they argue that communities "legislate conduct and behavior, establishing the eminently kosher as well as the unseemly and untoward" (p. 156). And Porter's succinct definition (1986) also suggests a dual nature: "A 'discourse community' is a group of individuals bound by a common interest who communicate through approved channels and whose discourse is regulated" (p. 38).

Balancing instigation with constraint and approval with restriction takes some sheen off the rosy view and more accurately describes the dynamics of community discourse. However, the use of opposing terms can create misleading dualities. Discourse regulations determine what *can* and *cannot* be discussed, as well as what *might* and *must* be discussed. In each case, the legislation controls the production of knowledge in writing. Regulations that instigate or approve a particular reality may well be as oppressive as those that constrain reality.

A community's discourse can be regulated in a variety of related ways: Set roles and relationships among writers and readers may determine who says what to whom, as well as when, where, why, and how it is said; standardized documentation may fix patterns in the collection, interpretation, and presentation of information; repeated activities associated with texts, such as meetings, interviews, and production or treatment procedures, may shape the form and use of those texts. Though some discourse regulations are acknowledged by the community, others are obeyed without thought; they are simply "the way things are done."

Whether explicit or implicit, recurring features of text and context can be understood as aspects of genre, according to Miller (1984), who defines genres as "typified rhetorical actions based in recurrent situations" (p. 159). Bazerman (1988) elaborates: "A genre is a socially recognized, repeated strategy for achieving similar goals in situations socially perceived as being similar. . . . A genre is a social construct that regularizes communication, interaction, and relations" (p. 62).

The regulatory function of community is not necessarily sinister or negative. Indeed, many conventional or generic features of text and context are designed to produce a fair and effective exchange of ideas or opinions. For example, the roles of adversary and advocate in law and legislature result, ideally, in discourse that helps participants arrive at the best course of action. Similarly, document cycling, draft review practices, and other regular collaborative strategies allow organizations to move toward consensus. Moreover, genres almost always make writing and reading easier.

However, a community's discourse conventions are more than mere etiquette or tradition, and they affect more than text production; they also determine the way the group and its individual members think. The pervasive influence of genre regularizes meaning by replicating, as closely as possible, the processes of composition and interpretation. By controlling discourse, the community controls knowledge: What cannot be said cannot be known. Conversely, the community can ensure certain knowledge by requiring it.

In addition, once adopted, the repetition of regulations can render them invisible. Smith (1974) explains this phenomenon: "Socially organized practices of reporting and recording work upon what actually happens or has happened to create a reality in documentary form, and though they are decisive to its character, their traces are not visible in it" (p. 257).

These are serious charges. They suggest the need for greater attention to the rules and routines of discourse. What blinkers do writers don when they voluntarily obey the writing regulations of their disciplines? Must they ignore, suppress, or compromise personal beliefs in order to fulfill their obligations to their discourse communities? When do the demands (and privileges) of membership threaten the integrity of personal knowledge? What happens when writers challenge community rules? These and other questions guided the study described in this chapter. Though the context and constraints may be unique to the social workers who experience them, some tension between individual vision and community expectations is a fact of life for all writers.

Context and Method

When an adolescent in Quebec is judged guilty of an offense under the Criminal Code, a chain of texts and events is set in motion. The most crucial text is the Predisposition Report (PDR), which is written by a social worker as an advisory report on the sentencing (disposition) of the adolescent. To prepare the PDR, the social worker takes the offending adolescent on as a client and conducts extensive interviews with the youth, his or her family, teachers, employers, and others. The inquiry the workers conduct through these interviews is determined, in large part, by the form of the PDR.

The structure and substance of the report itself are shaped, in turn, by guidelines all workers follow. The guidelines indicate the proper arrangement and relevant content of the report. The PDR includes various versions of the incident that led to the charge (from the police, the adolescent, the parents, and the victim, if there was one), a section detailing prior convictions (known as "Official Antecedents"), assessments of the adolescent and the family, a summary, and a recommendation for sentencing. Social workers can recommend incarceration but usually suggest some blend of probation, community work, and, if appropriate, financial restitution to victims. Inevitably, the PDR has a dramatic effect on the adolescent's life; one worker described it as "the rope that can hang the kid."

Copies of the Predisposition Report are made available to the judge, the defense and prosecuting lawyers, the adolescent, and the family. The social workers can be called to the hearing as witnesses. The legal status of the document forces the social workers to abide by a variety of regulations regarding the inadmissibility of certain types of information. Failure to comply with these restrictions can lead to public criticism from the judge and lawyers or even to contempt of court charges.

The examples that follow come from an extensive qualitative study of the writing done by these social workers. Eight workers were interviewed initially; subsequently, four of them provided lengthy protocols (up to seven hours long), collected while they wrote PDRs, and the same four sat for a discourse-based, retrospective interview. The workers' notes, case logs, rough drafts, and final reports were examined. In addition, many informal interviews took place over the telephone or when tapes and texts were being exchanged. The study took just over a year to complete.

No systematic method was used in the selection of the interview and protocol excerpts that follow. They were chosen from a much larger body of data simply because they provide overt comments on some of the community's discourse regulations or explicit examples of the effect of those regulations. In a sense, the total body of data charts the full extent of the community's control of discourse and the individual writer's compliance and conflict with those controls. Each moment in the protocols and every interview answer sheds light on how the community, through the regulated discourse of its members, produces the knowledge it requires. Many of the examples below represent conflicts with community expectations, because it is at the point of conflict that regulations become apparent. (Occasional infelicities in style or expression are due to some social workers using English as a second language.)

A note of caution before moving on: The following discussion is divided into two sections—admissible and inadmissible evidence. Though this classification makes the presentation of findings easier and neater, it obscures to some extent the dynamics of discourse regulations. For example, there are complex connections among the social workers, judges, lawyers, families, and clients, and that web of relationships helps explain some of the reporting rules the workers follow. However, for the sake of this discussion, only the most obvious and clearly defined of community regulations are presented, those governing what *can* be said and those governing what *cannot* be said.

Admissible Evidence

The four pages of guidelines for the Predisposition Report provide the writers with a detailed outline of the document. Even veteran social workers refer to them frequently. Headings and subheadings are indicated, and brief instructions describe appropriate commentary for each section. The "Assessment of Adolescent" section, for example, asks for the following:

1. Describe the adolescent according to age, maturity, character, and personality.
2. Evaluate adolescent's degree of motivation and his capacity to curb his delinquent behavior.
3. Assess any plans put forward by the adolescent to change his conduct or to participate in activities or undertake measures to improve himself.

In effect, the guidelines serve as a heuristic: They guide the writer to admissible evidence; that is, they indicate what the community considers permissible knowledge. In addition, by suggesting types of discourse—in this case, description, evaluation, and assessment—the guidelines regulate the writers' and readers' ways of thinking about the adolescent. Occasionally, the guidelines make an explicit link between the knowledge requested and its use by the community, as in this description of one section of the report: "The summary should give a global picture of the adolescent's evolution and of his interactions with his family and social milieus in order to help the court understand the adolescent's involvement in delinquencies."

The guidelines aim to organize the varied detail of each adolescent's life into a pattern of reporting. However, that pattern reflects the beliefs and procedures of the social workers' community; moreover, the community anticipates, indeed assumes, a certain type of adolescent. As Smith (1974) explains, "A highly complex socially organized practice mediates the relation of knower and known" (p. 257). The repeated practice of the juvenile court system, including the composition and interpretation of the PDR, presumes that the adolescent is a known object. Smith continues:

The object constituted as known is already socially constructed prior to the knower's entry into the relation. Her relation to it, the act in which she knows it, has thus already a determinate structure. She may appear as investigator, discoverer, or inquirer, but so long as this social determination remains unexamined, her enterprise is closed by a boundary which cannot be transcended. (p. 257)

Even before Sophie, the social worker, meets Louis, the adolescent, she *expects* he will fit a certain profile. This expectation justifies the PDR guidelines and the categories of admissible knowledge. Furthermore, the expectation is reinforced by a charge of guilty and by Sophie's first encounter with Louis in documentary form: the police report of his offense, which indicates that Louis was present during the robbery of $85 from another adolescent. Typically, Louis denies involvement, claiming to have been in the wrong place at the wrong time. Initially, at least, Sophie conducts the PDR process without apparent conflict. She acts "as investigator, discoverer, [and] inquirer," and, during the composing process, interprets and reports according to the PDR guidelines. But increasingly she feels some disjuncture, as these protocol excerpts suggest (quotation marks indicate text being read or written aloud; three dots [. . .] indicate a short pause, and four dots indicate a deletion):

- [Reviewing a section.] I'm on the wrong track again. There's just something wrong with this kid that's so hard to put together.
- What else can I say about this kid? Feel I still don't know him. Something intangible, but I just cannot get my hand on it . . . something weird.
- [Working on Assessment of Adolescent section.] "Louis is a 15.11 year old mulatto adolescent" . . . [Reads this back.] It's true, he's blank in my head. I spend my whole working day on this phantom.
- So many contradictions in this case. How can he be self-confident and self-assured and not be able to answer questions? Unbelievable! I've never had so many problems. Amusingly enough, the harder the kid, the better I am, but if it's everyday kids, I'm zilch.

The final sentence of the last excerpt reveals Sophie's recognition of a disruption in the usual knower-known relation. She is working on a "phantom" because she is attempting to write about the adolescent she and the community *expect*, not about the "everyday" one who actually exists. This conflict becomes apparent when Sophie completes a draft of the Summary section of the report, a rather negative overview of the adolescent. She turns the tape recorder off; when she turns it back on, she has this to say:

After discussing with a colleague there, discussing that the kid doesn't have to be bad, necessarily, fundamentally. In short . . . [Reads draft of Summary and rips page up.] Let's twist this into something . . . [Begins new, more positive Summary, which ends:] "No major areas of concerns could be identified in this adolescent's life which could explain his involvement or reaction with regards to the present matter." That's it, judge! Roll it and smoke it! If there's nothing to say, there's nothing to say.

Because she was "programmed to think of the kid as a bad boy," as she put it, Sophie had great difficulty writing this report. The adolescent's history did not match the progression of delinquency assumed by the community and implied by the guidelines. During her discourse-based interview, Sophie explained:

> I was trying to really dig into every zone or area of his life to try and find something else that would let us know or lead us to believe that we were right. Because it is unbelievable that a kid starts as a first charge—without antecedents, with no problem whatsoever—in getting involved in something like that, which was robbery. You start by shoplifting, breaking and entering, then you go into confronting people.

Sophie was attempting to prove that the community's expectations "were right." Because she could not, she examined those expectations and thus, in Smith's terms, crossed a "boundary" and transcended the "determinate structure" of her community's discourse and knowledge. However, she did so at some risk to her own status as a member of the community, as these excerpts from her discourse interview suggest:

- This [PDR was] really a royal pain to write and, I wonder, maybe because it wasn't a clear case, maybe because I was trying to prove something to justify my credibility in front of the court . . . And I think it became easier to write once I stopped trying to prove myself.
- I have to convince the court, at least let them know, that I'm sorry, but if you were expecting to find a rotten little kid, I didn't find it. But it has to be credible also.

In this situation, the "repeated strategy" of the PDR, codified in the report's guidelines, worked to eliminate the differences between the adolescent in question and the adolescent expected. Without Sophie's determination to understand her discomfort and her willingness to risk her credibility, Louis would have been known and treated as "a rotten little kid." This tendency of discourse to shape knowledge by overgeneralization is described by Smith (1984b): "Discourse develops the ideological currency of society, providing schemata and methods that transpose local actualities into standardized conceptual and categorical forms" (p. 65).

Thus, regulations meant to promote or instigate discourse by defining admissibility of evidence create a particular knowledge, an "ideological currency." And though these rules encourage discourse, they are infused with the community expectations and assumptions that produce them, and therefore they shape and control knowledge as surely as do regulations against discourse.

Inadmissible Evidence

Under the rules of law, certain kinds of information cannot be entered as evidence. In effect, these categories identify unwelcome discourse, and therefore they act as a negative heuristic: They discourage the search for and disclosure of some knowledge. Banned from Quebec's juvenile court, and therefore from the PDR, are three types of inadmissible evidence. One is self-reported delinquencies: The social workers cannot describe in the PDR any delinquencies reported to them by the adolescent but not officially recognized. This restriction prevents self-incrimination. A second, and similar, category of inadmissible evidence concerns charges pending against a client or charges on which the client was acquitted. This restriction guarantees that the adolescent will be judged only on the case before the court. The final inadmissible category is hearsay evidence, which is "evidence not proceeding from the personal knowledge of the witness, but from the mere repetition of what he has heard others say" (Black, Nolan, & Connolly, 1983, p. 368).

Unlike the guidelines, which control the production of knowledge in subtle, almost invisible ways, the inadmissible evidence regulations are relatively clear, as is the social workers' conflict with them. There are penalties for disobeying the rules: At the least, workers can receive a reprimand from the judge; at worst, they can be charged with contempt of court and be fined. Nevertheless, the workers take a risk when they believe the inadmissible evidence has a strong bearing on their client's offense or when they need it to justify their recommendation: in other words, when they feel the value of the knowledge surpasses the damage it can cause. The excerpts that follow provide examples of workers discussing or confronting the three types of forbidden information.

The first excerpt is from an interview. It came in response to a question about self-reported delinquencies. (Here, phrases in quotation marks indicate where the worker is speaking as if she were the client.)

By the third interview they feel more relaxed and they will start telling about, "Well, before I actually got caught for this B and E [breaking and entering] I was stealing bikes, I was doing this." You know, I know a kid that's gotten into B and E is not the first time he's done something. It's the first time he's been caught. And, you know, I had a kid who started stealing cars when he was eight, but wasn't caught until he was twelve. I mean, there were four years of outlandish stuff this kid was doing and I couldn't tell the court. And it was an obvious placement case, but I could not give enough facts to the court to prove it.

The worker believes that knowledge of the boy's past will allow the court to make an appropriate decision; however, regulations against the use of that information prevent her. In a sense, this is an example of "the value contradictions that arise when discourse communities overlap" (Bizzell, 1987, p. 3). As a member of the social service community, this worker values the knowledge because it indicates what she considers the appropriate social service response to the situation: removal of the boy from his home and placement in some form of residential custody, probably a group home. As a member of the juvenile court community, she is constrained from using information that is considered inappropriate because it is self-incriminatory.

A similar conflict often develops when the social workers write the Official Antecedents section of the report. Only those offenses for which the youth has been found guilty may be mentioned in this section. No matter how often an adolescent has appeared in court, and regardless of concurrent charges, the worker must stick to the offense for which the PDR was requested. Although the worker may use her knowledge of the youth's frequent court appearances in her assessment and in determining the direction of her ongoing relationship with, or treatment of, the client, she may not introduce that knowledge in court. In the following protocol excerpt, a social worker struggles with a PDR for a boy who appears to have used a variety of aliases and who, in addition, has been acquitted in the past and has other charges pending. (In the following excerpts, quotation marks indicate text being read or written aloud.)

Official Antecedents, here we go, that's easy. "Official Antecedents": The kid has been acquitted; two files have been closed in our services; I cannot mention them. He's been acquitted in court for a charge I cannot mention either. Is that considered to be an antecedent? Oh God, it's so bad that the court cannot know everything that happened prior to this. Technical stuff! Feel that this kid has so much hidden, and he's a liar. Okay, let's play by the book. "Official Antecedents: None."

"Technical stuff" and "play[ing] by the book" are references to the regulations governing evidence. The social workers seemed to respect the fact that these generic restrictions ensured that the PDR would be, in Bazerman's term, a "repeated strategy" and that all clients would be judged in a similar way. However, that respect did not prevent them from occasionally chafing under the limitations when they felt the need for full disclosure. In this excerpt, the worker returns to the same section sometime later:

> Okay, "Official Antecedents": I'm going to say [crosses out the word "None"], "Dennis [client] has no prior conviction before the Youth Court, however he is awaiting trial on a" minor charge? "however he is awaiting trial on a charge." Do I have the legal right to mention that it is a theft? "however he is awaiting trial on" an offense? Should I keep it vague or should I mention it? "however he is awaiting trial on a charge." Maybe I shouldn't even mention it. "on a charge." Oh, what the heck, I shouldn't do that. [Crosses out sentence.] No, this kid has the right to be considered innocent until he's undergoing trial so I'm going to keep it . . . he has no antecedent at this point. I have no right of mentioning anything. [Writes "None."]

Finally, just before sending the report for typing, the worker came back to this section again:

> "Official Antecedents: None." I feel like I should put something in Official Antecedents. The kid is having, like, phew! Am I allowed to say this? Oh, this is an eternal dilemma . . . "None, however Dennis is awaiting trial on another charge and awaiting arraignment on two (2) municipal by-laws." I think I would feel better because I look like a dummy. Kid's been too, like, you know, he's not a bird of paradise.

When asked to explain these excerpts during her discourse-based interview, the worker described the tension between knowledge needed and knowledge banned:

> Even self-reported offenses that were not even brought to the court tell you something about this kid. If he got out on a technicality, but he admits the fact, I think it should be in. So, obviously, I was debating it [in the excerpts above]. Sometimes I'm . . . for some kids I say, well, it's not really that important, but in some cases, like this one, he already got away with a wrong name, having a file here—two of them have been closed—now he's coming back and I say too bad the kid . . . the court cannot know more about this kid and I'm trying to really put it in, avoiding the legal trap.

"Avoiding the legal trap" means making the inadmissible evidence partly acceptable; in this case, by referring to but not naming the charges pending. This tactic is not always possible. The following protocol excerpt captures a worker wondering about the admissibility of something she is writing. The PDR she was working on was a difficult and painful report. Her client, an obviously troubled young man, was charged with beating his common-law wife, Linda. Although the worker felt Linda was frightened, she had not been told this directly:

> "It is to be noted that Linda's social worker, Martin Hanna, told this worker" . . . That's hearsay. Jesus, I wonder if I can put that in? It's just so important. She told her social worker that she was afraid of Howie [client]. [Stops tape recorder; turns it on again.] Okay, I've gotten several different opinions, but I think I'll put it in anyway. This is, like, hearsay, but it's important for the judge to know, so let it be struck from the record. . . . Boy, I'm going to get into trouble for putting that in, but I've got to.

For the worker, this knowledge was important enough to risk the ire of the defense lawyer and the censure of the judge. During her discourse interview about this PDR, the worker was asked if she would be willing to delete the hearsay evidence. She said no, and spoke at length about her decision; some excerpts:

- There's a lot of hearsay in the report which I'm not allowed to put in, in a court report, so I took the risk of putting it in, thinking that it's important for the judge to know. . . . I'm the one that's going to get it, you know, from the lawyers in court for having put that stuff in. But at least I'll know that the judge knows about these concerns. So that was pretty difficult, 'cause this is pretty unusual for me to go out of bounds, and put stuff in the report that you're not supposed to.
- I was very ambivalent about putting it in, because it's such a serious report. If the defense lawyer starts to discredit me for having put that in the report, then what's the judge going to think of the rest of the report? But I figured I'd take the chance because I figured it was important.
- It's weird to say, but when you write these reports, you often have in mind who's the judge that's going to be reading them. I think I was. Because I knew it was a woman judge, I think I gave myself a bit more leeway; maybe that's why I felt comfortable in putting some of the hearsay in, because of the judge. It's a bit weird to say, but maybe if it had been a different judge, very legalistic, I might have thought twice about that.

The worker assumes that a female judge will want to know about the young woman's fear of violence, despite the fact that disclosure of that knowledge breaks the discourse rules. She goes "out of bounds," beyond the boundary imposed by the community, to tell that knowledge. In so doing, she risks losing her credibility as a member of the community.

These examples of workers in conflict with discourse regulations are exceptions to the rule. In most cases, and necessarily, the PDR guidelines and legal constraints operate invisibly. Within the regulations (and the assumptions they embody), the social workers collect, interpret, and report the information that allows the juvenile court community to conduct its business. Occasionally, the community's rules clash with the individual's perceptions, and then the extent of the community's control of discourse and knowledge becomes apparent.

Conclusion

Reither (1985) puts it succinctly: "To belong to a discourse community is to belong to a knowledge community" (p. 624). The relationship between discourse and knowledge is reciprocal: Each shapes the other. In order to write successfully within a community, individuals must respect the discourse rules that produce the knowledge required by the community. Indeed, community membership is based, in large part, on adherence to such regulations.

As teachers, researchers, supervisors, consultants, and so on, we follow *and* promote regulations, consciously and unconsciously. Though some of those rules may seem inconsequential, others have profound results. Many of the stringent constraints in the reporting of experimental research, for example, ban traditionally undervalued ways of experiencing and knowing the world. The low value placed on narrative in much formal writing indicates a similar prohibition against certain ways of seeing and reporting. Such restrictions often reflect a distrust of hunch, intuition, opinion, or instinct—in other words, a distrust of personal or "subjective" knowledge (see Belenky, Clinchy, Goldberger, & Tarule, 1986). Even apparently mundane regulations, such as that against the use of the first person pronoun in formal writing, can influence the production of knowledge: The PDR writers cannot say, "I believe"; instead, they write, "It is believed." As a result, knower and knowledge are separated, and the text takes on a "documentary reality."

Of course, regulations are not inherently harmful. Limits on PDR reporting prevent the boastful adolescent from condemning himself, and guidelines focus the social worker's attention and free her from some difficulties of invention and arrangement. Not all rules that block discourse are necessarily bad, nor are those that encourage discourse automatically good. And regulations change; as this study came to an end, social workers and juvenile court lawyers were meeting to discuss revisions to the PDR guidelines.

However, discourse regulations do influence the composition and interpretation of texts, and therefore the thinking of community members. This study suggests the extent of that influence and raises important questions for research and pedagogy. We need to know more about how style guides, writers' manuals, and other discourse regulations determine the production of knowledge. We need to examine the conventions we impose on students, and we need to consider what power they have to reject them. In our own writing and reading, in this very book for example, we need to discover what rules are at play, and we need to know their consequences.

9 Graham Smart

Genre as Community Invention | A Central Banks' Response to Its Executives' Expectations as Readers

Research has begun to reveal how discourse communities in school and workplace settings use written genres to enable effective writing and reading (Bazerman, 1988; Campbell & Jamieson, 1990; Devitt, 1991; Freed & Broadhead, 1987; Freedman, 1987; Herrington, 1985; Myers, 1990b; Smart, 1992). This research, together with other theoretical scholarship (Bakhtin, 1986; Coe, 1987; Freadman, 1987; Maimon, 1983; Miller, 1984; Swales, 1988), suggests a reinterpretation of genre as a broad rhetorical strategy enacted, collectively, by members of a community in order to create knowledge essential to their aims.

This view of genre has guided my study of a community of executives and research staff at the Bank of Canada, where I have been an in-house writing trainer for the past eight years. As I observed the chain of rhetorical events through which specialized "written knowledge" (Bazerman, 1988) is developed by the research staff and then used by the executives in discussing corporate issues and making decisions, a focal question emerged: How does the community invent the particular genres it needs for creating the written knowledge required by the executives in their decision-making role?

In attempting to answer this question, my inquiry focused on the community's epistemology and knowledge making, on regularities in texts and in the composing processes and reading practices associated with these texts, and on contextual influences that appear to evoke such regularities. From my findings, I have developed a theory on how the community invents the genres it needs for creating written knowledge. According to this theory, four major contextual influences—the executives' issue-resolving mandate, several mental constructs that inform their thinking, a tacit understanding between the executives and the research staff about the delegation of problem-solving responsibility, and the intertextual resonance of prior written discourse—shape the executives' reading practices and consequent expectations. These expectations, conveyed and given authority through the institutional hierarchy, in turn exert a compelling force on the composing processes of the staff as they collaborate in preparing documents for the executives' use, thereby giving rise to a body of typified discourse. This theory can be used to account both for textual features common to all the community's genres and for textual features that differentiate these genres.

The Study

The Setting

As a central bank, the Bank of Canada's primary role is to formulate and implement Canadian monetary policy, with the aim of contributing to the country's overall economic performance. The Bank carries out this role in a context of broad public accountability, and therefore, to be effective, must preserve its credibility. This need for credibility requires that the Bank make, and be seen to make, carefully reasoned decisions, not only on issues related to monetary policy, but also on issues related to its own internal administration.

At the apex of the Bank's hierarchy is a management committee, composed of fifteen executives, that is responsible to an external board of directors for ensuring that the institution performs effectively. The executives make decisions on the broad objectives of monetary policy, as well as on how best to pursue these objectives. They also make, or recommend to the board of directors, decisions concerning the Bank's internal administration. Traditionally, the members of the management committee have been economists who have risen through the ranks. On the current committee, thirteen of the executives were trained in economics, one in business administration, and one in law.

Below the management committee in the Bank's hierarchy are twelve departments that, in addition to performing operational activities, carry out research for the committee. These departments include four on what is known as the "policy side" of the Bank, where economists conduct research related primarily to monetary policy, and eight on what is known as the "administrative side," where staff such as computer specialists, financial analysts, auditors, data-processing analysts, and personnel experts conduct research related to the institution's internal administration. In all, across the twelve departments, the research staff numbers approximately 250. Each department is headed by a chief, who is responsible for seeing that documents reporting research and analysis to the executives serve their needs.

The Theoretical Lens

Research in composition studies and related disciplines on the social nature of genre and on contextual factors that influence writing and reading provided me with a theoretical lens for observing the rhetorical activities of the Bank's executives and research staff. Miller (1984), in a ground-breaking article, argues against a formalist conception of genre, proposing instead to redefine genres, nonliterary as well as literary, as typified rhetorical actions arising within a society in response to recurrent situations. Swales (1988) situates genres more locally, describing them as a defining property of the discourse community, a result of the community's shared goals, forums, and expectations.

Bazerman (1988), in tracing the emergence and evolution of the experimental article in scientific disciplines, portrays written genre as a community-enacted rhetorical strategy. At the heart of Bazerman's argument is the claim that a research community's genres, in enabling effective writing and reading, play an important part in the creation of written knowledge. Although always evolving, a genre offers a community, at any historical moment, a measure of rhetorical stability through regularities in written texts and in the production and interpretation of these texts. According to Bazerman, "These regularities encompass . . . how one would go about reading a text, as well as how one would draw a diagram or frame an argument" (p. 314).

Work by other scholars complements Bazerman's notion of genre by exploring contextual factors that tend to regularize writing and reading within communities. Bizzell (1982, 1987) points to how discourse conventions shape thought and language use within social groups. Cooper (1986) describes a social web of ideas, purposes, norms, interactions, and textual forms created by and acting upon writers. Toulmin (1958, 1972) and Toulmin, Rieke, and Janik (1979) demonstrate that discipline-specific modes of argument inherent in academic or professional fields structure their discourse. Winsor (1989) illustrates how, within a professional organization, individuals' writing is invoked and shaped by corporate objectives. Porter (1986) and Devitt (1991) discuss how writers respond to the intertextual influences of a community's prior written discourse. And research by Ede and Lunsford (1986, 1990) suggests a correlation between social structure and patterns of collaborative writing. From their inquiry into reading, Fish

(1980) and Culler (1980) propose the notion of the interpretive community, a group of readers sharing similar aims, specialized knowledge, and tacit interpretive conventions. Vipond and Hunt (1989), Flower (1988), Schlotthaus (1989), Schwegler and Shamoon (1991), and Coe (1987), in identifying factors such as situation, purposes for reading, previous textual experience, disciplinary concepts, and text structure as influences on readers' strategies, suggest how members of a community come to share conventions for interpreting discourse.

Central to Bazerman's inquiry (1988) is the question of how a community develops the genres it needs for structuring the intellectual activity that leads to written knowledge. His historical analysis of scientific disciplines reveals how genres emerge from, and in turn influence, a matrix of shared goals, epistemological assumptions, empirical methods, and social practices. Bazerman emphasizes the need for further research into the development of genres within "the sciences and other knowledge-generating communities" (p. 332). He foresees such work contributing to the design of "intelligent curricula to meet the local rhetorical needs of students" (p. 332) entering such communities.

The theoretical assumptions underlying my study of how a community of executives and research staff at the Bank of Canada invents its genres are derived from the research outlined above. The study assumed that nonliterary genres, as broad, knowledge-building rhetorical strategies, are often the local inventions of particular discourse communities. The study also assumed that, within such a community, a genre can usefully be conceived as a distinctive profile of regularities across three dimensions: a set of written texts, the composing processes involved in producing these texts, and the reading practices used to interpret them. Finally, the study assumed that such regularities are not accidental, but rather result from contextual influences.

Research Methods

The study involved participant-observer research over eight years. As an in-house writing trainer, I work with members of the research staff on both the policy and administrative sides of the Bank to help them develop the specific, advanced literacy they need for documenting research and analysis for the institution's executives. In this role, I have coached forty-nine writers, of varying levels of experience, through the process of preparing an analytic paper for the management committee or one of its subcommittees. I also have consulted with thirty supervisors on how, as reviewers, to give writers useful feedback on plans and drafts. This experience has provided an excellent vantage point for observing the individual composing processes and the writer/reviewer collaboration that occur as a paper is taken through successive iterations until judged appropriate for an executive readership. I have kept field notes on my observations of writers and reviewers at work; collected copies of writers' drafts, reviewers' annotations, and final papers; and tape-recorded meetings between writers and reviewers.

In addition, I have explored both the reading practices and the expectations that the Bank's executives bring to analytic papers prepared by the research staff. I conducted standardized interviews, averaging an hour in length, with ten of the fifteen executives and collected a total of twelve reading protocols from six executives in sessions where I observed and tape-recorded a reader talking aloud while going through a paper. I also interviewed eleven of the twelve department chiefs, as well as one deputy chief, about their perceptions of the executives' expectations as readers. Finally, I collected fifty-four analytic papers, each described by either an executive or a department chief as well written.

In analyzing the data—audiotapes and transcripts of interviews and reading protocols, approximately eleven hundred pages of field notes, and a variety of written texts (drafts, reviewers' annotations, and final papers)— I worked from the premise that to discover how the community invents its genres, I needed to inquire into the community's epistemology and knowledge making; identify regularities in the community's texts, in the research staff's composing processes, and in the executives' reading practices; and locate contextual influences that appear to evoke such regularities. Although I observed individual differences in writers, readers, and texts, these differences were excluded from the analysis.

The Community's Epistemology, Knowledge Making, and Genres

The Bank's research staff and the executives on the management committee constitute, in Bazerman's terms, a knowledge-generating community (1988). In order to structure the intellectual activity underlying the production and interpretation of written knowledge used by the executives for resolving issues of monetary policy and internal administration, the community employs a family of genres.

The executives approach monetary-policy and administrative issues through a process of "collegial . . . discussion and debate" (W. A.).[1] "The members of management have a history of trying to understand the issues . . . whether it be monetary policy or new buildings . . . [by] discussing them, debating them" (P. J.). Whether the issue is, for example, how to respond to an impending legislated change in the Canadian banking system that could affect the implementation of monetary policy, or whether a proposed computerized data-processing system would be cost-effective, the executives' collegial discussion usually follows much the same pattern. First, the issue is defined and its implications are carefully explored; then, the advantages and disadvantages of alternative courses of action are assessed; and finally, a consensual decision is reached.

Because of a strong belief in the epistemic force of writing, the executives depend on written discourse, much of it produced by the research staff, to focus and structure their oral discussion of monetary-policy and administrative issues. The executives' belief in the epistemic value of writing has two facets. First, they believe that written knowledge provides a necessary foundation for in-depth discussion of difficult issues: "Many of the issues we deal with at the Bank are very complex, with a lot of ramifications that lead in many directions, and if you really want to sort these kinds of things out, then the only way you can do it is through written analysis and discussion" (W. A.). "Whenever we have a meeting [to discuss an issue], the rule of the game is that the paper is distributed well in advance. . . . You're given time to work through the ideas as best you can before the meeting. . . . In my view there's a tremendous advantage to written debate on complex issues. The discipline is great; the depth of understanding is enhanced" (C. F.). Consequently, the intertextual body of written discourse generated around issues is considered an important community resource: "We rely heavily on a history of thought, and the files . . . are really important. Questions keep recirculating . . . and having the written word is very important, at times, to go back to . . . to know what we've done before, and where we've started from" (D. R.).

Second, the executives believe that if the research staff are to provide the management committee and its subcommittees with sound analysis on monetary-policy and administrative issues, staff members need to use the writing process to develop and test their ideas: "There has been a very great reliance put on the written page around this institution . . . [because] it's in trying to write a piece, and putting it down where it stares back at you, rather coldly, that you really wrap your mind around the arguments . . . [so that] the work tends to be done with greater depth, and tends to be worth rather more than it would otherwise be" (W. W.). A related notion is that the intellectual effort required to "wordsmith [their prose into] straightforward terms that an interested layman can understand" (A. M.) helps the staff shift their analysis from the level of technical detail to the level of conceptual argument. The executives also think that textual collaboration among staff members improves the quality of their work: "[The members of the management committee believe that] if you . . . write the case down and circulate it among colleagues, and get some criticism of it before you send it on [to the committee], you do find that perhaps there are some considerations that haven't been dealt with, or there are some problems with the argument" (D. B.).

To acquire the written knowledge needed to support their oral discussion of a particular monetary-policy or administrative issue, members of the management committee often will ask a department to research a specific question and document its findings in an analytic paper. At other times, a department will take the initiative in studying and reporting on an issue known to concern committee members. In either case, the department's research staff gather, manipulate, and interpret relevant quantitative data reflecting economic or administrative events to develop knowledge commonly referred to by the executives as "written analysis." In its various instances, written analysis performs one or more of the following functions: identifying and interpreting trends in historical, current, or projected data; proposing, evaluating, or suggesting modifications to a theoretical model for interpreting data; defining a problem, along with its causes and consequences; assessing the advantages and disadvantages of alternative courses of action; and recommending, justifying, and planning for a particular action.

Written analysis is developed, conveyed, and interpreted through a family of genres, each of which provides the executives with the specific form of written knowledge they need for discussing a particular type of monetary-policy or administrative issue. Genres contributing to discussion of monetary policy include, for example, the note to management, which describes and interprets current economic or financial trends in Canada or other countries; the research memorandum, which presents macroeconomic work of a theoretical, often econometric, nature; and the staff economic projection, which provides forward-looking analyses of the Canadian, American, and global economies. Examples of genres contributing to discussion of the Bank's internal administration are the automation proposal, which presents a cost-benefit case for designing, purchasing, or upgrading a computerized system for processing data in some area of the Bank's operations; the project-update report, which describes progress, resource expenditures, problems, and strategy in project work; and the stewardship document, in which a department reports on its accomplishments over the past year and outlines initiatives planned for the year ahead.

Regularities in Texts, Composing Processes, and Reading Practices

Regularities in texts, in the research staff's composing processes, and in the executives' reading practices reflect the structure that the community's genres bring to the intellectual activity underlying the production and interpretation of written analysis. Further, these regularities point toward a theory that accounts for the invention of these genres. Certain regularities in texts, composing processes, and reading practices occur across all genres, while other regularities are genre-specific.

Texts in all genres exhibit a similar underlying rhetoric. They take a clear position on an issue of concern to the executives and support this position with a sustained argument: "There's a standard core to any paper you would write: It has to have an argument [and] . . . it has to have supporting evidence. . . . That's fundamental to what we trade in—we trade in arguments and synthesis" (W. A.). Typically, a text begins with an introduction that identifies the monetary-policy or administrative issue to be discussed, places this issue in a historical or conceptual context, states a position, and summarizes a supporting argument. Next, the supporting argument is presented in full, with its selected quantitative data, its economics-based reasoning, and its intertextual linkages with other community texts. Finally, any serious qualifications to the conclusions are mentioned. Texts within any single genre enact this common rhetoric through a unique configuration of communicative functions and linguistic forms that gives the texts their distinctive discourse structure.

The composing processes involved in the research staff's preparation of analytic papers for the executives also are regularized significantly. In all genres, composing processes are structured by a similar cycle of writer/reviewer collaboration. Typically, following a briefing from his or her supervisor on an issue of concern to the management committee or one of its subcommittees, a member of the research staff gathers and evaluates relevant data and composes a draft for review. The writer then incorporates rounds of spoken and written feedback from the supervisor into successive revisions until the latter is satisfied.[2] At this point, another round of collaboration usually occurs, involving the writer, the supervisor, and a more senior reviewer. As the collaborative cycle continues, unnecessary technical detail is filtered out, key concepts are clearly defined, and the argument becomes increasingly issue-centered, coherent, and succinct. When the chief of the department decides the text has been refined sufficiently, it is sent on to its executive readership.

Within single genres, regularities in the nature and sequence of an experienced writer's rhetorical maneuvers are linked to the discourse structure of the emerging text as well as to the genre's particular intertextual relationship with other genres. For example, a writer working on an automation proposal typically begins by drafting the recommendation and its justification, then returns to them repeatedly as a touchstone for developing other parts of the text, a process that, in turn, usually prompts ongoing revisions to the recommendation and justification. And a writer working on a department's annual stewardship document, when about to draft an account of the past year's accomplishments, typically will read over both the previous steward-ship document with its outline of initiatives for the year ahead, to see what the department had committed itself to, and documents reporting on major departmental projects, to see what has actually been achieved.

Reading protocols and interviews with the executives on the manage-ment committee revealed that the reading practices they use to interpret analytic papers prepared by the research staff are also significantly regular-ized, in three ways. First, the executives share a similar way of approaching texts, regardless of genre. Usually, an executive will select a paper, either to be read alone or along with other related papers, to prepare for a meeting where a particular monetary-policy or administrative issue will be discussed with other members of the management committee. Consequently, the executive turns to the paper with a clear goal: to construct the specific form of knowledge needed to play an active role in moving the discussion forward. Typically, this knowledge will include answers to questions raised by the issue at hand. One executive, asked prior to reading a departmental steward-ship document what he expected to learn from it, replied, "Well, I'm looking for several things. I'm certainly looking for some discussion of the past year: areas of success, problem areas, lessons that come out of that. . . . If there are problem areas, what are those? And what, if any, measures need to be taken to deal with them?" (P. J.)

Second, the executives share a similar procedure for negotiating their way through texts. Typically, an executive begins by previewing a paper—reading the introduction and flipping through the remaining pages—to infer a sense of the overall argument and to decide on a reading strategy, that is, what parts of the text to read carefully and what parts to skim. The executive then proceeds in an active, question-driven manner, working as quickly as possible to construct the knowledge required. Throughout this process, the executive takes a distinctly critical stance, demanding evidence for any assertions and continuously challenging the line of argument: "If I'm reading to make an important judgment on the basis of a paper . . . I need . . . to challenge it critically, and decide whether I agree with it or not, and whether it's missing things, or . . . how it relates to other issues that are of relevance to me. . . . Just because you say it, why should I believe it? Convince me!" (W. A.) When the executive has evaluated the argument, answered his or her questions, and noted any areas where further work by the research staff would be useful, the paper is put aside. As a time-pressured reader responsi-ble for a wide range of issues, and with a great amount of written material to get through, the executive settles for the specific knowledge needed and moves on to another task.

Third, the executives share similar interpretive frameworks—mental schemata of specialized concepts and other previously acquired knowledge (Rumelhart, 1980; van Dijk & Kintsch, 1983) that they use in constructing knowledge from texts. Here, a pattern of regularity exists both within and across the community's genres. The interpretive framework the executives apply in constructing knowledge from texts in a particular monetary-policy genre would have certain elements specific to that genre; certain elements common to frameworks applied to texts in other monetary-policy genres; and still other elements common to frameworks applied to texts in all genres, whether dealing with monetary-policy or administrative issues. The converse would be true of the interpretive framework the executives apply to texts in a particular administrative genre.

For example, in reading a note to management about world oil markets prior to a management committee discussion on midterm prospects for the North American economy and the implications for Canadian interest rates, the executives would apply an interpretive framework with certain elements unique to the note to management; they would apply other elements common to the framework to a research memorandum on what a monetary union in the European Community would mean for the world's central banks; and yet other elements common to the framework to an automation proposal presenting a case for upgrading a computerized data-processing system.

A Theory on How the Community Invents Its Genres

From regularities observed in texts, in the research staff's composing processes, and in the executives' reading practices, I have developed a theory on how the community invents the genres it needs for creating specialized written knowledge. According to the theory, four major contextual influences shape the reading practices the executives bring to analytic papers: the executives' issue-resolving mandate, several mental constructs that inform their thinking, a tacit understanding between the executives and the research staff about the delegation of problem-solving responsibility, and the intertextual resonance of prior written discourse. The executives' shared reading practices lead to common expectations for the discourse structure (that is, the configuration of communicative functions and linguistic forms) of these papers. In turn, the executives' expectations, conveyed and given authority through the institutional hierarchy, exert a compelling force on the staff's collaborative composing processes, thereby eliciting a range of typified discourse.

The overarching influence on the executives' reading practices is the management committee's mandate for conducting monetary policy and overseeing the Bank's internal administration. The committee's mandate continuously generates a circumscribed range of recurrent monetary-policy and administrative issues requiring decisions. To provide a framework for resolving these issues, the committee has defined decision making roles for its members and has established a schedule of plenary and subcommittee meetings as forums for discussion. Together, these roles and forums create the need for a supporting body of typified written knowledge that the executives derive, in large measure, from analytic papers prepared by the research staff. The committee's broad mandate also imposes constraints on the executives, such as the amount of time they can spend on any single paper, given the wide range of issues they must deal with.

A second influence on the executives' reading practices comes from several shared mental constructs. Specifically, these mental constructs inform the interpretive frameworks the executives apply to analytic papers in creating meaning from them. One construct the executives bring to all papers, whether about monetary policy or administration, is the disciplinary paradigm of economics, the theoretical structure used by economists to investigate and explain how a society organizes the use of scarce resources to produce and distribute goods and services: "If you're going to argue with someone you have to know what his professional background is, and what kinds of paradigms they're particularly attuned to. And in that sense most of our management is trained as economists. . . . That means things like maximizing arguments are clearly important. . . . We're trying to minimize costs [and] . . . maximize output, for a given level of input . . . [and] that's very fundamental to anything that economists talk about" (W. A.).

Within their paradigm, economists analyze the economic and financial forces underlying historical, current, and projected trends in statistical data. While explaining such trends is an important part of their analysis, economists are careful about attributing causality; when they do assert causality, they tend to assume, influenced by the dichotomy of supply and demand, that there are often a number of causes for any given phenomenon. When reporting their analyses, economists are trained to support interpretations of data with rigorous argumentation involving specific warrants (Toulmin, 1958, 1972) and, where relevant, to qualify their conclusions with a statement of "risk," pointing to other factors that could have been considered and indicating the degree of dependability that should, therefore, be assumed. As decision makers, economists are concerned with identifying the feasible alternatives available to them and with calculating relative costs and benefits: "When spending large amounts of money, one wants to have a very clearly delineated set of options, with a costing out of those options. And [this requires] a fairly detailed analysis of what you're talking about, in the way of expenditures and returns" (C. F.). In this calculation, economists take into account not only the explicit expenditure involved, but also the "opportunity cost," reasoning that resources used for one activity are unavailable for another.

Another mental construct shared by the executives, one that influences the interpretive framework they bring to any monetary-policy paper, is a conceptual model of the Canadian economy, as set in relief against the American economy and, at one remove, against the global economy. Linked to the management committee's broad monetary-policy objectives and to its assumptions about how to implement policy most effectively, this model provides a context for thinking about the causes and implications of current economic and financial trends and for projecting such trends into the future. Dynamic and provisional, the model is supported empirically by complex econometric equations used by the research staff on the policy side of the Bank to interpret statistical data on the Canadian, American, and global economies: "From a [monetary-]policy perspective, somebody on the management committee needs to have at all times in his mind a working model of the economy, and of the impact that various policy levers have on the economy—the domestic economy, the international economy. . . . [Analytic papers on monetary-policy issues] tend to be on [topics such as] wages . . . wage-setting behavior, or the CPI [Consumer Price Index], or the impact of a move in the exchange rate on interest rates. . . . It helps [to] . . . fit [these papers] into your model. . . . So [for example] if someone says . . . the price of oil has gone up . . . you [know] that's going to affect exports for Canada, and it may affect prices." (T. N.).

A mental construct that influences the interpretive framework the executives bring to analytic papers on administrative issues is the "corporate framework," a conceptual model of the Bank's five business functions and related work activities.[3] Initially developed, collaboratively, by the management committee and the research staff in the mid-1980s to foster a coherent, institution-wide approach to designing computer systems and data bases, the model has in recent years also begun to serve as a conventional frame of reference for discussion within the committee of the Bank's planning, budgeting, and accounting processes.

A third influence on the executives' reading practices—again, specifically on the interpretive frameworks the executives bring to analytic papers— comes from a tacit understanding between the executives and the research staff about the varying degree of problem-solving responsibility delegated to the staff. Through enculturation into the Bank's ways of working, the executives and the senior members of the research staff share an implicit sense of how far the staff are to take their analyses, depending on the type of issue involved. For example, in certain situations, the research staff are delegated the limited task of identifying and explaining trends in quantitative data; in other situations, the staff are to go further and assess alternative courses of action; and in still other situations, they are to make and justify a recommendation.

A fourth influence on the executives' reading practices is the intertextual resonance of the community's prior written discourse. Given the extent to which the executives' discussion of issues is document-supported, the interpretive framework brought to one analytic paper invariably includes knowledge previously acquired from other papers. For example, an executive reading a note to management on current commodity prices will attend to whether it confirms or challenges the most recent staff economic projection, with its forward-looking analyses of Canadian, American, and global economic trends. And an executive reading an automation proposal from a department would assess it in light of both the department's previous annual stewardship document, which described initiatives to be undertaken during the year, and recent automation proposals from other departments, with their competing resource requirements.

Shaped by these four major contextual influences, the executives' shared reading practices lead to shared expectations. The executives expect analytic papers from the research staff to accommodate their way of approaching texts, their procedure for negotiating their way through texts, and their interpretive frameworks for constructing knowledge. More specifically, the executives expect a paper, whether on monetary policy or administration, to be structured and visually formatted in a way that allows a reader to identify, at a glance, the issue addressed; to rapidly preview the paper, and thus infer the overall argument and decide on an appropriate reading strategy; and to construct, as quickly as possible, the particular knowledge required. The executives expect a paper to focus on a specific issue; to state a clear position and support it with a succinct argument grounded in carefully selected quantitative data and infused with the disciplinary logic of economics; to answer key questions associated with the issue; to indicate relevant intertextual links with previous papers; and to reflect the appropriate degree of problem-solving initiative. Further, the executives expect a paper on monetary policy to fit within the prevailing conceptual model of the Canadian, American, and global economies; and increasingly, they expect a paper on an administrative issue to fit within the "corporate framework" model of the Bank's five business functions.

And in fact, the executives do get what they expect. Their expectations, conveyed and given authority through the institutional hierarchy, exert a powerful force on the composing processes of the research staff. The principal social mechanism for transmitting the executives' expectations is the writer/reviewer collaborative cycle. Typically, as an analytic paper goes through successive revisions, reviewers of increasing seniority up to the level of the department chief provide the writer with spoken and written feedback. These reviewers, by virtue of their own experience as writers and their personal contact with members of the management committee, have learned to anticipate the executives' needs and reactions. As the reviewers' suggestions are incorporated into a paper, its discourse structure evolves towards the specific, generic form of written analysis that the executives require to support their discussion of a particular monetary-policy or administrative issue. This social mechanism for transmitting the executives' expectations is reinforced by the pattern of career advancement for the research staff: The ability to produce papers appropriate for an executive readership is an important factor when an individual is being considered for promotion.

Using the Theory to Account for Textual Features

This theory of how contextual influences, acting through the executives' reading practices and consequent expectations, lead to generic discourse can be used to account for the textual features of analytic papers. Certain influences hold constant for all genres and result in common textual features; other influences hold for some genres, resulting in particular textual features, but not for other genres. This interplay of contextual influences thus determines those features that the community's texts have in common as well as those features that differentiate them. To illustrate this, we will look at two genres, the automation proposal and the note to management.

The automation proposal presents a cost-benefit case for purchasing, designing, or upgrading a computerized system for processing data in some area of the Bank's operations. The proposal describes the current data-processing method; identifies problems inherent in the method; stipulates requirements related to system performance, security, timeliness, cost, and compatibility with existing systems that any acceptable solution must meet; assesses the advantages and disadvantages of the feasible automation alternatives; recommends and provides a justification for one of these alternatives; and proposes an implementation plan that includes resource requirements, work activities, and a schedule. The note to management analyzes recent economic or financial developments in Canada, the United States, or another part of the world. The note describes significant trends in current economic or financial data, explains why these trends are occurring, indicates meaningful correlations with other trends, and, where relevant, may suggest the implications for monetary policy.

First, we will look at textual features common to both the automation proposal and the note to management. Texts in both genres begin with an introduction that identifies and situates the issue to be addressed, states a position on this issue, and summarizes a supporting argument. In the body of the text, the full supporting argument is presented, with its interpretation of quantitative data, its economics-based reasoning, and its intertextual references, along with any "risks" (or serious qualifications) attached to the conclusions. These common textual features reflect contextual influences that hold across the community's family of genres, including the executives' broad mandate for resolving monetary-policy and administrative issues (with the time constraints this mandate imposes on them as readers), the central place that the paradigm of economics occupies in the Bank's intellectual life, and the importance of the intertextual antecedents of current discourse.

However, there are obvious textual differences between the two genres. To point to one: While the automation proposal makes a recommendation for administrative action, the note to management does not make a specific recommendation about the direction of monetary policy. The difference can be explained by the varying degree of problem-solving responsibility implicitly delegated to the research staff in different circumstances. On one hand, the management committee delegates to staff on the administrative side of the Bank responsibility for identifying cost-effective opportunities for computerizing the institution's data-processing operations and, in each case, for determining the best approach. Consequently, the executives expect an automation proposal to extend its analysis to the point of making and justifying a recommendation. On the other hand, the committee delegates to staff on the policy side of the Bank the task of monitoring and interpreting current economic and financial developments. However, because monetary policy is conducted from a longer-term perspective linked to the reduction of inflation in the economy, the committee does not expect the staff, in a note to management, to extend their analysis of current economic or financial data into a specific policy recommendation. Discussion between the executives and the staff about the orientation of monetary policy occurs in other forums.

Implications for Theory, Research, and Teaching

This chapter has described a study that asked how a community of executives and research staff at the Bank of Canada invents the genres it needs for creating written knowledge used by the executives in discussing corporate issues and making decisions. To address this question, the study examined the community's epistemology and knowledge making, identified regularities in texts and in the composing processes and reading practices associated with these texts, and located contextual influences that appear to evoke such regularities. Findings from the study support the theory that major contextual influences shape the executives' reading practices and that the executives' consequent expectations exert a compelling force on the collaborative composing processes of the research staff, thereby giving rise to a body of typified discourse.

The study has implications for genre theory, research, and teaching. Miller (1984) and subsequently Bazerman (1988) and Freedman (1989) have proposed that genre be reconceived as social action. The present study, in exploring one community's family of genres as broad, knowledge-building rhetorical strategies involving both writers and readers, continues this line of scholarship. More specifically, the study contributes to theoretical discussion on how genres are invented. Miller (1984) accounts for the emergence of genres by pointing to the generative power of recurrent situations. Bazerman (1988) and Campbell and Jamieson (1990) focus on the innovations of virtuoso writers and on intertextual influences to explain how genres arise. In highlighting the role of readers' shared expectations in the ongoing invention of a community's genres, the present study adds a further dimension to this aspect of genre theory.

In defining genre as a distinctive profile of regularities across texts, composing processes, and reading practices, the study offers a conceptual framework for naturalistic inquiry into genre. Specifically, the study raises two questions for further research. First, which of the regularities in texts, composing processes, and reading practices associated with a given genre are unique to that genre, which are common to other genres, and why? And second, how do such regularities intersect with individual differences in texts, writers, and readers?

The study also suggests that genre, conceived as a community-enacted, knowledge-building rhetorical strategy, can take a central place in writing instruction both for employees in the workplace and for students in university and college classrooms. As an in-house writing trainer in a corporate setting, I draw on a social view of genre in working with individual writers and with groups. As I coach a writer through the process of preparing a document, an awareness of the genre-specific rhetorical maneuvers of more experienced writers allows me to prompt the writer to experiment with composing strategies that have proven congruent with the genre's discourse structure. In so doing, the writer learns to deploy the heuristic power that the genre brings to the recurrent situation it addresses. Genre also provides a context for discussing how the writer's document will be used by particular readers with identifiable reading practices to construct specific knowledge important to the Bank's business. This understanding allows the writer to re-read drafts in a way that anticipates how the document will be read by its intended audience, an ability essential for effective revision.

A social view of genre also informs seminars involving groups of Bank employees and supervisors from work areas within individual departments. In these seminars, I lead the participants in discussing ways of refining their writer/reviewer collaboration for different types of documents. As well, a seminar provides writers who are experienced in composing in particular genres with a forum for sharing their rhetorical insights with less experienced colleagues. Frequently, participants also have an opportunity to talk with one of their executive readers, invited to the seminar as a guest, about expectations for the documents produced by the group.

In Writing Across the Curriculum programs, students learning a disciplinary discourse could explore the discipline's major genres as broad rhetorical strategies for creating different types of knowledge. Students could study connections between regularities of communicative function and linguistic form in texts and regularities in the composing processes experienced members of the field use to produce these texts and in the reading practices they use to interpret them. Such inquiry, in providing a rich context for practice in reading and writing generic discourse, would contribute to helping students develop the local rhetorical competence needed to take a turn in the genre-structured conversation of the discipline.

Acknowledgments

I am grateful to Aviva Freedman for responding to several early drafts of this paper and to Charles Bazerman for commenting on a later draft.

Notes

1. In this paper, the convention used to attribute quotes is to place the initials of the speaker immediately after the quotation. W. A., C. F., P. J., A. M, T. N., and W. W. are members of the management committee. D. B. and D. R. are department chiefs.

2. In many parts of the Bank, a writer would normally circulate a draft of a paper among his or her peers for comments prior to passing it on to the supervisor for review.

3. As defined by the "corporate framework," the Bank of Canada's five business functions are the following: conducting monetary policy, administering Government of Canada debt, issuing bank notes, providing banking services, and managing the Bank as an organization.

Geoffrey A. Cross

The Interrelation of Genre, Context, and Process in the Collaborative Writing of Two Corporate Documents

The most important value of group writing is the sharing of individual perspectives to produce, presumably, a better written product. Such multiple perspectives would seem encouraged more by some genres than by others. For example, one might think that the group-writing process of a short letter signed by two authors would involve fewer perspectives to integrate and take less time to produce than a longer report signed by four authors. Yet, in the group-writing processes described in this chapter, the opposite was true. Why would the group writing of a 504-word executive letter of an annual report take fifty-five days from first draft to approval, while the group writing of a 1,851-word corporate annual plan of the same organization, recounting largely the same story, take only fifteen days from first draft to approval?

Until the mid-1980s, to answer such a question, researchers in business and technical writing typically used the "textual perspective," focusing upon textual features such as genre (Faigley, 1985). But from this perspective, the letter-writing process would appear less difficult and less multifarious than the report-writing process. To answer our question, we need to go beyond isolated considerations of textual features to the social perspective advocated by many contributors to Odell and Goswami's landmark *Writing in Nonacademic Settings* (1985). As Faigley notes in this collection, the social perspective "forc[es] researchers to consider such issues as social roles, group purposes, communal organization, ideology, and, finally, theories of culture" (p. 236).

We need to consider how textual features are produced in organizational cultures by collaborators.

It is important to stipulate what is meant here by "genre" because, as Anderson (1989) notes, "there is no generally accepted term for the overall structural patterns conventionally used for communications" (p. 34). For the purposes of this discussion, "genre" is defined as a set of textual features and their implicit exigence that characterizes a particular kind of writing. Given this definition, generic functions and organizational purposes need to be differentiated. A genre that is a social convention, such as the executive letter, creates an exigence, such as recounting the previous fiscal year to outsiders. The genre often provides a largely neutral exigence—for example, recounting the year, good, bad, or mixed ("genre" in this sense emphasizing format more than some definitions; for example, see Miller & Selzer, 1985). Writers use a genre's exigence to fulfill organizational purposes, for example, to proclaim the company's success. So writers achieve organizational purposes in fulfilling broader generic functions.

Because different genres offer different textual constraints and opportunities for expression, composition researchers have called for studies to consider to what extent genre influences collaboration in a particular social context (Ede & Lunsford, 1983, p. 152; Faigley, 1985, p. 244). Such questions about collaborative writing are important to investigate, because group writing is a significant component of real-world work (Anderson, 1985; Lunsford & Ede, 1986) yet preliminary research indicates that over one out of three collaborations fail (Lunsford & Ede, 1986, p. 76). The following study considers the interrelation of genre, context, and process in the group production of the letter and report mentioned above.

To investigate how, if at all, genre shapes collaborative processes, a researcher initially might decide to study the production of documents of different genres by the same participants in the same cultural context (culture being a set of rules and behaviors that the examined community deems acceptable [Haviland, 1980, p. 29]). However, culture is not static, but dynamic; as ethnographers Bruner and Turner observe, culture is "always in production, . . . emergent" (Bruner, 1986, p. 12). Thus, culture is not a variable that can be controlled. Its development can have great influence on different group-writing endeavors because human thought is "consummately social," as Geertz notes (1973, p. 360). Considering the social dimension of writing, LeFevre (1987) points out that group invention is an ongoing process that "is occasionally manifested in an event such as a speech or a written text" (p. 42). Spilka (1990b) identifies this phenomenon in her investigation of orality and literacy in a "real-world" setting. The ongoing process of invention across collaborations and genres inevitably reflects continual cultural change.

Culture, text, and process, then, are not discrete facets of collaborative writing. All are connected by language being inscribed—with language at once social, generic, and dynamic. Taking these three facets into account, of course, is more complicated than simply focusing upon isolated textual features. The complexity of this perspective is why Faigley points out that researchers need to consider ideology and cultural theory. The language theory of Bakhtin (1981), which Faigley used in his description of the social perspective (1985, pp. 240–241), provides a conceptual framework that allows a focus upon social, generic, and dynamic features of language production.

Theoretical Underpinnings of the Study

Bakhtin identifies powerful, politically impelled unifying and dividing forces in language. Forces exerted by the center of power in a culture *"unify and centralize the verbal-ideological world* [Bakhtin's emphasis]" (p. 270). At the same time, however, forces exerted by persons oblivious to or resisting the power structure push toward disagreement and linguistic disunity. "The processes of centralization and unification," Bakhtin argues, "intersect in the utterance" with the forces of decentralization. Furthermore, this utterance is influenced not only by social forces, but also by "specific points of view, specific approaches, forms of thinking, nuances and accents characteristic of the given genre" (p. 289).

Bakhtin in these ways discusses the relations of context and genre to text. But process also may be considered from a similar vantage point (Cross, 1990). Bakhtin describes utterance as the *product* of a speech act. But we can consider "utterance" also as an "uttering," a *process* of articulation, in our case, as a social (group) process. By so doing, we can use Bakhtinian theory to help trace how generic conventions and social forces shape the group-writing process.

Bakhtin notes that the greatest clash between sociolinguistic points of view in a culture occurs where the power is unstable and somewhat dispersed (p. 344). Often, the product of this shouting match of multiple voices is cacophony. But when power becomes centralized, a unitary voice and point of view prevails. We might say that then monotone (that, too often, we may pronounce "monotony") ensues. Of course, documents and processes never can become completely multivocal or monovocal, because centralizing and decentralizing forces always exist in language. But the consolidation or dispersion of power often causes one set of forces to dominate a given process and text.

The only instance Bakhtin mentions in which we find multiple voices presenting views in authentic dialogue is in the genre of the novel, in which the novelist orchestrates all voices into an overarching whole that subsumes without stifling the multiple viewpoints. Going beyond Bakhtin's emphasis upon product to focus on utterance as an ongoing process, we can say that Bakhtin's discussion generates a tripartite view of group writing based upon the political situation and genre: group writing as cacophony, group writing as monotone, and group writing as symphony.[1]

The following examination of genre and context will reveal the chief reason the executive letter took much longer to write is the gradual consolidation of power occurring in the corporate culture, fostering cacophony in the initial and middle stages of the letter-writing process and then monovocality in the completion of the letter and in the production of the planning report. Neither process made the best use of its participants because important information was overlooked or removed as people talked past each other or repeated the viewpoint of the most powerful member of the hierarchy.

Methods

Object of Study

The site of research was the eight-hundred-employee home office of The Auldouest Insurance Corporation (a pseudonym), an organization comprising four insurance companies that underwrite both commercial and domestic clients. While publicly held companies send their executive letters to shareholders, Auldouest is a privately held company. But it also sent its letter to an important large audience: 500,000 policyholders were informed about the company's performance by an abridged annual report that contained the executive letter. This study describes the collaborative writing of the executive letter and planning report, documents typically produced (often collaboratively) in medium- to large-sized corporations.[2] The planning report is a particularly important document because it provides employees with information about the direction of the company over the next year. The executive letter is the best-read section of the annual report (Lewis, 1971, p. 20), which, in turn, is the most widely circulated type of report in industry (Vic, Wilkinson, & Wilkinson, 1990, p. 282).

Data Gathering and Analysis

Because the focus of ethnographic research is culture, and because the intention of this study was to describe the group writing of two different documents in a particular organizational culture, I employed ethnographic methods. I collected data nearly every working day during a twenty-week internship at the site and conducted four final interviews one month after my internship ended. Internship duties required two hours per day; the remaining four to six hours were spent on research. Several data-gathering techniques were used, including open-ended, contrast (Spradley, 1980, pp. 125–127), and discourse-based interviews. All writers and editors were interviewed except the CEO, whose actions were described by his secretary and other participants. I collected personal documents and both internal and external official communication (Bogdan & Biklen, 1982). I recorded my observations in field notes and an ethnographic process log. Since the focus of research was upon group interaction, I did not observe the writing of the first drafts, which were produced by one person. I observed three brainstorming sessions and observed and/or taped ten editing sessions. During sixteen discourse-based interviews, I identified all changes all editors made in each draft of the documents and asked them why they made each change. On four other occasions, I asked participants to make conclusions about the entire writing process after looking at several drafts.

One month into my fieldwork, using a technique described by Miles and Huberman (1984), I derived analytic categories from my field notes and conceptual framework and began coding notes and transcriptions. After leaving the site, I entered in a computer data base a condensed version of each of the editors' suggestions for changes or actual changes in the letter and report, the editors' stated reasons for these changes, the audiences (if any) that editors mentioned considering, hypothesized and grounded codes, and other information. I then sorted this data by codes, purpose, audience, whether the suggestion had been followed, and other fields. These sorts revealed important patterns, including which organizational purposes editors linked to which audiences, and which audiences were most important to which editors. Any patterns identified by the sorting were considered in light of all other data.

Because the ethnographer is the critical instrument of observation, I analyzed raw data alone (McCarthy, 1987, p. 241) rather than using outside raters. During the study, five procedures were used to authenticate the findings: (1) I spent a prolonged period at the site—over 735 hours; (2) because of a flexible work schedule, I attained the multiple time perspectives necessary in ethnographic observations (Doheny-Farina and Odell, 1985, p. 518); (3) an anthropologist, a rhetorician, and a business composition researcher critically reviewed my methodological procedures and the connections I drew between the data and rhetorical theory; (4) I compared several types of data; (5) I compared the perspectives of numerous informants. During the internship and interviews one month after leaving the site, I checked my interpretations with participants, sometimes directly, sometimes indirectly. Nevertheless, I pursued some questions that they did not believe were important, such as repeated questions about audience. I strove to provide the balanced interpretation described by Geertz (1973) as neither "imprisoned within [the subjects'] mental horizons" nor "deaf to the distinctive tonalities of their existence" (p. 53).

After I wrote a narrative account of the letter-writing process, it became apparent that the factors influencing the collaborations were subsumed by Bakhtin's theory of language; I then used this theory to interpret the collaborative processes.

Results

Generic and contextual differences helped create two very different collaborative processes.

Different Contexts

Different purposes. Conflicting organizational purposes emerging during the letter-writing process caused extended conflict and cacophony. The subsequent report-writing process, by contrast, was much less conflictive and much more monovocal, because some conflicts had been resolved in the letter-writing process, while the rest surfaced only after the report was approved.

In the letter-writing process, conflicts arose over how best to fulfill the document's generic functions of recounting the year. Group members produced two opposing accounts. Some members presented Auldouest as successful so that the company would attain peer-company recognition and more corporate customers. Other members represented the company as struggling within a troubled industry, to make its 500,000 policyholders receptive to rate increases. Auldouest's 1986 results supported both positions. In fiscal 1986, the favorable news was that Auldouest's assets had exceeded $400 million for the first time (to protect identities, this figure has been changed). Much of this amount, though, reflected the company's reserve kept for large claims that annual income could not cover. The bad news was that Auldouest had suffered an operating loss of $5 million in 1986, the seventh consecutive year of operating losses.

Only thirty days into the drafting and revising process did the conflict over these versions begin to be resolved, when the president convinced the CEO to present Auldouest's year as "positive" and requested subordinates to accept his view also. At this point, the "recovering" story that the company had told about itself previously was replaced by the "success" story.

Context and genre caused the report-writing process to be smoother than the letter-writing process. During the report-writing process, writers' organizational purposes appeared related rather than opposed. The genre described the previous year's performance, explained the plan for the new year, and tried to motivate readers to execute it. Because employees were an internal audience, the fact that the company had not made an operating profit could be revealed to them. While the top executives may not have wanted to disclose this information to agents, the other audience of the report, no discussion of this possible conflict ensued during the production process. Furthermore, the conflict over the recovering versus the successful versions of the year had already been resolved during the letter-writing process. Like the letter, the report emphasized success, though it plainly reported the operating loss.

Nonetheless, a different conflict over cross-purposes emerged after the report was approved. The troublesome issue was whether to disclose to agents the company's policy of providing more advertising and other support to areas assessed to have high-growth potential. At least one collaborator feared that agents might "draw a negative inference from that [that] we are not interested in the agents in medium-potential areas and low-potential areas." Addressed to both employees and agents, the approved draft mentioned the policy. But the president of Auldouest, after approving the document, chose not to send the report to agents. So conflict over purpose was avoided in the process at the expense of writers accommodating an audience that did not receive their text.

In this situation, generic functions and organizational purposes conflicted: While the report was designed to convey plans to the agents, the political context caused the president to dismiss this purpose. So the influence of the social context overpowered the influence of the genre in determining the outcome of the writing process.

Different audiences. Cacophony also occurred in the letter-writing process because collaborators perceived different audiences of the document. In addition, outside audiences required using standard English, and conflicts arose over different conceptions of standard English.

The letter had a composite external audience of fifteen different constituencies with conflicting interests, including agents, peer companies, and domestic and commercial policyholders. Consideration of audience caused the creation of both the "successful" and "recovering" stories that created turmoil and delay in the letter-writing process. Collaborators writing the recovery story were attempting to placate domestic policyholders receiving rate increases. By contrast, the new president, the chief proponent of the success story, was not aware that the letter was going to policyholders. He wanted to present the company as successful to persuade corporations to insure their considerable assets with Auldouest.

The letter-writing process was also more cacophonous because there were more editors (seven versus the five editors working on the report), who championed different audiences of the letter and who themselves were also critical internal audiences. So the letter had twenty-two different audiences, compared to the report's seven audiences. Cacophony in the letter-writing process was compounded because each member of the writing group expected the document to go to a different composite audience (Cross, 1990, p. 195). On the other hand, the report team expected the document to go to the same composite audience—agents and employees. The president reduced the audience to employees only after approving the document. Because there were fewer audience interests to consider, the report-writing process was more monovocal.

The processes also were influenced by the need to create different tones to accommodate the different composite audiences of the two documents. A formal tone is typical of the letter because it is sent to many external audiences. This tone demanded more attention to what the CEO and President perceived to be the conventions of standard English. While one may anticipate that a shared conception of tone would be a unifying factor, it was not. The need for formality brought in "grammar experts," the executive secretaries, who made some good editorial changes but who also imposed some idiosyncratic notions of standard English and thus created conflict. In one instance, for example, a secretary substituted "halt" for "stop" because she believed that to halt meant to stop temporarily. The report, on the other hand, addressed to employees and agents, had a more informal, newsletter style. Grammatical correctness was not a key concern.

Because of the report's few and familiar audiences, its production was more monovocal and less conflictive than was the production of the letter. The letter-writing process was cacophonous because writers unwittingly had different perceptions of the composite audience and standard English.

Different Genres

The combination of the changing corporate culture and the relatively monovocal genre caused letter writers to generate multiple and conflicting perspectives, though these viewpoints were often ignored in the product. A stable corporate culture, a more multivocal genre, and postproduction rerouting made the report-writing process less conflictive and more monovocal.

In their format, executive letters of annual reports are short messages, ostensibly from corporate leaders, requiring a unitary point of view. Writers and editors at Auldouest expected the letter to be "personal [and] subjective." But in actuality, eight people with different perceptions of audience contributed text to the letter and struggled for empowerment. Yet, less than one-third of the changes made by editors ended up in the final version of the letter. In fact, thirty days into the process, the letter was rewritten "from scratch" by three different people, and then two of these letters were quickly rejected. The cause of many rejections was the gradual shift of power and storytelling rights from the CEO and his advisors in Corporate Communications to the new president. Political instability facilitated cacophony—many voices trying to outshout each other. In the end, the president won, and the letter ultimately presented the monovocal "success" story.

The report, on the other hand, was what Lowenstein (Merrill & Lowenstein, 1973) calls "internally specialized" (pp. 40–41). It consisted of several compartmentalized subgenres, including a one-page interview with the president recounting the year; a one-page report of 1986 objectives and results; and a two-page article on 1987 goals, with interviews from the three members of the planning committee. Several voices were heard from in the finished document, but only within Auldouest. For agents, these voices were silenced because the report was not sent to them since it might have caused controversy. The report production process was also less conflictive because internal specialization made most editors not responsible for the entire document. One reason the Vice President-Information Systems and the Vice President-Personnel gave for closely editing just interviews was that the report was not "going out under their names." The smaller degree of ownership of those participants created less impetus to fight; for at least some editors, responsibility was compartmentalized.

In these ways, the interaction of genre and context caused a conflictive process with the letter and an accordant process with the report. In the letter-writing process, different voices struggled for the single opportunity afforded by the genre to tell the story of a company whose self-identity was shifting as power changed hands. In the report-writing process, the story of the company had been established already, and the internally specialized format allowed several collaborators to describe corporate strategy for the year without having to agree about the extent of disclosure. However, the document was not sent to its external audience.

Conclusion

This study suggests that while genre can have considerable influence upon a group-writing process, the influence of generic constraints should not be considered apart from their interaction with social forces in the document-writing context. If genre were the predominant influence upon group-writing processes and products, we might expect the short, unitary, coauthored letter to be the product of a relatively monovocal process and the internally specialized report to be multivocal. Largely the opposite occurred because of the relative strength of centralizing and decentralizing forces. If centralizing political forces such as the consolidation of power prevail, these forces, by setting precedent and limiting audiences, can make monovocal a text that ostensibly presents multiple perspectives. If decentralizing forces prevail, they can make the team writing of a monovocal letter multivocal and even cacophonous.

The interaction of genre and forces in the social context precipitated to a considerable degree the amount of conflict in each group-writing process. In the letter, powerful, opposing social forces competed for control of a very small, monovocal text, generating much conflict before territorial rights were established. The many audiences of the executive letter genre and their opposing interests made this writing process much more complex and problematic than the process of writing for the two audiences of the report. The report-writing process was more accordant, because the question of which story to tell was resolved by the time the plan was written. Also, the internal specialization of the report generated less conflict, because responsibility was compartmentalized. Further, the more informal report did not generate the conflict over real or alleged solecisms that the formal letter generated.

Both group-writing processes examined could have been improved considerably. The letter-writing process, involving highly paid managers, was inordinately long by Auldouest's standards, left at least two participants demoralized, and ended up ignoring 500,000 policyholders who received Auldouest's textual celebration of financial success along with an announcement of rate increases. The report-writing process was shorter, but still involved highly paid managers devoting time to addressing a nonaudience of the document. Neither the cacophonous letter process nor the monovocal report process made the best use of writing group members.

The problematic outcomes of the monovocal and cacophonous-then-monovocal processes elicit the question of what modes of collaboration are most effective. The alternative to cacophonous or monovocal approaches that is suggested by Bakhtin's language theory is collaboration as symphony. Here, voices are orchestrated into a totality that yields the power of focused, collective effort. But who should take on the role of Bakhtin's novelist who subsumes all voices into an overarching whole? Doheny-Farina's writers in an emergent organization (1986) found that the committee was better able than the individual to produce a text that met organizational needs. But on a literal level, at least, the Bakhtinian model presumes one novelist/conductor. One might argue like Machiavelli that governance by the wise individual manager is the best form of decision making. Unlike the newly instated president, however, this leader would have time to gain cognizance of vital information, such as the letter audiences, and would interact with all group members.

Small-group research supports both approaches. Fisher notes that consensual decision making is better for tasks that require group acceptance and for tasks "where no single answer may be externally validated as 'best' " (Fisher, 1974, p. 43). Fielder (1967) found consensual small-group decision most productive in situations that are moderately favorable for the highest-ranking member. Much research shows that consensual decision making creates more satisfaction among group members than does hierarchical decision making (e.g., Pood, 1980; Shaw, 1971).

However, small-group research also suggests that there are situations in which consensual decision making is not optimal. Two studies show that the quality of group performance decreases with the difficulty of the task (Shaw, 1963; Shaw & Blum, 1965). Perhaps this outcome is caused by the short attention span of groups: Berg (1967) found that groups typically spend just fifty-eight seconds on a single theme. Beyond that, group makeup influences efficiency. As its size increases beyond five members, the gap between productivity and potential widens (Williams & Sternberg, 1988, p. 353), as noted in the letter-writing process of this case. While heterogeneous groups have been found more effective than homogeneous ones, if groups are too heterogeneous, they cannot communicate sufficiently (Williams & Sternberg, 1988, p. 352).

Many problems of consensual small-group decision making may be avoided by one person soliciting the opinions of other group members and then deciding the course of action for the group. This hierarchical form of decision making is described by Machiavelli: The prince consults his advisers thoroughly and rewards them for candor, but makes the decisions himself (1532/1965, p. 86). Small-group research to some degree supports this mode of decision making. Research suggests that while hierarchically led groups are less satisfying, they are equally or more productive than consensually led groups (Shaw, 1971, p. 274). In their review of small-group research literature, Williams and Sternberg (1988) conclude that "groups seldom perform better than their best member would alone; more often, they do about as well as the second best member's ability would predict" (p. 352). Not only can some individuals make better decisions than groups, but such decision making is typically easier than trying to achieve consensus (Shaw, 1971). And in situations that are either particularly favorable or unfavorable to the leader, research suggests that directive leadership is more effective (Fielder, 1964, p. 146).

Yet, there are also many drawbacks to the conductor–orchestra model. The first problem is that the decision maker may not be capable. As Machiavelli notes, "A prince who is not wise never gets his advice unified" (1532/ 1965, pp. 87–88). A second drawback reported by studies of business executives and members of Congress is that the decision maker, though capable, may not have time to make the necessary evaluation of a large quantity of data needed to solve the problem (Clausen, 1973; Simon, 1965). Two other drawbacks are caused by the unequal power relationship between the synthesizer and other group members. First, research shows that subordinates tend to transmit only messages that enhance their image to their managers (Goldhaber, 1983, p. 159). Second, continuously giving decision-making power to one person may corrupt his or her judgment, as Lord Acton's caveat concerning absolute power tells us. Nonetheless, small-group research suggests that "high power" persons have more influence than "low power" persons in any group (Shaw, 1971, p. 285).

Clearly, we need to conduct more real-world studies of the group writing of different genres in different contexts to further investigate this question: Who in a given situation produces the combination of voices that yields the most rhetorical power—the committee or the "good prince"?

Notes

1. I use Bakhtin as a point of departure, developing a discussion of process out of his discussion of products. Bakhtin asserts that the most authentic multivocality occurs only in the novel and that rhetorical texts are typically monovocal, although they can incorporate opposing viewpoints (p. 325). In my view, the end rhetorical *product* frequently may be monovocal, but its writing *process* can include conflicting views to incorporate the best thinking of group members.

2. A related study (Cross, 1990) appears in *Research in the Teaching of English.*

| **Part Two** | Implications of Recent Research Findings for Theory, Pedagogy and Practice, and Future Research |

Part Two is a collection of chapters that assess the implications of recent research of workplace writing on theory, pedagogy and practice, and future research directions. Because this anthology focuses on professional writing research conducted in the past decade, its coverage of implications of this research is necessarily selective and does not attempt to be all-inclusive.

In the first three chapters, each author speculates on how writing research conducted in nonacademic settings during the past decade has influenced a particular theoretical approach to workplace writing. More specifically, the authors consider research implications for the notion of authorship (Debs), the notion of intertextuality (Selzer), and notions of discourse communities (Olsen).

Debs argues that the discipline needs to question its use of the terms "I" and "we," due to changing notions of authorship in workplace settings, and of the "significance of the organization's role in authorizing texts produced by its members." In her chapter, Debs uses Burke's concept of the marketplace (1937/1959) and other historical and more recent approaches to examine the notions of authorship and the "spokesperson" as they take shape in organizational cultures. She argues that "the relationship between the writer and the organization is essential to our interpretation of research on writing in the workplace" and that researchers need to examine more carefully that relationship, as well as its effects on workplace writing and writers.

Selzer traces and explores the notion of intertextuality as it has evolved from theoretical perspectives introduced by Bakhtin and Kristeva (who both use intertextuality to understand belletristic literature) to those perspectives implicit in recent professional writing research and scholarship. Selzer conceives a modern notion of intertextuality as "the sum total of all the voices drawn by a writer into his or her developing text and as all the voices heard by readers in the experience of that writing." According to Selzer, "technical and scientific and institutional writing might well be considered laboratories on intertextuality, places where the implications of intertextuality for our understanding of 'writer,' 'text,' and 'reading' might be teased out." For example, like Debs, Selzer asks where authorship in the workplace begins and ends; he also asks where a workplace "text" begins and ends, and argues that because intertextuality is a process for both writers and readers, the notion of "reader" needs to merge with that of an "author" when intertextuality is considered in terms of workplace writing.

Olsen reviews the literature representing three central contributions to the notion of "discourse community": those of social constructionists and "disciplinary definers," those of discourse and genre analysts, and those of process researchers. She argues that notable gaps exist in the research of discourse communities. According to Olsen, more attention needs to be paid "to many of the overwhelming realities of the American and international workplace," and more studies are needed "of non-Anglo-American contexts, of nonacademic and professional contexts, and of workers who include at least some, if not all, of the underrepresented demographic groups: nonwhites, older workers, females, handicapped workers, and nonnative speakers of English." Olsen points out, too, that more research is needed of how computer-based communication influences "the formation and maintenance of discourse communities" and that more detailed, ethnographic studies are needed "to confirm and extend present results" from studies on discourse communities in workplace settings. Future research, she argues, needs to regard the discourse community as an unstable, "fluid" entity rather than as static and stable and needs, as well, to determine the "limits" of a discourse community. Finally, Olsen notes the importance of further exploring issues of ethics, the role of the researcher in nonacademic research settings, and the sharing of knowledge across disciplines.

The authors of the next two chapters are concerned with the implications of recent research for continued attempts in the discipline to improve the training of writers both in academic and nonacademic settings, a necessary measure for improving workplace practice. Although the authors pay most attention to professional writing pedagogy in academia, they also discuss potential effects of that pedagogy on workplace practice.

154

Reither suggests that despite recent research findings that workplace writing is often a collaborative endeavor, writing-as-collaboration in the classroom typically involves "writing-as-literal-coauthoring," so that the focus of teaching "remains more on the production of texts to be evaluated than on ways in which texts arise out of other texts." He notes that writing instructors tend to focus on workplace practices and not on the conditions that gave rise to those practices. The result is that classroom collaboration takes place in an inhospitable environment "dominated by assumptions and motives that are antithetical to a vision of writing as collaborative, cooperative, social." In this chapter, Reither argues that writing instructors need to redesign their courses to make them scenes in the Burkean sense (1969a), in which collaborative activities arise from "natural or necessary ways to do the work that needs doing." He also suggests ways instructors can accomplish this goal.

Spilka continues Reither's discussion of how writing pedagogy in academia might be revised to respond better to changing research and theoretical approaches to "the social perspective." Given the modern, dual role of professional writers in the workplace as agents of both social accommodation and social change, or innovation, she asks, what becomes the primary charge of writing specialists in academia hoping to use pedagogy as a means of influencing workplace communication practices? To what extent should they train students to emulate workplace practices described in research reports or to analyze, critique, and change those practices? Building on Miller's argument (1989) that caution is needed in teaching nonacademic rhetorical practices, Spilka argues that educators of workplace writing need to maintain tension in their pedagogy between social accommodation and innovation, a goal that will require change in current pedagogical and research approaches. She explores how professional writing specialists in academia might use pedagogy as a means of improving workplace practice, how the results of qualitative studies of workplace writing might be taught, with caution, in professional writing programs in academia, and how researchers of workplace writing might design future qualitative studies to address not just theoretical, but also pedagogical aims in professional writing.

In the final four chapters, six professional writing specialists respond to recent trends in professional writing research and discuss their vision of how the discipline might alter its future approaches to workplace writing research in light of these trends.

Sullivan and Porter review the professional writing debate about the authority of "theory" versus that of "practice" and then consider the influence of this argument on researchers' notions of "methodology." They argue that the way workplace research typically is reported indicates the continuing influence of the view of methodology as a static and conventional set of strategies for observing practice, and that this view invests both methodology and theory with a privileged status relative to that of practice. They call for a new approach to the concepts of theory, practice, and methodology, one that regards them as "different types of socially constructed argumentative warrants" that should be regarded "as heuristic rather than foundational in nature, and therefore as dynamic and negotiable." They conclude that research methodology is "something we design out of particular situations and then argue for in our studies." This chapter therefore aims to move the discipline toward a notion of research as praxis, which they define as "a type of conduct that negotiates between positions rather than grounding itself in any particular position," and toward a notion of research methodology as heuristic.

In the next chapter, Debs considers which methods used in fields related to writing, such as organizational behavior, communication, sociology, and anthropology, hold promise for research in workplace writing. She also suggests how current debates about research in related fields might aid writing researchers in developing their methods of inquiry and returning "both to a renewed confidence and perhaps to a new caution in our own interpretive and critical stances." After examining how the choice of method can lead "to very different ends," Debs describes six methods from the social sciences that can aid workplace writing research, as well as criteria writing researchers can use to adapt methods from other fields to their own studies.

Doheny-Farina then points out the irony that, at a time when qualitative and ethnographic studies of workplace writing are escalating, some writing researchers are questioning underlying assumptions of traditional ethnography. His chapter responds to two types of critiques that have emerged in the literature: those concerned with how to do ethnography, and those concerned with how to write ethnography. Doheny-Farina argues that the discipline of professional writing needs to move closer to resolving these debates if it hopes to reach its maturity. According to Doheny-Farina, "the more we expose the arguments that guide our research actions, the more ethical our research can be. It is this ethical stance that will be our primary source of authority. That is, our strongest authority comes not from our representation of data, but in our attempt to do ethical research." To explore this proposition, he examines critiques of field research on writing and then analyzes ways to "construct our data through the rhetorical act of field research."

In the final chapter of Part Two, Bouldin and Odell argue that a theoretical perspective, such as Systems Theory, is needed to evaluate the strengths and limitations of research methodologies used in recent studies of workplace writing, and to determine how to integrate methodologies toward the development of a fuller understanding of workplace writing. In this chapter, the authors draw upon Systems Theory to assess the validity of some recent studies of workplace writing and to suggest how this theory can enable writing researchers to build on existing studies of workplace writing in their subsequent research. They conclude by arguing that "research is an ongoing transaction among researcher, prior conclusions, and new data. The goal of research on open systems is to continue to engage in that transaction, making sure that our minds remain at least as open as the systems we seek to understand."

Corporate Authority | Sponsoring Rhetorical Practice

In their article "Why Write . . . Together: A Research Update," Lunsford and Ede find that they cannot justify the low percentage of writing claimed by their respondents to be done collaboratively without calling into question modern notions of authorship: "Respondents think of writing almost exclusively as writing 'alone' when, in fact, they are most often collaborating on the mental and procedural activities which precede and co-occur with the act of writing as well as on the construction of the text" (1986, p.73). Surveying the amount of social activity that surrounds the production of any document in business and citing such common practices in industry as the use of boilerplate materials, the prevalence of technical and legal reviewers, and the recent development of information data bases, Lunsford and Ede state that "the concept of 'authorship' as most English teachers think of it, becomes increasingly fuzzy" (p. 73).

During the past seven years that I have been conducting research focusing on writers in what we now call nonacademic settings, I have come to believe that we should be paying closer attention to one particular (and perhaps peculiar) aspect of the responses writers often make in surveys and interviews: their use of the pronouns of authorship, the first person "we" and "I." Individuals easily use "I" and coauthors "we" when claiming responsibility for particular texts. Some of our research questions, however, particularly those used in discourse-based interviews, ask about specific choices a writer makes while composing a text. These questions elicit not only reasons for the choices, but also responses that suggest whether the authority for the decision has come from the individual or from a collective group such as the organization or division.

Consider, for example, the responses of the state agency writers in the study by Odell, Goswami, and Herrington (1983b). When asked why they preferred one choice in their writing over another, the state employees responded with statements such as the following: "I mean, we had written before, trying to clarify this whole thing" (p. 27); "We want them to realize that this is the reason" (p. 27); "As an accounting department, we have no authority to waive that" (p. 28); "We need this information so we can adjust his account" (p. 29). The documents on which these discourse-based interviews were based were written not by groups, but by individuals, yet many of the writers referred to an undefined "we" in justifying their decisions. Discourse-based interviews get at the tacit knowledge that a writer may employ in addressing a rhetorical situation; they also discover evidence that the writer often seems to work out of a sense of meeting a collective purpose determined by the agency.

I ran up against something similar when I used an adaptation of discourse-based interviews to research writing processes within a technology-producing organization (Debs, 1986). To my question, "Do you ever collaborate?" writers would inevitably say "no" or "rarely." Yet, when asked about specific features of a text, writers often would account for the feature by indicating how other members of the organization had influenced that particular choice. In one case, of eighty-seven of the text features (for example, the choice of cover, use of terminology, organization of the text, direct appeal to the audience) referred to during the interview, a writer had decided on sixty in discussion with at least one other person. But at the beginning of the interview, she had insisted that she "never collaborated on her writing."

Who is the "we" that authorizes these choices and decisions? Where did they come from? How and why does the "we" have the authority to intervene in and influence the writing without establishing themselves as coauthors? How does reference to this collective authority coexist with the modern notion of authorship as moving one's pen in solitude?

Rather than taking on the task of examining the concept of authorship, most studies of the social activities involved in writing in the workplace (my own included) have argued for a broadening of the definition of collaboration (recent articles include Allen, Atkinson, Morgan, Moore, & Snow, 1987; Couture & Rymer, 1989; Debs, 1989; Doheny-Farina, 1986). Thus, instead of meaning simply "writing together," collaboration would include all examples of what Couture and Rymer (1989) call "interactive writing." But are we continuing to dodge the real issue here? Isn't all writing to some extent interactive (a deliberately neutral term)? Is it collaboration if the people participating don't recognize it as such? Or are they participating in an activity that is intended to serve less the needs of the individual and more the needs of the organization, a kind of "collective authorship"? Certainly, enlarging the net created by the term collaboration has allowed us to capture and examine many more of the social interactions we find that make up composing and document production processes in the workplace and has helped to point out the usefulness of skills such as negotiation and small group participation for writers. Doing so, however, also has limited our understanding of authorship as it is shaped in the workplace and the signifi- cance of the organization's role in authorizing texts produced by its mem- bers. Thus limited, we have yet to begin examining how writing relates to the issues of social authority and the flow of power between individuals and groups in contemporary society. What I hope to do in this chapter is to outline the elements of a possible explanation of the concept of authorship as it takes shape within that part of society Burke termed "the marketplace" of rhetoric (1937/1959).

Rhetoric Employed by Modern Organizations

In their responses to surveys and interviews, many of the writers, whether career writers or people who write on the job, demonstrate what Bloom (1973) has called an "anxiety of influence." Bloom speaks of the literary artist's inability to acknowledge creative debts, particularly to other writers. LeFevre (1987) makes a similar point, noting that many collabora- tors, editors, and the like, especially if they are women, are not credited with coauthor status, but simply given thanks in the acknowledgments section. And in the workplace, individuals claim personal ownership of the words they have written, even when their names do not appear on docu- ments. Berlin's work (1987) suggests that the concern for proprietary claim over what one writes is a result of assumptions that inform the teaching of literature and writing, a remnant of the belletristic rhetorical tradition of the nineteenth century. Eisenstein argues that preoccupation with original authorship and attending matters such as property rights and plagiarism "undermined older concepts of collective authority" as a result of the fixity and publicity made possible by the printing press (1979, p. 122). Ong (1982) maintains that a transition from an oral to a literate culture brings with it an increased consciousness of personal autonomy and a greater distance be- tween author and audience as each becomes a fiction to the other.

In an oral culture, the "author," or rhetor (the root is the same), was immediately present and visible and spoke with autonomy, but as a member of the community being addressed. The concept of "making" or "creating" a speech was associated more closely with the credibility and acceptance needed to move an audience than with originality. Of the Hellenic courts, Lentz writes, "The spoken word remained the closest substitute for the knowledge in the minds of men who knew, for the truth of individual expression as it was to be measured in the court" (1983, p. 258). (Lentz's use of "man" is correct here; in general, women were required to be represented by men in court.) Thus, during the early history of rhetoric, when writing was suspect and one's ability to speak in a public forum was a condition of responsible citizenship, the authority by which someone spoke (particularly on things probable) rested with the community and the individual; one was responsible for the truth and "goodness" of his words. For the classical rhetorician, rhetoric was necessary as a kind of social equipment for an individual's participation in public life. Recall that in Athenian society the civic forum of public discourse evolved in or near the *agagora*, the marketplace.

Rhetoric, however, is directly a function of social needs and patterns. As part of the fabric of society, the practice of rhetoric will reflect changes in the structuring of that society. Speakers in the Athenian courts and classical rhetoricians did not have to contend every day with the multiplicity of social units that divide and structure modern society. The growth in number, size, and importance of formal organizations, particularly bureaucracies, during the past century has been documented by both sociologists and historians (see, for example, Jacoby, 1973). Sennett (1980) considers the use of authority by corporations and notes several ways he believes the discourse of an organization legitimizes the exercise of power without acknowledging individual responsibility: "The veiling of power, built into the foundations of administrative science in the work of Herbert Simon, also oils the links in the chain of command. . . . [Memos and directives] are texts with absent authors, . . . since they have no visible source and apply to the organization as a whole" (p. 174).

The society we participate in is made up of a proliferation of organizations, and part of the way in which we identify ourselves is made up of the multiple, often embedded, memberships we each hold. Although we may want to be cautious in recognizing it as such, the corporation, certainly the organization, has become the major arena for public life for the individual in modern Western civilization. One's concerns are often those of the economically prescribed marketplace; one's participation is shaped by the collective dialogues of the sponsoring organization; one's rhetoric is often of necessity (or at least of salary) a product of institutionalized corporate activities.

In 1937, shortly after the depression, Burke anticipated the "rhetorical effects" of an incorporated society (and offered his explanation of where writers' use of personal pronouns originate): "The so-called 'I' is merely a unique combination of partially conflicting 'we's.' Sometimes these corporate identities work fairly well together. At other times they conflict with disturbing moral consequences. Thus, in America, it is natural for a man to identify himself with the business corporation he serves" (1937/1969, p. 264). Burke then argues that unionism is a response to a failure of corporations and a survival of earlier corporate forms: the church, the guild, and the town or city. Accepting the idea that a "locus of authority" can rest within a group or organization, he relates the corporate identification of an individual with particular uses of language:

> There is a clear recognition of "corporate identity" in the "editorial we." The editor selects and rejects manuscripts and writes comments, with vague reference to his membership in an *institution*. (He also, of course, quickly learns to "cash in on" the privileges of such an identity, as he rejects your manuscript with a frank admission that "the editors" could not agree on it, without adding that he may have "deputized" for the lot.) A variant is the "we" of business correspondence, where the writer of the letter pronounces his *corporate* role, without so much as a thought on the matter. (p. 266)

An organization, at its simplest, is a group of people who reasonably assume that all members will at least comply with a common purpose and accept those goals that are commonly held. Organizational theorist Putnam offers a definition central to most of the work current in the field of organizational communication: "Organizations . . . are social relationships, that is, interlocked behaviors centered on specialized task and maintenance activities" (1983; see also Weick, 1979). In exchange for a guarantee of personal security and often of financial reward, a member gives up the exercise of certain personal powers to maintain a social contract with other members who form the organization. As with any organization, the primary goal of a corporation is to continue its existence. For most modern corporations, economic growth, even when it is at odds with some facet of social value, is part of that purpose. Meeting the purpose of the organization is a condition of membership. So is the loss of autonomy, according to Tompkins and Cheney: "[Members] literally decide to accept certain organizational premises and approach work-related decisions from the organization's perspective: that is, they assume the role of the organization. In this way the member acquires an organizational personality . . . accepting the values and goals of the organization as relevant to on-the-job decisions" (1983, p. 125). The variables of writing in the workplace offer a number of on-the-job decisions.

▌ Corporate Authority

The role of the organization may be taken on so well by individual writers that we find the corporation to be the only author visible in many documents today that address a consumer audience, such as annual reports (excluding the CEO's letter, which, in turn, is often written by an agency or committee), collection letters (these are often "personalized" with pseudonymous signatures), and advertising materials. Even in science, which is becoming increasingly incorporated, we continue to find concurrent evidence of collective authorship with articles signed by research teams of fifteen or more people, some of whom have not even seen the documents on which their names appear.

Manuals that accompany products demonstrate a range of ways in which corporations publicly acknowledge their authorship. Consider the appeal used by Hewlett-Packard on the inside cover of its *82143A Printer Owner's Handbook*: "When Messrs. Hewlett and Packard founded our company in 1939, we offered one superior product, an audio oscillator. Today we offer over 3500 quality products, designed and built for some of the world's most discerning customers. Since we introduced our first calculator in 1967, we've sold millions world wide, both pocket and desktop models. Their owners include Nobel laureates, astronauts, mountain climbers, business [sic], doctors, students, and homemakers" (1979). At the very least, the "we" used in this passage stands for "dramatized" authors, but this nonetheless calls forth a very different self-consciousness than that of one writing as an individual from a personal voice. It is a question of ethos, not of persona. There are also examples in which companies make use of "corporate appeals" in directly addressing other companies: "At a time when financial data is available almost instantly from a company's data processing center, it may take a week or more to type and edit a financial statement. . . . For many organizations, no system exists to handle information as the valuable resource that it is. . . . To help organizations handle information, IBM offers the IBM Displaywriter System" (IBM, 1982, p. 1–1). Throughout the text, the operator is never addressed, only discussed, as one organization talks to another about its employees.

In fact, most product manuals are published not under the individual writers' names, but under the corporation's name. In one way, this practice makes sense: We do not know who designed the Courier Model 110160–001; why should we know who wrote the manual for it? And many manuals are products of several people's contributions as well as series of revisions by different authors and editors. In contrast to this rather common practice, however, a number of Apple's "glamor" manuals do publicly identify the writers, designers, graphic artists, and project coordinators responsible for each publication.

The basic triad of elements (writer, audience, text) that we have distilled from classical theory is not sufficient to explain or to model the practice of rhetoric in today's economic world. What needs to be added is a fourth element, that of (for lack of better words) the sponsoring organization, and what needs to be stressed is not audience or writer or sponsor, but the relationships among these. It is from examining the variations of these relationships that we will understand how a particular kind of authorship is fashioned in the marketplace and how the individual writer participates.

The Role of Spokesperson

Much of the discourse produced in contemporary society, not just in the marketplace, is sponsored by organizations, and, to varying degrees, the individual writer acts as a spokesperson or representative. This is a key and problematic relationship—problematic, in part, because we tend to conflate audience and sponsor. The tendency in composition studies to see the choices writers make in their writing as depending solely on their interpretations of the traditional communication triangle (the writer addressing an audience, whether real or evoked, whether internal or external to the organization) diminishes our ability to see the investment of the organization in authorizing a text. Such a point of view also hides from examination the special relationship that develops between the writer and the organization, a relationship that varies depending on whether the context of the rhetorical act is internal or external to the organization.

An organization may have a physical location, identifiable if abstract characteristics, and even a history, but it will have no voice except through its members. The pragmatic importance of controlling this voice is reflected in the legal concept of "agency": A company can be bound legally by what an employee says or promises. Since the organization is held responsible for what an authorized employee says, it is important for the individual to "get it right." Since an organization is a sociological entity, "right" is usually a matter of collective or designated authority.

Unfortunately, little has been written about the actual communication aspects of this type of agency relationship or about the demands of being sponsored in one's writing, although, historically, we can find a number of practices that seem related: the orthographers of Greece, "ghostwriters" of political documents and speeches, modern advertising. But the role of the rhetor as spokesperson for an institution is at least suggested in Aristotle's *Rhetoric*. Considering the choices (means) available to deliberative speakers, Aristotle concludes: "Clearly, then, we must distinguish the tendencies, institutions, and interests which promote the end of each form of government, since it is with reference to this end that people make their choices" (*Rhetoric* 1.8). Jamieson extends this claim, arguing that genre constraints represent an institutional spokesperson's "sense of presentness of past." To her, genre "perpetrates a distinguishable institutional rhetoric by creating expectations which any future institutional spokesperson feels obligated to fulfill rather than frustrate" (1973, p. 165).

Following Aristotle's lead, Jamieson sees the rhetor acting as a spokesperson for the institution, community, or state while addressing the members of that same institution, community, or state. I would like to suggest, however, that in marketplace rhetoric, the rhetor acts as a spokesperson by representing one institution (the organization) to another broader community (the general public consumer or organizations of consumers). Thus, the role of spokesperson cuts two ways into production and act, adding a new dimension to Aristotle's claim: "As speakers we should have a command of the character of each form of government; since for each form its own character will be most persuasive; and these political characters must be ascertained by the same means as the character of individuals" (*Rhetoric* 1.8).

In the only other reference to the spokesperson role of a writer that I have been able to find, Murphy notes the "relationship of message-maker to king" described by Cassidorius Senator. Employed as a minister for an illiterate king in Italy during the early middle ages, Cassidorus included a job description in his popular work on letterwriting, *Variae*: "The Questor has to learn the king's innermost thoughts to utter them to the subjects. He has to be always ready for a sudden call, and must exercise the wonderful powers which, as Cicero has pointed out, are inherent in the art of an orator. . . . He has to speak the king's words in the king's own presence . . . with suitable embellishments" (*Variae* VI; cited in Murphy, 1974, p. 197).

If a writer negotiates a text within an organization, the choices that arise from the organization's own character or past practice will be most persuasive. If the writer speaks for an organization to an external audience, he or she must fulfill the expectations developed in the audience by previous organizational spokespersons. Note that this is different than epideictic discourse in which the rhetor would speak about—most likely praising— the organization. As a spokesperson, the writer draws from dialogue with members of the organization so that discourse addressed to an audience outside will be received as if the organization were speaking through the rhetor. It is natural, then, that visible members of an organization often are concerned with the ways in which their ethos reflects on that of the organization (and conversely). We must also recognize that the organizational image is a matter of both *technos* and *atechnos*.

The role of spokesperson affects, but does not necessarily eliminate, individual ethos. Discussing self-representation in fictional and nonfictional discourse, Cherry (1988) argues that a distinction should be maintained between ethos and persona, the concept of ethos going beyond and encompassing that of persona. The interplay between individual and corporate, between ethos and persona, does set up some interesting questions. For example, is it an organization's (rather than a writer's) decision to use passive over active voice? If so, does the company, in fact, have an impersonal (or professional/scientific) character which it wishes to maintain with its audiences? Does such an image contribute to how the character of its products is perceived? What are the writer's grounds for arguing against this decision? Given these expectations, how would the audience react to a shift made in a corporation's persona?

Rhetorical choice (and analysis) is a relatively straightforward matter when writer and audience are members of the same group or community. Such an assumption, however, diminishes the multiple roles an "incorporated" writer maintains in negotiating identifications and interpretations with audience, project teams, the corporation, and members of different groups and specialties. In industry, the choices a writer makes are often drawn from an understanding of the rhetorical situation as it is mediated by the organization. In writing, for example, about new products or policy decisions, the writer is acting as a spokesperson for the organization in transcribing what is, in effect, a preexisting reality (the product or policy developed by the organization): It is the company's message and to a large extent the organization's vision or knowledge that the writer is sending. Members of the organization have the authority to intervene to ensure that the document reflects the character of the company and its view of the text as it plays out in the marketplace.

We find examples of the complexity of this interaction when we look at technical writing addressed to an audience not made up of members of a technically-sophisticated community. In an article in which he defines technical writing as writing that accommodates technology to the user, Dobrin suggests that the question of "who is accommodating whom . . . depends on the power of each" (1983, p. 243). The ways of speaking identified with a product originate with the designers of the product. We can see this phenomenon most frequently in certain computer documentation, in which the aim often is not to converse with the audience (an aim reserved instead for marketing publications), but to make the audience conversant with the products' developers. Understanding the language and its use in a particular technology is a condition of participation in the user community.

As a consequence, we find that the rhetoric of computer documentation is often not sermonic, but catechetical. Repetition, directive tone, unequivocal statements, layout featuring questions and answers, frequent use of single unambiguous definitions, arrangement centered on division of objects and concepts—these are features we once associated with the Catholic church's *Baltimore Catechism*. The technical writer's role here may not be to translate, but to teach the dogma of the product (and technology) to create a community of people who will use the product and identify with it through their use of language. In this way, we find the reversal of Dobrin's definition, as he has indicated: The writer's job becomes one of accommodating the user to the technology, to the company's products. Historically, much technical writing has been instructional, but computer documentation now is being altered in response to both the sponsor's purpose, which the writer takes on, and the organization's corporate function of creating a market.

Means of Institutionalizing Rhetorical Practices

How can an abstract thing such as a corporation or any organization so actively participate in a process as concrete as writing a document, to the point that it can be said to sponsor and authorize the writing? An organization is an institution, and it authorizes documents by institutionalizing rhetorical practices. Although an organization exists by virtue of its members, the individual members are, to some extent, replaceable. Ford remained a company with and without Iacocca as president; It exists differently because of his departure, but it still exists. For many companies in the marketplace today, writing serves the same purpose as does any commodity: It is produced for use, sale, or trade. Writing may be an art form, but it is also a product by which a company earns profits, or an organization gains capital, or an agency conducts its transactions. It is also a way of communicating within the organization, and therefore of maintaining the organization. Thus, any company has a stake in what is written (effectively, for profit) and in how something gets written (efficiently, for resource conservation). Consequently, most organizations make some attempt to institutionalize rhetorical practice, to establish and fix a fairly orderly pattern of interactions and behavior related to the negotiation of texts and the production of documents.

Because, in most cases, the organization, not the individual, is responsible for what is contained in and communicated by a document it sponsors, it is in the interest of the company to encourage or even to require other members of the organization to interact with the writer, thus guaranteeing the organization's collective authorization. The locus of authority remains in the organization: Document cycling, review privileges, central data bases, and boilerplate material are indications of the increasing acceptance of and dependence on this authority. Various parts of the document or various parts of the process can be "departmentalized," assigned to different people. Since a document is "owned" by the company, the organization can, with little cause, replace the writer with another individual. The organization, then, employs what for it are standard procedures: production policies, division of labor, and hierarchical distribution of authority. We can anticipate that the more rigid and controlled the institutionalization of the writing process, the less individually responsible the writer will feel and the less likely change (in the document or in the process) can be brought about by the writer.

In their study of two management consultants, Broadhead and Freed take note of what they call "institutional norms": "[These] govern rhetorical decisions designed to make a text adhere to accepted practices within a company, profession, discipline, or the like. . . . In their broader application to the writing process, these institutional norms reflect a writer's overall environment for thinking, composing, and revising" (1986, p. 12). Although clearly indicating the pervasiveness of these institutional norms and practices in the site they studied, Broadhead and Freed relegate their analysis primarily to problems in the writer's physical environment and miss their significance as means for the organization to authorize documents.

When an individual joins an organization, there are many ways in which he or she will be influenced as a writer, simply because that individual has joined the daily ongoing dialogue that maintains the organizational culture. The recent and expanding series of interpretive analyses in the field of organizational research suggests that we should not underestimate the strength of the equivalence between organizations and culture (Javlin, Putnam, Roberts, & Porter, 1987; Putnam & Pacanowsky, 1983). Smircich, for example, proposes that, as "networks of meaning," organizations depend "on the emergence of shared interpretive schemes, expressed in languages and other symbolic constructions that develop through social interactions" (1983, p. 160). Writers develop a tacit knowledge of the company and its institutional norms through the processes of socialization and identification. Through training, collaboration, exposure to models and past successes, even stylebooks, they learn the expectations of the institution as they have been developed by past spokespersons.

But the identification process is a complex one because organizations themselves are made up of groups of people, aligned together by the division of labor and hierarchy of authority, and each group may elicit varying degrees of identification among its members. The choices an individual makes will depend on his or her participation in the activities and interactions different groups develop and maintain to get something done. Aldefer and

Smith argue that these groups work as communities: They "tend to develop their own language (or elements of language, including social categories), condition their members' perceptions of objective and subjective phenomena, and transmit sets of propositions—including theories and ideologies—to explain the nature of experiences encountered by members and to influence relations with other groups" (1982, p. 40). Individual differences in perspective and even in use of language can, to some extent, be accounted for by membership in different embedded groups.

Interactions with other members of a group or organization ensure that the writer can assume the role of the organization. Other members not only contribute their rules for writing, but they also voice the norms of the institution and, most importantly, share their interpretations of the rhetorical situation. They, too, represent the organization's view of itself; they, too, are concerned with the ways it is presented. This concern with representation creates a two-part test for any public discourse: It must fit the organization's internal definition or interpretation of the rhetorical situation before it can be delivered to the external audience. For a person writing in an organization, context may not be a simple thing—particularly with the organization screening the writer from the audience, intervening in the writing process, and actually shaping the text to represent its interests—and we may need to talk about two contexts: the one in which the writing is produced and the one in which it is addressed. (In a particularly careful analysis, Harrison [1987] examines organizations as rhetorical contexts, emphasizing their cultural and knowledge-making characteristics. Not all discourse, however, is addressed to audiences within the organization; thus, a rhetorical context may consist of the organization or may encompass the organization as it is socially embedded. Harrison's work suggests the ways in which organizational members may be separated from the larger community.) In an organization, a writer's authority has to do with one's advocacy of the audience; the writer's power, however, is related to an ability to fashion the organization's presence in the marketplace and to negotiate choices (and therefore change) in the organization. At its best, the relationship between writer and organization is dialectical. Authority can be disputed.

Conclusion

In this chapter, I have tried to suggest that the relationship between the writer and the organization is essential to our interpretation of research on writing in the workplace. With striking results, we have shifted successfully our attention from the writing processes of individuals exclusively to include those of a group. But in considering issues of authority, power, and responsibility, we need to unveil the organization, to identify more carefully the relationships that exist between the individual and groups within society, and to begin to explore the development and characteristics of those relationships and their effects on writing and the writer.

In considering the role of the writer, such a perspective offers new questions. How has the concept of authorship developed and in what ways does the authorship of nonliterary texts differ from literary ones? (For the beginnings of this discussion, see Ede & Lunsford, 1990.) When and why did the business organization assume a collective voice and when did the personal voice of the individual stop representing the organization? How do audiences perceive different organizations and corporations through texts? How are new writers socialized within a company? Are written documents simply artifacts of corporate culture, or do they play a role in shaping the organization (see Yates, 1989)? Are there differences in the ways that other members of the organization interact with the writer? If so, in what ways does the perception of their role as critic, collaborator, or audience affect the interaction? What is the responsibility of the writer to the organization? To the audience?

As we pursue this line of questioning, we may find that the writer plays an essential, though at this time unacknowledged, role within the organization that ought to demand a conscious examination of the terms of membership as well as an aggressive sense of social responsibility.

Intertextuality and the Writing Process

An Overview

> My own voice was the voice of the dead, for the dead had contrived to leave textual traces of themselves, and those traces make themselves heard in the voices of the living.
>
> —Stephen Greenblatt, *Shakespearean Negotiations*

In a large financial institution, new employees are initiated into a homogeneous culture comprised of hundreds of economists and financial analysts. How? They are immersed in the discourse practices of the community; the rites of initiation include plenty of writing, formal and informal reviews of that writing, management oversight over writing practices, the employment of a style guide and an editorial board, and lots of reading and discussion of the written work of experienced employees. At the end of a year or so, documents prepared by the initiates exhibit a host of particular traits characteristic of the institution and known as "the Bank of Canada style" (MacKinnon).

At the General Accounting Office (GAO), writers submit their work to lengthy in-house review. As a result, documents betray a strong institutional voice that reflects the caution and care that are characteristic of the institutional climate at GAO. As another result, the process creates frustration in staff members (Kleimann).

The author of an article in a medical journal, without ever being conscious of it, appropriates the language, syntax, ethos, and paternalistic and atomistic values that are conspicuous in articles in medicine that the author has never read (Segal).

A short executive letter appended to an annual report in the insurance industry takes two months to produce. Why? It takes that long for the writer and team of editors composing the letter to negotiate the letter among themselves, to satisfy warring political complexities within the organization, and to place the letter successfully in relation to other documents, such as the annual report itself and the company's corporate plan, reports by other companies, the previous years' annual reports and executive letters, and communications about company performance anticipated for the future (Cross).

These four episodes, of course, are paraphrased from chapters earlier in this book. What could they possibly have to do with the European psychoanalyst, feminist, and semiotician Julia Kristeva and the Russian socio-literary theorist Mikhail Bakhtin? It is a commonplace to note that scholarship on writing—including scholarship on scientific, technical, and business writing—used to regard writing as a private affair, the product of the interaction between an individual and a developing document. In the tradition of formalist literary criticism, texts were understood as more or less self-contained artifacts: They might betray the "influence" of other persons and traditions, or they might "allude to" prior texts, and they certainly might be "adapted to" particular audiences, but they nevertheless were seen as organic wholes that could be—and should be—understood without much reference to "outside" factors.

These days, by contrast, most scholarship on writing (whether it considers belletristic literature or student writing or institutional prose, whether it considers the writing process or the finished results of that process) regards written discourse as a public and social affair, the product (and process) of an individual's interaction with an environment, even when it is seemingly performed alone by people physically sealed off from others, but most obviously when it is performed in circumstances like the ones described above, where writers cooperate in ways both obvious and subtle to produce texts that enact complex social functions. In short, attention lately has shifted from individual writers and their finished products to the environmental factors that shape them. Of all those environmental factors, a primary one is, of course, other texts—texts that betray not merely vague and indirect "influences," but that together comprise complex, interconnected networks of meaning within which seen and unseen authors, readers, and texts cooperate and compete in the creation of knowledge and in the performance of social action. Indeed, "context" or "environment" or "setting" or "culture" might be understood as nothing more than a complex of language and texts, and individuals within an environment therefore might be understood as minds assimilated into its concepts and terminology.

And that is where Bakhtin and Kristeva come in. In an effort to understand and describe this network—to understand discourse not as a formal, static, self-contained object but as a dynamic interaction among writers, readers, and other texts—Kristeva coined the term "intertextuality." The occasion was a 1969 commentary on Bakhtin (translated in 1980 as "Word, Dialogue, and Novel" in her *Desire in Language*), whose work on "dialogism" seemed to her to provide an antidote to textual formalism and a means of locating texts within contexts. According to Kristeva (working from Bakhtin), "Any text is constructed as a mosaic of quotations; any text is the absorption and transformation of another" (p. 66). Far from being self-contained, far from being fixed, every text incorporates within itself an intersection, a dialogue, a network among writers and readers and other texts. And "intertextuality" is Kristeva's word for this dialogue, this complex interaction among texts that produces every new one.

Intertextuality is to be distinguished from the narrower concepts of allusion and source for two reasons. First, the terms "source" and "allusion" imply that only parts of a text are intertextual. After all, those who locate sources and allusions typically tie them off from the more "original" parts of a work. Second, those terms imply that influence works in only one direction. The broader notion of intertextuality (at least as Kristeva defines it) holds that texts in their entirety are transpositions of other texts and are understood in relation to those others, whether writers and readers are aware of those transpositions or not. Texts are inevitably read (as they are written) against other texts, so the question of "which text came first" becomes moot.

At the very least, texts are intertextual in their individual words, in that words carry a history. That is what Greenblatt (1988) means in saying that "the dead had contrived to leave textual traces of themselves, and those traces make themselves heard in the voices of the living" (p. 1). Segal's work on medical writing elsewhere in this volume details just how influential those voices of the dead can be. But it is not just a matter of history; in a kind of dialogue, words speak with other uses of those words in other contexts past, present, and future. As Kristeva notes elsewhere in *Desire in Language*, in an essay she ironically entitles "The Bounded Text," "A given textual arrangement [intersects] . . . with [all] the utterances . . . that it either assimilates into its own space or to which it refers in the space of exterior texts" (1980, p. 36). Or in Bakhtin's words, "The author exaggerates, now strongly, now weakly, one or another aspect of the 'common language,' sometimes exposing its inadequacies to its object and sometimes, on the contrary, becoming one with it" (1981, p. 302). In this sense, intertextuality comes very close to the Bakhtinian notion of "heteroglossia," the term he uses to denote the meeting of individual utterance and the broader social context present in every word.[1] "At any given moment," says Bakhtin, "language is heteroglot from top to bottom: it represents the contradictions between the present and the past, between different socio-ideological groups in the present, between tendencies, schools, circles, and so forth" (p. 291).

At the very most, intertextuality goes far beyond the resonances in individual words to denote every kind of network enacted in a text. Nuances in diction are part of intertextuality, to be sure, but so is every other "voice" contained in a work: sources and allusions, the incorporation of prior ideas and the common stock of cultural formulations for them, the implications of conflicting points of view that a text "answers," genre conventions, and so forth. As Barthes (1973/1985) has noted:

> Every text is an intertext; other texts are present in it, at variable levels, in more or less recognizable forms: the texts of the previous culture, and those of the surrounding culture. Every text is a new fabric woven out of bygone quotations. Scraps of code, formulas, rhythmic patterns, fragments of social idioms, etc., are absorbed into the text and redistributed in it, for there is always language prior to the text and language around it. A prerequisite for any text, intertextuality cannot be reduced to a problem of sources and influences; it is a general field of anonymous formulas whose origin is seldom identifiable, of unconscious or automatic quotations given without quotation marks. (p. 5)

The physical text, in sum, can be viewed as an occasion for multiple interactions. The text is not an entity but an event, a kind of dynamic collaboration among seen and unseen writers and readers and texts, all cooperating in the creation of meaning. In Kristeva's words, intertextuality is "a relationship materialized," or the sum of relationships materialized, in physical discourse (1980, p. 36). Or as Johnson writes, "The theory of intertextuality states that no text is a harmonious, organic whole in itself, and is therefore not to be considered an autonomous, isolated unit. It is rather the product of intersections of a whole corpus of texts which may be broadly defined as our 'culture' " (1988, p. 71). A given text cooperates not only with its predecessors, but also with its successors in a polyphonic and synchronic enterprise. And so "to investigate the status" of a text, writes Kristeva, "is to study its articulations with other texts" (1980, p. 65).

Perhaps a specific example will help clarify; let me borrow the one presented by Orr (1986, pp. 816–817), the example of *Hamlet*. Seeing that work intertextually might take us first to Shakespeare's sources in Kyd and Belleforest and to their own sources. Then we might work forward: We have *Hamlet* as a play in successive periods and countries. We also have Shakespeare (the real person), Shakespeare as a biographical (textual) subject, and Shakespeare's son Hamnet, known to us through texts. And then there is Shakespeare as a figure in Joyce's *Ulysses*, Shakespeare allusions in *Ulysses*, and the Hamlet-Hamnet theory of Stephen Dedalus. From there we might weave in the *Hamlet* allusions in Eliot's "Love Song of J. Alfred Prufrock" and in Pynchon's *The Crying of Lot 49*, Eliot's essay "Hamlet and His Problems," Stoppard's play *Rosencrantz and Guildenstern Are Dead*, Joyce as a character in Stoppard's *Travesties*, Joyce's work as a source for other books and poems, and so on and so on, ad infinitum. Note that each of these intertextual contacts resemanticizes the other elements all along the chain; and note that the order in which an individual reader enchains the items carries the semantic burden. That is, if one reads *Ulysses* before *Hamlet*, *Hamlet* will be different for that reader than for someone who reads the two items in the order in which they were actually written. Intertextuality is a function of readers as much as of writers; the focus should be on what both bring to bear on the activity. Thus, intertextuality is not to be confused with the mere origins of a text, though origins certainly are involved.[2] Kristeva and her followers are interested in other matters as well: the places where textual boundaries overlap or are broken. As Orr says, "Intertextuality is a confrontation between discourse from different frames; the confrontation effectively transforms the borders between the conflicting discursive universes" (p. 814).

Note, too, that although Bakhtin and Kristeva employ intertextuality in the service of understanding belletristic literature (Bakhtin was especially interested in the novel),[3] intertextuality is present in every discourse. Bazerman, for instance, has already begun to account for intertextuality in scientific discourse: He uses the term in *Shaping Written Knowledge* (1988); and in an essay in press he shows how an article in evolutionary biology participates in a network that includes Voltaire, scholarly discourse on sociobiology, prior texts by the same authors, cited and uncited scholarly literature, and an academic symposium. Similarly, Devitt (1991), McCarthy (1991), and Berkenkotter, Huckin, and Ackerman (1991) have detailed intertextual phenomena in professional writing in accounting, psychiatry, and English. Miller and I (1985) described some of the intertextual dynamics present in reports and proposals in transportation engineering. And Ede and Lunsford (1990) have catalogued intertextual dimensions in the explicitly and implicitly collaborative writing that occurs in so many settings.

Given the difficulty of Kristeva's writing (she blends semiotics with structuralism, Lacan and Freud with Marx), given the levels of abstraction in her use of the term, given her debt to Bakhtin (shadowy, contradictory, and elusive in his own right), and given the open-ended suggestiveness of the term, no wonder that so many others have been emboldened to make idiosyncratic use of "intertextuality." Roudiez in his introduction to *Desire in Language* complains that the term "has been much used and abused on both sides of the Atlantic [and] has been generally misunderstood" (p. 15); and Owen Miller (1985) has made a similar and consequent point: "There is no constituent feature, satisfactory to all, which would allow us to define the term" (p. 19).[4] Nevertheless, it seems fair to represent intertextuality as I have tried to do so here. as the sum total of all the voices drawn by a writer into his or her developing text and as all the voices heard by readers in the experience of that writing. Porter (1986), like Greenblatt and others, is drawn to the useful metaphor of "traces": "Every discourse is composed of 'traces,' pieces of other texts that help constitute its meaning. . . . Examining texts 'intertextually' means looking for 'traces,' the bits and pieces of text which writers [and I would add readers] borrow and sew together to create new discourse" (pp. 34–35).

While the concept of intertextuality still is radically undermining central notions in literary study, where the myths of the solitary writer and self-contained text and passive reader remain relatively entrenched, the notion of intertextuality probably seems relatively uncontroversial to those who study technical, scientific, and institutional discourse, because writing and reading in those settings are so overtly social. It may be difficult to wean ourselves from considering Austin or Chaucer or Blake or Faulkner as individual geniuses who created their masterpieces alone, difficult to take the experience of reading *Emma* or the "Songs of Innocence" out of the individual study; but it is quite routine (as many chapters in this volume demonstrate) to see writing and reading on the job as cooperative and social. For this reason, technical and scientific and institutional writing might well be considered laboratories on intertextuality, places where the implications of intertextuality for our understanding of "writer," "text," and "reading" might be teased out.

Who is the "writer" or "author" of a simple engineering proposal, for instance? According to my experience with one Chicago-based transportation engineer, authorship is anything but individual. Of course, a specific person's name usually can be found on the proposal, and, of course, particular words are crafted by individual people: A specific engineer might be in charge of compiling a final version of the proposal, incorporating along the way the contributions of other engineers (who might even draft specific parts), professional technical writers (who might concoct graphics, edit the engineer's draft, and manage the "look" of the final product), and even company managers (who might oversee and approve a specific proposal—and on occasion intervene in the composition of it). But behind these individuals might stand an army of unacknowledged others: the composers of "boilerplate" (portions of previously written documents appropriated and sometimes revised for the occasion now at hand); secretaries who type and silently amend; letter writers and telephoners and e-mailers whose advice gets incorporated along the way; "authors" of company style manuals; advisors who are called upon to make suggestions for the developing draft; colleagues whose ideas and practices have shaped the engineer's work.

All of this is pretty well established. Chapters in this volume by Spilka and Dautermann call attention to oral networks that come into play during the composing of documents at work; and Cross and MacKinnon acknowledge several of the other voices I have just mentioned. But intertextuality also requires the acknowledgment of still other "authors." Consider the reviewer who rejected the engineer's most recent proposal and who thereby motivated some changes in this one. Consider the specific request for proposal that motivated this proposal and influences its content and arrangement. Consider the hundreds of other RFPs that the engineer-author has seen and responded to and the previously written proposals that suggest to the author a ready supply of formulas, formulations, and other *topoi*. Consider the thousands of other proposals drafted by other transportation engineers over the past decade or so, proposals that together create generic expectations that any engineer is likely to observe. Consider the disciplinary terminology, values, patterns of thought, and habits of mind that result from an engineer's education, professional reading, attendance at conferences, and so forth—in other words, the engineer's initiation into and immersion in a particular disciplinary community. As Miller and I have shown (1985), all of these, too, "author" the fictional proposal under discussion here. Finally, consider the "real" audience, whose perceived values and circumstances shape the document profoundly: Cannot the audience be seen as author too?

All of this is just for starters. Several chapters in this volume detail in various and suggestive ways how authorship is communal and intertextual at work: For example, MacKinnon explains how writers are initiated into the web of discourse practices characteristic of a particular institution, and Cross describes how individual authorship is dominated by and subsumed under the power of an interventionist executive. (For more on how communities shape individual writers, see also Winsor, 1989.) Articulating this network of "authors" can be seen to diminish the status of the person whose name goes on the document in the end. In fact, Cross and Kleimann in this volume explain how dispiriting it can be when a practice like document cycling creates an institutional text that drowns out the contributions of individual writers. From another perspective, though, intertextuality simply offers a different, and not less diminished, view of authorship. Though some have proclaimed the death of the author (Barthes, 1977; Foucault, 1979), intertextual analysis can actually reinvigorate the appreciation of an individual's contribution by describing it more accurately, less mysteriously. It can change our understanding of "invention" and "creativity" without requiring the author's self-effacement into an anonymous and deterministic Foucauldian network.[5] Moreover, intertextual analysis of institutional authorship can reinvigorate literary theory, where the concept of intertextuality was born. That is, an appreciation of institutional authorship can invite greater recognition of heretofore unacknowledged "coauthors" of literary texts—the agents and publishing houses who serve as gatekeepers and hence supply particular constraints; the editors whose advice shapes so much of so many finished products; the reviewers and reviewing organs and publicity machines and success stories that shape public taste (and hence the practices of writers); and all the rest.

If figuring out where authorship begins and ends is problematized by the concept of intertextuality, that is probably because the notion of "text" is problematized too. For where exactly does the text of that mythical engineering proposal mentioned above begin and end? All texts, after all, are intertextual; they are created and consumed in relation to other ones. The "bounded text" is really quite unbounded. From the perspective of both writer and reader, individual texts blur into and join texts at their edges, and at some remove. On the one side, a given document (such as a proposal) is a response to a prior document (such as an RFP), without which it makes no sense. On the other side, the document motivates new ones (for example, acceptance letters, contracts, subsequent reports, perhaps articles and conference papers, not to mention the attendant letters, progress reports, internal memos, phone messages, and so on) that can be understood only in relation to it. Together, particular documents lose their particularity. What emerges instead are communication chains—networks, webs, fabrics (pick your metaphor)—that *together* comprise meaning or glimpses of meaning. Intertextuality invites us to look forward from a document as well as back, to consider not only those prior documents that generated it but also future documents inspired by it. It invites us to consider texts not as self-contained artifacts but as open-ended contributions to ongoing conversations, conversations that in their totality create and constitute meaning.

And what of the reader? What happens to notions of reader and audience under the assumption of intertextuality? On one hand, not much: The real reader continues as a concrete entity denoting the one who consumes a text. As Phelps (1990) has said, audiences and readers "do not disappear within heteroglossia and intertextuality, but remain vigorously present, active persons who engage in discourse events one at a time" (p. 169). Proposals, after all, get read by real people. On the other hand, audiences and readers cannot be easily extricated from writers and texts. As I have already begun to indicate, the reader merges with the idea of author in at least three senses: in the sense that in motivating and directing discourse, the reader "authors" the text; in the sense that reading is itself an active, "authoring" process; and in the related sense that from the perspective of intertextuality, the reading process is a writing process (my reading is always prologue to—part of— my subsequent writing). On that note, let me complete the passage from Phelps: Writer and audience "do not disappear within heteroglossia and intertextuality, but remain vigorously present, active persons who engage in discourse events one at a time, although the simultaneous and historical concatenation of human conversations gives any such event endlessly dia- logic overtones" (p. 169)—that is, writers and audiences change roles (as it were) endlessly throughout their exchanges; their words both coincide and conflict in the course of their debate.[6] Finally, intertextuality recognizes, as well, not just real audiences and audiences in the writer but also readers in the text, that well-known cast of fictive presences in the text that have been explicated by Booth, Ong, Prince, and others.

The readers of a proposal therefore affect writers (become, in fact, reified within writers), show up in the text itself (sometimes quite explicitly so), actively create their own texts for their own purposes (during the act of reading), and appropriate the proposal in the process of creating their own subsequent documents. We have been conditioned by formalist criticism and the assumptions inherent in traditional communication theory to seeing texts as fixed and permanent, as words on a page, the discrete product of a writer's effort, the autonomous object of a reader's scrutiny. But poststruct- uralism and reader-response criticism have broken down the hard distinc- tions among those concepts. Reading and writing, readers and writers: These dissolve into each other when text is considered as an event and not an object. And every such event is endlessly and intriguingly intertextual, endlessly and intriguingly implicated in other words and other contexts.

In sum, intertextuality is a process for both writers and readers. At bottom, it denotes the processes of thought and forms of expression that are carried along in the flow of a culture and that animate writing and reading. It matters not whether by culture you mean Culture writ large (as in the sum total of a people's customs, artifacts, or habits of mind) or culture writ small (as in the microculture of a specific technical or scientific enterprise): Readers and writers experience the flow of culture as a kind of collaboration among seen and unseen authors and texts and readers, all in the process of making sense. One job of the critic of culture—of the rhetorician, that is— is to uncover the various resonances inscribed in the tapestry of text and to account for their source, their intricacy, and their meaning.

Notes

1. For more on Bakhtin and "heteroglossia," see the introductory pages of Cross's chapter elsewhere in this volume.

2. For an enlightening analysis of intertextuality and the production of a document, see Porter (1986) on the authorship of the Declaration of Independence.

3. For a collection of useful essays on intertextuality and belletristic discourse, including overviews and a bibliography, see O'Donnell and Davis (1989).

4. Miller provides a detailed account of the difficulties of defining intertextuality that I highly recommend. See also Harris (in press).

5. Porter (1986) is eloquent on this point (see pp. 38–41). For a short history of the term "author," see chapter three of Ede and Lunsford's *Singular Texts/Plural Authors* (1990).

6. The postmodern phenomenon of "hypertext" dramatizes just how thoroughly distinctions between author and audience dissolve in the activity of reading. In this electronic medium, readers are as free as writers to reorient text. Lanham has written at some length about this phenomenon; see, for instance, his "Extraordinary Convergence" (1990).

13 | Leslie A. Olsen

Research on Discourse Communities

An Overview

> Scientific knowledge, like language, is intrinsically the common property of a group or else nothing at all. To understand it we shall need to know the special characteristics of the groups that create and use it.
> —Thomas S. Kuhn, *The Structure of Scientific Revolutions*

Recent research on discourse communities explores the way values, assumptions, and methods shared by readers and writers in a given community (that is, in an academic or professional field, an organization, a department, or some other group) affect the type and nature of communication produced and accepted by both the readers and the writers in that community. More narrowly, research on discourse communities in the workplace focuses on the communication between individuals or within groups in the workplace and on how the contexts in the workplace affect and are affected by the writing and speaking that occur. Such studies should become increasingly important, given the complexity of the modern workplace, our societies' needs to become more efficient and competitive in national and international markets, and the changing nature of both work and the workforce in both industrialized and nonindustrialized nations.

A discussion of the recent research on discourse communities in the workplace must consider a number of social and contextual factors affecting workplace communication and thus must, of necessity, consider research in several often overlapping areas: disciplinary definition and social construction conducted in sociology and rhetoric; discourse analysis (and its subfield genre analysis) conducted in linguistics and rhetoric; and process studies of communication in various workplace settings conducted mainly in composition and rhetoric, but also including work in psychology, sociology, and linguistics. This chapter will first briefly discuss research in these areas, moving from those dealing with the sociology of knowledge—the larger field issues of knowledge formation and organization (social construction)—to those dealing with the formal textual conventions that "organize" the discourse and reflect the field's social conventions (genre and discourse analysis) to, very briefly, those dealing with the problems faced and choices made by individual writers or speakers or groups wrestling with the social and textual conventions of a field (process studies). The chapter will then briefly summarize overall results from the collection of studies and finally discuss needed areas of research, the holes or gaps in our current knowledge.

Contributions of Social Constructionists and Disciplinary Definers

Studies in the sociology of knowledge could be seen to begin with Kuhn's *Structure of Scientific Revolutions* (1962, 2nd ed. 1970), in which he argued that science and scientific knowledge develop through a series of revolutionary changes in what a community accepts as knowledge, through changes from one world view (an acceptance of objects of investigation, experimental and analytical methods, types of conclusions, etc.) to another world view. Studies in the sociology of knowledge have been concerned with the social conventions, assumptions, and paradigms that organize a field and with the processes by which knowledge within a field is formed, organized, and disseminated. Such studies have moved recently to include those characterizing the nature of the discourse communities that exist within a field or enterprise—communities of scholars, scientists, managers, engineers, or other communicating "practitioners." These studies form the body of research most obviously associated with the concept of discourse community, because they overtly treat the formation, operation, and effects of discourse communities. In particular, they treat the construction of facts, texts, knowledge, and complex social and intellectual systems and methods, including languages, for important social activities.

Many of these studies and the umbrella sociological movement known as social construction are reviewed by Bruffee (1986) and Bazerman (1990), including early works that argued in a then-positivist world that knowledge is not just discovered but instead is constructed by groups of scientists (see Bazerman). Bazerman also reviews the citation analysis literature relevant to the definition and evolution of discourse communities. Both of these threads of research—social construction and citation analysis—culminate in seminal case studies that examine the writing of scientific research results and organizational communication and how claims and arguments are negotiated among writers, colleagues, referees, and other reviewers through sometimes extensive cycles of reviews and revisions. These include Gilbert (1977); Latour and Woolgar (1979); Knorr-Cetina (1981); McGrath, Martin, and Kulka (1982); Gilbert and Mulkay (1984); Light and Pillemer (1984); Myers (1985, 1990a, 1990b); Bazerman (1990); Winsor (1990a); and Doheny-Farina (1991b). A series of other studies argues that contextual factors significantly affect the appropriateness and effectiveness of communication within organizations as shown by Colomb and Williams (1985), Brown and Herndl (1986), Doheny-Farina (1988), Driskill (1989), and Suchan and Dulek (1990); within scientific communities as shown by Dubois (1981), Peters and Ceci (1982), Bazerman (1984, 1988), Myers (1985, 1990a, 1990b), and Huckin (1987); and within academic communities as shown by Armstrong (1980), Herrington (1985), Odell (1985), Cooper (1986), Freed and Broadhead (1987), and Olsen and Huckin (1990). Work on legal and medical contexts will be treated below, since most of these works have a primary focus on description or analysis from a discourse or genre point of view, even though they significantly treat contextual factors.

A second set of studies involves attempts to define characteristics within and differences between disciplines in terms of the natures of disciplinary knowledge. These include Becher's taxonomic studies (1987a, 1987b, 1989); Bazerman's comparative analyses of articles from English, biochemistry, and the sociology of science (1981) and his analysis of the physics article (1984, 1988); Geertz's study (1983b); Gross's collection (1990) on the rhetoric of science; McCloskey's study of the rhetoric of economics (1985); Nelson, Megill, and McCloskey's 1987 volume and Simons's 1989 volume on the rhetoric of the human sciences; and Tracy's 1988 analysis of discourse analysis papers from four related but different fields (discourse processing, anthropological linguistics, conversational analysis, and communication). In each of these papers, the background and training of the writers, the state of knowledge within the community, and the expectations of the readers—the characteristics of the discourse community—affect what is claimed and how it is argued.

A third set of studies attempts to define the context in which communication occurs in the nonacademic workplace. These include more general studies of nonacademic writing from the social perspective (Faigley, 1985; Odell, 1985; Odell & Goswami, 1985; and Odell, Goswami, Herrington, & Quick, 1983; Pellegrini & Yawkey, 1984) as well as studies of the context for communication within complex industrial and governmental organizations as shown by Winkler (1983), Miller and Selzer (1985), Spilka (1988a), Driskill (1989), Kleimann (1989), and the articles in Kogen (1989); within the law as shown by Gregory (1948), Smith (1947, 1967, 1973), White (1973), Leflar (1974), Witkin (1977), Stratman (1988), Gopen (1989), and Levi and Walker (1990); and within medicine (Kuipers, 1989; Frankel, 1989, in press) and in doctor-patient relationships in medicine (Frankel, 1989, in press; Stiles, 1978–1979; Waitzkin & Stoeckle, 1972) and in doctor-patient relationships in dentistry (Bochner, 1988; Moretti & Ayer, 1983; and Verheij, Horst, Prins, & Verkamp, 1989).

Finally, several articles dealing with the nonacademic workplace context focus on the role and characteristics of the important managerial audiences. In early work, Mintzberg (1973, 1975) provides a very accessible overview of the managerial role. In case studies, Mathes (1986) and Winsor (1990a) treat the role of management communication in the nuclear incident at Three Mile Island and the Challenger disaster, respectively, and Yates's book-length study (1989) treats the workings of the Illinois Central Railroad, Scovill Manufacturing, and Du Pont.

Academic writing has been comparatively well studied, including Joliffe (1988), Dieterich (1989), and the few articles listed in the following section. However, since the focus of this book is on nonacademic settings, this area will not be covered here.

Contributions of Discourse and Genre Analysts

Discourse and genre analysts attempt to define the grammatical and rhetorical features within a text that characterize an instance or type of discourse. Once these features are understood, they become parts of the context that help shape the final form of a text. Early but important linguistically-oriented studies of the use of language in professional contexts include those by Hudson (1978), Kittredge and Lehrberger (1982), and DiPietro (1982). Later work has concentrated on law, medicine, and education. Many of the law and medicine studies are reviewed below, though those on education are not since nonacademic settings are the focus of this book. Other discourse studies include those by McCloskey (1985) and Samuels (1990) on the language of economists; Linde (1988) on politeness and accidents in aviation discourse and Robertson (1988) on radiotelephony communication for pilots; Wowk (1989) on the organization of talk in an organization; Olsen and Johnson (1989) on a discourse-based approach to the assessment of readability; Rubin (1984a) on stylistic variations; and Swales on genre analysis (1990b) and on discourse communities, genres, and English as an international language (1988). In seminal statistical studies, Biber (1988) and Biber and Finegan (1989) analyzed a large corpus to identify statistically features associated with individual types of texts, including official documents and some work genres among a much wider range of text types.

Law. The best overview of social and linguistic studies of the law by professionals from a variety of disciplines appears in the excellent and comprehensive review by Levi (1990). Additional bibliographies of the literature include those by Leflar (1974), Collins and Hattenhauer (1983), Levi (1985), Kolin and Marquardt (1986), and Bhatia (1987). Leflar provides a blend of annotated bibliography and bibliographic essay by a law professor and former Associate Justice of the Arkansas Supreme Court on the "function and role of the appellate process and the part that opinion writing plays in developing the law" (p. iv). Finegan (1978) reviews the literature on comprehensibility in legal discourse, Swales (1990a) reviews recent studies "aimed at helping non-native speakers (NNSs) acquire legal communicative competence" (p. 105), and the authors in the excellent volumes edited by Coleman (1984, 1989) and Levi and Walker (1990) provide a series of extensive bibliographies on various research topics.

As outlined in Levi's overview (1990), research on the interrelationship between language and the law conducted by linguists and social scientists falls into three broad categories: "(1) the study of spoken language in legal settings; (2) the study of language as a subject of the law; and (3) the written language of the law" (p. 13). The following areas (quoted from Levi) have received the most extensive research attention:

1. Conversational analysis of language in legal settings, including studies of plea bargaining, courtroom discourse, and conversation as entered as evidence in criminal trials
2. Linguistic factors affecting reliability of eyewitness testimony
3. Plain English studies (especially concerning the written language of legal documents and the oral language of jury instructions)
4. Presentational style and language attitudes in courtroom testimony. (p. 12)

Another set of generally accessible works is written primarily by lawyers or law professors and deals with the special concepts, contexts, and language problems in legal discourse. Most of these works include discussions of contextual factors in addition to the genre features indicated. These works tend to be more "broadbrush" than those produced by the social scientists and linguists.

1. Outlines of genres in legal writing (Weihofen, 1980) and in special types of legal writing such as police reports (Wilson and Hayes, 1984).
2. Discussions of particular legal genres such as judicial opinions or, even more specifically, appellate court opinions (Gregory, 1948; Smith, 1947, 1967, 1973; Leflar, 1974; Stevenson 1975; Witkin, 1977). These typically include discussion of genre and style considerations and of special rhetorical problems

such as unfamiliarity with or misuse of the controlling precedents. Stratman (1988) provides a case study of rhetorical choices and factors affecting them in the composing processes of lawyers on opposing sides of an appellate case and of the reading and opinion drafting processes of court clerks dealing with the briefs.

3. Introductions to special problems with legal constructions and typical misuses of legal language (typically found in legal writing texts, such as those by Mellinkoff, 1982, and Gopen, 1981).

Other studies deal with what are quintessentially both legal and general topics, such as inequalities of power: Adelsward (1989); Spencer (1988) on pre-sentence investigative reports; Sharrock and Watson (1989) on police interviews; Uehara and Candlin (1989) on jury selection; and Harris (1989) on resistance to power and control in court.

Taken as a group, all of these studies show how—in particular instances—the setting, the situation, the participants, and their language use affect the form of the legal discourse. Perhaps more interestingly, they also provide very convincing instances of discourse forms that do or may affect the discourse community from which they come. For instance, consider the following:

1. The style in which a witness presented testimony affected later judgments about that witness's credibility (Erickson, Lind, Johnson, & O'Barr, 1978; Lind & O'Barr, 1979; O'Barr, 1982).
2. Jury instructions are so hard to understand that juries do not adequately understand them (and thus are likely to produce judgments at odds with the ideals of the system) (Charrow & Charrow, 1979; Elwork, Sales, & Alfini, 1977; Elwork, Alfini, & Sales, 1982).
3. Litigants in small claims court tell stories in a manner that adversely affects judgments made against them (O'Barr & Conley, 1990).
4. The language and legal philosophy used by divorce lawyers "may work to unwind the bases of legitimation that other levels [of the legal system] work to create" (Sarat & Felstiner, 1990).
5. The language and strategies used by court interpreters (Berk-Seligson, 1990) and court reporters (Walker, 1990b) affect the process and final record of court proceedings.
6. A legal brief's "textual techniques greatly affect [appeals] clerks' legal information-processing, especially their formulation of appeal issues" (Stratman, 1988).

Medicine. There are reviews of research on language use in medical contexts (Maher, 1986) and on discourse analysis of medical texts (Kuipers, 1989; Swales's shorter but somewhat more recent 1990a review). Studies of the discourse characteristics in interviews between a doctor (or other medical professional) and a patient include Maclean's review (1989) of five pioneering studies; discussions by Stiles (1978–1979), Mishler (1984), Todd (1989), and Frankel (1989, in press) on doctor-patient interviews; Verheij et al, (1989) on dentist-patient interactions; and Mason (1989) on interactions in a pharmacy. Ongoing sources include the *Medical Anthropology Quarterly* and the *EMP [English for Medical and Paramedical Purposes] Newsletter* (Bruce, 1984–continuing).

Other studies investigate the choice of units from the single word to the grammatical construction to the order and type of information required by genre conventions. Two early studies indicate the range of features identified in these discourse and genre studies. The first illustrates the effects on word choice and grammar; the second the effects on rhetorical structure. First, in 1981 Dubois reports on the techniques biomedical researchers use to "manage" or not evoke the potential pity one might have for experimental animals in reports of biomedical research. These include the use of euphemisms (such as "sacrifice" or "terminate" instead of "kill"), the use of minimizing syntactic constructions (such as the use of the passive to minimize the presence of a killing agent), or "countereffort" (such as the "deletion of specific mention of the research animal at points where the emotion is greatest" or "including items which reflect their [researchers] humaneness" [p. 254]).

Later studies showing the effects of contextual factors on the specific forms of written texts include Pettinari's book-length study (1988) of the surgical or "operative report as an institutional text from three perspectives. . . . (1) the relationship between the operative report and the surgical event: the relationship between the talk in the operating room and the dictation of the report. (2) The internal structure of the text: the relationship between prosodic and grammatical features and the episodic structure as perceived by the resident dictating the report. (3) The change in reporting styles over time: the contrast between reports dictated in the first and last years of residency training" (p. 129). These later studies also include research by Smith on how medical authors distinguish "objective statements of accepted fact from author-marked observations of opinion, hypothesis, or recommendation" (1984a, p. 25); by Dubois on numerical imprecision in biomedical slide talks (1987) and on citation patterns in biomedical journal articles (1988); by Salager-Meyer, Defives, Jensen, & De Filipis on genre analysis of English medical discourse (1989); by Salager-Meyer on metaphor in English, French, and Spanish medical prose (1990); by Drass on a comparison of the discourse of nurses practioners and physician assistants (1988); and by authors in Coleman (1985).

Contributions of Process Researchers

Process studies of communication in various workplace settings have been conducted mainly by researchers in composition and rhetoric, but also by psychologists, sociologists, and linguists, or by rhetoricians using methodologies from those fields. Many of the studies trace the composing process of a single author or of a group of authors composing individually but still constrained by external and social contexts. For instance, LeFevre (1987) treats invention in general as a social act. Since many of these studies have been cited in the other articles in this volume, they and this category will not be treated here.

I will, however, note that the composing processes of groups of writers composing collaboratively has become an increasingly popular research topic, partly because of its importance in the workplace and partly because of the emphasis on the social nature of communication being discussed here. Studies of collaboration in the workplace include those discussed in Ede and Lunsford (1990), Malone (1991), and Lay and Karis (1991). Studies of specific aspects of collaborative work include Webber (1991), Farkas's study (1991) of collaborative writing and software development, and Couture and Rymer's study (1991) of interaction between writer and supervisor.

Contributions from Previous Work

Taken as a whole, the research on discourse communities makes several points. First, when creating a piece of discourse, an author—especially a successful author—considers the discourse community or audience for the discourse; tries to tailor the discourse to the needs, values, assumptions, conventions, and expectations of the community; and is judged as successful partly in relation to the extent to which the discourse community has been satisfied. This consideration of audience may be seen as an effect of self-censorship or the clever ability of the author to execute the traditional audience analysis stage advocated by Aristotle and virtually every rhetorician since. Certainly this is nothing new.

A second point is that discourse from one organization, field, or other discourse community varies in ascertainable and understandable ways from the discourse in another community.

Third and fourth points made by the studies are that individuals in an organization or other discourse community review and suggest or mandate changes in an author's text and that contextual factors significantly affect the appropriateness and effectiveness of communication within organizations and within scientific, academic, and professional communities. Again, this is nothing new to the worker who has tried to get a supervisor's signature on a report or to the academic trying to deal with a journal reviewer's comments in preparing an article for publication.

What is more new is the extent to which many such reviews and revisions within a community define and continue the community's knowledge and ensure the continuation of the values, assumptions, conventions, and expectations of the community.

Thus, these studies show that there is indeed an effect—and often a profound effect—of the context and the values of the community of readers and listeners on the content and form of a document. Perhaps more unexpectedly, a few of the studies also suggest that there is sometimes an effect of the content and form of a document on its context, including helping to define the sense of community and to project its set of values and attitudes. Unfortunately, there are not nearly as many of these as of the former type.

A number of legal studies attest to some of these effects: altered judgments of a witness's credibility (Erickson et al., 1978; Lind & O'Barr, 1979; O'Barr, 1982); jurors who do not understand their instructions making decisions at odds with the ideals of the system (Charrow & Charrow, 1979; Elwork, Sales, & Alfini, 1977; Elwork, Alfini, & Sales, 1982); adverse judgments in small claims court resulting from stories that are psychologically satisfying but legally ineffective (O'Barr & Conley, 1990); undermining by divorce lawyers "of the bases of legitimation that other levels of the legal system work to create" (Sarat & Felstiner, 1990); effects on process and final record of courtroom proceedings from the language and strategies used by court interpreters and court recorders (Berk–Seligson, 1990; Walker, 1990b); effects on the legal information processing of appeals court clerks and their formulation of appeal issues (Stratman, 1988).

In addition to these studies from the legal system, Suchan and Dulek (1990) report results from studies of communication within the U.S. Navy that illustrate enormous impacts of external context on communication and of impacts of communication on the situation. Because of problems in dealing with the public, Congress, and other non–Navy discourse communities, the Navy has mandated new requirements for officers to write in the "normal" clear style taught in technical and business communication courses instead of in the typical Navy bureaucratic style full of abbreviations and acronyms.

> Although the correspondence manual orders naval officers to follow these new communication rules, and naval officers as a group are very responsive to authority, these changes have met with much resistance, particularly from more senior officers. One commander commented, "How can I respect myself and

get respect from my men by writing like an 18-year-old?" A captain voiced his resistance to the clear language rules by complaining: "I'll be damn [sic] if I'll write like an enlisted man." . . . Instead of seeing themselves as uniquely intelligent, professional decision makers when they wrote, officers saw themselves as common, everyday followers. (Suchan & Dulek, 1990, p. 94.)

Suchan and Dulek argue that the mandated language changes have "stripped officers of a way of signaling membership in a close-knit community and differentiating themselves from other communities—enlisted men and the private sector in general—of whom they are somewhat suspicious" (p. 94).

Needed Research

Research on types of work and workers. The articles referenced here and in the other articles presented in this volume deal almost exclusively with an Anglo-American context, with academic and professional contexts, and with the composing processes of white, usually young or middle-aged, male, nonhandicapped, native speakers of English. This situation is common in the research literature on discourse communities to date. There is relatively little attention from the discourse community perspective to many of the overwhelming realities of the American and international workplace:

1. that in North America and Western Europe, the workforce is becoming increasingly multicultural. Projections suggest that by the early twenty-first century, current minorities (Hispanics, Afro-Americans, Asians) will comprise 60% of the American workforce, and Europe has absorbed large numbers of workers from Africa, Asia, and Eastern Europe, with the probability of more to come.
2. that women comprise an increasingly large part of the workforce (that is, the nonhome workforce) in North America and Western Europe and an increasing part elsewhere.
3. that in North America, older workers comprise an increasingly large part of the workforce.
4. that many businesses rely on multinational sales, workforces, and communication.
5. that academic and professional contexts—such as those in law, medicine, engineering, and business management—while important and accessible and interesting, form a relatively small part of the total workforce (only 1 to 24.5 nonprofessional workers in Britain as cited in Coleman [1989]).
6. that the British Commonwealth and North America account for only a small portion of the international workforce.
7. that at least in the United States, handicapped workers have greater access to the workplace as a result of federal antidiscrimination law.

Research on Discourse Communities

It is true that there has been significant work in Europe and North America in providing English language training material for guest workers, including serious efforts in the military in upgrading the language skills of recruits to the armed forces. However, these language training efforts do not generally address the issues of discourse communities. (A notable exception that directly addresses the immigrant's membership in a professional discourse community is the work on language training for immigrant professionals in Australia reported in Burton [1989].)

Thus, one direction for future research would be to conduct additional studies on contexts and workers that are not represented or well represented already. These would include studies of non–Anglo-American contexts, of nonacademic and professional contexts, and of workers who include at least some, if not all, of the underrepresented demographic groups: nonwhites, older workers, females, handicapped workers, and nonnative speakers of English. They would also include studies of professionals who are not well represented in the current studies, such as architects, musicians, artists and other creative artists, ministers, social workers, or public health officials.

There has been an extensive amount of work on the composing habits of individual writers (not reviewed here) but comparatively little on the nature and effects of computer-based communication on the formation and maintenance of discourse communities. The work that does exist includes Murray (1988); Siegel, Dubrovsky, Kiesler, and McGuire (1986); Sproull (1986); and Sproull and Kiesler (1986).

Some aspects of the nature of international work have been reviewed by Swales (1990a) and Coleman (1989), including recent studies "aimed at helping non-native speakers (NNSs) acquire legal communicative competence" (Swales, 1990a, p. 105). Other work includes that by Berk-Seligson (1990) on bilingual court proceedings and the role of the translator, Parkhurst (1990) on the differences in composing processes of native and nonnative scientists, Clyne (1987) on the cultural differences in the organization of academic texts, and the authors in the excellent volumes edited by Coleman (1984, 1989). However, much additional work needs to be done on the differences between native and nonnative speakers in their composing processes to address discourse community issues, understanding of genre conventions, and community expectations.

An additional group to be investigated would be the elderly; Swales (1990a) has suggested the area of discourse analysis and gerontology. While this would not directly address the world of work, it would address the needs of those who do work with the elderly.

Research on the concept of discourse community and its signals. Although there has been some wonderfully detailed work on individual discourse communities and their markers, such as genres and other conventions, we need additional studies—especially detailed, ethnographic ones—to confirm and extend present results on the community-specific values, assumptions, conventions, and expectations that mark specific discourse communities and on the rationales to explain them. Useful discussion of such research occurs in Doheny-Farina and Odell (1985). In addition, we need to look at such features as metadiscourse and its function, as noted by Crismore (1989).

Another need is to extend the nature of the current work. Lyon has noted that standard discussions treat discourse community as if it were a relatively static, or at least stable, and monolithic entity and suggests that we might focus further attention on its unstable and diverse aspects: "Discourse studies would be advanced by focusing on the conflicts and finer distinctions within a groups' aims and actions, recognizing the structures and hierarchies within groups, acknowledging our own interpretive procedures, and discussing specific groups; this interpretive approach might well identify the contingent and fluid aspects of discourse formation." (Lyon, in press). It might also identify the "contingent and fluid aspects" of discourse community formation.

In a related vein, Miller (1984), Bazerman (1988), and Pettinari (1992) raise questions about the limits of a community, the means by which we identify one, and the relationship between discourse community and genre use. Pettinari notes that shared use of a nonstandard genre typically signals that a community exists, but points to instances in which people who do not talk together apparently share a genre. What are the implications of this apparently unusual genre use for our sense of both genre and discourse community?

Issues of ethics and the role of the researcher to intervene in research settings. As researchers work in organizational settings, it is inevitable that they will discover situations that are not optimum or are unethical, dangerous, or illegal. What should be done in such cases? There are conflicting demands on a researcher, including promises of confidentiality and the research goal of not altering the system being studied in the process of studying it, which often are at odds with one's responsibilities as a citizen and human being to warn others of danger. There is still little consensus about the responsibilities of potential whistle-blowers who are employees of a faulty organization, and that situation is surely better understood than that of the privileged researcher. Three discussions of the researcher's dilemma are in the contributions by Doheny-Farina in this volume, in Rogers and Swales (1990), and in part of the conclusion in Pettinari (1990):

One wonders to what extent researchers cast themselves in the role of criticizing "prior work" like dentists do. In this case the "prior work" is the ongoing communicative activity in the institutional context. In criticizing such prior work, do researchers thereby subtly cast themselves as being able to do better? Or, if not to do better, then certainly to know better? But since translating research findings into policy decisions is not always done, what happens with our findings?" (p. 269)

Additional research. In addition to replicating and extending our knowledge of communities—of community-specific values, assumptions, goals, theories, methods, conventions, and results—we need to share our current knowledge more fully across the various disciplines involved. Volumes such as this one will contribute to this goal. We also need to conduct more research on areas that are "social necessities." Such areas might include important professions that are not well represented in the current studies, such as architecture, music, art, and other "creative" fields; the ministry; social work; or public health. Other areas might include the problems in understanding product labels and warnings, the ways of producing more effective ones, and the following list of issues, originally raised by Walker (1990a) in terms of needed research in the legal community but here slightly rephrased for generalization into other contexts in which observers or decision makers are drawing conclusions and making judgments:

1. Identification of those rules of "communicative competence" in various testi-monial events (for example, depositions, trials, administrative hearings, small claims courts, or presentation of a scientific or organizational argument of fact or policy) that give communicators the greatest degree of control over the presentation of their own stories or arguments. One specific question to ask might be what linguistic techniques (independent of direct intervention by someone else) are most effective for countering an antagonist's version of "the truth."
2. Investigation of the interplay among the three variables of (a) ways of speak-ing, (b) impression formation, and (c) outcome of judgments or decisions. A corollary line of research could focus on written speech and presentations of someone's position, studying the relationship among the ways the speech or presentations are represented in the texts, impression formation, and the actual decisions made by influential readers of those texts.
3. Application of speech act theory to various judgmental issues. One specific research focus might be on what the mythically but legally relevant "ordinary prudent person" (or "reasonable man") understands a warning, threat, prom-ise, offer, etc., to be.

4. Investigation of the linguistic aspects of the hazards to due process or functionality in our organizational and social systems for the "language and
culture different," including very young children, the deaf, the developmen-
tally impaired, nonnative speakers of English, and non-English speakers.
(Adapted from Walker, 1990a, pp. 355–356)

Finally, although we know something about how communities form
and are maintained, there are a number of issues related to the life cycle of
discourse communities that need to be addressed: How do communities
dissolve or merge into a different form? What are the differences between
larger or weaker communities and their smaller or more intense counterparts
(what is the effect on a community of size and strength of interactions)?
How does a previous member of a community get "dropped" when the
community retains its subject focus, changes that focus, or dissolves?

Conclusion

It is ironic that ultimately these discussions lead us back, at the end, to
the place where we began, with the insights of Kuhn written in 1969 in the
postscript to *The Structure of Scientific Revolutions*:

> How does one elect and how is one elected to membership in a particular
> community, scientific or not? What is the process and what are the stages of
> socialization to the group? What does the group collectively see as its goals;
> what deviations, individual or collective, will it tolerate; and how does it control
> the impermissible aberration? A fuller understanding of science will depend on
> answers to other sorts of questions as well, but there is no area in which more
> work is so badly needed. Scientific knowledge, like language, is intrinsically the
> common property of a group or else nothing at all. To understand it we shall
> need to know the special characteristics of the groups that create and use it.
> (1970, pp. 209–210)

| **Bridging the Gap** | Scenic Motives for Collaborative Writing in Workplace and School |

The notion of writing as social, collaborative process has been developed into an extremely friendly idea, so much so that we see demonstrations of its extraordinary power to drive theory making and research every time we open a journal or thumb through the pages of a conference program. When we look to our classrooms, however, we cannot say they have proved generally hospitable to the idea. To be sure, more and more teachers are asking their students to engage in one form of writing-as-social—literal writing and revising together—but too often, writing-as-collaboration is allowed to mean merely writing-as-literal-coauthoring, and the pedagogical focus remains more on the production of texts to be evaluated than on ways in which texts arise out of other texts (Reither & Vipond, 1989).

Part of the problem, as I have argued elsewhere (Reither, 1989), is that institutional and disciplinary values, assumptions, and conventions constrain us to organize our classrooms top-down, teacher-to-student. Another part of the problem is that research findings (Ede & Lunsford, 1990; Lunsford & Ede, 1986), which note that 87% of the professionals they studied write collaboratively at least some of the time, have led some to reason that if team writing is common practice in certain kinds of workplaces, and if students are being prepared to take roles in those workplaces, then teachers should give students team writing and revising assignments. In our teaching, we have foregrounded workplace practices, while giving only secondary attention to workplace conditions that enable and motivate those practices. As a result, such narrowly collaborative practices as coauthoring and peer editing often are parachuted into environments that are not wholly friendly—into classrooms dominated by assumptions and motives that are antithetical to a vision of writing as collaborative, cooperative, social.

What makes these classrooms inhospitable is that they are driven by what Ede and Lunsford (1990) call "the commonsense view of writing as the physical act of putting pen or typewriter key to paper" (p. 60). When writing is defined this way, even when classroom practice emphasizes process over product, grades are assigned to students on the basis of teachers' evaluations of student-written texts as stand-alone entities. When this is the case, students are unlikely to experience motives for collaborating and writing that arise out of relationships among writers and others, out of relationships of texts among other texts, or out of the functions of texts within communicative, rhetorical, social networks—the kinds of considerations that become important when writing is conceptualized from within a "social perspective" (Faigley, 1985). What ultimately counts in these classrooms is writing that gets a good grade, and very little in the situation promotes considering whether or not a piece of writing actually succeeds in getting work done or in moving and bending readers to action, belief, and attitude (Burke, 1969b). Such issues can exist only in talk about writing, in simulation, or in imagined possibilities.

In classrooms where writing's ultimate function is to be graded, then, it is unlikely that such powerful activities as "planning, gathering information, drafting, and revising collaboratively" (Ede & Lunsford, 1990, p. 20) will be seen as much more than techniques for reinforcing lessons consistent with a view of texts as gradable artifacts. These classrooms prove inhospitable, incompatible environments for collaborative practices, understandings, or motives. In such classrooms, the need of the educational bureaucracy to assess and rank students continues to be served, but the students' rhetorical needs and aims are not necessarily better served than they were before team authoring and peer editing came into classroom use. What is missing from these classrooms are the circumstances that make possible and (thus) motivate writing as social process—the very conditions that make collaboration and cooperation appropriate, even necessary, in many business, governmental, and professional workplaces. What is missing are the rhetorical needs, aims, functions, and moves that organize and drive the production of written knowledge.

My thesis here is that if teaching writing as social, collaborative process is to have any reasonable chance of succeeding, teachers must radically redesign their courses to make them scenes (Burke, 1969a) where collaborative writing and revising are appropriate, efficient, even natural or necessary ways to do the work that needs doing.

To develop this thesis, I explore three issues. First, I examine further what it means to say that writing is collaborative and social. I argue for a view of collaborative writing that encompasses far more than literal writing-together, on the ground that an expanded notion of writing-as-collaboration will help teachers see more clearly the kinds of changes they need to make in their classrooms. Specifically, I argue that intertextuality (Porter, 1986) itself, or what I call "knowledge making" (Reither & Vipond, 1989), is a collaborative process, driven by a collaborative imperative. Second, I poke about in the literature of the field represented by this book to identify some of the "scenic motives" (cf. Burke, 1969b) that enable collaboration in a variety of professional and business workplaces. And third, by way of conclusion, I suggest some ways teachers can organize courses to provide students with the kinds of scenic motives that make collaborative writing happen in workplaces. I do not suggest teachers should try to replicate in their classrooms the all-too-often oppressively hierarchical, competitive, bottom-line mentality of the workplace. These conditions can force consensus (see Myers, 1986; Trimbur, 1989) rather than encourage constructive, multivocal pooling of experiences, styles, abilities, and knowing. I do suggest that making classrooms in some ways more like collaborative workplaces will help students understand better what writing is and does.

Writing as Collaboration

As Ede and Lunsford (1986) point out, writing is collaborative, cooperative, and social in at least two ways, each based on different views of what writing is, when writing begins and ends, and in what circumstances writing is collaborative. One view sees writing as producing a document, a process that begins with an intention to write and ends when a text is produced; and, therefore, writing is collaborative when writers literally coauthor or write in teams to produce a text. Often grounded in the work of Abercrombie (1960, 1970), Ede and Lunsford (1986, 1990), Mason (1970), and Bruffee's (1978, 1984, 1985) peer tutoring practice, this view dominates writing-as-collaboration thinking and practice.

The second view sees writing as beginning essentially in other (oral and written) texts and ending when people stop reading and writing—which is, effectively, never; and, whether or not authors literally write and revise together, writing is always collaborative, because writing always occurs as a dialogic process, in situations where everyone who writes does so with two implicit or explicit aims: first, to build on others' knowledge to make "new" knowledge or otherwise bring about change within discourse communities, and second, to provide "written knowledge" (Bazerman, 1988) for others to build on. This more comprehensive, more profoundly social view understands all knowledge making as collaborative (see Reither & Vipond, 1989). Often grounded in the work of Bakhtin (1981), Burke (1950, 1969b), Fish (1980), Fleck (1935/1979), Geertz (1973), Kuhn (1970), LeFevre (1987), Rorty (1979), Vygotsky (1978), and Bruffee's "conversation theory" (1984), we see this view encapsulated when Burke (1950) suggests that "a rhetorician . . . is like one voice in a dialogue. Put several such voices together, with each voicing its special assertion, let them act upon one another in co-operative competition, and you get a dialectic that, properly developed, can lead to views transcending the limitations of each" (p. 203).

Burke's construction is an important one, having in it a potential for merging the two notions. Burke's view allows us to see that sometimes multiple voices come together literally to coauthor or team-write single texts; but multiple voices *always* come together (even when texts are physically produced by single writers) in every text that constructs knowing or otherwise modifies the dialogue, dialectic, and conversation (Clark, 1990; see also Bakhtin, 1981; LeFevre, 1987) that constitute every field of practice. Moreover, and even more important, Burke's notion allows us to understand that the written knowledge that constitutes any field comes about dialectically, that is to say, collaboratively: Many authors contribute their unique ways of knowing and seeing to the process of making that knowledge.

The common element in both views of collaboration is multiple voices, each with its own rhythms, its own tones, its own special ways of knowing, its own contributions to make to the process. Every voice, different from every other, strives to find and define its own style, its own sources of authority, its own place in the field of practice. Every voice comes together collaboratively with every other voice, no matter how distant in place or time, to produce both the written knowledge that is a single text and the written knowledge that constitutes any field of knowing and practice. That is, writing is "social," "collaborative," "intertextual" in that authors challenge, modify, use, build on, and add to the utterances of others to join in "co-operative competition" with them in the process of text and knowledge making. The aims? To work to get things right, to keep the conversation going (Rorty, 1979), to advance individual and community belonging, identity, and knowing.

Scenic Motives for Collaborative Writing in the Workplace

When we look to the kinds of business, governmental, and other professional workplaces studied in the present volume and elsewhere, we find that collaborative practices abound in many of them, but never for their own sake. Such practices are always solidly grounded in conditions of situation—scenic motives—that are there by virtue of what these workplaces are, what they do, and how they work.

The most obvious of these motives is that such workplaces are scenes where writing is the means by which people do their work. No matter the specific nature of the enterprise, these workplaces are, at some level, scenes for research and development, for making and remaking written knowledge (see Reither, 1985, 1990). In such environments, writing is a means by which questions are posed and answered, information is disseminated, individual and institutional activities are planned, announced, and coordinated, situations and data are analyzed, and co-workers are educated (Anderson, 1985). Documents are used as "instruments for initiating projects, reporting on their progress, and bringing them to a conclusion" (Paradis, Dobrin, & Miller, 1985, p. 284). All of this work-in-writing (and work-in-reading) is of course both "social" and "intertextual"; and all of it serves to build and reinforce the sense of identification (Burke, 1969a) and community that come from mutual knowing and purpose (see also Spilka, 1990b). In addition, a good deal of this writing is collaborative in the narrower sense. People find it appropriate to write and revise in teams, Zimmerman and Marsh (1989) point out, when proposals and reports need to be written quickly and efficiently. As well, literal collaboration is built into the system by the very fact that people are hired for their differences in expertise; they are employed to perform specific, deliberately complementary roles within the workplace (Zimmerman & Marsh, 1989).

The impulse to divide the labor of writing and revising leads to the practice Paradis, Dobrin, and Miller (1985) call "document cycling," whereby several hands work on the writing and revising of a document as it moves through the workplace. A number of people with different competencies can, in the interests of accuracy and quality, write different sections, examine what others have written, suggest revisions, and comment on documents in ways that provoke further consideration and research. Document cycling is thus a means for getting the feedback working writers need as they write proposals, progress reports, and research reports.

If a primary motive for collaborative writing and revising is the need to get the work done, a strong secondary motive arises out of the need of managers and co-workers to monitor and stay attuned to the progress of that work. Document cycling and various forms of team writing (see Ede & Lunsford, 1990) help business people and professionals keep tabs on what is going on, to oversee the process, and to ensure, as far as possible, completeness and accuracy (Paradis, Dobrin, & Miller, 1985). These practices thus allow supervisors and more-experienced co-workers to bring their experience to bear to "shape the intellectual labor of the staff researcher" (Paradis, Dobrin, & Miller, 1985, p. 300).

A third scenic motive for writing and collaboration in workplaces, perhaps the most powerful of them all, is that writing, especially for and with co-workers, serves personal and social needs to be visible, to belong, to maintain internal networks, and to sustain a sense of community within the organization. Writing for and with co-workers enables business people and professionals to establish not only their own individual identities, authority, and place, but also to contribute to organizational identity and community. An engineer at Exxon ITD told Paradis, Dobrin, and Miller (1985) that "work I did at first was lost . . . because I didn't write it up" (p. 295). Writing thus "enabled . . . employees to package and project their physical and intellectual labor" (p. 295). But of course there is more here than a need to get credit. In the best of these organizations, everyone's contributions fit into larger enterprises—internal networks, the organization itself, and even a wider community that makes use of the resulting knowledge. The organization is a synergistic social system in which every member occupies a niche that is in some way important to the organization: When people are doing their own work, whether alone or in a team, they are also doing the organization's work. Their individual accomplishments benefit the community that includes them as members.

This leads to a fourth scenic motive, the need to develop and maintain an identity and culture for the institution itself. Because an organization's identity shapes and gives direction and focus to its members' projects, no organization can hold together without a knowable "corporate" identity, constituted in shared values, goals, methods, genres, and styles. Perhaps nothing is more important to that identity than "an in-house language and . . . local discourse conventions" (Faigley, 1985, p. 238). So powerful is this motive that, as Perelman (1986) puts it, individuals in workplaces "exist largely as projections of institutional roles rather than as idiosyncratic individuals," so that while "an individual can personalize an institutional role, or institutional roles can be performed in quite different ways, . . . the extent to which a role can be personalized or the number of ways the role can be acted out are always limited by institutional rules and goals" (p. 474). Thus, "the activity of writing [demands] that its practitioners develop a kind of social consciousness of the organizational environment" (Paradis, Dobrin, & Miller, 1985, p. 293; see also Spilka, 1990b). Writers become persuasive in a community as and when they assimilate for their own use the rhetorical strategies and moves that work in that community.

A final scenic motive is of a different order, in that it collapses all the others into one, even as it adds other dimensions. I can only describe it fragmentarily here. This motive resides in the fact that language itself and the ways people use language "contain" the collaborative motive. White (1985) puts it well when he tells first-year law students that

> in both language and law, learning has a double focus: if one is to live and act competently in a particular culture, one must learn how the language . . . is in fact spoken by others, by those whom one wishes to address, to persuade, to learn from, and to live with. . . . Your concern . . . is thus a double one: to learn as completely as you can how the legal culture functions; and to establish a place for yourself in relation to it from which you can attempt to use it in your own ways. (pp. 53–54)

Implicit in White's observations is the notion that terms, rhetorical moves, and persuasive means evolve collaboratively as people use public language to make meaning and otherwise bring about change.

This motive includes what seems to be an infinite range of ways language, and people's habitual uses of language, condition what and how people do what they do in the workplace (and everywhere else, for that matter). It accounts, for example, for the fact that the more important the document being written, and the more novel or complex the writing problem, the more likely it is that the document will be written collaboratively through a number of drafts. It accounts, as well, for the fact that writers necessarily always build on the work of those who have written before them, using their texts not only as sources of information and boilerplate text, but also as models for ways of accomplishing the work of the organization. Thus, according to Campbell and Jamieson (1990), "rhetorical types are linked to purposes; that is, they arise to perform certain functions, to accomplish certain ends in certain kinds of situations" (p. 104).

Bridging the Gap Between Workplace and Classroom

We must, I believe, confront the plain truth that these motives operate fully and healthily in too few of our students' writing scenes. Even when writing and collaboration are ways work gets done in classrooms, what finally matters for both teacher and students is too often not the work but the grade assigned to the work. Not often do students write with and for one another, to use one another's written knowledge to further their own and the community's projects by making more written knowledge. Except only superficially, students do not write and collaborate to define, augment, and assert their own identities within larger networks and communities. Except only rarely, classrooms do not develop their own genres, styles, and cultures. Finally, although we often find the trappings of collaboration in our students' writing scenes, we do not often find students enmeshed in "the complexities of the rhetorical situation, the political realities of exigencies and purposes, the tensions created by multiple audiences, the textual needs of readers, and the constraints imposed by cultural contexts" (Matalene, 1989, p. x).

To provide scenes hospitable to collaborative writing practices, teachers can look to ways to make three major changes in their classrooms. One is to engage students in ongoing learning projects that require them to ask the kinds of questions that drive research, gather information and ideas that answer those questions, and consolidate and share findings—creating written knowledge—by writing for others' use. So far as possible, it must be students, not teachers, who conceptualize the project and the process, who ask the questions that drive the project, and who do the gathering, organizing, and sharing. And, depending on the complexity and length of the documents needed to do the work, many of the texts might be written and revised in teams. For the scenic motive to be present, the situation must be organized so that projects cannot go forward unless the student researchers regularly pool their findings with one another, in both small groups and whole, so they can build on each other's intellectual labor. The key here is to work not primarily with what students already know, but with what they find out through research outside the classroom. The students' learning goals must be linked with what others have done, not only in the course they are taking, but also in the wider field of practice their project fits into. (See Reither & Vipond, 1989.)

What kinds of projects? One answer is that teachers can give students the same kinds of projects they themselves might undertake when they work in their fields—subject, of course, to time frames, resources, student backgrounds, and institutional constraints (obviously, the project has to be do-able). I once asked a year-long first-year writing class to undertake an ethnographic study of the rhetoric of teaching, in which the students' first task was to learn how to do ethnography, which they did by reading it and (with help from anthropologists they asked to serve as consultants) teaching one another how to do it; once they had done that preliminary learning and teaching, they went into classrooms to study and write about what teachers were doing to influence students to learn. In courses I teach in rhetoric, Shakespeare, and modern drama, for instance, I've organized projects for my students based on these kinds of questions: What can classical and modern rhetorical theory tell us about what people do with words? How and where did Shakespeare learn to do what he did? (See Reither, 1990.) What are the origins and nature of some of the main "schools" of modern Western drama?

Rather more directly relevant to the concerns of this book, at Clemson University, Young (1990) had students in an advanced business and technical writing course "actually *do* technical writing, rather than study and practice doing it" (p. 173). The project he gave his students asked them to draft, test run, and finally produce a users' manual for the Clemson University Forestry and Agricultural Network telecommunications system. The project involved learning how to use the system in order to write about it. When the students came into the course, they learned they "would work collaboratively, and . . . set agendas, deadlines and grading procedures only after [they] got into the project, understood its scope and possibilities, and figured out the best way [they] could work together to learn something about technical writing in the process of getting [their] project done" (p. 173). At Penn State, using a quite different collaborative-classroom model, Selzer (1990) organized a beginning technical writing course as "an arena of shared inquiry" (p. 191) where students learned how to do technical writing while they were "studying language and its uses in technical, scientific, and institutional settings" (p. 190).

But it may not be necessary, as these instances might lead one to believe, for teachers to organize whole courses as research-and-writing projects. Perhaps it is enough for teachers to organize only some of the work this way. Whatever the case, teachers can and probably should start small: Instead of beginning courses with background lectures, for example, they could ask students to generate initial research questions and then go to the library, in teams or task forces, to gather information and examples, pool findings, and construct their own overview out of what they find. From such a process, students can learn how to build on what they already know to learn something more about a field's major issues, themes, and problems. They can learn where the field came from, what its work and its texts look like, whom its major texts and authors are thought to be, and so on. More important, if teachers organize their courses so that this background knowing is then used as a source for further student questions, research, and pooling, the students can learn how knowledge is built on other knowledge and how individual knowing has its sources in collective knowledge and practice.

We can point to three key principles in all this: First, whenever students need information or examples that are available to them through research, teachers can ask them to conduct the appropriate research, alone or in small groups; swap information; organize their findings in written reports (proposals, feasibility studies, interim reports, and drafts); and then present their texts for the use of others. Second, when one student or a small group of students is given responsibility for finding out and reporting on a given question, problem, or topic, and when, to do their work, the other students in the class need what the student or group of students has learned—when there is no other efficient way to get it—the rhetorical-communicative situation itself provides scenic motives for writing and collaborating. And third, in such courses both content and writing (insofar as they are separable) are learned far less by direct study and instruction than by reading and writing what one learns: forms, content, values, assumptions, conventions, persuasive resources, rhetorical moves, kinds of questions asked in the field, kinds of research appropriate to the field, and kinds and sources of evidence available. Because they have real functions in learning, writing and content are learned primarily through use in a context of need. That is, writing and content are learned by reading and by writing with and for one another— just as we learn them and just as business people and professionals learn them.

Another change involves the extraordinarily difficult task of redefining the teachers' role in the classroom, so that they function as research-project managers instead of gatherers, organizers, and deliverers of knowledge. As Selzer (1990) suggests, if a course "is not merely a matter of imparting skills and competencies and efficiencies, the teacher is less likely to be a . . . 'delivery system'—and more likely to be a fellow student engaged in the body of knowledge" (p. 190). All competent teachers necessarily know how to ask the right kinds of questions and how to gather, organize, and deliver information to others; that is (perhaps unfortunately) their stock in trade. And most teaching practice seems founded on the assumption that, if teachers do the work, students will learn. But that logic is flawed not only in the obvious way. It is also faulty insofar as such an approach assumes that knowing consists primarily in the mastery of "content." It is of course true that students can, will, and do learn content from lectures and textbooks, but it is also true that they will have a tough time learning the social, collaborative, intertextual origins and nature of that content if all they have to go on is what they get from lectures and textbooks. What teachers need to do, I believe, is offer scenes that ask students to pose questions, gather information, and make knowledge so they can learn how to perform these tasks themselves. In fact, we could say that the whole point of teachers' reorganizing their classrooms into collaborative environments is to help students become question-driven gatherers, organizers, and sharers of knowledge.

The third change is aim and consequence of the first two changes: When teachers ask students to undertake real research projects that result in real advances in knowing (even if it is just their own), and when teachers function in classrooms not as founts of knowledge, but as managers of students' efforts to make knowledge, the result is that the students must change who they are. Teachers must help students recast their own roles in the classroom: from people who come to class to listen to lectures, read textbooks, and write term papers and exams to people who come to class having done some research outside of class, ready to pool their findings with those of others, evaluate the present status of their developing knowledge, and identify gaps in knowing that need to be filled. The project—producing knowledge through texts—needs to be arranged so that, if they are to participate and if the project is to go forward, the students must come to the classroom prepared to share the fruits of intellectual labor. Gathering information and creating knowledge make a person into an important kind of "expert": one who knows something others do not know or who knows something differently from others. Being an expert gives one something to say on a problem or issue and, therefore, status and place in the community. Gathering and pooling knowledge—collaborating, bringing knowing and texts together—enable people to identify and develop roles for themselves in communities. There are two key elements here: The first is that teachers must believe students can and should learn how to carry out and share the results of the inquiry that characterizes whatever field of practice their project fits into; the second is that students must see their task as producing texts others can take seriously, be changed by, and use as ground for further research and writing. When these things happen, texts will be treated not as artifacts, but as utterances in ongoing conversations.

There is probably no point pretending that classrooms can truly replicate the kinds of workplaces studied by Ede and Lunsford and by the researchers represented in the present volume, or even that we should want our classrooms to do so. We can, however, usefully recognize that the ultimate goal of the classroom is pretty much the same as that of the workplace: to make written knowledge. Recognizing that, and recognizing that knowledge is something people make with other people, we can then begin making our classrooms scenes that enable and motivate writing and knowing as social, collaborative, intertextual processes. Clearly, something more basic than asking students to write and revise in teams needs to happen. What we have to do, I believe, is organize classrooms as places where students can experience the same kinds of motives for writing and collaborating that many people experience in many workplaces. Students (and teachers) need to know what happens when there is work to do and when writing is the way to do that work. Students need to experience scenes where writing and collaborating are central ways for people to define themselves and their relationships with one another within networks and organizations. They need to experience ways they can use writing and collaborating to develop and maintain group identity and culture. They need, finally, to experience the pressures of community-specific language, rhetoric, methods, conventions, genres. Unless they do, it will be difficult for them to understand fully the ways in which, and the extent to which, writing and knowing are fundamentally social processes. Until classrooms embody these kinds of scenic motives, we will find it difficult, indeed, to bridge the gap between workplace and classroom.

Acknowledgments

I thank the following trusted assessors for commenting on drafts of this chapter: Jackie Reither, Douglas Vipond, Rachel Spilka, Lester Faigley, Graham Smart, and two anonymous reviewers.

Rachel Spilka

Influencing Workplace Practice

A Challenge for Professional Writing Specialists in Academia

"**A**s a technical communicator, I am the bridge between those who create ideas and those who use them." This quotation, which begins the "Code for Communicators" of the Society for Technical Communication (STC), suggests that a primary role of a technical communicator is to serve as a liaison, or bridge, between those who create ideas and the users of those ideas. Yet, the technical communicator's role has evolved dramatically in the past few decades.[1] Currently, the technical communicator is perceived as an information developer (see, for example, Schriver, 1989, p. 321) responsible for adapting to and perpetuating workplace culture, but also for working toward changing and improving workplace practices. The technical communicator, therefore, has become known as an agent both of social accommodation and social change, or innovation.

Given this dual role of technical communicators in workplace settings, what becomes the primary charge of scholars in academia aiming to use pedagogy as a means of influencing workplace communication practices? To what degree should educators in academia train students to adapt to and perpetuate the ongoing workplace communication practices described in research reports and other literature? To what extent should these educators encourage student writers to analyze, critique, and even change those workplace communication practices? How can they help students know how to act as agents of continuity or as agents of change, and to determine when to assume either role?

Miller (1989) argues that professional writing specialists[2] in academia need to use caution in teaching nonacademic rhetorical practices, because those practices described in research reports might not serve as ideal models for student writers to emulate. She also stresses that, although workplace practice has influenced the pedagogy (in academia) of workplace writing, academia has an important contribution to make, as well, to workplace communication practices and should be making that contribution more concertedly, for example, by training students to apply theory to a critique of workplace practice.

This chapter builds on Miller's argument that educators in academia need to exercise caution in their pedagogy to avoid indiscriminately translating results of workplace writing studies into professional writing pedagogy and need, also, to ensure continual inquiry into potential shortcomings of workplace practices. I argue that, at all times, these educators must maintain tension in their pedagogy between social accommodation and social innovation, and that such a goal will require changes in current pedagogical and research approaches. These educators need to become more sensitive to which workplace practices they include in their curricula. In addition, they need to work in greater harmony with each other toward the goal of strengthening the integrity of professional writing pedagogy, for example, by designing future qualitative studies that respond not only to theoretical needs in the profession, but also to questions that aim at improving professional writing pedagogy.

This chapter raises issues and questions intended to inspire further discussion and debate. My assumption is that at this stage, the issues for initiating a conversation must be established before professional writing specialists can speculate on answers or can pinpoint exactly academia's potential for influencing workplace practice. Specifically, my central aim is to explore the following questions: (1) How might professional writing specialists in academia use pedagogy as a means of improving workplace practice?; (2) How might the results of qualitative studies of writing in the workplace be taught, with caution, in professional writing programs in academia?; and (3) How might researchers design future qualitative studies that address pedagogical aims of professional writing?

How might professional writing specialists in academia use pedagogy to improve workplace practice?

Those practices preferred and accepted by workplace cultures, observed by writing researchers, and reported in the literature might be contrary to those rhetorical principles that have been preferred and accepted by academia. According to Miller (1989), professional writing specialists in academia seem "uncertain about where to locate norms, about whether the definition of 'good writing' is to be derived from academic knowledge or from nonacademic practices" (p. 15). While Tebeaux (1985) calls for professional writing pedagogy to change to conform to what has been observed in practice, Miller argues instead that these specialists need to exercise caution in their pedagogical choices and decisions, especially those concerning which workplace practices to teach and which ones to avoid teaching.

To date, perhaps because of the recency of qualitative studies of workplace writing (most of which have emerged just since the mid-1980s), professional writing specialists in academia are just beginning to include in their curriculum instruction of workplace practices as reported by researchers who have observed those practices in the workplace. Most reported research has been descriptive, with investigators observing how a workplace culture influences composing process behavior and decisions and how such workplace practices are deemed acceptable or unacceptable by particular workplace cultures.[3] Unfortunately, this descriptive emphasis leaves unresolved whether these observed writing practices are, in fact, immediately effective with primary readers or productive in the long run for the affected organizational contexts. Without such an analysis, professional writing specialists in academia too often assume that instruction should train students to mimic these observed, real-world practices without highlighting reasons for questioning some of them.

Miller (1989) is concerned about this uncritical stance toward documented workplace practices. She argues that professional writing specialists need to exert greater influence, through their courses and curricula, on workplace practice:

> The academy itself is also a set of practices, including those of observation, conceptualization, and instruction—practices that create their own kind of knowledge. Such knowledge allows the academy to provide a standpoint for inquiry into and criticism of nonacademic practices. We ought not, in other words, simply design our courses and curricula to replicate existing practices, taking them for granted and seeking to make them more efficient on their own terms, making our students "more valuable to industry"; we ought instead to question those practices and encourage our students to do so too. (p. 23)

Miller resists advocating that the workplace accommodate itself to the academic perspective; instead, she calls for a "necessary combination of academic and nonacademic contributions to curriculum" (p. 23).

As an important first step toward ensuring that perspectives from both academia and the workplace contribute to the professional writing curriculum, professional writing specialists, both in academia and in the workplace, need to acknowledge that academia and the workplace can and should serve as mutual constraints; that is, they need to agree that professional writing pedagogy in academia needs to be influenced, somehow, by those practices preferred and accepted in workplace cultures, while those practices, in turn, need to be influenced, somehow, by that knowledge preferred and accepted by academia.

On a relatively small scale, the workplace has benefited, already, from insights about communication provided by professional writing specialists (situated either in the workplace or in academia). Some workplace practitioners are unaware of effective or ineffective communication strategies within their organization until they receive from a researcher information and an evaluation of them, based on rhetorical and other theories. Sponsors of qualitative studies of workplace writing typically receive from researchers an analysis of communication in their particular workplace cultures, as well as an evaluation of communication processes and products, and, in some cases, advice for improvement. Some workplace practitioners also receive advice from conference presentations and proceedings, research reports, and other literature. In these cases, the advice they receive usually is influenced by theory and by what is considered "ideal practice" by those in academia.

Of course, what academia considers to be an "ideal" workplace practice might conflict with a workplace impression, and workplace practitioners certainly need to use caution themselves in evaluating even solicited advice. They can either strive to achieve that "more ideal situation," as presented by professional writing specialists, or reject it as inappropriate for their particular culture. For example, suppose that a workplace practitioner reads a research report demonstrating that delays in the composing process were detrimental to fulfilling project goals; should that practitioner believe that such delays are always detrimental? My own report in this volume suggests that silences and delays can facilitate invention and planning and can be quite helpful to fulfilling project goals. Believing the results of any one study, or even of a few studies, can be a risk for workplace practitioners, especially if those results are from studies taking place in other workplace cultures. Clearly, workplace practitioners can (and need to) bring much social knowledge to an evaluation of academic advice on workplace practices.

In turn, professional writing specialists in academia also need to determine which workplace practices to accept and reject from their pedagogy. Those more skeptical professional writing specialists in academia typically use theory to analyze practices observed in the workplace, and while applying that new perspective to their curriculum, they tend to filter out from instruction those observed practices that appear contradictory to what theory presupposes as "ideal" and to what academicians value. Yet, those observed practices filtered out from pedagogy in academia might be valued, still, by workplace cultures. Without considering that the workplace could have entirely different notions from their own of what might be ideal practice within their own cultures, these academicians risk training student writers to rely on theoretical perspectives as a sole guide to evaluating workplace practice instead of training them to rely on both theoretical and workplace perspectives for such an evaluation. Professional writing specialists and their students need to resist this tendency by deliberately conditioning their theoretical insights by the judgments and preferences of workplace cultures.

To achieve this goal, professional writing specialists in academia need to ensure that their curricula include training in both social accommodation and social innovation. They need, first, to prepare student writers to identify, analyze, and both adapt to and work within the constraints of any particular workplace culture. Second, student writers need training in rhetorical and social analysis so they can analyze and decide on which practices to emulate and which to critique and attempt to change, as well as when and how to emulate, critique, or effect social change in any given workplace culture. Students need to learn the "social boundaries" of a culture, that is, the extent to which social accommodation is necessary and social innovation is possible. With that type of social knowledge, students are unlikely to simply adapt to a workplace culture without questioning that culture's practices and are more likely to discover a special kind of social power: knowledge of the extent to which they can challenge workplace norms and initiate change in a workplace culture.

Several writing specialists can attest, already, to the potential effectiveness of instruction in social context research and analysis, as well as in social accommodation and innovation. For example, some specialists (including Reither, this volume, and Selzer, 1989) suggest that instructors in academia can equip student writers with the means of researching any workplace culture (including, Reither notes, that in an academic setting), which can be an important first step toward understanding what is unique and important to that culture. Also, initial attempts have been made to train students in both social accommodation and innovation:[4] Both Lutz (1989) and Anson and Forsberg (1990) describe training writing internship students in discovering and then coping with both effective and ineffective strategies of social accommodation and innovation. However, even with these early successes in the instruction of both social accommodation and innovation, much change still is needed in the curricula of professional writing programs in academia to provide more specific instruction in social analysis and in strategies for both social accommodation and innovation.

Some workplace practitioners already have recognized the value of including instruction in social analysis in the professional writing curriculum. According to Ross Squire, a founder of the search division of Documentation Development, Inc., Boston and New York (in a presentation to the Society for Technical Communication, Northern New England Chapter, 19 January 1989), training in social analysis is one of the fundamental competency areas New England employers are seeking in candidates for technical writing positions (other areas he listed are in basic technical writing and editing, graphics, desktop publishing, and interpersonal communication). Squire argues that candidates with training in understanding the social context or culture of an organization are especially competitive on the job market. Although Miller (1989) might argue against academic programs catering to workplace preferences, in this situation, academia would be working toward a goal it shares with the workplace: to graduate from its programs marketable professional writing specialists with superior cognitive ability and special skill in both rhetorical and social analysis. Adding training in social analysis to professional writing programs (and perhaps increasing its presence in the curriculum) therefore can be seen as a means of promoting cooperation between academia and the workplace, an important first step toward improved future relations between these ultimately mutually dependent polarities.

If academia makes a more concerted effort to train student writers in the research and analysis of social contexts and in both social accommodation and social innovation, it can progress toward the goal of exerting greater influence on workplace practice. Once student writers enter workplace cultures and then act in ways that not only perpetuate, but also shape and reshape those cultures, it will become more certain that academia will influence workplace cultures gradually, but significantly and responsibly.

How might the results of qualitative studies of writing in the workplace be taught, with caution, in professional writing programs in academia?

How is it possible to integrate research descriptions of workplace practice into curricula in ways that are suitably cautious? In this section, I will identify three strategies for exercising such caution in the pedagogy of professional writing in academia, with the hope that professional writing specialists will critique these strategies and identify alternative or additional strategies that might be more effective.

Training Students in Strategies for Social Innovation

As described earlier, if students are trained in academic professional writing programs to analyze and critique workplace practices and to apply strategies for effecting social change in the workplace, they will be less likely to value workplace practices that are ineffectual or detrimental in any given workplace culture. Both professional writing instructors and their students need to analyze carefully the strengths and weaknesses of those workplace practices reported in the literature and to consider in which social circumstances those practices are likely to be effective or ineffective. For example, instructors easily could ask students to work on an assignment collaboratively and require students to read articles on collaboration practices in the workplace; yet, they should also ask students to critique those practices reported in the literature, perhaps in light of which ones would be ideal for their own rhetorical and social situation. Without such discussion, students are less apt to develop the critical thinking and social analytic skills they will need to draw upon in future workplace settings to cope well with social expectations and to bring about needed social change.

Critiquing the Literature Before Designing a Course

Before including in a professional writing course instruction of a specific workplace practice, instructors need to analyze several aspects of the research report describing the workplace practice. First, they need to assess the validity of the research in reports describing that workplace practice: How sound are the original research questions? How sound is the researcher's study design and rationale for selecting methodology? Did the researcher rely upon methodological triangulation, both in data collection and data analysis? Next, they need to assess the quality of the researcher's analysis of research results: Did the researcher apply theory to the analysis, and competently? Did the researcher analyze results thoroughly and competently? Another important measure is to assess whether the workplace setting and situation observed by the researcher is similar to the types of settings and situations students are likely to encounter after graduation (or during an internship or course involving access to a workplace setting). If not, would it be helpful to instruct students in the workplace practices reported in the article? With this type of scrutiny and analysis, instructors will be more likely to instruct students in practices reported carefully and thoroughly in research reports and which are reasonably similar to those that the students are likely to encounter during or after the course.

Identifying Patterns in Workplace Practice Across Multiple Research Reports

Another strategy instructors can use is to include in their pedagogy just those workplace practices reported widely in the literature. By identifying patterns across research reports of particular workplace practices being effective or ineffective in fulfilling rhetorical or social goals, instructors can make a reasonable judgment whether it is helpful to instruct students in those practices. While it seems risky to accept, without question, a particular practice, concept, or model on the basis of what one researcher discovers in one or even a few studies,[5] it seems appropriate to teach a practice, concept, or model that has been discovered in a number of qualitative studies conducted by different researchers in a variety of workplace settings (and determined to be effective after careful data analysis in those studies).

An example is the practice of collaboration. Now that a number of researchers have observed the typical prevalence and potential effectiveness of collaboration in workplace settings (see, for example, Bosley, 1989; Couture & Rymer, 1989; Debs, 1986; and Ede & Lunsford, 1990), instructors can incorporate into their course designs instruction in collaboration, although this instruction should include, as well, student critiquing of specific strategies of collaboration. Similarly, since another frequent pattern reported in qualitative research studies is that of social interactions aiding professionals throughout the composing process (see, for example, Bocchi, 1991; Kleimann, 1989; Paradis, Dobrin, & Miller, 1985; Selzer, 1983; and Spilka, 1988a, 1990b), professional writing instructors need not hesitate to inform students that frequent interactions throughout the composing process can be a useful strategy of social context research and social analysis, accommodation, and innovation, or to require students to interact throughout the composing process of a particular document with such people as those with special knowledge about the problem or topic, those with special power in that rhetorical situation, and future users of the document. By identifying common patterns in a large body of qualitative research focusing on "the social perspective" (see Faigley, 1985), professional writing specialists can be reasonably certain that introducing these patterns to student writers has the potential to lead to improved practice, and improved ability or opportunity to critique that practice, in whatever workplace culture they encounter in the future.

How might researchers design future qualitative studies that address pedagogical aims of professional writing?

Traditionally, research in academia has aimed, primarily, at responding to theoretical exigencies, such as a problem posed by conflicting theoretical perspectives that research can attempt to resolve, or a gap in knowledge that research can attempt to fill. Doctoral programs certainly encourage new researchers to focus on theoretical problems and to pay less attention to meeting practical or pedagogical needs. The larger discourse community of professional writing specialists exerts the same sort of pressure on postdoctoral researchers of workplace writing. Beyond the political pressure, close attention to theory in research questions, design, and choice of methodology remains necessary to sustain and strengthen further the integrity of this specialty's intellectual inquiry.

Yet, as Miller (1989) argues, the need is also great to find ways to use research as a means of strengthening and ensuring the continued integrity of professional writing pedagogy. To move closer toward this goal, future research in professional writing needs to respond more strongly to needs in pedagogy, while continuing, as well, to respond strongly to needs in theory.

Achieving this goal promises to be a challenge. Major empirically based obstacles make it difficult to detect patterns across current qualitative studies on workplace writing, which, in turn, can discourage professional writing specialists from translating recent research findings into reliable pedagogical strategies. Qualitative researchers have developed different research designs, selected different methodology, and relied on different techniques for data analysis and evaluation. In addition, researchers have studied different populations (for example, engineers, other scientists, managers, nurses, social workers, government bureaucrats, technical writers) situated in different types of organizations (small companies versus corporations; public agencies versus private firms) that are characterized by different types of rhetorical and social configurations. For example, one researcher interested in studying the impact of conflict on composing behavior might choose to conduct a single case study in one division of a large corporation for one year, while another researcher interested in the same issue might choose to conduct multiple case studies in several government bureaus for three years. Tracing reliable patterns across studies with such disparate research designs is certainly difficult. Theoretical pressures also discourage generalizing across qualitative studies of writing in the workplace (for example, see Bouldin and Odell, this volume).

However, despite the diversity in empirical approaches and theoretical constraints, professional writing specialists, both in academia and in the workplace, need to find better ways to identify which workplace practices reported in the literature are likely to be effective or ineffective in certain rhetorical or social situations or in certain types of workplace settings. Such distinctions aid the dual purposes of building on theoretical knowledge and establishing a set of reliable pedagogical tools that can prepare novice writers better for future communication challenges in the workplace. Toward this end, professional writing specialists need to work in greater harmony while planning, conducting, and analyzing their studies. In this section, I will focus on how specialists might design their studies differently, in ways helpful for responding to pedagogical needs in professional writing but without diminishing the strength of these studies' theoretical foundations. Throughout this section, readers should keep in mind political, economic, and other practical constraints that might impair significant progress toward the goal of unifying researchers' efforts (see, for example, Berlin, 1988), as well as possible strategies for overcoming these constraints (such as making it more possible for both academia and industry to support these types of research efforts). Although this section does not discuss these constraints, nor ways to overcome them, I hope professional writing specialists will be discussing these concerns in the future.

More Attempts to Build on Existing Research

Since qualitative research of workplace writing is relatively recent, it is natural that, for the most part, researchers have been thinking and designing their studies independently, to the point at which their studies have little or no connection with others just completed or being conducted concurrently with their own. To date, efforts to build on knowledge gained from other qualitative studies have been minimal. To increase the validity of qualitative research of this type and to strengthen efforts to detect reliable rhetorical and social patterns across studies, more research is needed that builds on research findings recently discovered in completed studies. If most qualitative researchers continue to operate independently to the point of ignoring knowledge already gained or new claims emerging from completed studies, attempts to progress further in professional writing theory will be weakened, as will attempts to seek valid patterns to translate into effective strategies for professional writing practice and pedagogy.

More Longitudinal Studies

To broaden knowledge of the reciprocal relationship between the composing process and social contexts, over time, thereby increasing the validity of rhetorical and social patterns observed, researchers need to broaden the scope of what has become the typical design of qualitative studies of workplace writing. Most recent studies of this type have involved observing the evolution of a rhetorical situation for just a year. Yet, many workplace problems are not resolved within a year; many require negotiations over several years or more. Similarly, many social goals are fulfilled only after years of conflict resolution and social adjustment. Devoting just a year to this type of study might limit observations to just part of the composing process, or to just part of a larger rhetorical and social process. For those interested in observing the response of a culture (including the target audience) to composing process decisions and behavior, longitudinal studies seem especially important. To detect reliable and complete patterns of how social contexts influence composing process decisions and behavior (social accommodation), it might be important to trace a rhetorical situation to the point at which a workplace problem is resolved or composing processes are completed. Similarly, to detect reliable and complete patterns of composing process decisions and behavior influencing social contexts (social innovation), it might be necessary to devote several years or more to tracing the impact on a culture of social interactions and documents that, collectively, aim to effect needed social change in an organizational culture.

Also, since workplace cultures often change, sometimes dramatically, over time, observations of what occurs in that culture during just one year might provide a false impression of those rhetorical and social practices considered the "norm" and of those practices considered innovations. Longitudinal studies can enable researchers to detect whether patterns observed in the early stages of the project resemble those patterns observed later on, thereby strengthening the validity of pattern identification and description during data analysis at the study's completion.

More Large-Scale, Collaborative Studies Across Multiple Cultures

To date, most qualitative studies of writing in the workplace have been relatively small in scale, which aids in detailed, in-depth observation and analysis of rhetorical and social behavior. Most studies are conducted by a single investigator, who is solely responsible for analyzing and interpreting data; also, most of these studies focus on communication within a single case situated in a single culture.

These types of studies, although valuable in many respects, tend to limit the extent to which researchers are able to detect valid rhetorical and social patterns related to a rhetorical situation in the workplace. By focusing most or all observations on a single culture, researchers of these studies tend to ignore, or find it difficult to observe, collaborations taking place between all participants of a rhetorical situation, including those situated externally to the observed culture, and the response to composing process decisions and behavior on the part of any audience members situated outside the observed culture. Researchers of these studies also tend to observe just those documents and social interactions initated by the culture being observed and to ignore documents and social interactions initiated by other cultures involved in the rhetorical situation. Data collection efforts in these studies also tend to suffer from a single investigator attempting to observe all social interactions, new developments, and cultural change in a case.

More large-scale qualitative research projects are needed to enable fuller observation of complex rhetorical situations involving collaboration between rhetorical participants in multiple cultures and communication with a multiple audience situated in multiple cultures. Ideally, multiple investigators would collaborate on such large-scale projects.

More Cooperation Between Researchers

Finally, the profession needs increased cooperation between more researchers in its attempts to strengthen the design and methodology of qualitative studies of workplace writing, to improve data collection and analysis techniques, and to reach a greater consensus as to acceptable ways of reporting research data. Although this anthology joins an ongoing debate in the profession about these needs and ways to fulfill them, it would be ideal if a single, regular forum for this type of debate were established for professional writing specialists. Cooperation between professional writing researchers is a critical prerequisite to progress in translating research results into improved pedagogy, which, arguably, is a critical prerequisite to continued growth in this specialty.

Clearly, this chapter calls for a deliberate effort among researchers of workplace writing, who need to consider modifying previous approaches to research design to respond not just to theoretical needs, but also to those in the pedagogy of professional writing. Already, qualitative research of workplace writing has contributed greatly to the increasing maturity of professional writing, especially to its theoretical growth. An important next step is for this research to contribute, as well, to the maturity of both the practice and pedagogy of professional writing. Second, cooperation is needed between academia and the workplace so progress can be made in identifying common goals and then strategies for fulfilling those goals. Although professional writing specialists in academia can take measures now to ensure continued influence on workplace practice, at some point, representatives of academia and the workplace will need to work together to ensure that they continue operating as mutual constraints and, more importantly, that they find ways to depend more significantly on one another while striving to fulfill shared goals. In the meantime, professional writing specialists in academia will need to make careful judgments in deciding which workplace practices to include in their pedagogy and in deciding ways in which they might train student writers in both social accommodation and innovation to prepare them well to handle the challenges of communicating effectively within and across social contexts in future workplace settings and situations.

Acknowledgments

I thank Barbara Mirel and James E. Porter for commenting on earlier drafts of this chapter.

Notes

1. William Karis (1991) discusses the use of the word "bridge" in this code, contrasting it with the more common perception of technical communicators as collaborators in the making of knowledge in nonacademic settings.

2. In this chapter, "professional writing" refers to composing processes and products aimed at resolving workplace problems or fulfilling workplace goals, and "professional writing specialists" refers to rhetoricians focusing their empirical, theoretical, or pedagogical inquiries on those workplace composing processes and products.

3. Two notable exceptions to this trend are studies conducted by Dautermann and Paré (reported in Part One of this volume), who both focus on the use of communication as a means of effecting change in a community.

4. Although Couture (1991) predicts that training students in critiquing and initiating changes in workplace practice will be the major development in professional writing pedagogy in the 1990s, specialists in academia have made just initial steps toward altering pedagogy to accommodate this type of instruction.

5. It seems less risky, however, to instruct students in those patterns of workplace practice identified within large-scale, multiple case studies, such as within Ede and Lunsford's longitudinal, multimodal study of collaboration (1990).

On Theory, Practice, and Method | Toward a Heuristic Research Methodology for Professional Writing

This chapter begins by reviewing an old argument in professional writing—the debate about the authority of "theory" versus that of "practice"—and moves to consider what that argument has to do with researchers' notions of "methodology." What does the theory/practice dispute have to do with methodology? We believe that this longstanding binary has been maintained by the way workplace research is typically reported. We believe that however workplace researchers actually conduct their work—however they think about it, practice it, or talk about it at conferences—the way that research typically gets written up indicates the continuing influence of a foundational approach to methodology: that is, a view that sees methodology as a static and conventional set of strategies (even when "socially constructed") for observing practice and thereby generating "knowledge" about practice. Such a view is a way of investing methodology with a status similar to theory; both are given a privileged place relative to practice. Just as theory often purports to "explain" practice, methodology is presumed to allow a privileged observation of practice.

Our position is that the concepts "theory," "practice," and "methodology" as used in professional writing represent different types of socially constructed argumentative warrants. As such, they should be seen as heuristic rather than foundational in nature and therefore as dynamic and negotiable. To note that these concepts are socially constructed is hardly novel or surprising. We suspect that most workplace researchers in professional writing, whether they do qualitative or quantitative studies, will even agree in the abstract. However, the implications of this view for researchers' methodologies may be more controversial. This view leads to the conclusion that research methodology should not be something we apply or select so much as something we *design out of particular situations and then argue for* in our studies. This notion sees methodology as heuristic rather than determining: In this view, methodology intersects with and is perhaps changed by practice; it is more than simply a means of "reporting on" practice.

In this chapter, we start by critiquing the theory-practice binary as it operates in professional writing research, moving toward a notion of research as *praxis*. (Not to be confused with "practice," *praxis* refers to a type of conduct that negotiates between positions rather than grounding itself in any particular position.) We then call upon discussions of the research process as considered in methodology texts, working toward a notion of research methodology as heuristic, a notion we recommend as a more useful and flexible model for professional writing research.

Reconfiguring Theory/Practice as *Praxis*

A Critique of the Theory-Practice Binary

The theory-practice debate arises from the search for authority in professional writing. The cartoon version of this debate pits the working technical writer (who thinks that academics are theoretical people who are out of touch with the "real world" and who cannot program their VCRs) against the academic professional writing teacher (who sees working professionals as people who have no time to read, think, or reflect and who are more interested in what they are doing than in why).

Obviously, these caricatures represent the extremes of the binary. Yet the debate certainly was once significant. In 1979, Miller argued that teachers should develop that facet of technical writing that allies it with the humanities, focusing on "the reasons and values which underlie the rhetoric of technical writing" (Miller, 1979, p. 617). Tebeaux (1980) responded by saying that "the point of view of the business and industrial world of which the student will become a part is the only criterion which should be used to plan and teach [technical writing]. . . . The requirements of the real world and the departments whose students take the course should determine what is taught" (pp. 823, 824; see also Harris, 1980).

Has the issue died since 1980, the time of the Miller-Harris-Tebeaux debate? We think not. As recently as 1989, Miller has said that "technical writing has sought a basis in . . . nonacademic practices. . . . We ought not . . . simply redesign our courses and curricula to replicate existing practices" (pp. 17, 23). Knoblauch, in a 1989 article, argued that the workplace is the locus of expertise.

But perhaps most workplace researchers in professional writing have embraced the position that theory and practice interrelate: Both have a role to play. But the question still remains, a role to play in what? And how? The obvious and temptingly simple answer would be for some moderator to announce that theory and practice are both important, so obviously our curricula and research agenda should be guided by both. This resolution seems reasonable, except that depending on how this compromise is effected, it can insidiously maintain the binary. We can assign value to both but still situate them in separate camps, two sources of authority in two different places: Yes, theory is important and theory is the job of the university; and yes, practice is important, and we find out what practice is by observing writing in the workplace. Today, we'll have a class on theory, perhaps a discussion of Kinneavy's *Theory of Discourse*. Tomorrow we'll have a field trip to the workplace. Such compartmentalization can work to maintain theory and practice as separate activities: theory belonging to the realm of the academic, the university; practice to the realm of the nonacademic, the workplace (see Miller, 1989).

One way we see this binary at work in reports of workplace studies is in the tendency for theory to be treated mainly in the review of literature section (and perhaps the discussion/conclusion), but rarely as part of methodology or data analysis. Researchers might well *say* that theory and practice are both important, and even treat both seriously, yet compartmentalize theory and practice in the traditional sections of the research report and never allow them to interconnect, and use notions of theory and practice in particular ways that valorize theory (and method, as a kind of conventionalized theory)—sort of a separate-but-equal principle for segregating theory and practice.

The Dangers of Privileging Theory or Practice

Is there a general understanding about what is meant when we refer to theory and practice? Not really, though we would not go so far as to say that the terms have no meaning. Rather, as they are used in professional writing research, the terms have approximate and unstable meanings, often established in one term through reference to the other. In other words, they are usually opposites. "Theory" seems to refer to any general and/or abstract design, system, model, belief, or principle used to explain, interpret, prescribe, or critique practice. As applied to research, theory refers to the critical and methodological presuppositions one brings to a setting. It refers as well to a critical stance, an interpretive position. (Thus, we view research methodologies as theories.) "Writing practice" seems to refer to any particular activity of composing at a specific moment in time—that is, a local and specific instance of writing (for example, workplace writing). Our study of a developing documentation writer (to be discussed later) indicates that theory and practice each has its own particular enabling power and contribution to understanding. At the same time, each alone has its inadequacies, gaps, and limits, which we need to identify as far as that is possible.

Theory alone, by its very nature as abstraction, as generalization, cannot account completely for the situational, the specific instance of practice. That is not to dismiss theory, but simply to say that it ought not be perceived as all-determining or all-explaining.

Writers of technical instructions know this lesson well. Writing technical instructions is challenging because it is often difficult to address the needs of all users. The situatedness of a technology strongly influences how that technology is to be used and, therefore, how we write instructions for it (see Doheny-Farina, 1991a). An example will serve to illustrate: One of our graduate students at Purdue University wrote and then "tested" a piece of computer documentation for teaching undergraduates to use the Apple Scanner in one of the computer labs. (User testing is a research methodology developed to allow documentation writers to become acquainted with the situations of actual users.) The difficulty the writer encountered was that the scanner behaved differently depending on the computer it was connected to and the image the student was attempting to scan (for example, photographs behaved one way, simple line drawings another). Since he was writing the documentation for a particular computer lab, he knew what machine the scanner would be connected to. But he could not possibly guess what type of graphic the student would bring to the tutorial. The writer could not produce lockstep, foolproof instructions, because he could not control an important variable of the situation. The writer was then faced with a dilemma: How does he determine who the typical user will be? Does he write the documentation addressing a number of different likely scenarios, or an imagined generic scenario? User testing helped the writer decide what some likely practices might be, but user testing alone did not provide a definitive answer. In some sense, this example is true of all writing situations, because the writer can never know precisely what the reader will bring to the communication setting. Here is the limit of theory.

A number of researchers from a variety of fields, including professional writing, have noticed the dominant tendency in academic scholarship to privilege theory (often portrayed as "structure" or "method") over practice and have begun to challenge this presumed superiority, arguing for the significance of practice. Bourdieu's analysis (1977) of the theory-practice dynamic represents his break from what he refers to as the "positionality of the objectivist stance" he associates with traditional social science research. Bourdieu points out that to understand an activity, such as the gift-giving ritual of Kabyle culture, one must understand the timing of that activity. The static structuralist paradigm does not account for the timing, the situatedness of the ritual, what rhetoric terms *kairos* (see Phelps, 1988, pp. 230–231; Kinneavy, 1986). Theory, in this instance understood to be an all-encompassing structure or framework of understanding, does not account for the "positionality" of the ritual.

Suchman (1987) explores the relationship between plans (which function as theory or structure) and the situated actions of the users of a copying machine. She notes that "European navigators" (her analogy for the Western rationalist) tend to view plans as abstract and prior structures, as determining or at least guiding behavior. Her observations of office workers learning to use new copying machines indicate that such users proceed more like "Trukese navigators": They know where they want to go, but they do not have any prior navigational plan for getting there. They proceed in ad hoc fashion, letting the unfolding events of the situation (rather than the preconceived plan) determine what they will do next. The problem, according to Suchman, is that researchers seldom distinguish between the plan (as intention) and the explanatory structure. Her point is that as researchers, we must begin to understand structure as "an emergent product of situated action, rather than its foundation" (p. 67).

What these and other researchers are recognizing is that theory, in the common and various ways it is perceived and employed, is by itself inadequate to account for the particular, what we know as practice. Human action is situated action, according to Suchman. And that represents the limit of theory.

The practice warrant is a common one resting on the assumption that we can actually observe what writers do. Of course, most researchers recognize that there is no such thing as pure, unadulterated observation. Observation always proceeds with some hypothesis in mind, however well- or ill-formed it may be. The observer brings to the observing situation a hypothesis, tools for observation, and critical apparatuses, as well as prejudices and misconceptions of various sorts. These factors comprise a conceptual grid, allowing certain elements to be observed, while (few would deny) concealing other elements. This entire set of factors falls under the heading "theory."

The limits of practice pertain to generalizability and significance. How can we move from the particular instance to an understanding of what the instance is? Unless we do multiple observations, there is no guarantee that what we have observed is typical. But even multiple observations do not tell us whether the writing practices we are observing are effective or desirable. As Miller (1989) and others have pointed out, the limitation of the practice warrant is the difficulty of arguing the *should* from the *is*. To develop criteria, we need to supplement the practice argument with evidence from some other sphere. Our study of the developing documentation writer demonstrates that we always apply some kind of rhetorical orientation or critical judgment; we always observe practice through the lens of some kind of rhetorical theory, whether we are conscious of it or not.

Working Toward *Praxis*

The theory/practice division is a fictional construct, but nonetheless has quite real effects. It leads "practical people" to neglect or underestimate discussions of ideology or theory as too abstract, too academic, too political, and as neither necessary nor desirable in the workplace. It leads "theoretical people" to privilege lofty, abstract, and (usually) static principles without sufficient regard for their dynamic situatedness.

Our position is that the binary must be acknowledged, as Miller (1989) and Phelps (1988) have done. Both Miller and Phelps recognize the limitations of theory alone and practice alone and lay the groundwork for a dynamic *praxis* that recognizes the necessary contribution of each.

Phelps (1988) warns against assigning theory the status of "truth" or "scientific knowledge." Seeing theory in such terms can lead to two simplistic responses: the uncritical "naive assimilation" of theory, or its rejection as irrelevant or impractical. Phelps urges us to see theory "in terms of its capacity to redescribe . . . experience and point to new ways of being and doing" (p. 229). Within this scheme, theory does not function as a validating ground. Rather, it is an alternate "story" (p. 230), and perhaps an ideal story, against which we juxtapose other stories, for instance the stories of specific practices. Theory does not function, then, to explain practice, or to reveal the hidden elements of practice. Rather, in Phelps's words, "theory is a text to be mapped onto experience" (p. 235). The contribution of practice to theory, according to Phelps, is that practice "disciplines theory by demonstrating its limits, destroying its absolutist pretensions to be the sole foundation and ultimate reality on which practice depends. . . . Theory . . . is for composition praxis an enabling fiction" (p. 239) that assists us in organizing practice(s) in terms other than those of that specific practice.

While Phelps notes the value of both theory and practice, for her they are still separate spheres. Miller tries to bridge the binary by identifying *praxis* as a middle ground between theory and practice: *Praxis* is a higher form of practice, an "informed or conscious practice." For Miller, *praxis* is something more than a simple addition of or compromise between theory and practice; it represents a new kind of critical positioning. It is a practice conscious of itself that calls upon "prudential reasoning" (see Miller, 1989, p. 22) for the sake not only of production but for "right conduct" as well. It is informed and politically conscious action.

Praxis is a "practical rhetoric," focused on local writing activities (practice), informed by as well as informing general principles (theory), and calling upon "prudential reasoning." *Praxis* recognizes the "inseparable relation between reflection and action" (see Phelps, 1988, on Freire, p. 211; Schon, 1983, on professional action as reflection-in-action). As it applies to research activity, *praxis* refers to a kind of triangulation: not the kind by which you check results by using a variety of empirical or theoretical methods, or by collecting data through a variety of media, but a conceptual one that leads to research that privileges neither the theoretical foundation nor the observed practice. It is a research perspective willing to critique both theory and practice by placing both in dialectical tension, which can then allow either to change.

The judgment that enables this dynamic is referred to as "practical judgment," that is, *phronesis* (sometimes translated as "prudence"). According to Garver, this kind of reasoning recognizes the "inferential relation between rules and cases, precepts and examples" (1987, p. 12). It inserts itself into that gap "between apprehending a rule [*episteme*] and applying it [*techne*]" (p. 16). Prudence "requires that the writer [or researcher, we would say] find some middle ground between too much universality—the superfluous . . . proclamation of moralizing principles—and too much particularity" (p. 39). The art here requires a fine, balancing judgment that is inescapable and unavoidable (see Phelps, 1988, p. 228).

Case Study of a Developing Documentation Writer

We see the need for theory and practice to work interactively, not separately. But what would such a *praxis* look like? Floreak's description of his own composing process (1989) provides an example of the professional writer engaged in "reflective action" (or *praxis*) during composing. In his discussion of his work on "Project First Steps," Floreak intertwines theory and practice, not treating them in separate compartments but discussing his project from a kind of theory-in-practice perspective. He calls upon theories of audience and usability methods for assistance and advice, but his commitment is to "translating" this theory in terms of the situation out of which he writes.

Our own study of a developing documentation writer also illustrates the ways in which theory and practice become intertwined and interdependent. In 1989–1990, we conducted a longitudinal case study of a developing professional writer, who wrote, revised, tested, and then revised again a tutorial for learning Aldus PageMaker 3.01 (for details of this study, see Porter & Sullivan, in press; Sullivan & Porter, 1990a; Sullivan & Porter, 1990b). We focused particularly on how the writer ("Max") responded to the five usability tests he ran, looking at how he interacted with his users and how he revised his document based on user input. We observed that the writer's rhetorical orientation—that is, his implicit theory of rhetoric, in this specific case, a theory about how computer documentation is supposed to work—served as a terministic screen influencing what he saw the users doing and how he responded to user input.

Max tended to interpret user response in terms of the theoretical model he implicitly believed: "Max's view of documentation and his use of the user test information reflected his systems orientation and his bias toward content and correctness criteria" (Sullivan & Porter, 1990a, p. 34). Max's theory in this case is a conventional attitude that content is what counts most in writing and that content is something separate from and prior to writing. "Writing," to Max, is a means of packaging content, for which reason it may be important. But Max does not have anything like a social constructionist notion of writing. To Max, writing does not influence or interact with "content"; it simply transmits it. In other words, Max holds to an information transfer model (see Driskill, 1989, pp. 127–128). In addition, Max holds to values about computer documentation that arise from what we term an engineering "systems orientation": "Good documentation is comprehensive, covering all the necessary material and providing a complete and accurate description of a procedure. Users must be told everything to do; [Max's] tutorial provides lock-step directions for performing the tasks and either the users get it 'right' or they get it 'wrong' " (Sullivan & Porter, 1990a, p. 34).

We concluded from our study that Max's implicit communication theory in concert with his systems values led to his responding to user comments in certain predictable ways. For example, when users encountered problems, Max's answer typically was either to add clarifying information to existing sections or to fix unclear sentences. He did not regard possible global changes in system structure or document design, because these were "givens" in his orientation. His allegiance to the system (as given) and to the document superseded his commitment to users.

Max's situation is by no means uncommon in professional writing: he holds to an implicit theory that serves as an interpretive screen, so he responds only to certain types of user input, and he carefully classifies that input according to his rhetorical model, his notion of how instructional text works. We can diagnose this tactic from two perspectives: We could say that Max was not "attuned" enough to practice (see Phelps, 1988, pp. 220–

223, on "attunement"), not sensitive enough to his data, to his observations of users; we could also say that he was not conscious enough of his own theory. We would say that he expressed no awareness of it at all—it was simply a given of the setting.

We see two ways the writer in this situation could work out of the difficulty. Max's blind spot was that he viewed practice (in this case, what users actually did with his tutorial) as simply providing information, data. The more productive use of practice here would have been to see it as dialectically challenging theory, to regard the data of the user test as resistant to the dominant assumptions Max was bringing to the setting (see de Certeau, 1984, on the resistant nature of practice). The other way Max might have helped himself is by calling upon multiple theories. To admit that there are multiple theories is, in the first instance, to notice the inadequacy of Theory (with a capital *T*) conceived as a single and universal unifying structure.

The important point our study raises is that theory is not something "belonging to" the workplace observers and then "transported to" workplace practice (which "belongs to" the workplace writer being observed). Rather, theory is itself a type of practice and always already involved in the practices of both the researcher and writer being studied. From the other side, practice cannot be atheoretical, though it can perhaps be unconscious of its theory. In short, the binary is breachable.

Research Methodology as *Praxis*

All manner of research and scholarship deploys methodology. Given our discussion of theory and practice, we now ask how critically researchers in professional writing view their methodologies. Do they accept and apply precut methods to their research? Do they critique and revise methods as they apply/make them? Do they develop new methods or mix methods? Most reports of workplace research do not help us decide, because they tend to conventionalize the reports, asking us to think that they selected and applied methods appropriate for the study. They use the conventional rules of methodology as criteria against which they argue for the quality of their research design rather than by invoking the workplace setting (in the case of naturalistic field studies) or problematizing the vocabulary of the researchers (in the case of surveys and interviews).

We contend that in workplace studies methodologies are of necessity a *praxis*, though write-ups of such studies sometimes mask the heuristic nature of researchers' methods-in-practice. This tactic could be interpreted as a privileging of theory over practice, because we suggest here that methodology has theoretical dimensions. Treating methodology as a set of antiseptically applied rules governing the collection of practice strips the knowledge-making ("-ology") possibilities out of method.

Our aims in this section are to catalog some conventional approaches to method in workplace studies, as they are discussed and promulgated in methodology texts, and to argue that viewing research methodology as *praxis* requires methodology to function in a middle ground between theory and practice, as a heuristic set of filters (and not a static set either) for both theory and practice.

Conventional Approaches to the Practice of Research

Method-Driven Research

One common strategy for writing up research in professional communication is to proceed by assuming that the researcher has applied a standard methodology (for example, ethnography) to a workplace setting, with the aim being to understand workplace writing practice. The tactic is common and accepted, because it rests on two strategies we trust implicitly: a tried-and-true method, and the actual observation of a behavior. The researcher applies a given method to a new workplace setting to generate "findings," which the observer might use to advance theory, that is, to build new models or theories, challenge old models/theories, and/or establish pedagogy (see figure 16.1).

That this attitude toward research persists in professional writing research is indicated in a recent volume on research in business communication edited by Campbell, Housel, and Locker (1988), which offers advice that seems to encourage this formulaic approach, with a few exceptions. The collection's organization (several process-of-research chapters followed by discussions of samples, surveys, experimental design, analysis, field research, historical research, and so on) and discussion of research issues suggest the view that method is a matter of selection and application.

The implicit warrants in such an approach are that methods are given procedures, well-established and trustworthy bases for observing practice, and that properly applying method to practice can help us verify or generate models and theories. Models and theories are always imperfect, but contin-

Figure 16.1. Method-Driven Research

ued observation of practice can help them move to a greater level of reliability. The method–driven tactic is often what apprentice researchers perceive
as the proper use of methodology. They perceive the conventions as given,
by teachers or textbooks, and their task is to find a new application for a
tried-and-true method.

Problem-Driven Research: Practice

Most discussions of methodology of course do not support a method-
driven approach, arguing instead that new researchers should start with
topics and questions and let the inquiry into the topic guide the choice of
method (see Kothenbeutel, 1988; Miles & Huberman, 1984; Yin, 1989). The
researcher starts by noticing a problem or question in workplace practice or
theory, selects the method appropriate for inquiry into that question, and
then applies the method to practice to verify old theory or to generate new
theory (see figure 16.2).

Within this tactic, arguments about methodology typically focus on
which method yields a better answer to particular questions, still focusing
on "method" as a static construct that one applies to a setting in order to
reveal its principles of operation. They do not see method as something that
is shaped continuously by the practice of research or by the situation.

Problem-Driven Research: Theory

The privileging of theory uses the researcher's (as opposed to the workplace's) problem or question to drive the study. (We see this tactic as less
common in workplace studies than in general composition research.) The
researcher (1) begins with a general statement functioning as a starting point
or model (for example, "All writing promotes the ideology of the writer
against the ideology of the audience," a theoretical warrant, or "Writing has
stages but is recursive," a model-driven assertion); (2) from such assertions
develops a problem statement that could drive a research project; (3) selects
a method or methods that may yield appropriate solutions; and (4) applies
that method or methods to practice in order to reveal the essence of a
given practice (see figure 16.3). Such an approach sometimes has as its aim
changing the model or theory; often the aim is exploring and understanding

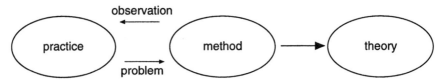

Figure 16.2. Problem-Driven Research (Practice)

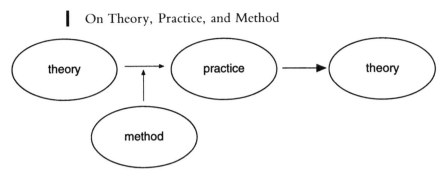

Figure 16.3. Problem-Driven Research (Theory)

something heretofore hidden in the practice. Flower, in her study of "writer-based" and "reader-based" prose (1979), took her cognitive-process model (a theory) and protocol analysis (a method) and used them to establish criteria through which to view reports.

Problematized Research Methods

Practitioners of the three methods discussed above may well appreciate the importance of theory, practice, and method. They may even, for instance, notice the ways in which practice can influence changes in methodology. They may accept that research methods are "socially constructed." Most researchers certainly accept that the research observer "brings" theory to the workplace setting. And yet researchers can hold these views and still not practice research as *praxis*, at least not in the sense we are describing. The key feature of *praxis* is the move to problematize method, part of which requires overthrowing the compartmentalization of theory, practice, and method.

"Method" needs to be problematized from at least two perspectives, one of methodological choice and one of the judgment of methodological quality. Earlier we challenged the conventional wisdom about choice when we asserted that too easy and unreflective a reliance on the stability of a method holds the danger of foundationalism; relegating method to choice fails to recognize that methodological rules are socially constructed as well as situationally adjusted as they are invoked. Eisner and Peshkin (1990) detail how choice of method can mask a complex set of decisions, at times even from the researcher, when they discuss how researchers use "problem-driven" to move past "method-driven" research design:

> One way . . . is to remind the skeptical or puzzled that the problem itself should be used to identify methods one knows how to use. Once the problem has been adequately conceptualized, the question or method can be easily answered. While such advice is comforting, it is too simple. First, what constitutes a

problem is not independent of the methods one knows how to use. Few of us seek problems we have no skill in addressing. What we know how to do is what we usually try to do. But the problem is still more complex. The methods into which we have been socialized provide powerful filters through which we view the world. . . . The complexities do not stop here. Being socialized into a method also means being socialized into a set of norms that define acceptable scholarship. (p. 9)

Eisner and Peshkin's discussion of "socialization into method" raises the second perspective on problematizing method, the question of methodological quality, which is often reduced to concepts such as rigor. Rigor is discussed frequently in disputes between qualitative and quantitative approaches to empirical research. Qualitative research can achieve rigor through its dense and detailed scrutiny of one or more cases, while quantitative research can achieve its rigor through careful application of measures and statistical checks. When the two methods try to merge their studies of a problem, theory, or issue, they stumble over the problem of how to connect such disparate activities. Eisner and Peshkin identify four stances: (1) that there are no differences between qualitative and "conventional" research (by which they mean experimental research, surveys, and other investigations aiming to uncover principles and trends they might generalize to explain or predict the behavior of a population), because they both are liable for the same criteria; (2) that conventional and qualitative methods complement each other, with each type suitable for a type of question; (3) that qualitative research is "soft" and less trustworthy than conventional research, and therefore can be used only for exploratory work; and (4) that conventional methods are suspect because they try to apply a natural science paradigm to human behavior. Eisner and Peshkin use variant notions of "rigor" to cooperate, or they deny the possibility of cooperation. The more completely some external sense of rigor (that is, drawn from the conventions of other disciplines) is imported into workplace research, the less likely workplace research is to acknowledge the ways in which the situation of the research affects the researcher's ability to invoke a textbook notion of "rigorous" method.

We find both perspectives—methodological choice and the judgment of methodological quality—important to research methodology for professional writing, particularly when considered in light of the theory-practice dispute. Can method be selected before the designation of a problem? Does method shape the problem or is it merely chosen after the designation of a problem? Are various types of methods, notably qualitative and quantitative (or conventional) methods, complementary or incompatible? Ought workplace research meet the textbook guidelines for rigorous application of method, or ought it develop arguments for the methodology of each study?

Multimodality as a Partial Answer

One way workplace research can problematize method usefully is by drawing on the notions of multimodality that Lauer has promoted in rhetoric and composition. Lauer and Asher (1988) argue for the advantage of multimodal methodologies for composition research (they refer to historical, rhetorical, and empirical), showing that multimodality is necessary for addressing the complex problems composition studies address. Their view is that the various methodologies are brought together and used to aid in a rhetorical inquiry; when they are used, the methods are imported and applied (see figure 16.4). They further hold that inside empirical research, qualitative and quantitative methods may also be used in harmony to complement each other. Though the researcher must stitch together the various methods needed to address the problem adequately, multimodal methods (Herrington, 1985 provides a good example of multimodality) require the researcher to do work that conforms to the norms of acceptable scholarship in several methodological camps.

In practice, multimodality may prove very difficult to achieve, particularly because some methodologies take the position that others are not appropriate (see Eisner and Peshkin's positions above), and it is difficult enough for a researcher to learn the conventions of a single methodology, much less several. Also, a danger of multimodality is that it introduces methodological complexity, the possible result of which could be overemphasis on the method to the exclusion of practice and theory, ultimately resulting in making methodology the police of practice.

Researchers relying on multimodality must take care to remember that methodology is also theory. How does research proceed when the very methods used are always open to scrutiny? Our answer is that methodology, in addition to becoming problematized and becoming an element of a study that must be argued for, can usefully become heuristic. We further think that by becoming aware of the theory-practice binary that operates inside methodology of research and scholarship, we can develop a set of methodologies for workplace studies that contribute creatively to workplace research.

Method as Explicitly Argued *Praxis*

Once we accept that the methods we normally choose to use provide powerful filters through which we view the world, we can adjust to a position of using those filters consciously. Our methodological concepts influence our perception (see Van Maanen, 1988); our task as researchers is

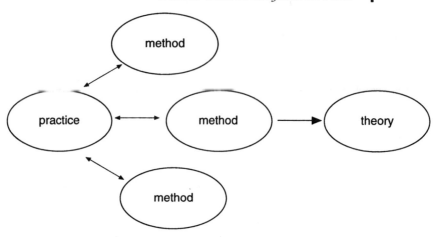

Figure 16.4. Problematized Method (Multimodality)

to be aware of that influence (as far as possible) and to use it heuristically to help shape our research. We think that most workplace researchers recognize this premise, at least in the abstract, and view it as that part of research that is "behind the scenes." Most researchers, however, still have not dared to articulate this premise as explicit *praxis*.

Multimodality, or methodological pluralism, can contribute, but it does not do so innocently. As Barone (1990) argues, "It is self deluding that claim for one's preference for systematic, analytical methods is beyond the realm of preference" (p. 361). He goes on to agree with Gouldner (1982) that "methodology is ideology" and argues that we cannot use rules to help us claim that we have uncovered nuggets of truth.

The power of methodology is in the boundaries and frameworks it invokes, and, yes, these boundaries are ideological and socially constituted (see Bruffee, 1986). However, what gives methods their knowledge-generating power is that they are community frameworks, constituted and agreed upon by researchers. We can accept these frameworks as given by the community or we can argue to the community that one or more particular frameworks, justifiably reshaped by this situation, provide helpful filters/ guides for this, and perhaps other, workplace research. Our preferred approach is the second, which we call methodology as *praxis* (see figure 16.5).

Both the "method first" and the "question/problem/theory first" approaches to research work from a select-and-then-apply-a-method approach to methodology. Typically, they do not explore how the question changes as differing methodologies embrace it, or how the method changes as the constraints of a particular research situation unfold. As workplace research-

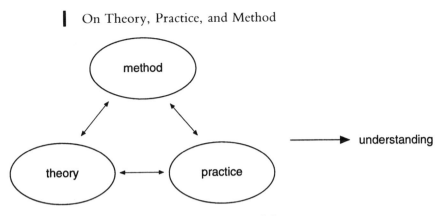

Figure 16.5. Problematized Method (Praxis)

ers attest, the situation exerts powerful constraints on the design of the research. For example, Huettman (1990) was unable to interview the audience for a consulting report because such action would have damaged the cooperation of the organization she was studying. In his study of legal influences on corporate composing practices, Porter (1990b) was able to report attorneys' viewpoints of cases only if he were careful not to identify the attorneys or their clients or write up the case in a way that would appear to assign blame or liability to any party involved. Dautermann (1991) had to emphasize the oral aspects of composing in her study of nurses' collaborative composing because so much of the composing in her eighteen-month study was oral in character. Simpson (1989) had to focus on revision because the most appropriate documentation for end-users was in revision when he worked for the computer book publisher. In all of these studies, the methodology (and in part the research questions) shifted as the situation affected the unfolding plan over time. We do not think this uncommon in ethnographic studies: Not only is it common, it is unavoidable. But researchers who do not acknowledge the impact of the situation and who do not use the heuristic quality of method to aid them in dealing with shifts over time run the risk of writing research reports that reaffirm the social norms of methodology, even when their own methods deviated from those norms in reasonable, defensible, even laudable ways. Methodology that is portrayed as a set of immutable principles, rather than as heuristic guidelines, masks the impact of the situation—of the practice—on the study in ways that could unconsciously reinscribe theory's dominance over practice. It seems to us that the real contribution of many workplace studies is to challenge the sanctities of method and theory and, yes, even practice. They need to acknowledge the fact that they are *praxis* in order to succeed.

If you see study of nonacademic writing as the activity of going "out there" and bringing information back to curriculum, you run the risk of accepting uncritically the methodologies associated with social sciences. You decide to do a survey, follow given survey methodology, and that methodology remains "pure." Research in this scenario is simply "information collection." The setting loses power to affect the theory or the method, the theory loses power to affect the method or the setting. If, rather, you see the activity as at least in part "constructing methodology," you become critical of methodology. You do not simply transport methodology, you adjust methodology to setting and the theory—and your explanation of this adjustment becomes a significant feature of your write-up of that study.

Conclusion

We have examined method, theory, and practice not to undermine their authority for professional writing research, but to consider the benefits and limitations of their authority. We suggest that none of these concepts is alone sufficient to develop or verify knowledge in professional communication research—or in any research field for that matter. Conceptual triangulation requires that we apply multiple concepts, not just retesting with a variety of methods but bringing different epistemologies (or different sorts of warrants) to bear on the same situations. We are calling this activity *praxis*, which requires balancing and juxtaposing warrants, bringing them into dialectic interaction.

To the extent that methodology is also theory, it becomes problematized and an element of a study that must be argued for in the reporting of the study. We further think that by becoming aware of the theory-practice binary that operates inside methodology of research and scholarship, we can develop a set of methodologies for workplace studies that creatively contributes to workplace research.

It may sound as though we are undermining the entire basis for any writing or rhetoric research, the very knowledge base of the discipline itself. We hope not. What we are trying to do is expose these terms as social constructs (which all argumentative warrants are) in the midst of an ongoing social process (that is, the development of a discipline) and award them a new status: as heuristic. This argument may undermine the basis of disciplinary knowledge as *episteme*, but in its place we offer "understanding," our suggestion being that "understanding" (we might perhaps call it "strategic knowledge") and not "knowledge" in the scientific sense should perhaps be the aim of a productive field like professional writing.

Our contentions, then, are these:

- We cannot just uncritically accept research methods as given to us in a "valid" form by the social sciences.

- We need to approach research as *praxis*, as a design activity involving the construction of a method worked out from the intersection of theory and situation, which leads not to knowledge (in the sense of total truth), but toward understanding, the basis for future rhetorical judgment.
- We need to acknowledge several points about methodology in workplace studies:
  1. Theory is already in the workplace (even if it is implicit, as it was in the Max study);
  2. Researchers bring theory to the workplace;
  3. Methodology is designed (not simply "selected") to suit a particular workplace setting.

We argue that researchers need to:

- develop more elastic notions of "case study," "ethnography," and so on, and adapt these methodologies to fit circumstances;
- be willing to discuss "divergences" (that is, points where their methodology departs from "socialized method");
- be willing to "reflect back on" the methodology, critique the methodology, and suggest changes. Conclusions might be those about the methodology as well as about the practice;
- be sensitive to the role of multiple theories in guiding researchers' and writers' activities and observations.

The question we raise here pertains to the identity of the researcher. Are you a theory person, a practice person, or a method person? The danger is leaning too much in any of these directions. To improve research, we have to learn to act with these perspectives—theory, practice, method—in dialectic tension.

| **Reflexive and Reflective Tensions** | Considering Research Methods from Writing-Related Fields |

I am an associate professor in a Department of English; I teach rhetoric and technical writing, and I conduct research in these areas. In this position, I have had some difficulty finding an appropriate label when "interfacing" with the rest of the world and the neighbors on the street in Florida where my parents live. My car bears a bumper sticker, "Support your local rhetorician"; no one mentions it. If I respond to the question "What do you do?" by answering, "I do technical communication," people ask how long I have worked for the phone company. The old standby "English teacher" evokes apologies for past errors in grammar. "Composition specialist" draws further discussion on newspapers and typesetting or furniture arrangement; "writing instructor" has been known to lead to a request to ghostwrite the listener's Great American Novel. Lately, I have been selectively trying out two new labels with some success: I answer with a straight face that I am a scientist studying languaging strategies or an artist who interprets what others believe.[1] Surprisingly, both play equally well in Pensacola.

Surprisingly, both play equally well in this book. A student of rhetoric and composition, using methods adapted from the social and human sciences to research writing as it is produced in the workplace, may be scientist, artist, or critic. When we write research, we create ourselves; one of our choices is what role we want to play.

As originally defined in discussions with the editor, the purpose of this chapter was to consider, for researchers in the field of writing, promising methods used in related fields such as organizational behavior, communication, sociology, and anthropology. But, as I reviewed the literature in other fields, a certain radicalism took hold. While I still intend to accomplish something like the purpose as originally set out, I also hope to show that current debates about research in other fields open up possibilities in developing our own methods of inquiry and can bring us to both a renewed confidence and perhaps a new caution in our own interpretive and critical stances.

The first part of this chapter, then, explores what relationships method holds with systems (or nonsystems) of research. At issue is not the definition of method, but an understanding of how the choice of method may lead to very different ends. An introduction to six specific methods from the social sciences that may prove useful to those researching writing in the workplace is presented in the second part of the chapter, along with general criteria to use in adapting methods from other fields.

Research Methods and Inquiry

What is research? For most, it is a search for knowledge, for understanding, for meaning—and, in some cases, it is a search for the ability to predict, and, thus, control. But that search can be conducted in a number of ways driven by philosophies, the events or phenomena being researched, and the context of the research. As Sullivan and Porter (this volume) argue, it is difficult to talk of method and theory separately. The methods of research—inquiry, observation, analysis, testing, and reporting—have a conserving effect. They are valued by specific communities, rather consistently, because they represent "system." Thus are we "disciplined."

Those who research writing in the workplace draw their inquiry paradigms (concepts, stances toward what is being observed, and methods; see Guba, 1990; Kuhn, 1977; and Toulmin, 1972) primarily from composition studies, education research, and rhetoric. The movement of composition studies from controlled empiricism—that is, from designs generally positivistic and often experimental, to naturalistic (primarily qualitative and sometimes truly ethnographic) studies—has been documented by Gere (1985) and Calkins (1985), among others. Calls for a rational system of research persist in composition journals through the 1980s. In an influential article advocating the term "inquiry paradigm" rather than "research for the field of composition," Emig explains that an inquiry paradigm "must be informed . . . by 1) a governing gaze; 2) an acknowledged, or at least conscious, set of assumptions, preferably connected with 3) a coherent theory or theories; 4) an allegiance to an explicit or at least a tacit intellectual tradition; and 5) an adequate methodology including an indigenous logic consonant with all the above" (1982, p. 65). In this view, research methods are only parts that must fit the whole of a particular system of inquiry. To make sense of the method, one must know the whole.

In attempting to identify existing paradigms, we find, however, that Emig's definition is an ideal, a construct. Competing paradigms coexist and overlap. In the social sciences, it is unlikely these paradigms will take a completed form. Currently, for example, composition studies can be categorized (and combined) into several possible paradigms or systematic approaches: cognitive, linguistic, social, or social-cognitive. Developmental studies that explore how a child acquires language may use all or any of those approaches, but a study founded on Vygotsky's work will differ in important ways from another owing to Piaget (for an example, see Bonk, 1990). One should note, in addition, that a researcher's ideology, philosophy, and "worldview" bear heavily on choices made in theory, method, and interpretation; thus, the way a phenomenologist does ethnography and reports on it can be quite different from the the way in which a symbolic interactionist or structuralist does it. Although these points of tension are challenged only infrequently as composition studies are being institutionalized, they have become foci for rich (and sometimes obstreperous) discussion in other fields. Consider, for example, the debates that have often reduced choice of research methods to battles between qualitative and quantitative (these continue, especially in education research). The positions are many: All research is qualitative (Eisner, 1981); qualitative and quantitative are complementary (Reichardt & Cook, 1979); qualitative methods must meet criteria of validity and reliability (Kantor, Kirby, & Goetz, 1981); the two do not fit together and will not (Smith & Heshusius, 1986; see Michel [1989] for a recent summary of many of these issues). Although critical to one's choice of research method as well as to the reporting of the research, these issues are not raised in key articles that offer guidelines for conducting qualitative research on writing in the workplace (see Doheny-Farina & Odell, 1985 and Halpern, 1988; Halpern does a more thorough job of indicating choices a researcher may make).

Because research on writing in the workplace is concerned with writers and writing in a definable social context (the organization), this research can also draw readily from the work of social scientists in anthropology, sociology, and communication. Each of these fields is concerned with a particular aspect or type of question about society. Sociology and anthropology have long traditions of inquiry that would be impossible to summarize effectively here; we can see, however, that each field has moved from deliberate attempts to create its own version of "the scientific method" to the creation and application of new methods as needed. Controversy occurs with the introduction of each new sampling technique, or statistical analysis, or survey response scale. With changes in method come changes in the questions that are asked; in other words, sometimes method drives theory. In each field, both theory and method are routinely and often hotly debated. In each field, competing paradigms emerge, reflecting different values, different ways of "catching" the processes of life. Though usually one or two paradigms are dominant, shifts are encouraged as theorists and researchers take on influence from philosophy, literary criticism, and other areas. Ironically, a system may be best judged from outside itself. Progress comes not from agreement, but from disparate or at least questioning voices; while power may rest with consensus, progress shows itself to be the consequence, not the resolution, of diversity.

The Plurality of Choice: Method as Rhetoric

Method, however, does not always have to mean system. That is, although choice of method will at some point always respond to the competition of paradigms, it may not always have to cohere logically to a single accepted system. In his analyses of science, philosopher Feyerabend attempts to problematize both the meaning and the role of method in science. In a passage remarkably parallel to the one quoted above from Emig, Feyerabend (1978) criticizes scientific education for the ways in which it limits by excluding:

> First, a domain of research is defined. The domain is separated from the rest of History (physics, for example, is separated from metaphysics and from theology) and given a "logic" of its own. A thorough training in such a "logic" then conditions those working in the domain; it makes *their actions* more uniform and it freezes large parts of the *historical process* as well. Stable "facts" arise and perservere despite the vicissitudes of history. An essential part of the training that makes such facts appear consists in the attempt to inhibit intuitions that might lead to a blurring of boundaries. A person's religion, for example, or his metaphysics, or his sense of humor (his *natural* sense of humor and not the inbred and always rather nasty kind of jocularity one finds in specialized professions) must not have the slightest connection with his scientific activity. His imagination is restrained, and even his language ceases to be his own. (p. 19)

In advocating a philosophy of "epistemological anarchy" (or "Anything Goes"), Feyerabend argues that a "playful" approach to theory and method has brought about the most dramatic paradigmatic shifts in the sciences. He advises, "A scientist who wishes to maximize the empirical content of the views he holds and who wants to understand them as clearly as he possibly can must therefore introduce other views; that is, he must adopt a *pluralistic methodology*. He must compare ideas with other ideas rather than with 'experience' and he must try to improve rather than discard the views that failed in the competition" (1978, p. 30). Admittedly radical in his view of what science is and what the scientist could be, Feyerabend argues that science—and method—is propaganda, useful within its appropriate context, but propaganda nonetheless. Method becomes an ideological question, and he calls upon the researcher to choose a path only after intensive reflection, conducted, in part, to build up a resistance to institutionalized authority.

Obviously influenced by Feyerabend but still holding empirical systems in regard, organizational theorist and researcher Morgan (1983) suggests we recognize that no method ensures "truth"; rather, we need to problematize methods to bind them together dialectically. In the dialectical interplay or "reflective conversation," as Morgan chooses to call it, we know more. Both Morgan and Feyerabend agree that progress is impeded if the conversation, the "dissensus," is not maintained. Morgan, however, is more comfortable with method as system. He offers a three-part framework for analyzing the logics of different research strategies made up of constitutive assumptions (paradigms), epistemologic stance (metaphors), and favored methodology (puzzle solving). In *Beyond Method*, an exceptionally useful collection that he edited, Morgan presents articles by twenty-one researchers illustrating different strategies, including positivist, structuralist, interpretive, feminist, and radical (political) approaches. Based on the approaches discussed in *Beyond Method*, figure 17.1 outlines types of choices researchers may make in developing a strategy. (I have added two areas that also should be considered: reporting and potential consequences.) In the face of such diversity, Morgan argues that one can uncover and challenge all assumptions, attempt to synthesize different works, and judge the pragmatic usefulness or effectiveness of some research as it adds to a discipline's understanding of situations and events; or, one can counterpose theories, methods, and findings in an attempt to develop a dialectical interplay. In the end, Morgan advocates the development of methods that are internally coherent but that lay claim to being only one way of knowing something—a version as good, perhaps, as any other, but no better.

Most researchers concerned with writing in the workplace adhere to the theory that knowledge is socially constructed, that language is constitutive to knowledge. Access to language and to social knowledge is one of the reasons ethnographic study conducted in organizations is so appealing. Yet, as several theorists have pointed out (Morgan, 1983; Rabinow & Sullivan, 1987; Simons, 1989, 1990), adherence to social construction theories destabi-

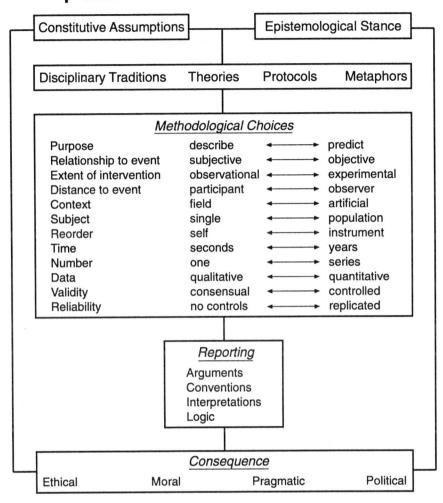

Figure 17.1. Framework for Developing Inquiry Strategies

lizes our own (that is, in this discussion, the researcher's own) knowledge, authority, and belief. Thus, calls for validity and reliability "tests" of qualitative methods may be based on what has constituted "good" inquiry in the past, or can be dismissed as irrelevent given the understanding that these methods get at different "kinds" of knowledge in different ways than do surveys and experiments. For example, validity and reliability can be seen as value tests developed by a community to judge the generalizability of results drawn from certain kinds of data. On the other hand, ethnographic research that deals with the representation of data differently and toward different ends (specificity or interpretation in lieu of generalizability) need not meet the test. It must, however, meet the very different test of reflexivity or self-consciousness (Herndl, 1991). Reporting becomes indistinguishable, certainly inseparable, from method.

In two collections of works by a number of scholars on the rhetoric of inquiry, Simons (1989, 1990) suggests that we take this additional step in any research: to see method as rhetoric and rhetoric as method. Simons argues, "In such ongoing debates as between objectivitists and relativists, postpositivists and antipositivists, foundationalists and antifoundationalists, monists and pluralists, rhetoric has emerged, not as a single perspective, but as a way of reconceiving the debates themselves" (1990, p. 5). Simons notes that we can look at "human behaviors, cultures, entire historical epochs" as texts and apply methods of rhetorical analysis, criticism, and reconstruction. Demonstrating that the contemporary cultural anthropologists "have become unprecedentedly self-conscious about their own work as writing, and their products as rhetorical or literary documents" (1990, p. 12), Pearce and Chen (1989) note four features they believe characterize the writing of anthropologists Geertz and Clifford: explicitly self-relexive, determinedly flexible in its logic, explicitly open-minded, and transparently rhetorical (p. 130; for other discussions of reporting in anthropology, see Brady, 1990). Thus, representations are presented as integral to the research method, not separate from the inquiry itself. Given our own debt to rhetoric, it is perhaps surprising that we only now are beginning to see articles in composition studies (Herndl, 1991) and on research in writing in the workplace (Doheny-Farina, this volume) advocating similar criteria in exploring, presenting, and evaluating our own inquiries.

Culture and Organizational Studies: What Method Implies

A particular example taken from organizational studies illustrates several ways in which concepts and methods adapted within competing paradigms may have rhetorical, and therefore political, implications.

Putnam (1983) posits two distinct approaches to research as it exists in organizational studies today: the functionalist and the interpretive. Directly related to the methods of natural sciences, the functionalist approach treats "social phenomena as concrete, materialistic entities" (1983, p. 34); the organization, often viewed as static and separate from its members, is the unit of study. The interpretive approach seeks to understand, and sometimes, to critique, "the subjective and consensual meanings that constitute social reality" (p. 32). Organizations are coalitions, sustained by symbolic (especially communicative) interactions; the focus of research shifts to the process of organizing. Both may use qualitative and quantitative methods, but Putnam suggests the interpretivist is more likely to use pluralistic methodologies, primarily qualitative ones in naturalistic settings.

It is a little difficult to tell which came first into organizational studies: ethnographic methods or the concept of organizational culture. (*Administrative Science Quarterly* published a special issue, vol. 24, edited by Van Maanen, on qualitative methods in 1979; an article by Pettigrew on organizational culture appeared in the same issue. However, the first use of the concept of culture to guide research on organizations is generally attributed to Turner, 1971.) That they arrived close to each other in time is not a surprise. What may be surprising, however, is the speed with which culture was first adapted within the functionalist approach as a variable that could be manipulated and the speed with which it was then popularized as a tool for control by management. Since organizational communication studies also have long depended on the social science of psychology for many of its methods, measuring instruments abound. It is not surprising, then, to find more than one instrument fully validated and accepted as a measure of organizational culture (Hofstede, Neuijen, Ohayv, & Sanders 1990; see also Greenbaum, DeWine, & Downs, 1987). This is metaphor and method adapted within the functionalist approach.

Smircich and Calas note that this research "seeks to define a relationship between objectified cultural events (for example, storytelling, rituals, language) and objective circumstances (productivity, turnover)" (1987, p. 234). In contrast, as Smircich and Calas argue, culture serves as a root metaphor in the interpretive approach: "Focus shifts to the processes of organizing as the enactment of cultural development" (p. 234). The lens of culture aids the researcher in exploring organizations as "structures of knowledge," "patterns of symbolic discourse," and "reflections of unconscious processes."

A researcher, then, can choose to "operationalize" culture as a dependent or independent variable. It can be measured; instruments for measuring culture can be validated; and, perhaps most importantly, reports can suggest to management ways in which cultural variables within an organization can be manipulated to affect productivity. The language used to describe organizations is that used to describe cultures, but the assumptions continue to be positivist in that generalizations, not the particulars of the individual, are ultimately sought. On the other hand, a researcher may choose to see culture as a metaphor for the daily processes of the organization, the enactment, for example, of what it means for someone to belong to an organization. The metaphor of culture becomes an extended one, because tools of analysis used by anthropologists to study culture are taken and applied to study the organization. The researcher also looks for myths, stories, rituals, artifacts, and language-in-use, but what is important are the participants' own individual interpretations of events and discourses. For the researcher, the choice of approach in considering organizational culture has social power, but it also has political and economic consequences. (On these concerns, see also Frost, Moore, Louis, Lundberg, & Martin, 1985.)

Six Methods

Having summarized some of the general concerns currently being discussed in writing-related fields when method is considered, I would like to turn to several specific methods that have not received as much attention as might be appropriate in the context of research on writing in the workplace, but that could be readily adapted to some advantage. I have selected six methods from fields that study socially complex activities: organizational studies, sociology, communications, and education (composition). What characterizes each of these methods is their demand for interplay between researcher and participant and their reliance on qualitative data. (Each of these methods is discussed more fully in the sources provided.)

Documentary Processes

Discussed in Mishler's well-known article "Meaning in Context: Is There Any Other Kind?" (1979) and brought to the attention of composition specialists in Emig's "Inquiry Paradigms" article (1982), documentary processes are a strictly phenomonological method, primarily used now in field studies of children. As developed by Carini (1975; see also Engel, 1975; Himley, 1991; and Patton, 1975), documentation requires extensive observation of an individual in a natural setting by a researcher over time. Time may be one of the key elements here; reports I have seen have been conducted for years. A strong theoretical foundation informs the method, but multiple interpretations of observations (and texts) are encouraged through collaborative "reflections" by observers and others. In a sense, this research never "ends": Participants and researchers may change, or a single researcher may employ the same process, continually positing possibilities against existing theories. What is derived from the series of observations, however, is constantly and collectively searched and searched again. Thus, the traditional interplay of reliability and validity becomes moot; each is achieved through consensus, but the conclusions are open to reinterpretation. More importantly, perhaps, such close and repeated examination allows for the themes and patterns to emerge from the observational data (rather than the data being massaged to fit predetermined categories) and the researchers are continually engaged, as well, in analyzing their own assumptions. I suspect this approach method, used by researchers with the proper training, would be especially effective in examining the developmental aspects of writers in an organization.

Account Analysis

Demanding much less time on the part of the researcher than does documentation, account analysis is a method that does not require observation, yet it allows people to speak for themselves. Their words and their stories become the data. Its theoretical base is symbolic interactionism: What people say is important; their accounts verbalize their motives, beliefs, and attitudes. Although a person may not seem to describe accurately an event, their words reveal accurately at least one dimension of what that event meant to that individual. Scott and Lyman (1968) define an account as a "statement made by a social actor to explain unanticipated or untoward behavior—whether that behavior is his own or that of others, and whether the proximate cause for the statement arises from the actor himself or from someone else" (p. 46). Harre and Secord (1973) and Tompkins and Cheney (1983) offer account analysis as a method that acknowledges a person's ability to monitor, comment on, and criticize his or her own actions in retrospect. Accounts are essentially reports: "the actor's statement about why he or she performed certain acts and what social meaning he or she gave to the actions" (Tompkins & Cheney, 1983, p. 129). The question "What really happened?" becomes "What happened that was meaningful for this person?," an entry to the ways in which individuals have constructed their views of the events or interactions. Other researchers work with accounts identified as concurrent with ongoing activities. They can be "listened for" in the field or elicited: "A symbolic interactionist might examine contemporaneous or retrospective account giving as a means of understanding the rules for appropriate behavior in an organization" (Bantz, 1983, p. 62). Tompkins and Cheney use accounts to discover decisional premises and their sources and to explain the nature of an individual's identification within an organization (1983, p. 131; see Levine's criticism of accounts, 1977, and Tompkins and Cheney's response, 1983). If we believe that in the act of writing, a person makes choices (deliberated or not), then we can see a number of possible applications of this method. For example, accounts of specific events and decisions given by the people involved in various collaborative writing activities could be compared. Such a comparison would help lay out the dimensions of what constitutes collaboration as distinct from interaction and how authority for a text is transferred among organizational members. Obviously, as stories, accounts readily lend themselves to rhetorical analysis.

Discourse-based interviews (Odell, Goswami, & Herrington, 1983b;

see criticisms in Hayes & Flower, 1983) can elicit accounts with relatively simple changes in the way questions are asked and responses negotiated and analyzed. For example, the initial question would be similar in both methods: pointing out a text feature and asking if the respondent would be willing to change or delete it. Based on this answer, the researcher would ask other questions to elicit full accounts of any interventions or negotiations that had occurred and were related to the writing (or feature) being examined. I have used this method with some success to identify the range of social interactions that occur during the writing of technical manuals and the premises that are used to negotiate textual decisions (Debs, 1986). I believe account analysis would further the detailed study of document cycling, a key finding in the Paradis, Dobrin, and Miller study at Exxon (1985), and it would allow researchers to compare results across cases (individual and organizational).

Account analysis is not without critics, however. Traditional research considers self-reporting unreliable; respondents may guard against giving certain responses and modify responses according to cues from the researcher, or the researcher may negotiate what is actually a misunderstanding. Supporters of account analysis, however, argue that the method admits ambiguity and does not need to exclude the subjectivity of the researcher as it is posited with that of the participant.

Life History Methods

Life history methods first were developed to meet the requirements of traditional scientific research (Frank, 1979; Langness, 1965; Langness & Frank, 1981). In the hands of interpretivists, however, the methods have been adapted to create an interplay, "to find a balance between the theory in the real world and the theory in the researcher's head, the research material modifying and developing the theory, and the theory interpreting, condensing, and transforming the themes that emerge from the material" (Jones, 1983, p. 152). The attempt is to create texts from people's words; the analysis conducted is not unlike that of a literary historian. (In 1991, Erlbaum Associates began publishing the interdisciplinary *Journal of Narrative and Life History*.)

The data, which are essentially elements of biography, may be gathered in several ways: existing records, documents, correspondence, and other materials; contemporaneous sources, that is, documentation of life-in-progress, through observations and interviews; or retrospective narratives in which individuals recall meaningful events in the past, again through interviews. Life histories may be constructed for individuals or for groups; they also may be used for comparison across groups. Depending on the purpose of the study, life histories may be taken of a number of people, as a one-time snapshot, or they may be taken over the course of years, with comparisons made as the narrative of each individual and the collected stories of a group change over time.

In using the life history approach to study organizations within an interpretive framework, Jones (1983) recommends that five criteria be met: "1) The person must be viewed as a member of a culture; 2) The role of significant others in transmitting culture must be recognized; 3) The nature of social action and the basis of social reality and culture must be specified; 4) The continuous, related character of experience over time must be a focus of analysis; 5) The social context must be continually associated with the action" (pp. 153–154). Jones outlines the way in which the process of employee socialization could be studied using a life history approach. The researcher would look for oppositions within members' accounts (looking particularly at critical events within the socialization process), between members' accounts (interviewing those responsible for the socializing), and between members' accounts and the researcher's own reconstruction. Validation by participants is, in fact, one of the key ingredients of this method.

Life histories, particularly taken over time, offer a unique method to study the effects and stages of the socialization process a writer faces in an organization. Another possibility for the application of this method would be to develop a life history of a document, from inception to production to readership, over time. No case study to date that I know of has first tracked the complete cycle of development and then gone on to encompass distribution, audience interactions, readers' responses, and the extended uses and routes of a document. Something that comes close to life history method is the recent *Control through Communication* (1989), in which Yates demonstrates the power of traditional archival research. While she calls her work case studies, they are, indeed, life histories, not of particular documents, but of the forms and roles of written communication in three organizations.

Three Visualizing Methods: Networks, Maps, and Q-Sorts

Since researchers studying writing in the workplace must deal with the social relationships and interactions that make up the organizational and writing processes, they may be interested in techniques that create, in effect, visual (and numeric) sketches of patterns. These sketches admittedly reduce the complexity of data based on social interactions, thereby losing accuracy, but that is also their advantage, since they serve as general statements that capture a breadth of data. Simplicity makes comparison of the data easier.

Network analysis consists of a rather well-developed group of empirical sociometric methods, used to study "social environments . . . as a structure of relations among actors in an environment. Actor attributes and behaviors are then explained in terms of the structure of relations in which they occur" (Bart & Minor, 1983, p. 9). Data (essentially, who talks to whom and why) can be obtained through surveys, interviews, or records (Knoke & Kuklinski, 1982). A number of sophisticated computer programs are available for analyzing the data, and since the statistics can be quite daunting, I would recommend that anyone attempting this type of analysis work with a specialist. However, I would also suggest that something as primitive as the sociogram, that is, a graph of social connections, first introduced in 1934, or a network profile (Sokolovsky, 1986) would benefit some studies of writing in the workplace.

Drawing a map of "social territory" is a useful idea if one recognizes that some accuracy is lost; for example, with qualitative data, a researcher could map the relationships among the themes that emerge. Both cognitive mapping and cause mapping have been used in social science research. Bougon describes cognitive maps as schema registering "all possible types of relations occurring in patterns of concepts (e.g., contiguity, proximity, continuity, resemblance, implication, causality, and their derivitive verbs)" (1983, p. 177). He limits cause maps to the drawing or mapping of causality relations. Already, there are established conventions regarding the development of maps, but they have been used effectively to display belief systems of individuals and of group members (see, especially, Bougon, Weick, & Binkhorst, 1977). Again, the elements of the map—the concepts and relationships—are offered by the participants; the structure shown in the representation is managed by the researcher.

Q-Sort (question-sorting interviews) and Q-Methodology (self-questioning interviews) are techniques that have continued to gain in popularity in social science research, particularly in organizational and interpersonal communication studies, though they were considered controversial when first introduced (Wittenborn, 1961). As currently used, the methods allow people to speak for themselves, that is, to attach their own meanings to complex concepts and situations, but in a way that also allows a reading of how individuals may or may not group together (Roloff & Miller, 1987). There are several variations of these methods. In one, participants make statements about a particular concept or situation. These statements are then processed (for example, redundant statements are removed or collapsed), and each statement is written on a card. Participants then sort (multiple-ranking) the cards according to the researcher's directions. Responses are then statistically analyzed using a technique similar to factor analysis. Q-factor, however, reveals which individuals had similar responses, not just the dimensions of the concept.

Conclusion

Referring to figure 17.1 again, we can see that tinkering with any element listed will produce methodological variation. And, in every field related to ours, variation is what we are seeing. We find, for example, in discussions of ethnography, advocates of extensive literature reviews and theoretical discussion "up front," placed before the presentation of the study, while other methodologists recommend limited literature reviews and advise the researcher to wait until the patterns and generalizations emerge from the data. There are advocates for theoretically grounded research and reporting, for atheoretical (and for antitheoretical) approaches to research and reporting, and for multiplied theoretical interpretations. (To my knowledge, only one study of a writer has deliberately presented more than a single interpretation of the findings; see Clark & Doheny-Farina, 1990.) We find that we may study one case or several; we may make a single observation or many over extended time spans. We may conduct research by ourselves or collaboratively, not only with other researchers but with participants as well (for a variation of this, see Couture & Rymer [this volume] for their use of an advisory group).

These variations of method are beginning to appear in our field, but with little of the exposition we find taking place in other fields. In reporting our research, we seem to have defaulted to the generic format of the "research report," including citing authorities (particularly methodologists) to authorize our choices in methods but, unfortunately, without discussing those choices. In other fields, however, several researchers are going so far as to experiment with the report format itself, developing, in particular, narrative as representation. Thus, we find the deliberately artistic attempts by Pacanowsky (1983) and Jermier (1985); these are short stories constructed to represent "what was found." The boundaries of art and science blur.

If our research continues to focus on the individual's act of authorship as it is played out as part of the social fabric, then I believe diversity will always exist in our field, as it exists in any of the humanities and the social sciences. What comes to issue is the ability to deal with that diversity, to make informed choices when not only theories but also methodologies, ideologies, and responsibilities compete.

As a field, we can begin by attending to the debates in other disciplines and to encourage forums for our own debates and discussions. The purpose I would advocate is to conserve through dialectic, not dictate. We would be well served to explore professional and material constraints faced in doing research in the workplace. As a field, we need to ensure the rigor of self-consciousness, encourage the adaptations made possible by reflection, and challenge conventions instituted without debate. Why? Because research is much more difficult than it used to be, or it should be more difficult as we develop a sensitivity to what we are about. As a researcher, the student of rhetoric also practices rhetoric, but the researcher must go one step further and turn that study back on his or her own practice as well—that is, to examine his or her research as a rhetorical act and to recognize the consequences of that act. Only in this way can we begin to develop and use, with some assurance and some resistance, methods we need to continue our research of writing in different contexts and social units.

For the individual researcher, this process begins with questions addressed not to a problem, but to oneself. What is my view of knowledge at this time, in this project? What claims can be made in research? Do I see through a lens of metaphor? If I change that metaphor, how do I see differently and what does that say to me? Is the primary focus of my study the individual? My understanding? Our interaction? Or the intersection of these with configurations offered by others in this field? Can I employ more than one method in my inquiry? To what advantage or disadvantage? What consequences might my study have to the participants? To the field? What have people said in other fields that relates to my study? How would I enter that conversation? These questions—and there are more—may seem simple in the asking, but they will prove difficult in the answering. But by helping to create tensions in our work, these questions represent the type of reflection and articulation needed to inform our choices, and uses, of method and to ensure that our inquiry is well conceived.

In the end, what we can learn of method from other fields is this: Choice means consequence. This is the overriding point, I think, being made by feminist, Marxist, and postmodern critics. For me, this is the point at which that "certain radicalism" occurred that I mentioned at the beginning of this chapter. What should guide us in our research choices is not simply an expectation of internal coherence, but a self-conscious reflection as to their consequences, as well. What should guide us in our appreciation of research well done is not its allegience to institutionalized norms, but a respect for the way in which it has met its rhetorical "turn" in the conversation carried forward in this and other fields of scholarship. As students of rhetoric, we are obligated to examine the rhetoric of our own methods as well and to seek to understand the tensions they create.

Note

1. For specific discussions of this relationship, see Carrithers (1990), Eisner (1981), and Kuhn (1977).

18 | Stephen Doheny-Farina

Research as Rhetoric | Confronting the Methodological and Ethical Problems of Research on Writing in Nonacademic Settings

With the publication of this book and others like it, we are witnessing the rise of qualitative and ethnographic studies of writing in nonacademic settings. The results of such studies have helped expand our conceptions of the domains of rhetoric, better ground our theories of composing, and inform the teaching of business, professional, technical, and scientific writing. Yet, ironically, this approach to studying writing has taken hold among writing researchers just when some are questioning the underlying assumptions of traditional ethnography (Clifford & Marcus, 1986; Punch, 1986; Van Maanen, 1988). So while we are building a body of research into writing in nonacademic settings, others are questioning some of the assumptions upon which our methodologies are based.

Some of these critiques point out that what an ethnographer writes is not an objective account of what actually happened within a research setting, but instead is a creation, a realistic fiction. These critiques argue that what ethnographers do is create texts, which, as Clifford and Marcus (1986) state, are manifestations of "the constructed, artificial nature of cultural accounts." Ethnography, they say, "is always caught up in the invention, not the representation, of cultures" (p. 2). If we accept such a statement, then those of us who study writing in nonacademic settings suddenly find ourselves in an inherent tension. On one hand, we are going into the field and making claims about what we see and do there. Those claims may inform the way others do their jobs (for example, when our claims inform those whom we study) and may very well inform the ways we teach technical, business, and professional writing. However, now we are becoming aware that those claims we make, even though we may argue otherwise, are not grounded in the data, but instead are constructed by our disciplinary biases and our methods. Our "results" are not what is "out there" in the field. Our results are, in a large part, what we, as researchers, bring to the research event.

Thus, the very sources of our authority are undermined. Those sources are our accounts of what happened on our watch. If we cannot claim that our accounts accurately represent what went on in the field, then on what foundation do we place our claims about the field? What does it mean to "always be caught up in the invention, not representation of cultures"? Useful answers to these questions center on the proposition that all of our research activities are rhetorical in nature. The more we expose the arguments that guide our research actions, the more ethical our research can be. It is this ethical stance that will be our primary source of authority. That is, our strongest authority comes not from our representation of data, but in our attempt to do ethical research. I will explore this proposition by first examining five critiques of field research on writing and then by analyzing some of the ways we can construct our data through the rhetorical act of field research.

Five Critiques of Field Research on Writing

If we consider studies of writing in academic classrooms as "field" research (and we should), we must recognize that field studies of writing have been around for a number of years. But a distinct rise in the number of such studies occurred in the 1980s. One part of this rise of field research has been the growth in studies of writing in nonacademic settings (from early investigations like Odell and Goswami's 1982 and Selzer's 1983 studies to those found in this book). While this type of research has proliferated over the last ten years, it is only recently that we are beginning to see some critiques of field studies of writing.

In this section, I will consider five critiques of various forms of qualitative field research on writing. Three of the critiques focus specifically on studies of writing in nonacademic settings: Dobrin (1987) reconsiders one of the most oft-cited studies of writing in nonacademic settings in the late 1980s, "Writing at Exxon ITD: Notes on the Writing Environment of an R&D Organization" (Paradis, Dobrin, & Miller, 1985). Kleine (1989) discusses his motivations as researcher on three different studies, two of which were conducted in nonacademic settings. Herndl (1991) analyzes the problematic nature of ethnographic texts and focuses in part on a study of mine, "Writing in an Emerging Organization: An Ethnographic Study" (1986).

The other two critiques that I want to review do not make writing in nonacademic settings their primary focus. Even so, the issues they raise are quite important for nonacademic applications of the methodologies in question. North (1987) analyzes the several problems with ethnographic research by discussing several studies, including Odell and Goswami's "Writing in Non-academic Settings" (1982), in a chapter of his book *The Making of Knowledge in Composition*. Finally, Smagorinsky (1989) attacks the validity of Graves's studies of children writing in school settings (see Smagorinsky's references for a lengthy list of the Graves studies that Smagorinsky attacks). While I will use these critiques to inform my own analysis of the challenges that face researchers conducting writing in nonacademic settings, I do so because this book focuses on nonacademic writing. Even so, the issues that I discuss below span the study of writing in academic as well as nonacademic settings.

Taken as a whole, the five critiques focus on three major issues: the role of the researcher, the manipulation and/or interpretation of data, and the construction of research texts.

The Role of the Researcher

In field research, investigators usually hope to have as little effect as possible on the events and people under study. Of course, we accept that it is impossible to have no effect whatsoever. Our presence alone, even if we hardly interact with the natives, can influence what natives do and say. In my experience, I have attempted to become actively engaged with participants when I am in the field. Yes, I want to observe, but I also want to get to know the native participants personally, and to do that, I need them to get to know me as well. I would like them to know that I am not a threat. But two problems arise: (1) even though I do not want to be a threat, my work may threaten the participants in ways that I cannot anticipate, and (2) I may change the way that the participants act and, in doing so, become myself an active participant in the events of the field. The former problem I will discuss in detail in a later section. The latter issue is discussed in detail by Smagorinsky in his critique of the work of Graves.

Smagorinsky argues that Graves's research reports reveal that Graves and his research colleagues actively determine the outcomes of their studies by intervening in the events under study. According to Smagorinsky, the Graves team claims "to observe, rather than control, student behavior" (p. 333). However, other statements in Graves's reports indicate "that the writing of these students does not in fact develop naturally, but is highly influenced by the biases and interventions of the researchers" (p. 333). As evidence, Smagorinsky quotes Graves's description of the relationship of the researchers with the teachers who were under study. That description reveals a melding or blurring of the roles of researcher and researched. Graves says, "Over coffee, at lunch, at breaks when gym, art, and music were taught, teachers asked questions about their children and the relation of the data to their teaching. . . . In a short time the mystique of 'research and researcher' were removed" (Graves quoted in Smagorinsky, p. 339). With researchers who intervene in the events that they are studying, readers, says Smagorinsky, "should not be surprised that these students develop as Graves predicts they will" (p. 335).

Therefore, any claims that Graves and his colleagues make regarding the writing development of the students under study must be suspect because of the researchers' subtle influences on the students through the teachers: "Yet the conclusions that the children come to are always predicted by the researchers. Is it possible that the researchers, and the teachers in the classrooms they are studying, are providing subtle and unconscious approval of certain decisions made by their students, and disapproval of undesirable decisions?" (p. 338). The ultimate point of Smagorinsky's critique is not that Graves's position on what makes good writing or good teaching is wrong. What Smagorinsky objects to is calling Graves's work research. Instead, Smagorinsky wants to call it "reportage." One does not do research when one engages in substantive interactions with those under study. Clearly, Smagorinsky rejects the research role that could be described as researcher-as–interventionist.

This issue of intervention is analyzed further by Kleine in a self-critique of his efforts at qualitative field research. Kleine, however, does not reject field researcher intervention, but instead argues that we need to recognize and reveal the types of interventionist roles that we will play whenever we do qualitative field research. He describes three roles that he has played:

1. Researcher-as-missionary: When doing a field study in a corporation (see Anderson & Kleine, 1988), Kleine and his research colleague attempted to promote changes in the corporation. They saw the natives as powerless, and they wanted to promote writing critically as a way to empower them. The researchers' ethnography thus became an ideological commentary on the corporation.
2. Researcher-as-apologist: During a study of faculty writing across the curriculum at his university, he uncritically promoted a line of thinking about the nature of the enterprise that he and the participants agreed upon. That is, he validated the institutional status quo, which, he says, was the noncontroversial, easy thing to do.

3. Researcher-as-sympathizer: When teaching writing to prison inmates, he attempted to study writing in a prison setting. As he collected data and learned the points of view of the participants, he began to see the needs for prison reform. When he informed the prisoners that his ethnography may be used to promote prison reform, the inmates told him that they did not want to be in a study that may identify them as rebelling against the prison authority. As a result, Kleine never reported the study in fear that the information could be used against the participants.

Kleine offers this critique as an example of the kind of self-analysis or self-perception that is typically lacking from our research reports. Rather than reject intervention as Smagorinsky does, Kleine wants us to reject the "scientific pretenses" to which many of our third-person ethnographic accounts aspire; that is, we must focus not just on our "subjects," but also on our actions with the participants with whom we are involved in the field.

Of course, the differences between Smagorinsky and Kleine relate to the different approaches that one may bring to field research. Does one enter the field to apply treatments to a population and run tests to see if those treatments had their effects? Or does one enter a field to "participate" in an experience in order to gain an understanding of the natives' views of that experience? The demands of the former approach seem the source of Smagorinsky's complaint against Graves, while the demands of the latter approach are consistent with Kleine's three research roles. The distinction between these two different approaches highlights one of the more confusing elements of what we call "research on writing in nonacademic settings": While many researchers may go out into the field to study nonacademic writing, some go there to employ a variety of social scientific, hypotheses-testing procedures, while others attempt to produce some sort of ethnography. The problems come when the claims that researchers make do not match the approach that they took in conducting the study. North (1987) raises this issue when he analyzes Odell and Goswami's oft-cited study (1982) of writing in nonacademic settings. North argues that Odell and Goswami could not have learned what the natives' rhetorical actions could mean because the researchers did not participate in the setting with them. According to North, this nonparticipation limits the claims that the researchers can make about their data:

Odell and Goswami simply characterize (their study) as "naturalistic." What kind of authority can their findings finally claim? . . . Odell and Goswami might be said, via their interviews, to get a glimpse of the workers' imaginative universe, but from an Ethnographic point of view they have no way to make sense of what they see. That is, while the writing may have been produced in context, the researchers have no access to how it comes to mean there—no apparent interest in when or where or why or for whom it was written, nor in how it was subsequently received, read, and acted upon. (p. 302)

North emphasizes that the above analysis is not a criticism of Odell and Goswami's research, because, he notes, they did not make claims as if they had conducted ethnographic, participant/observation. Even so, North discusses other studies that seemingly do make claims that are not warranted by the methods employed, which is precisely Smagorinsky's complaint against Graves. Thus, the goal of writing researchers should not be to limit nor extend their participatory role in field research. Their goal should be for their role to be consistent with the claims that their studies ultimately make.

The Manipulation and Interpretation of Data

When discussing the active role of the field researcher, we must mention the ways that researchers interpret and/or manipulate data. Smagorinsky's major complaint with Graves's work lies in the way that he perceives Graves manipulating data. Graves considers only data, according to Smagorinsky, that confirm Graves's own position on rhetorical and pedagogical issues: "He and his colleagues do not look for negative evidence for their hypotheses. All of their reported results give an enthusiastic endorsement of the theories that they are testing; nowhere do we see them raising questions about whether the evidence does in fact support their hypotheses" (1989, p. 339). In other words, through selectivity or manipulation, the researchers focus on only the instances that support the researchers' biases. As I noted above, a comment such as this reveals a fundamentally different perspective than, for example, the perspective of Kleine. Whereas Smagorinsky judges Graves upon a scientist paradigm that includes the convention of hypothesis testing, Kleine wants us to admit that the work of ethnographers does not lie within that paradigm. Ethnography by its very nature ensures that researchers will select or manipulate data, and ethnographers, according to Kleine, should attempt to reveal the sources of their manipulation and selectivity (1989). In other words, those of us who attempt to do ethnography cannot avoid manipulating data, so let us try to understand how we do it and bring that understanding to the fore in our studies.

This issue of data manipulation in field research of nonacademic writing is central to Dobrin's self-critique (1987) of the research process behind the well-known "Writing at Exxon ITD" article by Paradis, Dobrin, and Miller (1985), an article that makes a number of interesting and useful generalizations about the phenomena under investigation. These generalizations are useful because those of us interested in writing in nonacademic settings can apply these generalizations to other studies to other companies' practices, or to the ways that we teach classes in technical and business communication. Yet, these generalizations, according to Dobrin, are quite misleading. What Dobrin reveals in his critique (published two years after the original study was published) was that the phenomena under investigation were ungeneralizable.

Dobrin explains how the investigators' constructions of trends or patterns of writing-related behavior were deceptive. For example, he points out that their data indicate that supervisors wrote as much as their employees and edited as much as their superiors. What the data does not reveal, says Dobrin, is that while some supervisors wrote a great deal, others wrote very little. Such a situation can represent a thorny problem for researchers who enter a site with the intention of studying writing. As North (1987) notes, when faced with a situation in which writing does not play a significant role with a participant or organization, a researcher must decide whether or not to continue studying that situation. If the decision is to continue, the researcher must decide how to explain the lack of significance, thereby continuing to treat writing as significant through that explanation. This type of manipulation in field studies of writing is noted by North when he argues that ethnographers who enter a setting with the intention of studying writing will either find something significant about writing in that setting, or abandon the setting altogether: "The narrower the focus provided by a disciplinary-based predisposition, the greater the danger of unaccounted investigator bias, on the one hand, and of under-framed accounts leading to distorted perspective for outsiders, on the other. It is a matter that requires considerable caution by all parties" (p. 289). In the Exxon study, according to Dobrin, the investigator bias was there but unaccounted for, and this problem was only one of several.

Dobrin offers other ways that he and the others used to generalize the employees' writing patterns (for example, "writing ability affects job performance") and shows how all of those generalizations were deceptive. In addition, he argues that such problems would span approaches or methods in any case study: "Now I think our experience would have been the same if we had studied business writers or if we had done protocol analysis of the group's writing or if we had collected statistics about the forms being used. In each case, what we found out would be inextricably linked to the situation. Generalizations would seriously falsify, or else be unilluminating, or both" (1987, p. 7). His evidence for this conclusion is the report that he and his colleagues wrote and published. It was deceptive, he says, because it shaped this amorphous, situation-specific, ungeneralizable experience into a story designed for us who are interested in writing in nonacademic settings: "It was an attempt to provide disciplinary knowledge. It contained generalizations, tables, a certain veneer of jargon. It may even have proved useful to some people. But I'm afraid that it proved useful only for the reasons that certain mediocre fictions are useful. They present a story about the world which is more manageable and irresistible than fact" (p. 7). What Dobrin seems to assume, here, is that there could be an account that is not limited or manipulative.

An account geared toward a specific academic audience—say, an account attuned to those interested in the study of writing in nonacademic settings— would necessarily be a limiting, shaping construction that is no longer situation-specific, but instead has become disciplinary-specific. Even if the "results" are geared toward the situation-specific concerns and perceptions of the engineers and managers of Exxon ITD, the account still will be a construction that limits and shapes a vast array of phenomena. Is either approach less than truthful? It depends on what one claims. If the researchers claim that they present the truth as it was, without attempting to reveal their own biases, then the account is intellectually dishonest. But how can we know whether another account, the account that Dobrin would like to have presented, "one that," as he says, "was both true to the complexities and removed from the quotidian" (p. 7), may be more factual than the one that appeared in print?

One answer to this question may be to hold up our data—our selections from and representations of the complex environment we study—to experts who will judge the quality of that data. That is, one way to determine whether our data are "both true to the complexities and removed from the quotidian" may be to share it with the participants in order to test its validity. I have done this on occasion, and when the participants say, in effect, "Yeah, I think that's true," I have always felt pretty good about what I am doing. Unfortunately, the hope that one's collection and interpretation of data is somehow more valid if it is closer to the perceptions of the participants represents what I would call the *myth* of internal validity.

North (1987) defines internal validity and presents it as the highest type of verification of validity: "The ideal goal of Ethnographic verification, then, and so the standard against which it needs to be measured, lies in this matching up: to make the final interpretation one that the participants, understanding the investigator's aim of carrying it back to her own imaginative universe, would approve. This is obviously an ideal not often within easy reach" (p. 311). Whether or not this goal is difficult to achieve is one issue, but what North fails to consider is that this goal determines a screen that must influence the researcher's data collection and interpretations. Whether or not we refer to that screen as a check on validity or as a means of distortion is, in my mind, an open question. Does satisfying the natives balance the distortions that we may bring to events as a result of our discipline-specific agendas? Dobrin certainly laments the effects of discipline-specific influences on the interpretations of what he and his colleagues saw at Exxon; but he also notes that with some issues, there were those at Exxon who believed certain interpretations of the researchers. Unfortunately, one of those interpretations Dobrin later denied and characterized as a distortion. (This interpretation dealt with the claim that writing ability influenced job performance and evaluation.) Does this mean that this so-called internal validity is to be avoided? No. The screen of internal validity, just like discipline-specific screens, is one of several means of interpretation. And all interpretation is manipulation.

How, then, can anyone judge the validity of our research? That validity is judged continually throughout the research process from inception through publication. It is what I would call a practical validity that is determined through the responses of a variety of audiences. In this sense, validity is determined through a range of readings by audiences located within the researcher's discipline, as well as those located within the research sites. While the ways in which these audiences influence research reports will be discussed in a later section of this chapter, I want to emphasize here that my conception of a practical validity is legitimized by an adherence to a particular ethical stance in the construction of research texts. The following critiques inform this stance.

The Construction of Research Texts

An ethical research report will attempt to identify the rhetorical strategies that the author as researcher employs. Such a practice rarely is seen in research reports because many of us still (unknowingly?) subscribe to a residue of the positivists' objective research report. That is, an ethical research text will attempt to make explicit the ways in which the author is attempting to persuade readers through the use of the objectivist conventions of research reporting. Because this is an admission of the utter subjectivity of those conventions, researchers (and journal editors) may tend to reject such a practice.

This adherence to the objectivist myth in ethnographic studies of writing in nonacademic settings recently has been explored by Herndl (1991) in a critique of my research report "Writing in an Emerging Organization: An Ethnographic Study" (1986). Herndl analyzes the implicit rhetoric of my ethnographic account of writing in a new corporation in order to understand where my text's authority resides and how some of the sources of that authority may be hidden through the objectivist conventions: "My point is to suggest the amount of rhetorical work that goes into producing an ethnographic account of writing and the way it too is legitimized through socially maintained conventions. Other studies of professional writing or of classroom contexts might organize their descriptions around different topoi or employ a text structure other than that associated with problem solving, but they will be no less embedded in the discourse of their research community" (p. 326). Thus, all of the research reports in this book are equally embedded in the discourse of the community of writing researchers. It may be enlightening to examine them to understand how they each are "legitimized through socially maintained conventions." Herndl provides an example of such an analysis by criticizing the conventions he sees legitimizing my text. His analysis reveals five key textual strategies:

1. Make a "state-of-art" research claim: The text locates the study within a tradition and at the same time assumes the value of a new approach to solving problems within that tradition: "In the first three pages, Doheny-Farina cites thirteen recent articles in writing research to generate the two questions that guide his work. In doing so, he identifies himself as a member of his tradition and embraces the value of new, state-of-the-art research common in the research ethos" (p. 324).

2. Set up a problem solving framework: In order to present answers to the guiding questions, the text is structured to solve the problems posed by the questions: "This sets his text up as 'problem solving,' and the report gains credibility through the power and familiarity of this schema in composition theory" (p. 324).

3. Base analysis on certain privileged terms: Throughout the research text, I used certain terms to, in Herndl's term, "familiarize" the specifics of the phenomena under study. These are terms like "rhetorical context" and "exigence for writing." In addition, I concluded that the research supports current pedagogical models, thereby further attaching the phenomena to our discipline. These privileged terms provide a source of authority for the text.

4. Represent a dual researcher persona of participant/observer: My research text reveals that I witnessed all that I describe as happening at the research site, giving a veracity to the "data" upon which I make claims. At the same time, I did not present myself as participating in any of the ongoing activities that I described in the research report, so my data is imbued with a scientific objectivity that gives it further authority. Herndl notes that "this double movement maintains both the grounding in personal experience and the objectivity of description" (p. 326). Such a combination of roles "functions as a warrant for the authenticity and validity of the author's interpretation" (p. 326).

5. Cite irretrievable field notes: To support an objectivist "I was there" construction, I often included in the text quotations that came from my field notes.

After each such quotation, I would append a citation, such as "(ON, 10/5/83)," which indicates an observational note taken on 10/5/83. This practice, notes Herndl, supplies authority from an accepted practice but masks the real intent of that accepted practice:

> The gesture of citation derives, of course, from the parenthetical reference in APA style. The standard use of parenthetical documentation, however, is supported by the reader's ability to retrieve the appropriate article, read the material for herself, and form her own conclusions about the reality of the situation. Clearly, Doheny-Farina's notes are not available to readers of this article, but the gesture appropriates the same documentary power. That power, however, rests not in our ability to retrieve the "original text," as in my own self-legitimating gesture above, but in the claim that Doheny-Farina was there and that had we been there we too would have seen the same thing. The effect of the parenthetical reference is to maintain the separation of the participant's "being there" from his observation. (p. 326)

This point is echoed by Smagorinsky's complaint (1989) against Graves that he makes claims based upon data that is not in the research text. This limitation, according to Smagorinsky, allows for biases that cannot be checked by the reader. Thus, this limited, potentially biased presentation of data allows for only two responses from a reader. Either one accepts the researchers' interpretations or one doubts them, but either response is based on faith (p. 340). We either trust the researcher or we do not. The researcher builds trust through the careful use of rhetorical devices that are accepted by targeted readers, devices such as what Herndl calls "the trope of participant/observer" (p. 326). In this light, then, my research text manipulated constructs like data, field notes, and research role in order to gain adherence to an argument. Thus, while I embedded my ethnographic text within an objectivist tradition of ethnography, I clearly used those conventions as a source of authority for my argument.

The primary lesson of all five of the above critiques is that researchers' actions and their texts are rhetorical acts that need to be identified as such. Ethical researchers will attempt to lay bare their rhetorical intents. Researchers must identify as rhetorical devices those practices that heretofore were considered methods of scientific control. What we see, then, is a methodology that is largely a rhetorical enterprise. We are building arguments as we work in the field and construct our analysis and inscribe our interpretations. To repeat Clifford and Marcus (1986), we are involved in "the invention, not the representation, of cultures" (p. 2).

Thus, if we are to consider seriously the thrust of these critiques, we must ask ourselves how we invent as we record the activities of participants in our studies. Upon reflection, it seems that I invent in subtle ways when I both collect data and write research reports.

Data Collection as a Rhetorical Act: Gaining Control in the Field

I invent as I conduct research, because I attempt to explore conflict, and by doing so, I exert a measure of control, influencing what participants say to me. This practice counters a commonly held conception of the amount of control that an ethnographer has when in the field. A typical description of that common conception is described by Doheny-Farina and Odell (1985):

> If researchers want to conduct inquiry in naturalistic settings, they must change their notions about the respective roles of researchers and the people who take part in researchers' studies. Researchers may no longer think of their work as a matter of manipulating variables and trying to predict or influence behavior. Nor may researchers continue to think of themselves as working with subjects who simply perform tasks with no real understanding of those tasks. Instead, the researcher's principal job becomes one of trying to describe and explain phenomena over which the researcher has no direct control. (p. 507)

Do I actually give up control when I conduct such research? I often say that I do. I often feel as if I do. But it seems more accurate to say that I enter environments in which I have little or no control at the start and then am continually engaged in a subtle, tactful struggle to gain control over the aspect of that environment that I am focused on. I begin exerting control by trying to obtain things: I want access. I want information. I want documents. I want participants to share their thoughts with me, sometimes in detail beyond what they would share with fellow participants, sometimes different types of information than they would normally share with fellow participants. And as I am obtaining these things, I am directing participants' attentions to me (my researcher persona) and my agenda. I want them to believe that I am trustworthy and therefore offer anonymity (but can I always deliver it?) and a nonthreatening ear (but am I encouraging creative venting?). I want to focus on writing, and by doing so, I increase its visibility among participants. Even if I do not intend to, I make my concerns their concerns.

As I gain participants' trust and as my research agenda becomes accepted, the domain of my interest expands. I begin by observing and recording the routine. I try not to interrupt that routine. As my place becomes more secure—as I gain control—I seek conflict. I look for it and probe it. Why? Because it is by exploring conflicts, small and large, that I can explore previously tacit knowledge and learn some of the meanings participants attribute to their actions and to the actions of others. It enables me to get a glimpse at what they "know without saying," or seemingly do without conscious thought.

And when I do not find conflict, I subtly create it. How? Through some of our best methods, such as discourse-based interviews (Odell, Goswami, & Herrington, 1983a) and compose-aloud protocols. These methods are designed to pose choices, oppositions, or impediments to the participants in order to stimulate their thinking. Thus, by the time I have gained enough trust to be able to use these methods routinely or to ask participants routinely about some conflicts that have arisen among them, I am very much in control of my agenda, even though I have no control over the course of nearly all other events continually occurring at the research site. The key question thus becomes, How do I represent my role in the research process? Where do I locate myself in the research text? That all depends on my perceptions of my intended audiences.

The Research Text as Rhetorical Act: Anticipating Our Audiences

If in my research report, I mask my controlling role by presenting my findings from a third-person impersonal stance (which I have done several times), I am telling what Van Maanen (1988) calls the "realist's tale," which reveals

> a field worker-author who more or less disappears into the described world after a brief, perfunctory, but mandatory appearance in a method footnote tucked away from the text. The only other glimpse of the ostrich-like writer is a brief walk-on or cameo role in which he puts into place the analytic framework. The voice assumed throughout the tale is that of a third-party scribe reporting directly on the life of the observed. The tone suggests anonymity, a characteristic of science writing where the fieldworker is self-cast as a busy but unseen little fellow who is confident that the world as represented in the writing is the real one. Authority rests largely on the unexplicated experience of the author in the setting and the "feel" he has apparently developed for the time, place, and people. . . . "It is not my perspective," says the author, "but theirs." (p. 64)

But now we know that telling the realist tale is a rhetorical stance that attempts to establish authority based upon a notion of scientific rigor. Van Maanen argues that there is a more desirable type of tale that we should tell. He calls it the "impressionist tale" and defines it as a representational means of cracking open the culture and the fieldworker's way of knowing it, so that both can be examined jointly. Impressionist writing tries to keep both subject and object in constant view. Thus, such a study should focus not solely on the actions of the participants, but also on the researcher's role in examining the actions of the participants.

I do not believe, however, that this opposition means that the realist tale is somehow deceitful and that the impressionist tale tells the truth. The key difference between these two tales lies not in their relative truthfulness, but in their differing sources of authority. The realist tale derives its authority from forums that value objectivist, scientist rigor. The impressionist tale derives its authority from forums that reject that positivistic notion of scientific objectivity and are seeking alternative ways to represent what researchers do and learn. That is, I want to argue that research on writing in nonacademic settings is shaped significantly by researchers' rhetorical agendas and their perceptions of the expectations of their potential audiences. Indeed, those of us who do this type of research will find ourselves shaping our studies to adapt to a variety of audiences. The following is a speculative analysis of five different types of audiences and the demands that each may exert on a researcher.

1. The actual participants in the study: Often, one of our primary tasks is to mask the identities of the participants, their organizations, and their actions. Doing so is especially important when we are studying writing within business or industrial settings, because we may record proprietary information of which an organization may claim ownership. In addition, we may uncover actions that participants or their superiors may not want to be known about them or the organization. Therefore, sometimes we must not only mask but also "sanitize" our reports so that they are not controversial from the point of view of the participants. Sometimes these types of accommodations are trade-offs: We get to explore certain specific participant/organizational issues in our agenda as long as we stay away from, or excise, other issues that the participants deem potentially damaging.

2. Our disciplinary colleagues: One of our primary goals is to shape the complex and largely indeterminate events that we witness in the field so that those events speak to current disciplinary issues. To paraphrase a concern noted earlier, we go into an organization looking for writing and we damn well better find it! Furthermore, we need to characterize what we find in terms that enable us to take part in the current conversations of our discipline. And usually, we must include in those discussions a connection to pedagogy. These goals will lead us to ignore some events that we see in the field, but place others under the microscope.

3. The gate-keepers: In addition to shaping our interpretations so that they engage in the current conversations of the discipline, we need to highlight the uniqueness of our research. These two goals represent our argument for publishing our work. Do we ever see a research report that claims to provide

nothing new? Of course not. We must provide some new knowledge, and that becomes a primary goal of data collection and analysis.

4. The nonnative practitioners: Many of us study writing in nonacademic settings with the intention of informing a larger practitioner audience, for example, technical writers, managers, and other nonacademic readers who may be interested in our studies. These readers usually demand that our research offer some practical advice that may help them improve the ways that they do their jobs. Therefore, in addition to shaping our interpretations to satisfy the demands of our other audiences, we often try to reduce certain aspects of a study to some practical suggestions.

5. Our bosses: Those of us in academe know that the audiences who may be the most significant for us personally are the department chairs, college deans, and evaluation committees who will review our research publications. For those audiences, who will probably know very little about our discipline, we are compelled to show theoretical and scientific rigor in order to achieve sufficient academic gravity and be rewarded by tenure, promotion, and raises. Thus, whatever it is we study, we must argue that it is significant.

I do not offer these speculations as a way to condemn my own or anyone else's research. I offer them as a few of the most obvious forces that play a role in the way our research questions, methods, and results are formed. Our interpretations of these forces affect the ways that we construct our research arguments. In this light, I want to re-emphasize that ethical field researchers will attempt to make explicit that their projects are multifaceted arguments geared to address a variety of readers. But, I also must emphasize the obvious limitation of this self-consciousness: Researchers will never be able to lay bare all of these agendas and unmask all persuasive strategies at work in research text. Some will be too trivial to discuss, some will be too controversial to reveal, while others will be too embedded for researchers to see. But some agendas can be presented explicitly. If writers of field studies of writing in nonacademic settings make clear to themselves from the start that their entire research processes—from entering sites through publishing research reports—are rhetorical enterprises that should be identified as such, then those researchers can act ethically.

One potential danger with this move toward self-reflexiveness is that it can lead us away from the important issues that we need to study. It can turn us too far inward. Excessive navel-gazing will not help us learn more about people and cultures, nor will it enable us to help others who can learn from our studies. Because there is work to be done in the world, we need to walk that tightrope between ethical self-consciousness and our attempts to observe and analyze systematically and perceptively what is going on around us.

| **Tyler Bouldin and Lee Odell**

**Surveying the
Field and
Looking Ahead**

A Systems Theory Perspective
on Research on Writing
in the Workplace

Chapters in this volume, taken together with other studies of writing in the workplace, reveal a burgeoning field of research, one that fifteen years ago was virtually nonexistent (see Odell & Goswami, 1985, p. vii). During these fifteen years, researchers have begun to use a variety of methodologies to study writing done in such diverse nonacademic settings as engineering firms, computer companies, social work offices, insurance companies, and hospitals. Although still a relatively young enterprise, the study of writing in the workplace is sufficiently well established to invite, perhaps to require, researchers to consider two basic questions: What has been accomplished thus far? And how does one build on past accomplishments in planning future work?

To answer such questions, researchers will need a theoretical vantage point, a perspective that will enable them to understand the strengths and limitations of different research methodologies and to see how those methodologies can be integrated in developing a comprehensive understanding of writing in the workplace. In this chapter, we want to describe one such vantage point, a set of assumptions that comprise General Systems Theory. After illustrating these assumptions with references to recent work in composition studies, we will survey selected studies that relate to a single theme and then will show how Systems Theory enables researchers to build on these studies in subsequent research.

Establishing a Vantage Point: Systems Theory

During the first two decades of this century, researchers in biology found themselves in a predicament that should seem quite familiar to composition researchers. In attempting to understand certain complex phenomena (for example, cellular metabolism or the evolution of new populations of organisms), researchers realized they were dealing with objects of study that interacted in unpredictable ways with the surroundings in which they were placed. Further, researchers discovered that these phenomena displayed apparently purposeful behavior, modifying their physical characteristics or patterns of behavior as a result of interactions with their surroundings. Consequently, it became clear that researchers could not always follow conventional experimental procedures of isolating and controlling variables to make predictions and generalizations that would hold true in all contexts.

In order to resolve this predicament, researchers in biology developed a set of assumptions referred to as Systems Theory (for a more detailed discussion of Systems Theory, see Von Bertalanffy, 1968, and also Monge, 1977). The first of these assumptions is that *any phenomenon can be viewed as a system,* a set of interrelated component parts or processes arranged in such a way that a change in any one component is likely to lead to changes in other components. These components interact not only with each other, but also with the various contexts in which they appear.

This assumption seems especially appropriate for both written texts and the larger meaning-making processes of which they are a part. The text itself consists of components, such as lexicon, syntax, propositions, and cohesive devices, that are so interrelated that a change in any one component or, indeed, a change in the environment in which the text exists is likely to require a change in other components or in the environment. Similarly, the meaning-making process in writing consists of a number of components: writer(s), reader(s), text(s), and institutional context—the values, history, and processes that are characteristic of a particular organization. Any of these components can be seen as a system, and all of them interact with each other and with the various rhetorical, interpersonal, and organizational contexts in which they exist.

Since these systems are so highly interactive, Systems Theory also assumes that *one's understanding of a phenomenon must be holistic rather than atomistic.* One cannot concentrate on any one of the phenomenon's components (or subsystems) and ignore ways in which it affects and is affected by other components. From the perspective of Systems Theory, then, one should not focus on, for instance, the interpersonal aspects of the composing process without relating them to such matters as the lexical or propositional features of an initial draft, the changing features of successive drafts, or the cognitive activity that goes on while the writer is sitting alone, stringing words across a yellow pad or a computer screen. In order to understand these relationships, Systems Theory assumes that one needs to look for, or formulate, broad theoretical concepts that will suggest functional or structural relationships among apparently disparate components. For example, Cross's discussion of centripetal and centrifugal forces (1990) may help researchers account for much of what goes on throughout the composing process.

Another basic assumption in Systems Theory is that *systems range from the relatively "closed" to the relatively "open."* A closed system is one that has little interaction with its environment or that shows relatively little ability to adapt to changing conditions. Researchers can predict or generalize confidently about such a system without worrying that the influence of different contexts might affect the claims they want to make. An open system, by contrast, displays comparatively great ability to regulate its own behavior and respond unpredictably to its surroundings.

It is difficult to think of situations in which research on writing might focus on truly closed systems. Granted, some types of writing may have characteristics that seem relatively well defined (see, for example, Odell and Goswami's discussion of "pink memos" and "white memos" in a social service agency [1982].) Also, style manuals sometimes establish prescriptions (for example, never use the passive voice) that seem intended for application in all contexts. However, it is not possible to predict that a specific feature will appear at a given point in a given piece of writing; even within the same genre, specific texts are likely to vary somewhat according to the rhetorical context in and for which they are written. And, of course, the composing process is even more unpredictable and responsive to the circumstances in which a writer is working.

Because Systems Theory assumes that systems may vary widely, it also assumes that *research must be characterized by what Sutherland (1973) has called "instrumental congruence."* That is, rather than simply electing a method of research because it is well accepted, researchers must use inquiry methods appropriate to both the kind of system they are investigating and the kind of knowledge they possess at any given time. Sutherland identifies four levels of investigation corresponding to the degree of "openness" believed to characterize the system to be investigated: speculative, deductive, inductive, and experimental modes of inquiry. Each level of inquiry results in valuable knowledge, although these forms of knowledge vary in terms of their precision and reliability.

Speculative inquiry involves rational guesses—speculations—about the character of highly open systems, guesses that may be required simply because one's current knowledge is relatively limited, or because the object of study may appear (or may actually be) unique and indeterminate. Speculative work may use close readings of specific texts to draw inferences for which no other empirical data are readily available (see, for example, Miller and Selzer's inferences about invention processes reflected in the topical structure of one set of engineering reports [1985]) or reflections upon processes that seem important but are not readily accessible to empirical analysis (see Emig's comments on the role of intuition in the composing process [1964]).

Deductive inquiry may entail the application of a general theoretical framework to a particular instance or problem (see Flower and Hayes's assimilation of the composing process into the categories of problem solving and cognitive processes [1980]). Or it may entail an effort to analyze and synthesize existing theories to develop new theories that will reconcile conflicts among existing positions (see Kinneavy's *Theory of Discourse* [1971]). Deductive inquiry is appropriate for phenomena that are highly variable but that reveal relatively consistent patterns in a range of contexts.

Inductive inquiry entails both the close examination of specific texts or contexts for writing and also the generalized description of what has been observed. Inductive inquiry may take two forms: qualitative induction, which relies heavily upon interviews and observation and is represented in the majority of current studies of writing in the workplace; and quantitative induction, which entails the collection and statistical analysis of numerical data.

Experimental inquiry is characterized by the effort to control variables and make statistically reliable predictions and generalizations. Early discussions of composition research (e. g., Braddock, Lloyd-Jones, & Schoer, 1963) assumed that experimental inquiry was synonymous with research. However, true experimentation is not widely represented in composition research. Most studies that involve statistical analysis are examples of quantitative induction; they do not display the rigorous control of variables needed for the confident generalization and prediction that are the goals of experimental inquiry. In the field of composition studies, perhaps the closest approximation to what Systems Theory would label experimental inquiry appears in Langer and Applebee's *How Writing Shapes Thinking* (1987).

For Sutherland (1973), these levels of inquiry form a distinct hierarchy. He does acknowledge that the four levels of inquiry may be related—that, for example, theory derived from deductive inquiry might guide experimental work and results of experimental work might inform theory. He also acknowledges that speculative knowledge may be the only possible knowledge one can have of completely open systems. However, Sutherland clearly privileges the precision and reliability of experimental knowledge. He assumes that the final goal of research is the degree of certainty that he associates with experimental research.

Sutherland's assumption about the hierarchy of levels of inquiry is the one point at which we think writing researchers may need to diverge somewhat from Systems Theory. We believe that for purposes of studying writing in the workplace, relations among these levels of inquiry should be viewed as dialectical rather than hierarchical. That is, work with any type of inquiry may be refined, critiqued, or enriched by relevant work with other types. Writing researchers must be prepared to draw on the type of inquiry that seems most appropriate in a given context, without assuming that one type of inquiry is inherently more valuable than others.

Surveying Current Work: Insights into the Process of Invention

Even a cursory review of existing studies of writing in nonacademic settings reveals that this research is too extensive and diverse to do justice to in the space available here. Consequently, we decided to focus on a single topic: invention, the processes by which readers and writers gather and reflect upon information in an effort to construct meaning.

We chose this topic for reasons that we think should guide researchers' decisions to focus on any topic. The process of invention is important for writers in all contexts, since writing entails the formulation of new ideas as well as the expression of existing ideas. As researchers come to understand this topic, they will understand a significant portion of the domain of workplace writing. Also, this topic will allow researchers to take a holistic perspective on the phenomena they encounter. That is, it can enable researchers to integrate work on interpersonal interaction with analysis of textual features, the study of revisions, and analysis of corporate culture. Moreover, the study of invention can lead researchers to integrate the study of writing with the study of reading, since both readers and writers are engaged in the process of reflecting upon information and formulating ideas.

Finally, we chose to focus on invention because the process, if not the term itself, is prominent in a number of studies, many of which provide insights into the strategies writers use in formulating ideas or constructing meaning and the ways in which the meaning-making process is influenced by rhetorical, interpersonal, and cultural or organizational contexts. These studies provide a strong basis for planning long-range programs of research.

Strategies for Invention

Experienced writers in nonacademic settings are likely to have internalized a number of strategies that help them develop their ideas. Some of these strategies may seem procedural. For example, writers may have learned that for a particular type of task, they will be well advised to consult with specific individuals or review certain types of documents (Odell, 1985).

Other strategies seem more clearly conceptual; they represent mental activities that are useful in trying to think through a given topic. Miller and Selzer (1985), for instance, show how a group of engineering reports reflect sets of *topoi*—"concepts," "methods of analysis," or "patterns of thought" that are essential for effective writing in a particular engineering firm. Although they do not use the term *topoi,* other writers support Miller and Selzer's point. Broadhead and Freed (1986) note that different sections of reports they studied must address specific topics or issues, such as "analysis of the client's problems," the "specific need for the firm's services," or "monetary costs" (p. 93). Similarly, Odell (1983, 1985) has reported that writers in some governmental agencies know that in doing certain types of writing, they must respond to specific questions (for example, Are there any unintended consequences of a particular piece of legislation? How are various interest groups likely to react to the legislation?).

Although these studies use different terms to describe the invention process, all of them identify *topoi* or issues or questions that have heuristic and epistemological significance. None of these strategies is a simple algorithm, and none is grounded in a fully developed theory of invention. But all of them direct the writer's attention and thus contribute to what the writer has to say on a given topic.

Contextual Influences on Invention

Traditionally, discussions of invention have proceeded along the lines of the previous section, focusing on topics or analytical strategies individuals might use in formulating their ideas (see Young, 1976). More recently, however, scholars (see LeFevre, 1987; Young, 1987) have begun to look beyond the individual writer, considering ways in which rhetorical, interpersonal, and organizational/cultural contexts might influence the invention process.

Rhetorical context. Although the term "rhetorical context" may refer to the writer's ethos and rhetorical purpose as well as to the writer's sense of audience, most writing in the workplace studies of rhetorical context have focused principally upon audience. Some scholars (e. g., Redish, Battison, & Gold, 1985) have suggested that writers in nonacademic settings can be insensitive to the needs and interests of their readers. A number of other scholars (e.g., Mirel, this volume; Selzer, 1983), however, have demonstrated not only that considerations of audience are important in workplace writing, but also that a sense of audience guides the meaning-making pro-

| 273

cess, often leading writers to rearrange or reconceptualize their subject matter.

Interpersonal context. A number of studies indicate that writing in nonacademic settings often is characterized by extensive interaction between writers and their colleagues and between writers and at least some of their potential readers. Indeed, interpersonal interaction is so frequently remarked upon that, as Spilka (1990b) has suggested, researchers need not ask whether these interactions do occur as part of the composing process, but can ask when and why these interactions occur.

These interactions take a variety of forms, ranging from the "formal and informal conversations" that Selzer (1983) refers to as "communal brainstorming" to relatively formal interviews (Odell, 1985) or reviews (Winsor, 1990b). Whatever form they take, these interactions may serve a variety of functions: helping writers gather and assess information (Odell, 1985; Selzer, 1983), allowing writers and supervisors to negotiate the points that are to be emphasized in a given piece of writing (Paradis, Dobrin, & Miller, 1985), or helping writers determine which topics need to be elaborated further (Winsor, 1990b). These interactions may occur throughout the composing process, from writers' earliest efforts to gather and reflect on information to the very end of the process when writers and colleagues review a completed text with an eye to improving future work (Broadhead & Freed, 1985).

Organizational/cultural context. Both theory and research suggest that invention is influenced by the organizational and cultural contexts in which writers work. LeFevre (1987) presents a good introduction to theory in this area, and several studies illustrate ways in which the values, knowledge, and practices (that is, the "culture") of an organization can guide the invention process. For example, the organization may give writers access to existing texts that provide models of form and argumentation and that can serve as sources of content (Winsor, 1989). Further, an organization may influence the invention process by setting up review procedures, in which various members of the organization may raise questions or make comments that help shape the substance of what a writer has to say. And finally, the organization may provide its writers with a common frame of reference— shared values, experiences, purposes, even strategies for examining topics and developing ideas (see Odell, 1985; Winsor, 1990b).

Building on Current Work

The studies we have just summarized epitomize the richness and diversity of research on writing in the workplace. They have been conducted in a wide range of settings and employ a variety of methodologies, including interviews, naturalistic observation, and textual analysis. They also show how Systems Theory enables researchers to build on current work by

- engaging in different levels of inquiry rather than emphasizing one level to the virtual exclusion of others;
- making a more consistent effort to take a holistic view of the phenomena under investigation;
- developing long-range programs of research that would let researchers understand a given concept by observing the different ways it is manifested in a variety of settings.

Levels of Inquiry

Most of the research we cited earlier has entailed one level of inquiry: induction, usually qualitative induction. Researchers have observed writers in a variety of contexts, recording empirical observations and occasionally gathering survey data in order to generalize local findings. Inductive research procedures are appropriate for such a highly variable phenomenon as writing. But these procedures are most likely to be effective when researchers pursue concepts, such as invention, that allow integration of diverse empirical studies. To develop such concepts and thereby enrich their inductive investigations, scholars in the field also need to engage in speculative and deductive inquiry.

With respect to invention, speculative and deductive inquiry might proceed in several directions. For example, speculative inquiry might focus on intriguing topics that have been mentioned in individual studies but never developed in great detail. One such topic might be what Winsor (1989) refers to as the process of inscribing, which she defines as "the process by which groups come to agreement on what symbols should be assigned to reality" (p. 271). How does this process work? What are the interpersonal and conceptual activities that attend people's efforts to represent experience with a range of symbols that includes numbers and formulae, as well as natural language? How does this process shape one's understanding of the topic at hand?

Researchers speculating on such questions as these might draw on a number of different sources for important concepts. They might turn to philosophical studies of symbols (e.g., Langer, 1951), to theories of cognitive psychology (e.g., Vygotsky, 1966), or to studies of semantics (e.g., Hayakawa, 1963). Researchers might also draw upon their own experience to present the kind of personal account Elbow gives of his own composing process in *Writing Without Teachers* (1973). That is, people working in a given setting might try to describe their individual and collaborative efforts to symbolize and thereby understand the subject matter they routinely deal with. Such accounts might differ from Elbow's in that they focus on spoken as well as on written language and on the use of numbers or abstract symbols as well as on the use of natural language. These speculative accounts might give rise to concepts—comparable, for instance, to Elbow's notion of a "center of gravity"—that might be explored in both deductive and inductive studies.

In addition to speculative inquiry, there is a need for deductive work that both draws together existing work, much as we have attempted to do in the preceding discussion of invention, and also explores theoretical issues that are left unresolved in this work. For example, we have reason to believe that invention is guided at least in part by inquiry strategies. We also know that various "models" of invention—for example, the *topoi* of classical rhetoric (see Corbett, 1965), the Pentad of Kenneth Burke (see Kneupper, 1979), the categories of tagmemic theory (see Young, Becker, & Pike, 1970)— recommend strategies for examining information and formulating ideas. How adequately do these models account for the strategies researchers find when they examine written products or the composing process? Does one model have more descriptive or explanatory power than the others? Can they—*should* they—be synthesized? Or are there theoretical reasons for abandoning altogether the notion that a single model can usefully describe the wide range of activities people engage in when they try to construct meaning?

Other deductive work might focus on the ways context influences the invention process and might draw on theory and research in related disciplines. Harrison (1987), for example, suggests that studies of writing might well be informed by theory and research from the field of organizational communication. Specifically, Harrison refers to such concepts as an "organizational cognitive map," or to organizational worldviews and belief systems (pp. 12–13; see also Debs, this volume). Studies of writing in the workplace have shown that organizational culture (Odell, 1985) or constraints (Paré, this volume) influence the invention process of writers.

Intuitively, it would seem that this influence might be exerted through an organization's "cognitive map." But what is the nature of such a map? What theoretical basis is there for believing that such a map exists? How do writers acquire, follow, or depart from such a map? As researchers assess and synthesize existing work in this area, they should understand better how they might gather and interpret information about the meaning-making processes of writers in a given organization.

These references to existing work may seem to run counter to a widely expressed view of qualitative research methodology, the view that both concepts and the analytic categories that enable researchers to formulate concepts should "arise from the data." This view is important because it reminds researchers that they cannot simply impose concepts or categories on data, ignoring or distorting data that do not fit a Procrustean bed of existing concepts. As is true of the process of writing, the process of research is most interesting when it is most surprising, when researchers find themselves coming to new, unexpected insights.

But the phrase "arise from the data" is misleading. Concepts or categories do not arise from data any more than they spring full-blown from the brows of Zeus-like researchers. They arise, rather, from a transaction (see Rosenblatt, 1978) between data and the researcher's image (see Boulding, 1964) of the world—that is, between data and all the assumptions, prior knowledge, values, disciplinary concepts, and so on that lead a researcher to select certain data and to interpret them a particular way.

Unfortunately, it can be difficult to understand the image of the world that underlies a researcher's work. Sometimes this image of the world is tacit; and, like all forms of human knowledge, it is subject to ongoing analysis and revision. Further, as Schon (1983) has argued, this image may not exist apart from the specific decisions that "practitioners" (in this case, researchers) make in the process of carrying out their work. To modify E. M. Forster's famous comment about writing, researchers may not fully understand what they think until they see what they do. Consequently, one cannot assume that a given research project is guided by a fully articulated set of assumptions that exist separately from, and prior to, a particular project; doing the project may be the means by which one comes to understand fully those assumptions.

Yet a researcher's image of the world is a powerful force in research, so powerful, in fact, that Denzin (1989) suggests it may be necessary to "deconstruct" existing conceptions of the phenomena under consideration. Not only do those conceptions exist, they are also likely to govern a researcher's efforts even if, or especially if, the researcher has not made those conceptions explicit, subjected them to careful analysis, and related them to important disciplinary concepts in his or her field. Consequently, the field of writing in the workplace needs the speculative and deductive inquiry that would clarify existing knowledge, if only to let researchers see more clearly what they do not want to take as a given. From the perspective of Systems Theory, research on writing in nonacademic settings will be enriched if scholars in the field carry out deductive and speculative studies as well as inductive studies, using each type of inquiry to build upon, test, and modify insights derived from the other.

Holistic Perspectives

The studies summarized above often leave one with a sense of incompleteness. For example, two of the studies that identify strategies for invention omit information that should complement and perhaps extend conclusions based on the information they do examine. Odell (1985) provides a detailed analysis of analytic strategies reflected in one writer's discussions with a colleague. But he does not try to determine whether those strategies might have appeared elsewhere in the composing process—in writers' assessment of reviewers' comments on their writing, for example, or in the text of their writing itself. Conversely, Miller and Selzer (1985) make a convincing argument that a written document reflects various types of strategies that seem useful in gathering and assessing subject matter. But they do not attempt to determine whether or how those strategies might have appeared in writers' discussions with their peers or in writers' processes of drafting or revising their documents.

Similarly, discussions of audience either omit information or neglect relationships that seem critical to an understanding of how audience relates to the invention process. Although a number of studies discuss writers' conception of or attempt to accommodate an audience, those studies typically do not provide information about what happens when writers' texts are actually read by their intended audiences (for notable exceptions, see Bazerman, 1985; Kleimann, Mirel, and Smart, this volume; and Spilka, 1988a). How do readers construct meaning from those texts? Are their efforts guided by invention strategies? If so, how do readers' strategies compare to those used by writers of the texts or to strategies used by readers when they compose their own texts? To what extent or in what ways are readers influenced by their awareness of rhetorical, interpersonal, or organizational contexts?

In addition to omitting information about readers, some studies ignore relationships between different types of information. Broadhead and Freed (1986), for example, report exhaustive syntactic analyses of writing produced in a management consulting firm. Moreover, they describe not only writers' interactions with their audiences but also the goals writers hope to achieve with their audiences. Yet these different types of information are not integrated. For instance, how might an analysis of syntax inform or be informed by an understanding of writers' interactions with or goals for their audiences? How do writers' interactions with readers shape the goals they hope to accomplish, and how are those goals reflected in or influenced by those interactions?

It will not be easy to integrate analyses of social factors, written texts, and individuals' writing and reading processes. But from the perspective of Systems Theory, this sort of integration is essential. According to Systems Theory, one understands a phenomenon only when one has a holistic view of that phenomenon, a view that integrates all of its known components and all of its known manifestations. If researchers want to understand the process of invention, they will have to examine all the different activities that comprise invention, and they will have to study these activities in all the diverse contexts in which they go on. That is, researchers will have to examine such matters as writers' conversations with others; writers' notes (see Haas, 1990); writers' drafts and revisions; readers' efforts to create meaning from writers' texts; and writers' efforts to make sense of readers' comments on early drafts of a text. Are there any common features to these activities? Do different types of activities make unique contributions to the invention process? In what ways does the invention process vary (or remain the same) from one context to another?

Programs of Research

Cross-contextual research is especially important if researchers are to understand the concepts that are derived from deductive scholarship on meaning making. Although Systems Theory indicates that those concepts should help researchers integrate the findings of diverse empirical studies, Systems Theory also suggests that researchers' understanding of those concepts will be modified (challenged, refined, enriched) as the concepts are studied in different settings. Consequently, Systems Theory leads logically to programs of research in which researchers, working separately or in collaboration, try to study the same concept in different settings.

Consider what this might mean for studies of invention. As noted earlier, there is evidence that relatively systematic, conscious plans for invention may be important for writers in some contexts. But is the notion of systematic invention equally valid for other contexts? Or do other settings invite writers to rely more on intuition or on the epistemic power of talking and writing? Further, there is reason to think that different academic contexts value different sorts of systematic meaning-making strategies (Bazerman, 1988; Herrington, 1985). Would a similar observation hold true for different workplace settings? Would it hold true for different groups of writers (males/females; supervisors/workers; novices/veterans) or different types of tasks (for example, different genres or routine tasks and special tasks) in a given nonacademic setting?

A similar line of questioning pertains to other concepts, such as Bakhtin's notion of "centrifugal" and "centripetal" forces acting on the composing process. Cross (1990) has shown how these forces affect the composition of documents in one particular business setting. We suspect that the concepts of centrifugal and centripetal forces will help researchers integrate much of the diverse activity that goes on during the invention process. But to understand these concepts, researchers need to consider a variety of further questions: Do these conflicting forces appear in other workplace settings? If so, do they operate as they do in the setting Cross describes? Do different organizations have different ways of reconciling these conflicting forces? And, most important, how do answers to the preceding questions refine Cross's understanding of centrifugal and centripetal forces?

By asking these questions, we may seem to be advocating a practice that is common to experimental research, the practice of replicating existing studies in the hope of confirming or refuting their claims and thereby contributing to a discipline's confidence that research is leading to objective truth about the world. As we noted earlier, Systems Theory does value experimental work that leads to widely applicable predictions and generalizations about an object of study. However, systems theorists point out that this sort of research is possible only in the investigation of closed systems, which have limited ability to interact with their environments. In the case of open systems—and the process of meaning making is about as open as any system we can imagine—experimentation and the replication of prior experiments is neither possible nor desirable.

Instead of arguing for replication of experimental studies, we are advocating programs of research that seek to determine what Young, Becker, and Pike (1970) refer to as the "range of variation" of the concepts that are important for writing in the workplace. That is, we need to examine a given concept in the widest possible range of contexts, asking such questions as, In how many different ways may a given concept be manifested? How widely may it vary from one context to the next? Answers to such questions may clarify or refine scholars' understanding of the concept. Or they may lead to concepts that have even more explanatory power, concepts that allow scholars to account more fully, more reasonably, for the phenomena they have observed.

Goals

Implicit in these suggestions for research is an assumption about the goals of research on writing in the workplace. Since we believe that the meaning-making process is a relatively open system, it seems unlikely to us that studies of writing in the workplace will lead to the universally applicable predictions and generalizations that, from the perspective of Systems Theory, are the goal of experimental research. But we also believe that there is a basic human need to make generalizations and predictions—however provisional, however subject to ongoing scrutiny and revision.

To resolve this dilemma, we think it is useful to draw on Geertz's distinction (1973) between a researcher's "locus of study" and the researcher's "object of study" (p. 22). The researcher's locus of study may be a particular office or classroom or native village, but the researcher's object of study is a process that transcends, in some form, any specific setting. For Geertz, a researcher cannot use the data from one study to substantiate generalizations or predictions about the meaning-making process in other settings. One study will not "prove" another.

But Geertz points out that the conclusions drawn from observing in one setting can have diagnostic value. They can provide a perspective from which a researcher may view interaction that takes place in unexplored settings. As long as those conclusions help researchers interpret and account for new phenomena, they are likely to continue being used and elaborated. When those conclusions "cease being useful, they tend to stop being used and are more or less abandoned" (p. 27). In other words, research is an ongoing transaction among researcher, prior conclusions, and new data. The goal of research on open systems is to continue to engage in that transaction, making sure that our minds remain at least as open as the systems we seek to understand.

**Bibliography
Contributors
Index**

Bibliography

Abercrombie, M. L. J. (1960). *Anatomy of judgment*. London: Hutchinson.

Abercrombie, M. L. J. (1970). *Aims and techniques for group teaching*. Guildford: University of Guildford.

Adelsward, V. (1989). Defendent's interpretation of encouragements in court: The construction of meaning in an institutionalized context. *Journal of Pragmatics, 14*(1), 25–38.

Aldefer, C., & Smith, K. (1982). Studying intergroup relations embedded in organizations. *Administrative Science Quarterly, 27,* 45–65.

Allen, N., Atkinson, D., Morgan, M., Moore, T., & Snow, C. (1987). What experienced collaborators say about collaborative writing. *Journal of Business and Technical Communication, 1,* 70–90.

Anderson, C. M. (1989). *Richard Selzer and the rhetoric of surgery*. Carbondale: Southern Illinois University Press.

Anderson, J. (1981). *Acquisition of cognitive skill* (Tech. Rep. No. 81–1). Pittsburgh: Carnegie Mellon University, Office of Naval Research.

Anderson, J. (1987). Cognitive principles in the design of computer tutors. In P. Morris (Ed.), *Modelling cognition* (pp. 93–133). New York: John Wiley.

Anderson, P. V. (1984). What technical and scientific communicators do: A comprehensive model for developing academic programs. *IEEE Transactions on Professional Communication, PC–37,* 161–167.

Anderson, P. V. (1985). What survey research tells us about writing at work. In L. Odell & D. Goswami (Eds.), *Writing in nonacademic settings* (pp. 3–83). New York: Guilford.

285

Anderson, P. V. (1986). *Business communication.* New York: Harcourt Brace Jovanovich.

Anderson, W. W., & Kleine, M. (1988). Excellent writing: Educating the whole
corporation. *Journal of Business and Technical Communication, 2*(1), 49–62.

Andrews, D. C., & Andrews, W. D. (1988). *Business communication.* New York:
Macmillan.

Anson, C. M., & Forsberg, L. L. (1990). Moving beyond the academic community: Transitional stages in professional writing. *Written Communication, 7,* 200–
231.

Aristotle. (1960). *The rhetoric* (L. Cooper, Trans.). Englewood Cliffs, NJ: Prentice-
Hall.

Armstrong, J. S. (1980). Unintelligible management research and academic prestige.
Interfaces, 19, 80–86.

Attewell, P., & Rule, J. (1984). Computing and organizations: What we know and
what we don't know. *Communications of the ACM, 27,* 1184–1192.

Bakhtin, M. M. (1981). *The dialogic imagination* (M. Holquist, Ed.; C. Emerson &
M. Holquist, Trans.). Austin: University of Texas Press.

Bakhtin, M. M. (1986). *Speech genres and other late essays* (C. Emerson & M. Holquist,
Eds.; V. M. McGee, Trans.). Austin: University of Texas Press.

Bantz, C. (1983). Naturalistic research traditions. In L. L. Putnam & M. Pacanowsky
(Eds.), *Communication and organizations: An interpretive approach* (pp. 55–71).
Beverly Hills: Sage.

Barabas, C. (1990). *Technical writing in a corporate culture: A study of the nature of
information.* Norwood, NJ: Ablex.

Barclay, W. R., Southgate, M. T., & Mayo, R. W. (1981). *Manual for authors and
editors.* Los Altos, CA: Lange Medical.

Barnum, C. M., & Fischer, R. (1984). Engineering technologists as writers: Results
of a survey. *Technical Communication, 31*(2), 9–11.

Barone, T. E. (1990). Response to the commentary of Miles and Huberman. In
E. W. Eisner & A. Peshkin (Eds.), *Qualitative inquiry in education* (pp. 358–363).
New York: Teachers College, Columbia University Press.

Bart, R. S., & Minor, M. J. (1983). *Applied network analysis: A methodological
introduction.* Beverly Hills: Sage.

Barthes, R. (1977). *Image music text.* New York: Hill and Wang.

Barthes, R. (1979). From work to text. In J. V. Harari (Ed.), *Textual strategies:
Perspectives in post-structural criticism* (pp. 73–81). Ithaca: Cornell University Press.

Barthes, R. (1985). Texte [theorie die]. Quoted in M. Gresset & N. Polk, *Intertextuality in Faulkner.* Jackson: University Press of Mississippi. (Original work published 1973)

Bataille, R. R. (1982). Writing in the world of work: What our graduates report.
College Composition and Communication, 33(3), 226–283.

Bazerman, C. (1981). What written knowledge does: Three examples of academic
discourse. *Philosophy of Social Science, 11,* 361–387.

Bazerman, C. (1983). Scientific writing as a social act. In P. Anderson, R. Brockman,

& C. Miller (Eds.), *New essays in scientific and technical writing* (pp. 156–184). Farmingdale, NY: Baywood.

Bazerman, C. (1984). Modern evolution of the experimental report in physics: Spectroscopic articles in *Physical Review*, 1893–1980. *Social Studies of Science, 14,* 163–196.

Bazerman, C. (1985). Physicists reading physics: Schema-laden purposes and purpose-laden schema. *Written Communication, 2,* 3–25.

Bazerman, C. (1988). *Shaping written knowledge: The genre and activity of the experimental article in science.* Madison: University of Wisconsin Press.

Bazerman, C. (1990). Discourse analysis and social construction. *Annual Review of Applied Linguistics, 11,* 77–83.

Bazerman, C. (in press). Intertextual self-fashioning: Gould and Lewontin's representations of the literature. In J. Selzer (Ed.), *Understanding scientific prose.* Madison: University of Wisconsin Press.

Beach, R., & Anson, C. M. (1988). The pragmatics of memo writing: Developmental differences in the use of rhetorical strategies. *Written Communication, 5,* 157–183.

Beade, P. (1987). Comment. *College English, 49,* 708.

Becher, T. (1987a). Disciplinary discourse. *Studies in Higher Education, 12*(3), 261–274.

Becher, T. (1987b). The disciplinary shaping of the profession. In B. R. Clark (Ed.), *The academic profession* (pp. 271–303). Berkeley: University of California Press.

Becher, T. (1989). *Academic tribes and territories: Intellectual inquiry and the cultures of disciplines.* Milton Keynes, UK: The Society for Research into Higher Education & Open University Press.

Belenky, M. F., Clinchy, B. M., Goldberger, N. R., & Tarule, J. M. (1986). *Women's ways of knowing.* New York: Basic.

Bereiter, C. (1980). Development in writing. In L. W. Gregg & E. R. Steinberg (Eds.), *Cognitive processes in writing* (pp. 73–93). Hillsdale, NJ: Lawrence Erlbaum.

Berg, D. M. (1967). A descriptive analysis of the distribution and duration of themes discussed by task-oriented small groups. *Speech Monographs, 34,* 172–175.

Berkenkotter, C. (1989). The legacy of positivism in empirical composition research. *Journal of Advanced Composition, 9*(1&2), 69–82.

Berkenkotter, C., Huckin, T. N., & Ackerman, J. (1991). Social context and socially constructed texts: The initiation of a graduate student into a writing research community. In C. Bazerman & J. Paradis (Eds.), *Textual dynamics of the professions* (pp. 191–215). Madison: University of Wisconsin Press.

Berk-Seligson, S. (1990). Bilingual court proceedings: The role of the court interpreter. In J. N. Levi & A. G. Walker (Eds.), *Language in the judicial process* (pp. 3–35). New York: Plenum.

Berlin, J. (1987). *Rhetoric and reality: Writing instruction in American colleges, 1900–1985.* Carbondale: Southern Illinois University Press.

Berlin, J. (1988). Rhetoric and ideology in the writing class. *College English, 50,* 477–494.

Bhatia, V. (1987). Language of the law. *Language Teaching, 20*(4), 227–234.

Biber, D. (1988). *Variations across speech and writing*. Cambridge: Cambridge University Press.

Biber, D., & Finegan, E. (1989). Styles of stance in English: Lexical and grammatical marking of evidentiality and affect. *Text, 9*(1), 93–124.

Bitzer, L. F. (1968). The rhetorical situation. *Philosophy & Rhetoric, 1,* 1–14.

Bitzer, L. F. (1980). Functional communication: A situational perspective. In E. E. White (Ed.), *Rhetoric in transition: Studies in the nature and uses of rhetoric* (pp. 21–38). University Park: Pennsylvania State University Press.

Bizzell, P. (1982). Cognition, convention, and certainty: What we need to know about writing. *PRE/TEXT, 3,* 213–243.

Bizzell, P. (1987, July). *What is a discourse community?* Paper presented at the Penn State Conference on Rhetoric and Composition, University Park, PA.

Bizzell, P. (1989). Review of *Social construction of written communication. College Composition and Communication, 40,* 483–486.

Black, H. C., Nolan, J. R., & Connolly, M. J. (1983). *Black's law dictionary* (abridged 5th ed.). St Paul, MN: West.

Bloom, H. (1973). *The anxiety of influence: A theory of poetry*. London: Oxford University Press.

Bocchi, J. S. (1991). Forming constructs of audience: Convention, conflict, and conversation. *Journal of Business and Technical Communication, 5*(2), 151–172.

Bochner, S. (1988). *The psychology of the dentist-patient relationship*. New York: Springer-Verlag.

Bogdan, R. C., & Biklen, S. K. (1982). *Qualitative research for education: An introduction to theory and methods*. Boston: Allyn & Bacon.

Bonk, C. J. (1990). A synthesis of social cognition and writing research. *Written Communication, 7*(1), 136–163.

Bosley, D. (1989). *A national study of the uses of collaborative writing in business communications courses among members of the ABC*. Unpublished doctoral dissertation, Illinois State University, Normal, IL.

Bougon, M. G. (1983). Uncovering cognitive maps: The self-Q technique. In G. Morgan (Ed.), *Beyond method* (pp. 147–159). Beverly Hills: Sage.

Bougon, M. G., Weick, K., & Binkhorst, D. (1977). Cognition in organizations: An analysis of the Utrecht Jazz Orchestra. *Administrative Science Quarterly, 22,* 606–639.

Boulding, K. E. (1964). *The image*. Ann Arbor: University of Michigan Press.

Bourdieu, P. (1977). *Outline of a theory of practice* (R. Nice, Trans.). Cambridge: Cambridge University Press.

Braddock, R., Lloyd-Jones, R., & Schoer, L. (1963). *Research in written composition*. Urbana, IL: NCTE.

Brady, L. (Ed.). (1990). *Anthropological poetics*. Savage, MD: Bowman and Littlefield.

Britton, J. (1978). The composing processes and the functions of writing. In C. R. Cooper & L. Odell (Eds.), *Research on composing: Points of departure* (pp. 13–28). Urbana, IL: NCTE.

Bibliography

Britton, J., Burgess, T., Martin, N., & Rosen, H. (1975). *The development of writing abilities (11–18)*. London: Macmillan.

Broadhead, G. J., & Freed, R. C. (1986). *The variables of composition: Process and product in a business setting*. Carbondale: Southern Illinois University Press.

Brown, J. L. (1988). A survey of writing practices in management. *English Quarterly, 21*(1), 7–18.

Brown, R. L., & Herndl, C. G. (1986). An ethnographic study of corporate writing: Job status as reflected in written text. In B. Couture (Ed.), *Functional approaches to writing: Research perspectives* (pp. 11–28). Norwood, NJ: Ablex.

Bruce, N. (1984–continuing). EMP *[English for Medical and Paramedical Purposes] Newsletter*. Kuwait: Kuwait University Faculty of Medicine.

Bruffee, K. A. (1978). The Brooklyn plan: Attaining intellectual growth through peer-group tutoring. *Liberal Education, 64*, 447–468.

Bruffee, K. A. (1984). Collaborative learning and "The Conversation of Mankind." *College English, 46*, 635–652.

Bruffee, K. A. (1985). *A short course in writing* (3rd ed.). Boston: Little, Brown.

Bruffee, K. A. (1986). Social construction, language, and the authority of knowledge: A bibliographical essay. *College English, 48*(8), 773–790.

Bruner, E. M. (1986). Experience and its expressions. In E. Bruner & V. Turner (Eds.), *The anthropology of experience*. Urbana: University of Illinois Press.

Burke, K. (1950). Rhetoric—old and new. *Journal of General Education, 5*, 202–209.

Burke, K. (1959). *Attitudes toward history* (3rd ed.). Berkeley: University of California Press. (Original work published 1937)

Burke, K. (1969a). *A grammar of motives*. Berkeley: University of California Press.

Burke, K. (1969b). *A rhetoric of motives*. Berkeley: University of California Press.

Burton, J. (1989). Keeping language in its place. In H. Coleman (Ed.), *Working with language: A multidisciplinary consideration of language use in work contexts* (pp. 85–105). Berlin: Mouton de Gruyter.

Calkins, L. M. (1985). Forming research communities among naturalistic researchers. In B. W. McClelland & T. R. Donovan (Eds.), *Perspectives on research and scholarship in composition* (pp. 125–143). New York: MLA.

Cameron, K. S. (1986). Effectiveness as paradox: Consensus and conflict in conceptions of organizational effectiveness. *Management Science, 32*, 539–553.

Cameron, K. S., & Whetten, D. A. (1981). Perceptions of organizational effectiveness over organizational life cycles. *Administrative Science Quarterly, 26*, 525–544.

Campbell, D. T., & Stanley, J. C. (1966). *Experimental and quasi-experimental designs for research*. Chicago: Rand McNally.

Campbell, K. K., & Jamieson, K. H. (1990). *Deeds done in words: Presidential rhetoric and the genres of governance*. Chicago: University of Chicago Press.

Campbell, P. G., Housel, T., & Locker, K. O. (1988). *Conducting research in business communication*. Urbana, IL: ABC.

Campbell, P. N. (1975). The *personae* of scientific discourse. *The Quarterly Journal of Speech, 61*, 391–405.

Card, S., Moran, T., & Newell, A. (1980). Computer text-editing: An information-processing analysis of a routine cognitive skill. *Cognitive Psychology, 12*, 32–74.

Carini, P. (1975). *Observation and description: An alternative method for the investigation of human phenomena.* Grand Forks: University of North Dakota Press, North Dakota Study Group on Evaluation Monographs.

Carini, P. (1979). *The art of seeing and the visibility of the person.* Grand Forks: University of North Dakota Press, North Dakota Study Group on Evaluation Monographs.

Carrithers, M. (1990). Is anthropology art or science? *Current Anthropology, 31*(3), 263–272. Comments and reply, 272–282.

Carroll, J. M., & Aaronson, A. P. (1988). Learning by doing with simulated intelligent help. *Communications of the ACM, 31*, 1064–1079.

Carroll, J. M., Smith-Kerker, P., Ford, J., & Mazur-Rimetz, S. (1986). The minimal, manual. *Human Computer Interaction, 2*, 287–317.

Caviness, V. S., & O'Brien, P. (1980, 21 February). Current concepts: Headache. *New England Journal of Medicine*, 446–449.

Chang, H.-T. (1982). Roles of acupuncture in medicine. *American Journal of Chinese Medicine, 10*, 1–4.

Charney, D., Reder, L., & Wells, G. (1988). Studies of elaboration in instructional texts. In S. Doheny-Farina (Ed.), *Effective documentation: What we have learned from research* (pp. 47–72). Cambridge: MIT.

Charrow, R. P., & Charrow, V. R. (1979). Making legal language understandable: A psycholinguistic study of jury instructions. *Columbia Law Review, 79*(7), 1306–1374.

Cherry, R. (1988). Ethos and persona: Self-representation in written discourse. *Written Communication, 5*(3), 251–276.

Chisholm, R. M. (1988). Improving the management of technical writers: Creating a context for usable documentation. In S. Doheny-Farina (Ed.), *Effective documentation: What we have learned from research* (pp. 299–316). Cambridge: MIT.

Cicourel, A. V. (1986). The reproduction of objective knowledge. In G. Bohme & N. Stehr (Eds.), *The knowledge society* (pp. 87–122). Dordrecht, Holland: D. Reidel.

Clark, G. (1990). *Dialogue, dialect, and conversation: A social perspective on the function of writing.* Carbondale: Southern Illinois University Press.

Clark, G., & Doheny-Farina, S. (1990). Public discourse and personal expression. *Written Communication, 7*(4), 456–481.

Clausen, A. (1973). *How congressmen decide: A policy focus.* New York: St. Martin's.

Clifford, J., & Marcus, G. E. (1986). *Writing culture: The poetics and politics of ethnography.* Berkeley: University of California Press.

Clyne, M. (1987). Cultural differences in the organization of academic texts. *Journal of Pragmatics, 11*(2), 211–247.

Coe, R. M. (1987). An apology for form; or, who took the form out of the process? *College English, 49*, 13–28.

Bibliography

Coleman, H. (Ed.). (1984). Language and work 1: Law, industry, education [Special issue]. *International Journal of the Sociology of Language, 49.*

Coleman, H. (Ed.). (1985). Language and work 2: The health professions [Special issue]. *International Journal of the Sociology of Language, 51.*

Coleman, H. (Ed.). (1989). *Working with language: A multidisciplinary consideration of language use in work contexts.* Berlin: Mouton de Gruyter.

Collins, T. & Hattenhauer, D. (1983). Law and language: A selected, annotated bibliographer on legal writing. *Journal of Legal Education, 33*(1), 141–151.

Columb, G., & Williams, J. M. (1985). Perceiving structure in professional prose: A multiply determined experience. In L. Odell & D. Goswami (Eds.), *Writing in non-academic settings* (pp. 87–128). New York: Guilford.

Cooper, M. M. (1986). The ecology of writing. *College English, 48*, 364–375.

Cooper, M. M. (1989). Why are we talking about discourse communities? Or, foundationalism rears its ugly head once more. In M. Cooper & M. Holzman (Eds.), *Writing as social action* (pp. 202–220). Portsmouth, NH: Boynton/Cook.

Cooper, M. M., & Holzman, M. (1989). *Writing as social action.* Portsmouth, NH: Boynton/Cook.

Corbett, E. P. J. (1965). *Classical rhetoric for the modern student.* New York: Oxford University Press.

Couture, B. (1991, March). *Empiricism and interpretation in studies of professional writing.* Presentation at the Conference on College Composition and Communication, Boston.

Couture, B. (1992). Categorizing professional discourse: Engineering, administrative, and technical/professional writing. *Journal of Business and Technical Communication, 6*(1), 5–37.

Couture, B., Goldstein, J. R., Malone, E. L., Nelson, B., & Quiroz, S. (1985). Building a professional writing program through a university-industry collaborative. In L. Odell & D. Goswami (Eds.), *Writing in nonacademic settings* (pp. 391–426). New York: Guilford.

Couture, B., & Rymer, J. R. (1989). Interactive writing on the job: Definitions and implications of "collaboration." In M. Kogen (Ed.), *Writing in the business professions* (pp. 73–93). Urbana, IL: NCTE & ABC.

Couture, B., & Rymer, J. R. (1991). Discourse interaction between writer and supervisor: A primary collaboration in workplace writing. In M. M. Lay & W. M. Karis (Eds.), *Collaborative writing in industry: Investigations in theory and practice* (pp. 87–108). Farmingdale, NY: Baywood.

Cragan, J. F., & Shields, D. C. (1981). *Applied communication research: A dramatist approach.* Prospect Heights, IL: Waveland.

Creditor, M. C. (1986, 14 October). Me and migraine. *New England Journal of Medicine*, 1029–1032.

Crismore, A. (1989). *Talking with readers: Metadiscourse as rhetorical act.* New York: Peter Lang.

Cross, G. A. (1990). A Bakhtinian exploration of factors affecting the collaborative writing of an executive letter of an annual report. *Research in the Teaching of English, 24*(2), 173–203.

Culler, J. (1980). Literary competence. In J. P. Tompkins (Ed.), *Reader-response criticism: From formalism to post-structuralism* (pp. 101–117). Baltimore: Johns Hopkins University Press.

Cypher, A. (1986). The structure of users' activities. In D. Norman & S. Draper (Eds.), *User-centered system design* (pp. 243–263). Hillsdale, NJ: Lawrence Erlbaum.

Daft, R. L., & Lengel, R. H. (1986). Organizational information requirements, media richness and structural design. *Management Science, 32*, 554–571.

Damodaran, L. (1981). The role of user support. In B. Schackel (Ed.), *Man-computer interaction: Human factors aspects of computers and people* (pp. 13–19). Alphenaan den Rijn, the Netherlands: Sijhoff and Noordhoff.

Dautermann, J. (1991). *Writing at Good Hope Hospital: A study of negotiated discourse in the workplace.* Unpublished doctoral dissertation, Purdue University, W. Lafayette, IN.

Davis, R. M. (1977). How important is technical writing? A survey of the opinions of successful engineers. *The Technical Writing Teacher, 4*(3), 83–88.

Debs, M. B. (1986). *Collaboration and collaborative writing: A study of technical writing in the computer industry.* Unpublished doctoral dissertation, Rensselaer Polytechnic Institute, Troy, NY.

Debs, M. B. (1989). Collaborative writing in industry. In B. E. Fearing & W. K. Sparrow (Eds.), *Technical writing: Theory and practice* (pp. 33–42). New York: MLA.

de Certeau, M. (1984). *The practice of everyday life* (S. Rendall, Trans.). Berkeley: University of California Press.

Denzin, N. K. (1989). *Interpretive interactionism.* Newbury Park, CA: Sage.

Devitt, A. J. (1991). Intertextuality in tax accounting: Generic, referential, and functional. In C. Bazerman & J. Paradis (Eds.), *Textual dynamics of the professions* (pp. 336–357). Madison: University of Wisconsin Press.

Diamond, S. (1987). Treatment of chronic headache: A non-pharmacologic approach. *Postgraduate Medicine, 81*, 206–210.

Diamond, S., & Blau, J. N. (1986). Diet and headache: Is there a link? *Postgraduate Medicine, 79*, 279–286.

Dieterich, D. (1989). Writing by academic professionals. In M. Kogen (Ed.), *Writing in the business professions* (pp. 174–184). Urbana, IL: NCTE & ABC.

Dijk, T. A. van, & Kintsch, W. (1983). *Strategies of discourse comprehension.* New York: Academic.

DiPietro, R. (Ed.). (1982). *Linguistics and the Professions: Proceedings of the Second Annual Delaware Symposium on Language Studies.* Norwood, NJ: Ablex.

DiSalvo, V. S., & Larsen, J. K. (1987). A contingency approach to communication skill importance: The impact of occupation, direction, and position. *Journal of Business Communication, 24*(3), 3–22.

Dobrin, D. N. (1983). What's technical about technical writing? In P. V. Anderson,

J. R. Brockmann, & C. R. Miller (Eds.), *New essays in technical and scientific communication: Research, theory, practice* (pp. 227–250). Farmingdale, NY: Baywood.

Dobrin, D. N. (1987). Writing without disciplines. *Journal of Business and Technical Communication, 1*(1), 5–8.

Doheny-Farina, S. (1984). *Writing in an emergent business organization: An ethnographic study.* Unpublished doctoral dissertation, Rensselaer Polytechnic Institute, Troy, NY.

Doheny-Farina, S. (1986). Writing in an emerging organization: An ethnographic study. *Written Communication, 3*(2), 158–185.

Doheny-Farina, S. (Ed.). (1988). *Effective documentation: What we have learned from research.* Cambridge: MIT.

Doheny-Farina, S. (1991a). *From lab to market: A case study of the role of instructional texts in the transfer of technology.* Unpublished manuscript.

Doheny-Farina, S. (1991b, March). *Multiple interpretations and the publication of ethnographic texts.* Presentation at the Conference on College Composition and Communication, Boston.

Doheny-Farina, S., & Odell, L. (1985). Ethnographic research on writing: Assumptions and methodology. In L. Odell & D. Goswami (Eds.), *Writing in nonacademic settings* (pp. 503–535). New York: Guilford.

Drass, K. A. (1988). Discourse and occupational perspective: A comparison of nurse practitioners and physician assistants. *Discourse Processes, 11*(2), 163–182.

Driskill, L. P. (1989). Understanding the writing context in organizations. In M. Kogen (Ed.), *Writing in the business professions* (pp. 125–145). Urbana, IL: NCTE & ABC.

Driskill, L. P., & Goldstein, J. R. (1986). Uncertainty: Theory and practice in organizational communication. *Journal of Business Communication, 23*(3), 41–56.

Dubois, B. L. (1981). The management of pity in biomedical speeches. *The Seventh LACUS Forum 1980, 249–255.*

Dubois, B. L. (1987). Something of the order of around forty to forty-four: Imprecise numerical expressions in biomedical slide talks. *Language in Society, 16*(4), 527–541.

Dubois, B. L. (1988). Citation in biomedical journal articles. *English for Special Purposes, 7*(3), 181–194.

Duffy, T., Mehlenbacher, B., & Palmer, J. (1989). The evaluation of online help systems: A conceptual model. In E. Barrett (Ed.), *The society of text: Hypertext, hypermedia, and the social construction of information* (pp. 362–387). Cambridge: MIT.

Eason, K. D. (1977). The potential and reality of task performance by man-computer systems. In A. Pakin (Ed.), *Computing and people* (pp. 55–62). London: Edward Arnold.

Ede, L., & Lunsford, A. A. (1983). Why write . . . together? *Rhetoric Review, 1,* 150–157.

Ede, L., & Lunsford, A. A. (1986). Collaborative learning: Lessons from the world of work. *Writing Program Administration, 9,* 17–26.

Ede, L., & Lunsford, A. A. (1990). *Singular texts/plural authors: Perspectives on collaborative writing*. Carbondale: Southern Illinois University Press.

Edmeads, J. (1984, November). Placebos and the power of negative thinking [Editorial]. *Headache*, 342–343.

Eisenberg, D., & Wright, T. L. (1985). *Encounters with qi: Exploring Chinese medicine*. New York: Norton.

Eisenstein, E. (1979). *The printing press as an agent of change* (2 vols.). Cambridge: Cambridge University Press.

Eisner, E. W. (1981). On the differences between scientific and artistic approaches to qualitative research. *Educational Review, 10*(4), 5–9.

Eisner, E. W., & Peshkin, A. (Eds.). (1990). *Qualitative inquiry in education: The continuing debate*. New York: Teachers College, Columbia University Press.

Elbow, P. (1973). *Writing without teachers*. New York: Oxford University Press.

Elwork, A., Alfini, J. J., & Sales, B. D. (1982). *Making jury instructions understandable*. Charlottesville, VA: Michie/Bobbs-Merrill.

Elwork, A., Sales, B. D., & Alfini, J. J. (1977). Juridic decisions: In ignorance of the law or in light of it? *Law and Human Behavior, 1*, 163–190.

Emig, J. (1964). The uses of the unconscious in composing. *College Composition and Communication, 21*, 6–11.

Emig, J. (1982). Inquiry paradigms and writing. *College Composition and Communication, 33*(1), 64–75.

Engel, B. S. (1975). *A handbook of documentation*. Grand Forks: University of North Dakota Press, North Dakota Study Group on Evaluation Monographs.

Erickson, B., Lind, E. A., Johnson, B. C., & O'Barr, W. M. (1978). Speech style and impression formation in a court setting: The effects of "powerful" and "powerless" speech. *Journal of Experimental and Social Psychology, 14*, 226–279.

Faigley, L. (1985). Nonacademic writing: The social perspective. In L. Odell & D. Goswami (Eds.), *Writing in nonacademic settings* (pp. 231–248). New York: Guilford.

Faigley, L. (1986). Competing theories of process: A critique and a proposal. *College English, 48*, 527–542.

Faigley, L., & Miller, T. P. (1982). What we learn from writing on the job. *College English, 44*, 557–569.

Farkas, D. K. (1991). Collaborative writing, software development, and the university of collaborative activity. In M. M. Lay & W. M. Karis (Eds.), *Collaborative writing in industry: Investigations in theory and practice* (pp. 13–30). Amityville, NY: Baywood.

Feinberg, S., & Goldman, J. (1985). Content for a course in technical communication: Results of a survey. *Technical Communication, 32*(2), 21–25.

Feyerabend, P. (1978). *Against method*. Theford, Norfolk, Great Britain: Verso Edition, Thetford.

Fielder, F. E. (1964). A contingency model of leadership effectiveness. In L. Berkowitz (Ed.), *Advances in experimental social psychology* (Vol. 1, pp. 149–190). New York: Academic.

Bibliography

Fielder, F. E. (1967). *A theory of leadership effectiveness.* New York: McGraw Hill.

Finegan, E. (1978). *Comprehensibility in legal discourse.* Paper delivered at the Conference on "Voice Analysis on Trial," Salt Lake City.

Fish, S. (1980). *Is there a text in this class? The authority of interpretive communities.* Cambridge: Harvard University Press.

Fisher, B. A. (1974). *Small group decision making.* New York: McGraw-Hill.

Fleck, L. (1979). *Genesis and the development of a scientific fact.* Chicago: University of Chicago Press. (Original work published 1935)

Floreak, M. J. (1989). Designing for the real world: Using research to turn a "target audience" into real people. *Technical Communication, 36*(4), 373–381.

Flower, L. (1979). Writer-based prose: A cognitive basis for problems in writing. *College English, 41,* 19–37.

Flower, L. (1981). *Problem-solving strategies for writing.* Chicago: Harcourt Brace Jovanovich.

Flower, L. (1988). The construction of purpose in writing and reading. *College English, 50,* 528–550.

Flower, L., & Hayes, J. (1980). The dynamics of composing: Making plans and juggling constraints. In L. W. Gregg & E. R. Steinberg (Eds.), *Cognitive Processes in Writing* (pp. 31–50). Hillsdale, NJ: Lawrence Erlbaum.

Foss, D., Smith-Kerker, P., & Rosson, M. B. (1987). On comprehending a computer manual: Analysis of variables affecting performance. *International Journal of Man-Machine Studies, 26,* 277–300.

Foster, D. (1987). Comment. *College English, 49,* 709–711.

Foucault, M. (1979). What is an author? In J. V. Harari (Ed.), *Textual strategies: Perspectives in post-structuralist criticism* (pp. 141–160). Ithaca: Cornell University Press.

Frank, G. (1979). Finding the common denominator: A phenomenological critique of life history method. *Ethos, 7*(1), 68–94.

Frankel, R. (1989). Microanalysis and the medical encounter: An exploratory study. In D. T. Helm, W. T. Anderson, A. J. Meehan, & A. W. Rawls (Eds.), *The interactional order: New directions in the study of social order.* New York: Irvington.

Frankel, R. (in press). The medical record and the social construction of clinical reality. In R. Frankel (Ed.), *Language at work: Studies in situated interaction.* Norwood, NJ: Ablex.

Freadman, A. (1987). Anyone for tennis? In I. Reid (Ed.), *The place of genre in learning: Current debates* (pp. 91–124). Geelong, Australia: Deakin University Press.

Freed, R. C., & Broadhead, G. J. (1987). Discourse communities: Sacred texts and institutional norms. *College Composition and Communication, 38*(2), 154–165.

Freedman, A. (1987). Learning to write again: Discipline-specific writing at university. *Carleton Papers in Applied Language Studies, 4,* 95–114.

Freedman, A. (1989). Reconceiving genre. *Texte, 8,* 279–292.

Frost, P. J., Moore, L. F., Louis, M. R., Lundberg, C. C., & Martin, J. (Eds.). (1985). *Organizational culture.* Beverly Hills: Sage.

Gage, J. T. (1984). An adequate epistemology for composition: Classical and modern perspectives. In R. J. Conners, L. S. Ede, & A. A. Lunsford (Eds.), *Essays on classical rhetoric and modern discourse* (pp. 152–169). Carbondale: Southern Illinois University Press.

Garver, E. (1987). *Machiavelli and the history of prudence.* Madison: University of Wisconsin Press.

Geertz, C. (1973). *The interpretation of cultures.* New York: Basic.

Geertz, C. (1980). Blurred genres: The refiguration of social thought. *The American Scholar, 49,* 165–179.

Geertz, C. (Ed.). (1983a). *Local knowledge: Further essays in interpretive anthropology.* New York: Basic.

Geertz, C. (1983b). The way we think now: Toward an ethnography of modern thought. In C. Geertz (Ed.), *Local knowledge: Further essays in interpretive anthropology* (pp. 148–163). New York: Basic.

Gere, A. R. (1985). Empirical research in composition. In B. W. McClelland & T. R. Donovan (Eds.), *Perspectives on research and scholarship in composition* (pp. 110–124). New York: MLA.

Gettis, A. (1987, February). Serendipity and food sensitivity: A case study. *Headache,* 73–75.

Gilbert, G. N. (1977). Referencing as persuasion. *Social Studies of Science, 7,* 113–122.

Gilbert, G. N., & Mulkay, M. (1984). *Opening Pandora's box.* Cambridge: Cambridge University Press.

Glaser, B. G., & Strauss, A. L. (1967). *The discovery of grounded theory: Strategies for qualitative research.* Chicago: Aldine.

Glaser, E. R. (1987). Measuring and interpreting organizational culture. *Management Communication Quarterly, 1*(2), 173–198.

Goetz, J. P., & LeCompte, M. D. (1984). *Ethnography and qualitative design in educational research.* New York: Academic.

Goldhaber, G. (1983). *Organizational communication* (3rd ed.). Dubuque, IA: Brown.

Gopen, G. D. (1981). *Writing from a legal perspective.* St. Paul, MN: West.

Gopen, G. D. (1989). The state of legal writing: Res ipsa loquitur. In M. Kogen (Ed.), *Writing in the business professions* (pp. 146–173). Urbana, IL: NCTE & ABC.

Gopnick, M. (1973). *Linguistic structures in scientific texts.* The Hague: Mouton.

Gordon, M. (1985). Nursing diagnosis. *Annual Review of Nursing Research, 3,* 82–101.

Gould, J. D. (1980). Experiments on composing letters: Some facts, some myths, and some observations. In L. W. Gregg & E. R. Steinberg (Eds.), *Cognitive processes in writing* (pp. 97–127). Hillsdale, NJ: Lawrence Erlbaum.

Gouldner, A. (1982). Sociology: Contradictions and infrastructure. In E. Bredo & W. Feinberg (Eds.), *Knowledge and values in social and educational research* (pp. 324–354). Philadelphia: Temple University Press.

Graham, J. R. (1986, February). Headache as cranial angina [Guest editorial]. *Headache,* 104–105.

| Bibliography

Green, M. M., & Nolan, T. D. (1984). A systematic analysis of the technical communicator's job: A guide for educators. *Technical Communication, 31*(4), 9–12.

Greenbaum, H. H., DeWine, J., & Downs, C. W. (1987). Management and organizational communication measurement. *Management Communication Quarterly, 1*(1), 129–144.

Greenblatt, S. (1988). *Shakespearean negotiations.* Berkeley: University of California Press.

Gregory, H. B. (1948). Shorter judicial opinions. *Virginia Law Review, 34,* 362–369.

Gresset, M., & Polk, N. (1985). *Intertextuality in Faulkner.* Jackson: University Press of Mississippi.

Gross, A. G. (1988, Fall/Winter). Discourse on method: The rhetorical analysis of scientific texts. *PreText, 9* (3–4), 169–185.

Gross, A. G. (1990). *The rhetoric of science.* Cambridge: Harvard University Press.

Guba, E. G. (Ed.). (1990). *The paradigm dialog.* Beverly Hills: Sage.

Guinn, D. M. (1983). Ethos in technical discourse. *The Technical Writing Teacher, 11*(1), 31–37.

Gumperz, J. J. (Ed.). (1982). *Language and social identity.* London: Cambridge University Press.

Gunderson, C. H. (1986, January). Management of the migraine patient. *American Family Physician,* 137–143.

Haas, C. (1990). Composing in technological contexts. *Written Communication, 7,* 512–547.

Halliday, M. A. K. (1978). *Language as social semiotic: The social interpretation of language and meaning.* London: Edward Arnold.

Halliday, M. A. K. (1985). *An introduction to functional grammar.* London: Edward Arnold.

Halpern, J. (1988). Getting in deep: Using qualitative research in business and technical communication. *Journal of Business and Technical Communication, 2*(2), 22–43.

Harding, S. (1986). *The science question in feminism.* Ithaca: Cornell University Press.

Harre, R., & Secord, P. F. (1973). *The explanation of social behavior.* Totowa, NJ: Littlefield, Adams.

Harris, E. (1979). Applications of Kinneavy's *Theory of Discourse* to technical writing. *College English, 40*(6), 625–632.

Harris, E. (1980). Response to Elizabeth Tebeaux. *College English, 41*(7), 827–829.

Harris, J. (1989). The idea of community in the study of writing. *College Composition and Communication, 40,* 11–22.

Harris, S. (1989). Defendent resistance to power and control in court. In H. Coleman (Ed.), *Working with language: A multidisciplinary consideration of language use in work contexts* (pp. 131–164). Berlin: Mouton de Gruyter.

Harris, W. V. (in press). Intertextuality. *A Dictionary of Literary Concepts.* Westport, CT: Greenwood.

Harrison, T. (1987). Frameworks for the study of writing in organizational contexts. *Written Communication, 4*(1), 3–23.

Harrison, T. M., & Debs, M. B. (1988). Conceptualizing the organizational role of technical communicators: A systems approach. *Journal of Business and Technical Communication, 2*(2), 5–21.

Haviland, W. A. (1980). *Cultural anthropology* (3rd ed.). New York: Holt.

Hayakawa, S. I. (1963). *Symbol, status, and personality.* New York: Harcourt Brace World.

Hayes, J. R., & Flower, L. (1983). Uncovering cognitive processes in writing: An introduction to protocol analysis. In B. Rosenthal, L. Tamor, & S. Walmsley (Eds.). *Research in writing: Principles and methods* (pp. 206–220). New York: Longman.

Herndl, C. G. (1991). Writing ethnography: Representation, rhetoric, and institutional practice. *College English, 53*(3), 320–332.

Herrington, A. (1985). Writing in academic settings: A study of the contexts for writing in two college chemical engineering courses. *Research in the Teaching of English, 19,* 331–361.

Hewlett-Packard (1979). *82143A Printer Owner's Handbook.*

Himley, M. (1991). *Shared territory: Understanding children's writing as works.* New York: Oxford University Press.

Hofstede, G., Neuijen, B., Ohayv, D. D., & Sanders, G. (1990). Measuring organizational cultures: A qualitative and quantitative study across twenty cases. *Administrative Science Quarterly, 35,* 286–316.

Huckin, T. N. (1987, March). *Surprise value in scientific discourse.* Paper presented at the Conference on College Composition and Communication, Atlanta.

Hudson, K. (1978). *The jargon of the professions.* London: Macmillan.

Huettman, E. (1990). *Writing for the unknown reader: An ethnographic case study in a business setting.* Unpublished doctoral dissertation, Purdue University, W. Lafayette, IN.

Hymes, D. (1972). Models of the interaction of language and social life. In J. J. Gumperz & D. Hymes (Eds.), *Directions in sociolinguistics: The ethnography of communication* (pp. 35–71). New York: Holt, Rinehart, & Winston.

IBM (1982). *The IBM Displaywriter System General Information Manual.*

Jacoby, H. (1973). *The bureaucratization of the world* (L. Kanes, Trans.). Berkeley: University of California Press.

Jamieson, K. (1973). Generic constraints and the rhetorical situation. *Philosophy & Rhetoric, 6*(3), 162–170.

Janda, M. A. (1989). Talk into writing: Writers in collaboration. *Dissertation Abstracts International, 49,* 10A. (University Microfilms No. 88–27, 226)

Javlin, F., Putnam, L., Roberts, K., & Porter, L. (Eds.). (1987). *Handbook of Organizational Communication.* Beverly Hills: Sage.

Jermier, J. M. (1985). When the sleeper wakes: A short story extending themes in radical organizational theory. *Journal of Management, 11,* 67–80.

The job outlook in brief. (1982, Spring). *Occupational Outlook Quarterly,* 7–25.

Johnson, C. (1988). Intertextuality and the psychic model. *Paragraph, 2,* 71–89.

Johnson, R. (1990). User-centeredness, situatedness, and designing the media of computer documentation. In *Proceedings of SIGDOC '90* (pp. 55–61). New York: ACM.

Johnson, T. S. (1986). Comment. *College English, 48*, 76.

Joliffe, D. A. (Ed.). (1988). *Advances in writing research. Vol. 2: Writing in Academic Disciplines.* Norwood, NJ: Ablex.

Jones, G. R. (1983). Life history methodology. In G. Morgan (Ed.), *Beyond method* (pp. 129–146). Beverly Hills: Sage.

Journet, D. (1990). Forms of discourse and the sciences of the mind: Luria, Sacks, and the role of narrative in neurological case histories. *Written Communication, 7* (2), 171–199.

Kalmbach, J. E., Jobst, J. W., & Meese, G. P. W. (1986). Education and practice: A survey of graduates of a technical communication program. *Technical Communication, 33*(1), 21–26.

Kantor, K. J., Kirby, D. R., & Goetz, J. P. (1981). Research in context: Ethnographic studies in English education. *Research in the Teaching of English, 15*(4), 293–309.

Karis, W. (1991, March). *To be a bridge or to be a collaborator: A problem for professional writers in the '90s.* Presentation at the Conference on College Composition and Communication, Boston.

Keeler, H. (1990). Portrait of a technical communicator: A bibliographic review of current research. *Technical Communication, 37*(1), 41–48.

Keller, E. F. (1985). *Reflections on gender and science.* New Haven: Yale University Press.

Kelton, R. (1984). The internal report in complex organizations. *Proceedings of the 30th International Technical Communication Conference* (E50–E55). Washington, DC: Society for Technical Communication.

Kieras, D., & Bovair, S. (1985). *The acquisition of procedures from text: A production-system analysis of transfer of training* (Tech. Rep. No. 16). Ann Arbor, MI: Office of Naval Research.

Kieras, D., & Polson, P. (1985). An approach to the formal analysis of user complexity. *International Journal of Man-Machine Studies, 22*, 365–394.

Kinneavy, J. L. (1971). *A theory of discourse.* Englewood Cliffs, NJ: Prentice-Hall.

Kinneavy, J. L. (1986). *Kairos:* A neglected concept in classical rhetoric. In J. D. Moss (Ed.), *Rhetoric and praxis: The contribution of classical rhetoric to practical reasoning* (pp. 79–105). Washington, DC: The Catholic University Press.

Kirn, T. (1987). Migraine: Many things to many patients. *Journal of the American Medical Association, 257*(1), 12–13.

Kirtz, J. K., & Reep, D. C. (1991). A survey of the frequency, types, and importance of writing tasks in four career areas. *The Bulletin of the Association for Business Communication, 53*(4), 3–4.

Kittredge, R., & Lehrberger, J. (Eds.). (1982). *Sublanguage: Studies of language in restricted domains.* Berlin: Walter de Gruyter.

Kitzinger, S. D. (1980). *The complete book of pregnancy and childbirth.* New York: Alfred A. Knopf.

Kleimann, S. D. (1989). *Vertical collaboration and the report review process at the United*

States General Accounting Office. Unpublished doctoral dissertation, University of Maryland, College Park.

Kleimann, S. D. (1991). The complexity of workplace review. *Technical Communication, 38*(4), 520–526.

Kleine, M. (1989, March). *Beyond triangulation: Ethnography, writing, and rhetoric.* Paper presented at the Conference on College Composition and Communication, Seattle.

Kneupper, C. (1979). Dramatistic invention: The pentad as heuristic procedure. *Rhetoric Society Quarterly, 9,* 130–136.

Knoblauch, C. H. (1980). Intentionality in the writing process. *College Composition and Communication, 31,* 153–159.

Knoblauch, C. H. (1989). The teaching and practice of 'professional writing.' In M. Kogan (Ed.), *Writing in the business professions* (pp. 246–264). Urbana, IL: NCTE & ABC.

Knoke, D., & Kuklinski, J. H. (1982). *Network analysis.* Beverly Hills: Sage.

Knorr-Cetina, K. D. (1981). *The Manufacture of knowledge: An essay on the constructivist and contextual nature of science.* Oxford: Pergamon.

Kogen, M. (Ed.). (1989). *Writing in the business professions.* Urbana, IL: NCTE & ABC.

Koh, T. C. (1982). Tai chi and anklylosing spondylitis—a personal experience. *American Journal of Chinese Medicine, 10,* 59–61.

Kolin, P. C., & Marquard, R. G. (1986). Research on legal writing: A bibliography. *Law Library Journal, 78,* 492–517.

Kothenbeutel, K. L. (1988). Planning and conducting research. In P. G. Campbell, T. Housel, & K. O. Locker (Eds.), *Conducting research in business communication* (pp. 1–15). Urbana, IL: ABC.

Kraut, R., Dumais, S., & Koch, S. (1989). Computerization, productivity, and quality of work-life. *Communications of the ACM, 32,* 220–238.

Kristeva, J. (1980). *Desire in language* (L. S. Roudiez, Ed.; T. Gora, A. Jardine, & L. Roudiez, Trans.). New York: Columbia University Press.

Kuhn, T. S. (1970). *The structure of scientific revolutions* (2nd ed.). Chicago: University of Chicago Press.

Kuhn, T. S. (1977). *The essential tension.* Chicago: University of Chicago Press.

Kuipers, J. C. (1989). Medical discourse in anthropological contexts: View of language and power. *Medical Anthropology Quarterly, 4*(1), 99–123.

Lane, P. L., & Ross, R. (1985, September). Intravenous Chlorpromazine—Preliminary results in acute migraine. *Headache,* 302–304.

Langer, J. A., & Applebee, A. N. (1987). *How writing shapes thinking.* Urbana, IL: NCTE.

Langer, S. K. (1951). *Philosophy in a new key.* New York: The New American Library.

Langness, L. L. (1965). *The life history in anthropological science.* New York: Winston.

Langness, L. L., & Frank, G. (1981). *Lives: Anthropological approach to biography.* Novato, CA: Chandler & Sharp.

| Bibliography

Lanham, R. (1990). The extraordinary convergence: Democracy, technology, theory, and the university curriculum. *South Atlantic Quarterly, 89*, 29–50.

Latour, B. (1987). *Science in action: How to follow scientists and engineers through society.* Cambridge: Harvard University Press.

Latour, B., & Woolgar, S. (1979). *Laboratory life: The social construction of scientific facts.* Beverly Hills: Sage.

Lauer, J. M., & Asher, J. W. (1988). *Composition research: Empirical designs.* New York: Oxford University Press.

Lauer, J. M., Montague, G., Lunsford, A., & Emig, J. (1985). *The four worlds of writing* (2nd ed.). New York: Harper and Row.

Lave, J. (1985). Introduction: Situationally specific practice (The social organization of knowledge and practice: A symposium). *Anthropology and Education Quarterly, 16*, 171–176.

Lave, J. (1988). *Cognition in practice.* Cambridge: Cambridge University Press.

Lay, M. M., & Karis, W. M. (Eds.). (1991). *Collaborative writing in industry: Investigations in theory and practice.* Amityville, NY: Baywood.

LeFevre, K. B. (1987). *Invention as a social act.* Carbondale: Southern Illinois University Press.

Leflar, R. A. (1974). *Appellate judicial opinions.* St. Paul, MN: West.

Lengel, R. H., & Daft, R. L. (1988). The selection of communication media as an executive skill. *Academy of Management Executive, 2*, 225–232.

Lentz, J. (1983). Spoken versus written inartistic proof in Athenian courts. *Philosophy and Rhetoric, 16*(4), 242–261.

Levenstein, J. H., Brown, J. B., Weston, W. W., Stewart, M., McCracken, E., & McWhinney, I. (1989). Patient-centered clinical interviewing. In M. Stewart & D. Roter (Eds.), *Communicating with medical patients* (pp. 107–123). Newbury Park, CA: Sage.

Levi, J. N. (1985). Rights of linguistic minorities in the United States: An introductory bibliography. *Language Planning Newsletter, 11*(3), 2–5.

Levi, J. N. (1990). The study of language in the judicial process. In J. N. Levi & A. G. Walker (Eds.), *Language in the judicial process* (pp. 3–35). New York: Plenum.

Levi, J. N., & Walker, A. G. (Eds.). (1990). *Language in the judicial process.* New York: Plenum.

Levine, R. H. (1977). Why the ethogenic method and the dramaturgical perspective are incompatible. *Journal for the Theory of Social Behavior, 7*, 237–247.

Lewis, R. A. (1971). *Annual Reports.* Zurich: Graphics.

Light, R. J., & Pillemer, D. B. (1984). *Summing up: The science of reviewing research.* Cambridge: Harvard University Press.

Lincoln, Y. S., & Guba, E. G. (1985). *Naturalistic inquiry.* Beverly Hills: Sage.

Lind, E. A., & O'Barr, W. M. (1979). The social significance of speech in the courtroom. In H. Giles & R. N. St. Clair (Eds.), *Language and social psychology.* Baltimore: University Park.

Linde, C. (1988). The quantitative study of communicative success: Politeness and accidents in aviation discourse. *Language in Society, 17*(3), 375–400.

Linde, L. (1989). An information-seeker's mental model of the context and search principles in a database. In F. Klix, N. A. Streitz, Y. Waern, & H. Wandke (Eds.), *Man-computer interaction research* (pp. 149–159). Amsterdam: Horth-Holland.

Little, S. B., & McLaren, M. C. (1987). Profile of technical writers in San Diego County: Results of a pilot study. *Journal of Technical Writing and Communication, 17,* 9–23.

Lunsford, A. A., & Ede, L. (1986). Why write . . . together: A research update. *Rhetoric Review, 5*(1), 71–81.

Lutz, J. A. (1989). Writers in organizations and how they learn the image: Theory, research, and implications. In C. B. Matalene (Ed.), *Worlds of writing: Teaching and learning in discourse communities of work* (pp. 113–135). New York: Random House.

Lyon, A. (in press). Representing communities: Teaching turbulence. *Rhetoric Review.*

Machiavelli, N. (1965). *The prince.* In A. Gilbert (Trans.), *Machiavelli: The chief works and others* (Vol. 1, pp. 5–96). Durham, NC: Duke University Press. (Original work published in 1532)

Maclean, J. (1989). Approaches to describing doctor-patient interviews. In H. Coleman (Ed.), *Working with language: A multidisciplinary consideration of language use in work contexts* (pp. 263–296). Berlin: Mouton de Gruyter.

Maher, J. (1986). State of the art article: English for medical purposes. *Language Teaching, 19*(2), 112–145.

Maimon, E. (1983). Maps and genres: Exploring connections in the arts and sciences. In W. B. Horner (Ed.), *Composition and literature: Bridging the gap* (pp. 110–125). Chicago: University of Chicago Press.

Malone, E. L. (1991). Facilitating groups through selective participation: An example of collaboration from NASA. In M. M. Lay & W. M. Karis (Eds.), *Collaborative writing in industry: Investigations in theory and practice* (pp. 109–119). Amityville, NY: Baywood.

Marker, C. (1988). *Setting standards for professional nursing: The Marker model.* St. Louis: C. V. Mosby.

Mason, D. (1989). An examination of authentic dialogues for use in the ESP classroom. *English for Special Purposes, 8*(1), 85–92.

Mason, E. (1970). *Collaborative learning.* London: Ward Lock.

Matalene, C. B. (Ed.). (1989). Introduction. *Worlds of writing: Teaching and learning in discourse communities of work.* New York: Random House.

Mathes, J. C. (1986). Three-Mile Island: The management communication role. *Engineering Management International, 3,* 261–268.

Mathes, J. C., & Stevenson, D. W. (1976). *Designing technical reports: Writing for audiences in organizations.* Indianapolis: Bobbs-Merrill.

McCarthy, L. P. (1987). A stranger in strange lands: A college student writing across the curriculum. *Research in the Teaching of English, 21*(3), 233–265.

McCarthy, L. P. (1991). A psychiatrist using DMS-III: The influence of a charter document in psychiatry. In C. Bazerman & J. Paradis (Eds.), *Textual dynamics of the professions* (pp. 358–378). Madison: University of Wisconsin Press.

McCloskey, D. M. (1985). *The rhetoric of economics*. Madison: University of Wisconsin Press.

McGrath, J. E., Martin, J., & Kulka, R. A. (1982). *Judgment calls in research*. Beverly Hills: Sage.

Mellinkoff, D. (1982). *Legal writing: Sense and nonsense*. St. Paul, MN: West.

Merrill, J. C., & Lowenstein, R. L. (1973). *Media, messages, and men*. New York: David McKay.

Michel, S. L. (1989). *Writing and learning to write in a bicultural, corporate setting*. Unpublished doctoral dissertation, University of Cincinnati, Cincinnati, OH.

Miles, M., & Huberman, A. M. (1984). *Qualitative data analysis: A sourcebook of new methods*. Beverly Hills: Sage.

Miller, C. R. (1979). A humanistic rationale for technical writing. *College English, 40*(6), 610–617.

Miller, C. R. (1980). Response to Elizabeth Tebeaux. *College English, 41*(7), 825–827.

Miller, C. R. (1984). Genre as social action. *Quarterly Journal of Speech, 70*, 151–167.

Miller, C. R. (1985). Invention in technical and scientific discourse: A prospective survey. In M. G. Moran & D. Journet (Eds.), *Research in technical communication: A bibliographic sourcebook* (pp. 117–162). Westport, CT: Greenwood.

Miller, C. R. (1989). What's practical about technical writing? In B. E. Fearing & W. K. Sparrow (Eds.), *Technical writing: Theory and practice* (pp. 14–24). New York: MLA.

Miller, C. R., & Selzer, J. (1985). Special topics of argument in engineering reports. In L. Odell & D. Goswami (Eds.), *Writing in nonacademic settings* (pp. 309–341). New York: Guilford.

Miller, O. (1985). Intertextuality identity. In M. J. Valdez & O. Miller (Eds.), *Identity of the literary text* (pp. 19–40). Toronto: University of Toronto Press.

Miller, S. (1983). Rhetorical maturity: Definition and development. In A. Freedman & I. Pringle (Eds.), *Reinventing the rhetorical tradition* (pp. 119–127). University of Central Arkansas: L&S Books.

Miller, S. (1989). *Rescuing the subject: A critical introduction to rhetoric and the writer*. Carbondale: Southern Illinois University Press.

Mintzberg, H. (1973). *The nature of managerial work*. New York: Harper & Row.

Mintzberg, H. (1975, July–August). The manager's job: Folklore and fact. *Harvard Business Review*, 49–61.

Mirel, B. (1989). The politics of usability: The organizational functions of an in-house manual. In S. Doheny-Farina (Ed.), *Effective documentation: What we have learned from research* (pp. 277–297). Cambridge: MIT.

Mirel, B., Feinberg, S., & Allmendinger, L. (1991). Designing manuals for active learning styles. *Technical Communication, 38*, 75–87.

Mishler, E. G. (1979). Meaning in context: Is there any other kind? *Harvard Education Review, 49*, 1–19.

Mishler, E. G. (1984). *The discourse of medicine: Dialectics of medical interviews*. Norwood, NJ: Ablex.

Monge, P. R. (1977). The systems perspective as a theoretical basis for the study of communication. *Communication Quarterly, 25,* 119–129.

Moretti, R., & Ayer, W. A. (1983). *The president's conference on the dentist-patient relationship and the management of fear, anxiety, and pain.* Chicago: American Dental Association.

Morgan, G. (Ed.). (1983). *Beyond method: Strategies for social research.* Beverly Hills: Sage.

Morgan, G. (1986). *Images of organizations.* Beverly Hills: Sage.

Morgan, M., Allen, N., Moore, T., Atkinson, D., & Snow, C. (1987). Collaborative writing in the classroom. *Bulletin of the Association for Business Communication, 50*(3), 20–26.

Mulrow, C. (1987). The medical review article: State of the science. *Annals of Internal Medicine, 106,* 485–488.

Murphy, J. (1974). *Rhetoric in the middle ages.* Berkeley: University of California Press.

Murray, D. (1988). The context of oral and written language: A framework for mode and medium switching. *Language in Society, 17*(3), 251–374.

Myers, D. G. (1980). *The inflated self: Human illusions and the biblical call to hope.* New York: Seabury.

Myers, G. (1985). Text as knowledge claims: The social construction of two biologists' proposals. *Written Communication, 2*(3), 219–245.

Myers, G. (1986). Reality, consensus, and reform in the rhetoric of composition teaching. *College English, 48*(2), 154–174.

Myers, G. (1990a). Stories and styles in two molecular biology review articles. In C. Bazerman & H. Paradis (Eds.), *Textual dynamics of the professions* (pp. 45–75). Madison: University of Wisconsin Press.

Myers, G. (1990b). *Writing biology: Texts in the social construction of scientific knowledge.* Madison: University of Wisconsin Press.

Nelson, J. S., Megill, A., & McCloskey, D. N. (Eds.). (1987). *The rhetoric of the human sciences: Language and argument in scholarship and public affairs.* Madison: University of Wisconsin Press.

Norman, D. (1986). Cognitive engineering. In D. Norman & S. Draper (Eds.), *User-centered system design* (pp. 31–65). Hillsdale, NJ: Lawrence Erlbaum.

North, S. (1987). *The making of knowledge in composition: Portrait of an emerging field.* Upper Montclair, NJ: Boynton/Cook.

Northey, M. (1990). The need for writing skill in accounting firms. *Managerial Communication Quarterly, 3,* 474–495.

Nystrand, M. (1986). Introduction. *The structure of written communication: Studies in reciprocity between writers and readers.* Orlando, FL: Academic.

Nystrand, M. (1989). A social-interactive model of writing. *Written Communication, 6*(1), 66–85.

O'Barr, W. M. (1982). *Linguistic evidence: Language, power, and strategy in the courtroom.* New York: Academic.

O'Barr, W. M., & Conley, J. M. (1990). Litigant satisfaction versus legal adequacy in small claims court narratives. In J. N. Levi & A. G. Walker (Eds.), *Language in the judicial process* (pp. 3–35). New York: Plenum.

Odell, L. (1983). The discourse-based interview: Procedure and rationale. In P. Mosenthal, L. Tamor, & S. Walmsley (Eds.), *Writing research: Methods and procedures* (pp. 220–236). London: Longman.

Odell, L. (1985). Beyond the text: Relations between writing and social context. In L. Odell & D. Goswami (Eds.), *Writing in nonacademic settings* (pp. 249–280). New York: Guilford.

Odell, L., & Goswami, D. (1982). Writing in a nonacademic setting. *Research in the Teaching of English, 16,* 201–223.

Odell, L., & Goswami, D. (1984). Writing in a nonacademic setting. In R. Beach and L. S. Bridwell (Eds.), *New directions in composition research* (pp. 233–258). New York: Guilford.

Odell, L., & Goswami, D. (Eds.). (1985). *Writing in nonacademic settings.* New York: Guilford.

Odell, L., Goswami, D., & Herrington, A. (1983a). The discourse-based interview: A procedure for exploring tacit knowledge of writers in non-academic settings. In P. Mosenthal, L. Tamor, & S. Walmsley (Eds.), *Research on writing: Principles and methods* (pp. 220–236). New York: Longman.

Odell, L., Goswami, D., & Herrington, A. (1983b). Exploring writers' tacit knowledge: Research procedures and rationale. In P. Mosenthal (Ed.), *Writing research: Methods and procedures* (pp. 221–236). New York: Longman.

Odell, L., Goswami, D., Herrington, A., & Quick, D. (1983). Studying writing in non-academic settings. In P. V. Anderson, J. R. Brockmann, & C. R. Miller (Eds.), *New essays in technical and scientific communication: Research, theory, practice* (pp. 17–40). Farmingdale, NY: Baywood.

Odell, L., Goswami, D., & Quick, D. (1983). Writing outside the English composition class: Implications for teaching and for learning. In R. W. Bailey & R. M. Fosheim (Eds.), *Literacy for life* (pp. 175–194). New York: MLA.

O'Donnell, P., & Davis, R. C. (Eds.). (1989). *Intertextuality and contemporary American fiction.* Baltimore: Johns Hopkins University Press.

Olsen, L. A., & Huckin, T. N. (1990). Point-driven understanding in engineering lecture comprehension. *English for Special Purposes, 9,* 33–47.

Olsen, L. A., & Huckin, T. N. (1991). *Technical writing and professional communication.* New York: McGraw Hill.

Olsen, L. A., & Johnson, R. (1989). A discourse-based approach to the assessment of readability. *Linguistics and Education, 1,* 207–231.

Ong, W. J. (1982). *Orality and literacy: The technologizing of the word.* London: Methuen.

Orr, L. (1986). Intertextuality and the cultural text in recent semiotics. *College English, 48,* 811–823.

Pacanowsky, M. (1983). A small-town cop: Communication in, out, and about a crisis. In L. L. Putnam & M. E. Pacanowsky (Eds.), *Communication and organizations: An interpretive approach* (pp. 261–282). Beverly Hills: Sage.

Pace, W. (1983). *Organizational communication: Foundations for human resource development*. Englewood Cliffs, NJ: Prentice-Hall.

Paradis, J., Dobrin, D., & Bower, D. (1984). Personal correspondence. Cited in L. Odell & D. Goswami (Eds.), (1985), *Writing in nonacademic settings* (p. 68). New York: Guilford.

Paradis, J., Dobrin, D., & Miller, R. (1985). Writing at Exxon ITD: Notes on the writing environment of an R&D organization. In L. Odell & D. Goswami (Eds.), *Writing in nonacademic settings* (pp. 281–307). New York: Guilford.

Paré, A. (in press). Ushering "audience" out: From oration to conversation. *Textual Studies in Canada, 1,* 45–64.

Parkhurst, C. (1990). The composition process of science writers. *English for Specific Purposes, 9*(2), 169–180.

Partridge, S. (1986). So what is task orientation, anyway? *IEEE Transactions on Professional Communications, PC–29,* 26–32.

"Patient." (1971). *Compact edition of Oxford English Dictionary,* (Vol. 2). New York: Oxford Press.

Patton, M. Q. (1975). *Alternative evaluation research paradigms*. Grand Forks: University of North Dakota Press, North Dakota Study Group on Evaluation Monographs.

Pearce, W. B., & Chen, V. (1989). Ethnography as sermonic: The rhetorics of Clifford Geertz and James Clifford. In H. W. Simons (Ed.), *Rhetoric in the human sciences* (pp. 119–132). London: Sage.

Pellegrini, A., & Yawkey, T. (Eds.). (1984). *The development of oral and written language in social contexts*. Norwood, NJ: Ablex.

Perelman, C., & Olbrechts-Tyteca, L. (1969). *The new rhetoric*. Notre Dame: Notre Dame University Press.

Perelman, L. (1986). The context of classroom writing. *College English, 48*(5), 471–479.

Peters, D. P., & Ceci, S. J. (1982). Peer-review practices of psychological journals: The fate of published articles, submitted again. *The Behavioral and Brain Sciences, 5,* 187–255.

Pettigrew, A. M. (1979). On studying organizational cultures. *Administrative Science Quarterly, 24,* 570–581.

Pettinari, C. J. (1988). *Task, talk, and text in the operating room: A study in medical discourse*. Norwood, NJ: Ablex.

Pettinari, C. J. (1990). Review of "Discourse and institutional authority: Medicine, education, and law." *English for Special Purposes, 9*(3), 266–270.

Pettinari, C. J. (1992). *The problem of the interactional construction of accounts in a theory of genre*. Paper presented at the International Colloquium: Rethinking Genre, Ottawa.

Phelps, L. W. (1985). Dialectics of coherence: Toward an integrative theory. *College English, 47,* 12–29.

Phelps, L. W. (1988). *Composition as a human science: Contributions to the self-understanding of a discipline*. New York: Oxford University Press.

Bibliography

Phelps, L. W. (1990). Audience and authorship: The disappearing boundary. In G. Kirsch & D. Roen (Eds.), *A sense of audience in written communication* (pp. 153–174). Newbury Park, CA: Sage.

Piazza, C. L. (1987). Identifying context variables in research on writing: A review and suggested directions. *Written Communication, 4*(2), 107–137.

Piché, G. L., & Roen, D. (1987). Social cognition and writing: Interpersonal cognitive complexity and abstractness and the quality of students' persuasive writing. *Written Communication, 4*(1), 68–89.

Pinelli, T. E., Glassman, M., Barclay, R. O., & Oliu, E. W. (1989). *Technical communications in aeronautics: Results of an exploratory study—An analysis of profit managers' and nonprofit managers' responses* (NASA Report No. TM–101626). Washington, DC: National Aeronautics and Space Administration.

Pood, E. A. (1980). Functions of communication: An experimental study in group conflict situations. *Small Group Behavior, 11,* 76–87.

Porter, J. E. (1986). Intertextuality and the discourse community. *Rhetoric Review, 5,* 34–47.

Porter, J. E. (1990a). *Divisio* as em-/de-powering topic: A basis for argument in rhetoric and composition. *Rhetoric Review, 8,* 191–205.

Porter, J. E. (1990b, March). *The influence of the law suit on corporate composing processes.* Paper presented at the Conference on College Composition and Communication, Chicago.

Porter, J. E., & Sullivan, P. (1992). Repetition and the rhetoric of visual design. In B. Johnstone (Ed.), *Repetition in discourse: Interdisciplinary perspectives* (Vol. 2). Norwood, NJ: Ablex.

Prelli, L. J. (1989). *The rhetoric of science: Inventing scientific discourse.* Columbia: University of South Carolina Press.

Punch, M. (1986). The politics and ethics of fieldwork. *Qualitative Research Methods Series* (Vol. 3). Beverly Hills: Sage.

Purves, A. C., & Purves, W. (1986). Viewpoints: Cultures, text models, and the activity of writing. *Research in the Teaching of English, 20,* 174–197.

Putnam, L. L. (1983). The interpretive perspective: An alternative to functionalism. In L. L. Putnam & M. E. Pacanowsky (Eds.), *Communication and organizations: An interpretive approach* (pp. 31–54). Beverly Hills: Sage.

Putnam, L. L., & Pacanowsky, M. E. (Eds.). (1983). *Communication and organizations: An interpretive approach.* Beverly Hills: Sage.

Rabinow, P., & Sullivan, W. (Eds.). (1987). *Interpretive social science: A second look.* Berkeley: University of California Press.

Rafoth, B. A., & Rubin, D. L. (1988). *The social construction of written communication.* Norwood, NJ: Ablex.

Ray, H. (1985). A study of the effect of different data models on casual users' performance in writing database queries. *International Journal of Man-Machine Studies, 23,* 249–262.

Redish, J. C. (1988). Reading to learn to do. *The Technical Writing Teacher, 15*(3), 223–233.

Redish, J. C., Battison, R., & Gold, E. S. (1985). Making information accessible to the reader. In L. Odell & D. Goswami (Eds.), *Writing in non-academic settings* (pp. 129–153). New York: Guilford.

Reichardt, C., & Cook, T. (1979). *Qualitative and quantitative methods in evaluation research*. Beverly Hills: Sage.

Reither, J. A. (1985). Writing and knowing: Toward redefining the writing process. *College English, 47*(6), 620–628.

Reither, J. A. (1989). Teaching reading and writing: Texts, power, and the transfer of power (or, what if they had a revolution and nobody came?). *Inkshed, 8*(4), 3–8.

Reither, J. A. (1990). The writing *student* as researcher: Learning from our students. In D. A. Daiker & M. Morenberg (Eds.), *The writing teacher as researcher: Essays in the theory and practice of class-based research* (pp. 247–255). Portsmouth, NH: Heinemann-Boynton/Cook.

Reither, J. A., & Vipond, D. (1989). Writing as collaboration. *College English, 51*(8), 855–867.

Rieke, R. D., & Sillars, M. O. (1984). *Argumentation and the decision-making process* (2nd ed.). Glenville, IL: Scott, Foresman.

Robertson, F. (1988). *Airspeak: Radiotelephony communication for pilots*. Englewood Cliffs, NJ: Prentice-Hall.

Rogers, P. S., & Swales, J. (1990). We the people? An analysis of the Dana Corporation's policies document. *Journal of Business Communication, 27*(3), 293–314.

Rogoff, B. (1984). Introduction. Thinking and learning in social context. In B. Rogoff & J. Lave (Eds.), *Everyday cognition: Its development in social context* (pp. 1–8). Cambridge: Harvard University Press.

Roloff, M., & Miller, G. R. (Eds.). (1987). *Interpersonal processes: New directions in communication research*. Beverly Hills: Sage.

Rorty, R. (1979). *Philosophy and the mirror of nature*. Princeton: Princeton University Press.

Rosenbaum, S., & Walters, R. D. (1986). Audience diversity: A major challenge in computer documentation. *IEEE Transactions on Professional Communication, PC–29*, 48–55.

Rosenblatt, L. (1978). *The reader, the text, the poem: The transactional theory of the literary work*. Carbondale: Southern Illinois University Press.

Roth, P. (1987). *Meaning and method in the social sciences: A case for methodological pluralism*. Ithaca: Cornell University Press.

Roundy, N., & Mair, D. (1982). The composing process of technical writers. *Journal of Advanced Composition, 3*, 89–101.

Roy, R. (1986, July). Marital conflicts and exacerbation of headache: Some clinical observations. *Headache*, 360–364.

Rubens, P. M. (1981). Reinventing the wheel: Ethics for technical communicators. *Journal of Technical Writing and Communication, 11*, 329–339.

Rubin, D. L. (1984a). The influence of communicative context on stylistic variations in writing. In A. Pelligrini & T. Yawkey (Eds.), *The development of oral and written language in social contexts* (pp. 213–232). Norwood, NJ: Ablex.

Rubin, D. L. (1984b). Social cognition and written communication. *Written Communication, 1*(2), 211–245.

Rumelhart, D. E. (1980). Schemata: The building blocks of cognition. In R. J. Spiro, B. C. Bruce, & W. F. Brewer (Eds.), *Theoretical issues in reading comprehension* (pp. 33–58). Hillsdale, NJ: Lawrence Erlbaum.

Russell, D. R. (1990). Writing across the curriculum in historical perspective: Toward a social interpretation. *College English, 52,* 52–73.

Rutter, R. (1982). Teaching writing to probation officers: Problems, methods, and resources. *College Composition and Communication, 33,* 288–295.

Rymer, J. R. (1988). Scientific composing processes: How eminent scientists write journal articles. In D. A. Joliffe (Ed.), *Writing in academic disciplines* (pp. 211–250). Norwood, NJ: Ablex.

Sacks, O. (1985). *Migraine: Understanding a common disorder.* Berkeley: University of California Press.

Salager-Meyer, F. (1990). Metaphors in medical English prose: A comparative study with French and Spanish. *English for Specific Purposes, 9*(2), 145–160.

Salager-Meyer, F., Defives, G., Jensen, C., & De Filipis, M. (1989). Principal component analysis and medical English discourse: An investigation into genre analysis. *System, 17*(1), 21–34.

Samuels, W. H. (Ed.). (1990). *Economics as discourse: An analysis of the language of economists.* Boston: Kluwer.

Sarat, A., & Felstiner, W. L. F. (1990). Legal realism in lawyer-client communication. In J. N. Levi & A. G. Walker (Eds.), *Language in the judicial process* (pp. 3–35). New York: Plenum.

Savory, T. (1958). *The language of science: Its growth, character and usage.* London: Deutsch.

Schindler, G. E. (1975). Why engineers and scientists write as they do—Twelve characteristics of their prose. *IEEE Transactions on Professional Communication, PC-18* (1), 5–10.

Schlotthaus, W. (1989). Conditioning factors of textual understanding. In D. Meutsch & R. Viehoff (Eds.), *Comprehension of literary discourse* (pp. 74–88). New York: Walter de Gruyter.

Schneider, M. L. (1984). Ergonomic considerations in the design of command languages. In Y. Vassilou (Ed.), *Human factors and interactive computer systems.* Norwood, NJ: Ablex.

Schon, D. A. (1983). *The reflective practitioner: How professionals think in action.* New York: Basic.

Schon, D. A. (1987). *Educating the reflective practitioner.* San Francisco: Jossey-Bass.

Schriver, K. (1989). Document design from 1980 to 1989: Challenges that remain. *Technical Communication, 36*(4), 316–331.

Schriver, K., Hayes, J., Danley, C., Wolff, W., Davies, L., Graham, D., Cerroni,

K., & Bond, E. (1986). *Designing computer documentation: A review of the relevant literature* (Tech. Rep. No. 31). Pittsburgh: Communications Design Center, Carnegie Mellon University.

Schwegler, R. A., & Shamoon, L. K. (1991). Meaning attrition in ambiguous texts in sociology. In C. Bazerman & J. Paradis (Eds.), *Textual dynamics of the professions* (pp. 216–233). Madison: University of Wisconsin Press.

Scott, M. B. & Lyman, S. M. (1968). Accounts. *American Sociological Review, 33*, 46–62.

Scribner, S., & Cole, M. (1981). Unpackaging literacy. In M. F. Whiteman (Ed.), *Writing: The nature, development, and teaching of written communication* (Vol. 1, pp. 71–87). Hillsdale, NJ: Lawrence Erlbaum.

Scudder, J. N., & Guinan, P. J. (1989). Communication competencies as discriminators of superiors' ratings of employee performance. *Journal of Business Communication, 26*, 217–230.

Selzer, J. (1983). The composing processes of an engineer. *College Composition and Communication, 34*, 178–187.

Selzer, J. (1989). Composing processes for technical discourse. In B. E. Fearing & W. K. Sparrow (Eds.), *Technical writing: Theory and practice* (pp. 43–50). New York: MLA.

Selzer, J. (1990). Critical inquiry in a technical writing course. In D. A. Daiker & M. Morenberg (Eds.), *The writing teacher as researcher: Essays in the theory and practice of class-based research* (pp. 188–218). Portsmouth, NH: Heinemann-Boynton/Cook.

Sennett, R. (1980). *Authority*. New York: Vintage.

Sharrock, W. W., & Watson, D. (1989). Talk and police work: Notes on the traffic in information. In H. Coleman (Ed.), *Working with language: A multidisciplinary consideration of language use in work contexts* (pp. 431–450). Berlin: Mouton de Gruyter.

Shaw, M. E. (1963). *Scaling group tasks: A method for dimensional analysis* (Tech. Rep. No. 1, ONR Contract NR 170–266, Nonr–580[11]), Gainesville: University of Florida.

Shaw, M. E. (1971). *Group dynamics: The psychology of small group behavior*. New York: McGraw-Hill.

Shaw, M. E., & Blum, J. M. (1965). Group performance as a function of task difficulty and the group's awareness of member satisfaction. *Journal of Applied Psychology, 49*, 151–154.

Shelby, A. N. (1988). A macro theory of management communication. *Journal of Business Communication, 25*(2), 13–27.

Shuy, R., & Robinson, D. G. (1990). The oral language process in writing: A real-life writing session. *Research in the Teaching of English, 24*, 88–100.

Siegel, J. Dubrovsky, V., Kiesler, S., & McGuire, T. W. (1986). Group processes in computer-mediated communication. *Organizational Behavior and Human Decision Processes, 37*(2), 157–187.

Bibliography

Silberstein, S. D. (1984, September). Treatment of headache in primary care practice. *American Journal of Medicine*, 65–72.

Simon, H. A. (1965). *Administrative behavior* (2nd ed.). New York: The Free Press.

Simons, H. H. (Ed.). (1990). *The rhetorical turn: Invention and persuasion in the conduct of inquiry*. Chicago: University of Chicago Press.

Simons, H. W. (Ed.). (1989). *Rhetoric in the human sciences*. London: Sage.

Simpson, M. (1989). *Shaping computer documentation for multiple audiences: An ethnographic study*. Unpublished doctoral dissertation, Purdue University, W. Lafayette, IN.

Simpson, M. (1990). How usability testing can aid the development of online documentation. In *Proceedings of SIGDOC '90, 8* (pp. 41–47). New York: ACM.

Smagorinsky, P. (1989). Graves revisited: A look at the methods and conclusions of the New Hampshire study. *Written Communication, 4*, 331–342.

Smart, G. (1992). Exploring the social dimension of a workplace genre, and the implications for teaching. *Carleton Papers in Applied Language Studies, 9*.

Smeltzer, L. R., & Gebert, K. A. (1986). How business communication needs differ among professions. *The Bulletin of the Association for Business Communication, 49*(3), 4–7.

Smircich, L. (1981). Concepts of culture and organizational analysis. *Administrative Science Quarterly, 28*, 339–358.

Smircich, L. (1983). Studying organizations as cultures. In G. Morgan (Ed.), *Beyond method* (pp. 160–172). Beverly Hills: Sage.

Smircich, L., & Calas, M. (1987). Organizational culture: A critical assessment. In F. M. Jablin, L. Putnam, K. R. Roberts, & L. W. Porter (Eds.), *Handbook of organizational communication* (pp. 228–265). Beverly Hills: Sage.

Smith, D. E. A. (1974). The social construction of documentary reality. *Sociological Inquiry, 44*, 257–268.

Smith, D. E. A. (1984a). Medical discourse: Aspects of author's comment. *The ESP Journal, 3*(1), 25–36.

Smith, D. E. A. (1984b). Textually mediated social organization. *International Social Science Review, 36*, 59–75.

Smith, G. R. (1947). The current opinions of the supreme court of Arkansas: A study in craftsmanship. *Arkansas Law Review, 1*(2), 89–107.

Smith, G. R. (1967). A primer of opinion writing for four new judges. *Arkansas Law Review, 21*, 197–212.

Smith, G. R. (1973). A primer of opinion writing for law clerks. Judicial clerkships: A symposium on the institution. *Vanderbuilt Law Review, 26*, 1203–1210.

Smith, J., & Heshusius, L. (1986). Closing down the conversation: The end of the quantitative-qualitative debate among educational inquirers. *Educational Researcher, 15*(1), 4–12.

Sokolovsky, J. (1986). Network methodology in the study of aging. In C. Fry & J. Keith (Eds.), *New methods for old-age research: Strategies for studying diversity* (pp. 231–262). South Hadley, MA: Bergin and Garvey.

Solomon, G. D., Steele, J. G., & Spaccavento, L. J. (1983). Vermapamil prophylaxis of migraine. *Journal of the American Medical Association, 250,* 2500–2502.

Souther, J. W. (1989). Teaching technical writing: A retrospective appraisal. In B. E. Fearing and W. K. Sparrow (Eds.), *Technical writing: Theory and practice* (pp. 2–13). New York: MLA.

Spencer, J. W. (1988). The role of text in the processing of people in organizations. *Discourse Processes, 11,* 61–78.

Sperling, M. (1989). The writing conference as a collaborative literacy event: Discourse analysis and descriptive case studies of conversations between ninth grade writers and their teacher. *Dissertation Abstracts International, 49,* 11A. (University Microfilms No. 89-02 278)

Spilka, R. (1988a). *Adapting discourse to multiple audiences: Invention strategies of seven corporate engineers.* Unpublished doctoral dissertation, Carnegie Mellon University, Pittsburgh, PA.

Spilka, R. (1988b). Studying writer-reader interactions in the workplace. *The Technical Writing Teacher, 15*(3), 208–221.

Spilka, R. (1990a, March). *Accommodating research design and methodology to the social constraints of nonacademic settings.* Paper presented at the Conference on College Composition and Communication, Chicago.

Spilka, R. (1990b). Orality and literacy in the workplace: Process- and text-based strategies for multiple audience adaptation. *Journal of Business and Technical Communication, 4*(1), 44–67.

Spradley, J. P. (1980). *Participant observation.* New York: Holt, Rinehart, & Winston.

Spretnak, C. M. (1982). A survey of the frequency and importance of technical communication in an engineering career. *The Technical Writing Teacher, 9,* 133–136.

Sproull, L. (1986). Using electronic mail for data collection in organizational research. *Academy of Management Journal, 19,* 159–169.

Sproull, L., & Kiesler, S. (1986). Reducing social context cues: Electronic mail in organizational communication. *Management Science, 32,* 1492–1512.

Squire, R. (1989, January). *Technical writing/training: The New England job market and you.* Presentation at the Society for Technical Communication monthly meeting, Northern New England Chapter, Lowell, MA.

Starr, P. (1982). *The social transformation of American medicine.* New York: Basic.

Stevenson, D. W. (1975). Writing effective opinions. *Judicature, 59*(3), 134–139.

Stewart, M., & Roter, D. (Eds.). (1989). Introduction. *Communicating with medical patients.* Newbury Park, CA: Sage.

Stiles, W. B. (1978–1979). Discourse analysis and the doctor-patient relationship. *International Journal of Psychiatry in Medicine, 9*(3&4), 263–274.

Stratman, J. (1988). *The rhetorical dynamics of appellate court persuasion: An exploratory comparison of advocates' brief composing process with court clerks' brief reading and review process, Parts 1 and 2.* Unpublished doctoral dissertation, Carnegie Mellon University, Pittsburgh, PA.

Suchan, J., & Dulek, R. (1988). Toward a better understanding of reader analysis. *Journal of Business Communication, 25*(2), 29–46.

| Bibliography

Suchan, J., & Dulek, R. (1990). A reassessment of clarity in written managerial communications. *Management Communication Quarterly, 4*(1), 87–99.

Suchman, L. (1987). *Plans and situated actions: The problems of human-machine communication.* Cambridge: Cambridge University Press.

Sullivan, P. (1990, March) *Composing as the negotiation of management, engineering, and teaching views.* Paper presented at the Conference on College Composition and Communication, Chicago.

Sullivan, P., & Porter, J. E. (1990a). How do writers view usability information? A case study of a developing documentation writer. In *Proceedings of SIGDOC '90, 14,* 29–35.

Sullivan, P., & Porter, J. E. (1990b). User testing: The heuristic advantages at the draft stage. *Technical Communication, 37,* 78–80.

Sutherland, J. W. (1973). *A general systems philosophy for the social and behavioral sciences.* New York: George Brasiller.

Swales, J. (1988). Discourse communities, genres, and English as an international language. *World Englishes, 7,* 211–220.

Swales, J. (1990a). Discourse analysis in professional contexts. *Annual Review of Applied Linguistics, 11,* 103–114.

Swales, J. (1990b). *Genre analysis: English in academic and research settings.* Cambridge: Cambridge University Press.

Szekely, B., Botwin, D., Eidelman, B. H., Becker, M., Elman, N., & Schemm, R. (1986, February). Treatment of menstrual headache: Relaxation-biofeedback behavior therapy and person-centered insight therapy. *Headache,* 86–92.

Tebeaux, E. (1980). Let's not ruin technical writing, too: A comment on the essays of Carolyn Miller and Elizabeth Harris. *College English, 41*(7), 822–825.

Tebeaux, E. (1985). Redesigning professional writing courses to meet the communications needs of writers in business and industry. *College Composition and Communication, 36,* 419–428.

Tiefel, H. O. (1978, December). The language of medicine and morality. *The Hastings Center Report, 8,* 11–19.

Todd, A. D. (1989). *Intimate adversaries.* Philadelphia: University of Pennsylvania Press.

Tompkins, P. K., & Cheney, G. (1983). Account analysis of organizations: Decision making and identification. In L. Putnam and M. E. Pacanowsky (Eds.), *Communication and organizations: An interpretive approach* (pp. 123–146). Beverly Hills: Sage.

Toulmin, S. (1958). *The uses of argument.* Cambridge: Cambridge University Press.

Toulmin, S. (1972). *Human understanding.* Princeton: Princeton University Press.

Toulmin, S., Rieke, R., & Janik, A. (1979). *An introduction to reasoning.* New York: Macmillan.

Tracy, K. (1988). A discourse analysis of four discourse studies. *Discourse Processes, 11*(2), 243–259.

Trimbur, J. (1989). Consensus and difference in collaborative learning. *College English, 51,* 602–616.

Troolin, P., & Sahlin, C. (1990). *A descriptive study of the behavior of new users of Unicos Man Pages* (unpublished Tech. Rep.). Eagan, MN: Cray Research.

Turner, B. (1971). *Exploring the industrial subculture.* London: Macmillan.

Uehara, R. J. K., & Candlin, C. (1989). The structural and discoursal characteristics of *voir dire.* In H. Coleman (Ed.), *Working with language: A multidisciplinary consideration of language use in work contexts* (pp. 453–474). Berlin: Mouton de Gruyter.

Van Dyck, B. (1980). *On-the-job writing of high-level business executives: Implications for college teaching.* (ERIC Document Reproduction Service No. ED 185 584)

Van Maanen, J. (Ed.). (1979, December). *Administrative Science Quarterly, 24,* 360.

Van Maanen, J. (1988). *Tales of the field: On writing ethnography.* Chicago: University of Chicago Press.

Vatz, R. E. (1973). The myth of the rhetorical situation. *Philosophy and Rhetoric, 6,* 154–161.

Verheij, J. G. C., Horst, G. ter, Prins, P. J. M., & Veerkamp, J. (1989). General method for analysing dentist-patient interaction. *Community Dentistry and Oral Epidemiology, 17,* 173–176.

Vik, G. N., Wilkinson, C. W., & Wilkinson, D. C. (1990). *Writing and speaking in business.* Homewood, IL: Irwin.

Vipond, D., & Hunt, R. A. (1989). Literary processing and response as transaction: Evidence for the contribution of readers, texts, and situations. In D. Meutsche & R. Viehoff (Eds.), *Comprehension of literary discourse* (pp. 155–174). New York: Walter de Gruyter.

Von Bertalanffy, L. (1968). *General systems theory.* New York: George Brasiller.

Vygotsky, L. S. (1966). *Thought and language.* Cambridge: MIT.

Vygotsky, L. S. (1978). *Mind and society.* Cambridge: Harvard University Press.

Waitzkin, H., & Stoeckle, J. D. (1972). The communication of information about illness. *Advances in Psychosomatic Medicine, 8,* 180–215.

Walker, A. G. (1990a). Epilogue: Where do we go from here? In J. N. Levi & A. G. Walker (Eds.), *Language in the judicial process* (pp. 353–357). New York: Plenum.

Walker, A. G. (1990b). Language at work in the law: The customs, conventions, and appellate consequences of court reporting. In J. N. Levi & A. G. Walker (Eds.), *Language in the judicial process* (pp. 3–35). New York: Plenum.

Webber, J.R. (1991). The construction of multi-authored texts in one laboratory setting. In M. M. Lay & W. M. Karis (Eds.), *Collaborative writing in industry: Investigations in theory and practice* (pp. 64–81). Amityville, NY: Baywood.

Weick, K. (1979). *The social psychology of organizing* (2nd ed.). Reading, MA: Addison-Wesley.

Weihofen, H. (1980). *Legal writing style* (2nd ed.). St. Paul, MN: West.

White, J. B. (1973). *The legal imagination: Studies in the nature of legal thought and expression.* Boston: Little, Brown.

White, J. B. (1985). *Heracles' bow: Essays on the rhetoric and poetics of the law.* Madison: University of Wisconsin Press.

Whitefield, A. (1989). Constructing appropriate models of computer uses: The case of engineering designers. In J. Long & A. Whitefield (Eds.), *Cognitive ergonomics and human-computer interactions* (pp. 66–94). Cambridge: Cambridge University Press.

Williams, R. (1976). *Keywords: A vocabulary of culture and society.* New York: Oxford University Press.

Williams, W. M., & Sternberg, R. J. (1988). Group intelligence: Why some groups are better than others. *Intelligence, 12,* 351–377.

Wilson, J. B., & Hayes, S. P. (1984). *A competence-based approach to police report writing.* Englewood Cliffs, NJ: Prentice-Hall.

Winkler, V. M. (1983). The role of models in technical and scientific writing. In P. V. Anderson, R. J. Brockmann, & C. R. Miller (Eds.), *New essays in technical and scientific communication: Research, theory, practice* (pp. 111–122). Farmingdale, NY: Baywood.

Winograd, T., & Flores, F. (1986). *Understanding computers and cognition: A new foundation for design.* Norwood, NJ: Ablex.

Winsor, D. A. (1989). An engineer's writing and the corporate construction of knowledge. *Written Communication, 6,* 270–285.

Winsor, D. A. (1990a). The construction of knowledge in organizations: Asking the right questions about the Challenger. *Journal of Business and Technical Communication, 4*(2), 7–20.

Winsor, D. A. (1990b). Engineering writing/writing engineering. *College Composition and Communication, 41*(1), 58–70.

Witkin, B. E. (1977). *Manual on appellate court opinions.* St. Paul, MN: West.

Witte, S. P. (1985). Revising, composing theory, and research design. In S. W. Freedman (Ed.), *The acquisition of written language: Response and revision* (pp. 250–284). Norwood, NJ: Ablex.

Wittenborn, J. R. (1961). Contributions and current status of Q methodology. *Psychological Bulletin, 58,* 132–134.

Woolgar, S. (1988). *Science: The very idea.* New York: Tavistock.

Wowk, M. T. (1989). Talk in an organization: Organization in talk. In H. Coleman (Ed.), *Working with language: A multidisciplinary consideration of language use in work contexts* (pp. 541–564). Berlin: Mouton de Gruyter.

Yates, J. (1989). *Control through communication: The rise of system in American management.* Baltimore: Johns Hopkins University Press.

Yin, R. K. (1989). *Case study research: Design and methods* (rev ed.). Newbury Park, CA: Sage.

Young, A. (1990). Storytelling in a technical writing class: Classroom-based research and community. In D. A. Daiker & M. Morenberg (Eds.), *The writing teacher as researcher: Essays in the theory and practice of class-based research* (pp. 168–187). Portsmouth, NH: Heinemann-Boynton/Cook.

Young, K. (1989). Narrative embodiments: Enclaves of the self in the realm of medicine. In J. Shotter & K. J. Gergen (Eds.), *Texts of identity* (pp. 152–165). Newbury Park, CA: Sage.

Young, R. (1976). Invention: A topographical survey. In G. Tate (Ed.), *Teaching composition: 10 bibliographical essays* (pp. 1–43). Fort Worth: Texas Christian University Press.

Young, R. (1987). Recent developments in rhetorical invention. In G. Tate (Ed.), *Teaching composition: 12 bibliographical essays* (pp. 1–38). Fort Worth: Texas Christian University Press.

Young, R., Becker, A., & Pike, K. (1970). *Rhetoric: Discovery and change.* New York: Harcourt Brace Jovanovich.

Ziman, J. (1968). *Public knowledge: An essay concerning the social dimension of science.* Cambridge: Cambridge University Press.

Zimmerman, M., & Marsh, H. (1989). Storyboarding an industrial proposal: A case study of teaching and producing writing. In C. B. Matalene (Ed.), *Worlds of writing: Teaching and learning in discourse communities of work* (pp. 203–221). New York: Random House.

Zuboff, S. (1984). *In the age of the smart machine: The future of work and power.* New York: Basic.

Contributors

Tyler Bouldin serves as the coacting senior coordinator of the University Composition Board at the University of Arizona and as the codirector of the Southern Arizona Writing Project. His research involves theoretical and empirical study of the social, psychological, and conceptual dimensions of writing as a symbolic process. Currently, he and a cross–disciplinary team of researchers are studying ways writing can be used to foster creativity and community in an advanced engineering course.

Barbara Couture, an associate professor of English at Wayne State University, is the editor of and a contributor to *Functional Approaches to Writing: Research Perspectives* (Ablex, 1986) and *Professional Writing: Toward a College Curriculum* (Association of Teachers of Technical Writing, 1986). She is the coauthor, with Jone Rymer, of *Cases for Technical and Professional Writing* (Little, Brown, 1985) and the author of articles on composition, professional writing, and linguistic approaches to written discourse.

Geoffrey A. Cross, an assistant professor of English, teaches in the doctoral program at the University of Louisville. He has published a related study in *Research in the Teaching of English* and a human factors study of basic writers in *Computers and Composition*. He is working on a book under contract for Hampton Press, entitled "Collaboration and Conflict," about ethnography of collaboration in the workplace.

Jennie Dautermann is an assistant professor of technical and scientific communication at Miami University of Ohio. Her work has focused on qualitative research in nonacademic settings and pedagogies of professional writing. She has recently been involved with documenting the software program ISETL, which is used in experimental calculus classes throughout the country. Her chapter in this book is based on research she conducted for her Ph.D. in English at Purdue University.

Mary Beth Debs is an associate professor of English at the University of Cincinnati, where she teaches graduate and undergraduate courses in rhetoric and professional writing. Her articles have appeared in two collections, *Technical Writing: Theory and Practice* (MLA, 1989, eds. B. Fearing and W. S. Keats) and *Effective Documentation: What We Learn from Research* (MIT Press, 1989, ed. S. Doheny-Farina) and in *Technical Communication*, the *Journal of Business Communication*, *The Technical Writing Teacher*, and the *Journal of Business and Technical Communication*. She is working on a book that explores the political dimensions of rhetoric sponsored by and within the organization.

Stephen Doheny-Farina is an assistant professor of technical communication at Clarkson University. He has published in *Written Communication* and *Technical Communication* and has contributed to *Worlds of Writing* (Random House, 1989) and *Textual Dynamics of the Professions* (University of Wisconsin Press, 1991). His anthology, *Effective Documentation: What We Have Learned from Research* (MIT Press, 1989), was named by the NCTE as Best Collection of Essays in Scientific and Technical Communication. His second book, *Rhetoric, Innovation, Technology* (MIT Press, 1992), is a rhetorical critique of the role of technical communication in technology transfer. His current research interests involve the role of rhetoric in the development of technological innovations.

Susan Kleimann is a senior instructional systems specialist for the United States General Accounting Office, Washington, D.C. Within the GAO's Training Institute, she is responsible for developing content and managing logistics for GAO courses. She has worked with GAO's writing curriculum and is involved with its implementation of total quality management. In 1987–1988, she was appointed a fellow in GAO's Doctoral Research Program. She has taught at the University of Maryland and has published in *Technical Communication*. Currently, she is planning a study of a collaborative writing project within the GAO.

Jamie MacKinnon is an in-house business-writing consultant. He has also taught literature at the high school level in Nigeria and English as a second language to adults in Argentina and Canada. His "Toward a Canadian Rhetoric" appeared in the inaugural issue of *Textual Studies in Canada*. His chapter in this book is based on research he conducted for his M.A. thesis at Carleton University in Ottawa.

Barbara Mirel is an assistant professor in the School for New Learning at DePaul University. Her research on documentation inquires into the instructional content and design that best accommodate users' mental models and approaches to their complex, strategic tasks at work. She has been a professional documentation writer and now conducts workshops for information development groups at IBM. She has also contributed to *Effective Documentation: What We Learn from Research* (MIT Press, 1989, ed. S. Doheny-Farina), and her articles have appeared in *IEEE Transactions on Professional Communication*, the *Journal of Computer Documentation*, the *Journal of Technical Writing and Communication*, *Management Communication Quarterly*, *Technical Communication*, and *Technical Communication Quarterly*.

Lee Odell is a professor of composition theory and research at Rensselaer Polytechnic Institute. His current interest is in describing the cognitive strategies that underlie not only the process of writing but also the processes of reading and talking. He is also editing a collection of essays entitled *Composing Theory* (Southern Illinois University Press) that suggests ways the day-to-day experience of teaching and writing can inform theory.

Leslie A. Olsen is an associate professor and the director of the Technical Communication Program at the University of Michigan. She is the coauthor of *Technical Writing and Professional Communication* (2nd ed., 1991) and *Technical Writing and Professional Communication for Non-Native Speakers* (2nd ed., 1989) both published by McGraw-Hill, New York, and she has won awards for these two books from the Society for Technical Communication. Her research interests and other publications are in technical communication, discourse analysis, computer-based writing, and professional communication for nonnative speakers of English. She is also involved in a project to put computer learning centers, featuring instructional gaming, computer technology, and communication activities, into public housing projects.

Anthony Paré is the assistant director of the Centre for the Study and Teaching of Writing at McGill University. He is also an assistant professor in the Department of Curriculum and Instruction at McGill, where he teaches students in the secondary English education program and is coeditor of *Inkshed*. His teaching and research interests include the relationship between genre and knowledge making, writing in social service agencies, and writing in the academic disciplines.

James E. Porter is an associate professor of English and the director of business writing at Purdue University. His research bridges his interests in rhetoric theory (especially audience, ethics, and invention) and professional writing. He has published work in *Rhetoric Review*, *Technical Communication*, *IEEE Transactions on Professional Communication*, and the *Journal of Teaching*

Writing. His book, *Audience and Rhetoric: An Archaeological Composition of the Discourse Community* (Prentice-Hall, 1992) examines treatments of audience in rhetoric, composition, and professional writing.

James A. Reither teaches rhetoric and literature at St. Thomas University in Fredericton, New Brunswick. He has published in *PRE/TEXT*, *College English, Inkshed,* and elsewhere. Founder and former editor of *Inkshed,* he is a coeditor of *Textual Studies of Canada.* He is particularly interested in exploring radical new ways of thinking about practice in response to radical new ways of thinking about writing, texts, authorship, reading, community, and collaboration that have come into currency in rhetoric and composition studies.

Jone Rymer (formerly Goldstein), an associate professor in the School of Business Administration at Wayne State University, was recently a visiting associate professor in the Anderson School of Management at UCLA. Her current publications focus on professional writing processes, collaborative writing, and professional writing assessment. She coauthored *Cases for Technical and Professional Writing* (Little, Brown, 1985) with Barbara Couture.

Judy Z. Segal is an assistant professor of English at the University of British Columbia. She specializes in composition theory and pedagogy and in rhetoric(s) of science. She has recently published "The structure of advocacy: A study of environmental rhetoric" in the *Canadian Journal of Communication* and, with Andrea Lunsford and Robert Connors, the *St. Martin's Handbook for Canadians* (Nelson Canada, 1991). She is currently writing about the rhetoric of health policy and about medical persuasion and patient compliance.

Jack Selzer is an associate professor of English at Penn State University, where he directs the composition program and teaches a variety of graduate and undergraduate courses in rhetoric, literature, and technical and scientific writing. He was president of the Association of Teachers of Technical Writing from 1990 to 1992. The author of many journal articles and contributions to books, he recently edited *Conversations: Readings for Writers* (Macmillan, in press). He is putting together a collection of essays by many scholars, entitled *Understanding Scientific Prose* (University of Wisconsin Press), an effort to demonstrate the utility of particular methods of rhetorical analysis.

Graham Smart is the coordinator of writing training at the Bank of Canada in Ottawa, where he consults with employees individually to help them develop their writing ability and leads writing seminars for groups of employees. He has also taught applied linguistics in the Department of Linguistics at Carleton University and in the Faculty of Education at the University of Ottawa. His current research interest is in using genre theory, reader-response theory, and discourse analysis to explore how various aspects of social context influence writers, readers, and texts.

Rachel Spilka is an assistant professor of English at Purdue University, where she specializes in rhetoric and professional writing. She has published in *Technical Communication, The Technical Writing Teacher*, and the *Journal of Business and Technical Communication*. Her 1990 article in *JBTC* was named by NCTE as Best Article Reporting Formal Research in Scientific and Technical Communication. Her current research project is a longitudinal study of rhetoric across multiple cultures in government contexts.

Patricia Sullivan is an associate professor of English and the director of technical writing at Purdue University, where she teaches research method courses in the graduate rhetoric program. Her research interests combine rhetoric theory, methodology, computers, and professional writing. She has published in *IEEE Transactions on Professional Communication, The Technical Writing Teacher, College Composition and Communication, Technical Communication*, and the *Journal of Technical Writing and Communication*.

Index